Edited by Dennis R. Herschbach
and Clifton P. Campbell

WORKFORCE
Preparation:

An
International
Perspective

Tech Directions Books
Prakken Publications, Inc.

*To the men and women worldwide
who devote their professional lives
to education and training for work*

CONTENTS

Part II: Case Studies of Selected Country Practices

Acknowledgments

The editors wish to extend their sincere appreciation to the authors who committed their extensive knowledge and professional experience, as well as extraordinary insights, to writing these chapters. They are also deeply indebted to Linda L. Campbell, who generously provided invaluable assistance by checking and completing references, word processing, preparing tables, proofreading the many manuscript revisions and page proofs, compiling the final document, developing the index, as well as performing a host of clerical duties.

The editors are grateful to their colleagues at the University of Maryland and The University of Tennessee for their understanding while this project was underway. In addition, they thank their many colleagues spread across the globe with whom they have been engaged, over the years, in discourse on the topics of this book. For their viewpoints and encouragement regarding the worth of this international project, the editors express genuine gratitude. The support of colleagues and family was vitally important to the successful completion of this book.

The editors proudly acknowledge that the authors and others, whose creative work and combined efforts resulted in this book, generously donated their time and talents. The International Vocational Education and Training Association receives all royalties from the sale of this book, for use in improving and advancing workforce preparation worldwide.

Finally, the editors and authors thank Susanne Peckham, Managing Editor of Prakken Publications' Tech Directions Books, for her enthusiastic support, comprehensive editing, and diligent efforts in making the book a reality.

Preface

This book is about educating and training people for work. It is about how different countries use their schools and public and private resources to prepare citizens for work; it is about the different policy issues that shape education and training practices; and it is about the practical as well as unresolved issues surrounding how participants are selected, programs are designed, and instruction is conducted. It discusses linkages between schools and employers, as well as issues of poverty, opportunity, efficiency, and equity. It examines different education and training modes. And it explores the relationship between kinds of skills training programs and social and economic development priorities.

The reason for this book is simple. Perhaps at no other time in recent history has workforce preparation been viewed as so critical to the social and economic well-being of nations. There is a general, international consensus that better forms of work preparation are instrumental in the search for ways to achieve and sustain a higher standard of living. Perhaps in a simpler time, workforce preparation could be examined solely from a national perspective, but this is no longer the case: preparation for work has taken on an important international dimension.

The young person seeking work today enters a labor market very different from a decade ago, and the labor market a decade in the future will no doubt be quite different from today's. Work and preparation for it are changing rapidly. The defining influences have been global economic integration and competition, and the accompanying revolution in information and communication technology. Labor markets are no longer isolated—innovation and change are the norm. As we move into the future, we will need less labor to perform many tasks, and the combinations of necessary job skills will vary. The structure of work and the demand for skills are changing along with the conditions of employment. These trends will only accelerate with the increasing integration of national economies into a world economy.

It is not surprising that many countries have fundamentally restructured the ways that youth and adults prepare for work. Countries the world over have embarked on reform efforts to strengthen their education and training capability. And even though changes in national workforce preparation systems have emerged unevenly throughout the world, common developments are occurring. This does not mean that all systems of work preparation are becoming the same, but it does mean that fundamental social and economic changes worldwide are leading planners and policymakers to address common policy issues.

These issues include, for example, strengthening education and training programs' responsiveness to employment requirements, achieving a closer integration of work-education programs and academic preparation, forging closer public/private links, broadening the constituency groups served, diversifying financing, and achieving greater accountability. The various chapters in this book serve as the backdrop against which these and other issues surrounding workforce preparation are examined.

In a world increasingly dominated by the international marketplace, it is important to gain insights into how education and training systems worldwide are being restructured to address the challenges of globalization. Considerable intellectual leverage is thus gained by examining workforce development problems and issues.

Significant improvements in education and training performance, as well as changes in the strategies for preparing young people and adults for work, are required in a global economy that will increasingly have less room for the ill-prepared. The overall intent of the reading included in this book is to help form the foundation on which more informed decisions can be made regarding how best to prepare all people for work.

Dennis R. Herschbach
Clifton P. Campbell

Part I: Policy Perspectives on Workforce Preparation

Introduction

The outcomes of work preparation programs are shaped by the policy objectives planners and decision makers establish. This may seem a straightforward principle, but it is not. There are conflicting and competing claims on the uses of both public and private resources, and on the uses of the various institutional forms for workforce preparation. These claims are rooted in fundamental differences regarding the respective functions of academic and vocational instruction; ways to address issues of gender, ethnicity, and poverty; ways to best deliver education and training; and the relationship of schools to work and to larger social concerns. Some of these differences relate to market competition and to the extent to which workforce preparation programs should be designed for and judged by standards of economic efficiency. Others relate to the control of resources and issues of empowerment, social justice, and opportunity, while some are situated within the context of the public debate over social policy and government reform. Outcomes of workforce preparation programs are not value free, but are entwined in larger public policy issues regarding schools, society, opportunity, and work.

The chapters included in Part I examine major underlying policy issues that planners and decision-makers must grapple with as they seek to define the outcomes of work preparation programs. These issues are introduced and discussed in the context of six specific chapters, providing both breadth and depth of coverage. The cross-national framework of each chapter makes it possible to bring a broad international perspective to the discussion. At the same time, the individual chapters focus on major issues of workforce preparation. Each chapter also balances policy discussion with an examination of the practical aspects of implementation.

The first chapter in Part I uses planning as the context to establish and discuss fundamental policy positions regarding the purpose and design of programs for work. Rational planning models and their objectives are contrasted with political and consensual approaches to program development. The underlying value perspective of each planning approach is uncovered and examined. The authors conclude that the designed outcomes of workforce preparation programs are themselves a product of value-based decisions.

The next chapter, "Women, Education, and Training: Old Challenges in a New Age," by Daines, Hartenstein, and Birch, defines a value-position regarding women and work. Adopting a critical perspective toward the design of work education programs, the authors argue that women continue to encounter barriers to education and training, as well as to employment. When considered worldwide, the dimensions of discrimination are considerable and complex, yet workforce access for girls and women is increasingly viewed as a key element in social and economic development. An agenda is proposed for vocational and technical education that revisits the issue of how to address concerns of equity and individual opportunity.

Similarly, in Chapter 3, "Education and

Training Partnerships: An Enabling Framework," Coursey examines the construction of education and training partnerships and concludes that a consensual/critical policy perspective will most likely result in successful long-term collaboration. A distinction is made between the functional and structural aspects of partnerships, and attention is drawn to the differing views of business and education regarding their expected outcomes. A pluralistic, interactive perspective to partnership formation is presented.

Chapter 4, "Education, Training, and the Economy," examines vocational education and training from the perspective of economic efficiency. Using a human capital development perspective, Young looks at the roles of the state and the private sector in providing preparation for work. Rate-of-return analysis is applied to demonstrate one approach to decision-making and resource allocation. Examples from various countries are used to illustrate different education and training paths taken on the route to labor market development.

Chapter 5, "Workforce Certification," covers the development and administration of certification systems. Certification links different forms of education and training into a coherent system that can respond to both economic and social development objectives. Economic development and restructuring targets can be identified and skill requirements translated into education and training programming. But it is also possible to address concerns of occupational mobility and opportunity in ways that promote efficient workforce preparation, while accommodating the interests and aspirations of different constituency groups. Certification systems provide a framework in which to balance the competing claims of the rational, political, and consensual planning perspectives discussed in Chapter 1.

The final chapter in Part I addresses "Financing Workforce Preparation Programs." Regardless of policy objectives, vocational and technical education programs cannot be successfully designed and implemented without adequate financial resources. In most countries, policymakers struggle with ways to diversify the financing of work preparation programs. Public funding can no longer be expected to provide a high proportion of the necessary resources. Different funding alternatives, however, have conflicting impacts on policy and the ability to implement programs. Objectives of efficiency have to be balanced with concerns for equity, opportunity, adaptability, and stability. Chapter 6 examines both the constraints and opportunities associated with financing alternatives.

1

Planning, Efficiency, and Equity: A Conceptual Framework

By Dennis R. Herschbach and Cynthia Davis

Educational planning is essential for sound program development. Just about every educational organization, no matter how simple or complex, engages in some form of planning. In the case of vocational and technical education, programs must respond to changing social and economic circumstances and be cost-efficient. Planning addresses these concerns. Yet, despite the centrality of planning, the education profession lacks full agreement on how it should be done, which results in disappointment.

One reason for the disappointment is that planning is not a neutral activity. It is a normative activity, implemented in the pursuit of goals or objectives. Planning embodies value judgments about the purpose and importance of education and training programs, who should be served, and how best to provide services. Judgments also must be made about allocating resources, and inevitably, some individuals and groups benefit more than others. In addition, educational environments are generally complex and changing, whereas most planning models are static and simplified in both form and application.

Finally, vocational and technical education can no longer be viewed as a closed system operating independently of other school subjects or the larger community. Rather, planning must be viewed as a process that interfaces with the total education and employment framework within a community—it has become more complex and open to public scrutiny.

This chapter provides a conceptual framework for examining vocational and technical education planning. It is organized around three basic planning models: the technicist, political, and consensual/critical. The value base underpinning each model, how each applies to planning questions, and the various associated constraints are identified and examined. International examples of how each model applies also are presented.

Like education in general, workforce preparation policy is in a state of flux. Overall, internationally, there has been a shift away from the purely economic goals of vocational education to more social objectives. These include providing basic education needs; extending opportunity; enhancing the quality of life; and addressing issues of gender, ethnicity, and poverty. As the end purposes of vocational education and training are conceived differently, planning itself must be viewed in a different light. Planning, however, is not simply a technical exercise. Rather, it involves complex issues concerning the purpose and substance of vocational education and training; and as suggested, there is no neutral, or value-free approach to educational planning.

DECISION-MAKING LEVELS

Planning for workforce preparation involves three distinct levels of decision-making: macro-level, micro-level, and curriculum-level. Macro-level planning examines aggregated data on a national or regional scale to determine how to best make educational investments. What proportion of public expenditures, for example, should go to elementary education? To secondary and vocational education? How much public money should go to community college technical programs? How much to programming for the disadvantaged?

Planning at this level helps determine the optimal allocation of resources. The public sector largely controls the supply and—to a lesser degree, depending on the political and economic structure—demand side of education. Thus, market forces alone cannot be relied on for allocating resources.

On the other hand, macro-planning has not had much success. The lack of good, overall planning models, the inability to collect and use reliable data, and administrative insufficiencies all contribute to less-than-adequate results. Assuming that future economic growth patterns can be predicted accurately enough to base education investment decisions on them may itself be faulty.

Macro-Planning

Macro-planning is most widely applied in countries with centralized, planned economies, such as in the former Eastern Block—Russia, Poland, and Hungary, among other countries—where educational planning and control measures are amenable to close supervision and

regulation (Farrell, 1997). It is used less in countries with market-based economies, such as the United States. Some European countries, like the Netherlands, which has a tradition of social planning, have successfully steered a somewhat middle course.

Method (1979) nevertheless suggests that a major problem with macro-planning is that assessments are conducted "at such a high level of aggregation (national, regional, sectoral) that alternatives for training or skill utilization at the level of the firm, project or local organization cannot be considered directly" (p. 13). And planning must often commence at this level, since specific decisions must be made about allocating general resources. Usually, choices at the higher levels are taken as given, and local planners must make the best decisions possible within the budget allocation handed down from above.

Macro-level planning draws from three basic methods: rate-of-return, manpower forecasting, and social demand. Rate-of-return, which reflects neoclassical economic theory, assumes that the free market will indicate the demand for, and consequently influence the allocation of resources for, education and training. Investments that yield the greatest social and individual return are considered the best (Psacharopoulas, 1985). Manpower forecasting, at the opposite end of the economic theory spectrum, maintains that government should intercede in predicting future jobs and in training and educating people to fill those jobs (Richter, 1984). Finally, social demand attempts to relate anticipated or desired outputs of the education system with the supply side of education. The decisions made are basically political, rather than economic. Rate-of-return and manpower planning are technicist models, whereas social demand is a political model. Manpower planning and (to a lesser degree) rate-of-return analyses assume strong government intervention in education and training.

Micro-Planning

Micro-planning involves working with desegregated data on a local or regional level. It looks at the productivity quotient of such issues as resource allocation, student groups, teacher training, student-teacher interaction, and curriculum. Decision-making at this level relates to vocational and technical institutions within different areas of occupational programming. The decision-making emphasis shifts from determining the optimal use of resources across the total educational sector to identifying the most effective education and training alternatives for workforce preparation. Should funds, for example, be directed to tech prep programs at the community college level, or should they support collaborative school/employer initiatives? What are the main target populations served through programming? What is the optimal student outflow? What skill categories and levels should receive priority? While macro-planning data and analytical techniques are useful, it also is essential to consider the local potential to deliver training, as well as the range of workforce preparation alternatives that can be reasonably considered, given the available resources and employment climate.

Social demand considerations also come into play at the micro-planning level. Among the technicist, or rational, approaches, cost-effectiveness and cost-benefit analyses are widely used. These approaches are discussed later in the chapter. Other political and consensual/critical perspectives include contingency and interactive approaches to planning (Hudson, 1979).

The terms macro- and micro-planning are also used in connection with organizational and strategic planning. In this context, macroplanning addresses an organization's effect on external clients, while micro-planning refers to an organization's effect on small groups and individuals within the organization.

Farrell (1975) maintains that use of the terms macro- and micro-planning in education stems from economists having "captured" the field. He asserts that the economists' vocabulary has limited education, and argues for a broader interpretation of the term *macro-planning*. Macro, he claims, should refer to the overarching philosophies and theories determining the values, design, and methodology of a planning intervention. Macro-planning, in this sense, refers to both qualitative and quantitative approaches. Micro-planning, on the other hand, refers to specific operational or programmatic elements of an intervention, such as financing, management strategies, staffing, organizational structures, instructional resources, the specific model used, and the implementing context. These are senses in which the terms *macro-* and *micro-planning* are used in this chapter.

Curricular Planning

Another level of planning—curricular—occurs primarily at the local or institutional level. Curricular planning attempts to answer such questions as: What courses and programs will be offered, and for whom? What specific skills will be taught, and how are they best identified? What is the optimal program design? How will programs within and between occupational areas relate to each other and to work? This aspect of planning includes training duration, skill level(s) taught, instructional format, and so forth.

To make decisions at this level, a needs assessment at the workplace is often used. Program effectiveness directly depends on local decision-makers getting sufficient data to make good choices (Campbell, 1996). Curricular planning tends to use more interactive planning perspectives than do macro- or microplanning. Moreover, planning at this level should be continuous. However, when carried out at higher organizational levels, static instructional programs usually result. Planning at higher levels cannot capture local conditions or stay abreast of change. Most higher organizational levels concern themselves with preparing a planning document, largely conceived as a one-way process, whereas decision-making at this level requires continuous analysis and action related to local conditions.

Decisions about curriculum, however, involve value judgments about which content is most important to teach, to whom, and why. Social sorting occurs through curriculum. As is the case at all three levels of planning, one must recognize the underlying values embodied in the various analytical tools applied to decision making. The following section examines and compares three planning perspectives: technicist, political, and consensual/critical.

PLANNING PERSPECTIVES COMPARED

Planning means different things to different people. Davis (1994), working from a rationalist perspective, states that "educational systems planning is the development of clear goals and the design of efficient and effective education to achieve those goals" (p. 1825). Adams (1990), reflecting a normative perspective, asks whether "efficiency can be treated as a single index around which plans may be judged" (p. 382). In a similar vein, Farrell (1975) questions the meaning of such value-based terms as "equity" and "development" in educational planning. In this context, Klees (1991) maintains that economic bias and the rationalist paradigm have distorted the meaning of planning concepts, and have dominated educational planning since its inception.

Hudson (1979) draws attention to three fundamental planning perspectives that apply to workforce preparation, each with its own set of values and objectives. The human capital, neoclassical model holds that vocational and technical education programs primarily aim to promote the development of competitive skills among youth and adults. It assumes that individuals experience workforce problems because they lack the appropriate skills at the level of proficiency required in the workplace. Skills that individuals acquire through education and training, moreover, can be viewed as investments in human capital, and the larger economy functions both as the source of program-development data and the basis for justifying investments in education and training.

To make decisions, proponents of this planning perspective use technicist, or rationalist, planning models, represented by manpower forecasting, rate-of-return, and cost-effectiveness studies. A rationalist model assumes a stable reality, a relationship between means and ends and causes and effects, a value-free science, and the quantifiability and replicability of data (Adams, 1988). It refers to economic growth goals or cost criteria. The requirements for educated and trained workers, for example, derive in manpower planning from economic growth targets.

A second perspective, undergirded by the theory of segmented or multiple-tiered labor markets, assumes a divided or segmented labor market rather than a completely open one. Individuals enter and progress based on their backgrounds, education, and experience. Some workers find primary jobs; others find only low-paying, peripheral, or irregular work.

Education and training are valued, in part, because they help break down barriers to occupational mobility. Nevertheless, according to segmented labor market theory, social class differences, ethnic and gender biases, and the application of selection criteria unrelated to skills generated by education and training continue to exert a powerful influence on the life chances of individuals. Vocational and technical education forms but one aspect of the support required to help disadvantaged segments of the population work themselves out of low-wage, secondary jobs with little future. To be most effective for marginal populations, such measures as job restructuring, career development, anti-discrimination measures, and placement services must reinforce vocational and technical education. Planning itself must incorporate a broader range of support services impacting workforce preparation (Adams, 1988).

Yet a third perspective, informed by critical theory, builds from the concept of segmented labor markets, focusing on the political, economic, and social structures affecting training, job creation, and work. It emphasizes the transformation value of vocational and technical education. This more radical approach claims that class, gender, and ethnic differences rooted in the very structure of the capitalist system condition the employment prospects of individuals. Proponents of this perspective point out that rational planning models tend to ignore the organizational, political, and social context, and assume that planning is based on reason, free from influence, controversy, and faulty judgment. The resolution of planning problems best comes from individuals' interactions as they seek representative compromise and solutions. Plans for vocational and technical education are hammered out of contending and conflicting interests rather than cast cleanly from a mold of technical procedure. The objective of planning, moreover, is to promote social transformation, not just the transmission of skills.

The critical perspective also draws from labor market reproduction theory, as represented in the works of Giroux (1983) and numerous others. Why do poor minority youth and, often, women end up with low-paying, low-status jobs? Social reproduction theory suggests that social and economic factors, and specifically schools, reinforce existing inequalities. The education system reflects the economic and social class structure, subordinating the young to this structure and producing reserves of workers with differing skill profiles.

Schools, and vocational and technical education, in particular, help stratify groups, theorists contend, conditioning youth to the social relationships of dominance and subordination in the economic system. Elites train to take their place at the top of the social and economic ladder, while the poor are conditioned to accept lower status. Moreover, cultural capital, in the form of background, knowledge, disposition, aspiration, values, and skills, passes from generation to generation, aided by the school. Vocational and technical education transmits cultural capital that helps direct youth into occupations that are often of mar-

ginal social and economic value. The upper class acquires the tools appropriate for success in school and "good" work. The poor remain in low-level and marginal jobs.

A small but growing number of critical theorists (Kincheloe, 1995; Simon, Dippo, & Schenke, 1991) within vocational and technical education are exploring the implications of social reproduction theory. Gregson (1995), for example, argues that the school-to-work movement in the United States has focused too much on transmitting instrumentally useful work skills and, as a consequence, has failed to recognize its transforming potential. Vocational education, including cooperative workplace learning, Gregson contends, has considerable potential "for uncovering unjust contradictions, questioning . . . assumptions about how work is done, and exploring possible alternatives so that work can become more democratic and human" (p. 17). Similarly, Lakes (1994) suggests that work preparation must be reformulated to involve learners in resolving inequality and injustice in our social institutions. Furthermore, Carter (1994) observes that vocational education has not succeeded at ridding itself of gender stereotyping.

Within the European Union, considerable attention currently goes to establishing "parity of esteem" between vocational and academic subjects. A number of countries have made provisions to enable students to continue from workforce preparation programs to advanced postsecondary and university education. The intent is to erase, or at least reduce, social and class bias.

Both the political and consensual/critical perspectives use interactive planning models and assume an unstable, changing reality and a diversity of knowledge claims and value positions. They typically employ planning at the micro- and curriculum-levels of decision-making. These models also employ qualitative data, which does not always replicate from one planning situation to another.

A critical approach to planning that emphasizes participation, decentralization, value specificity, and qualitative data exemplifies interactive planning. Not surprisingly, "the planning paradigm chosen dictates, to a large extent, the rules of the game in making planning decisions" (Adams, 1994, p. 1805). The following three sections examine how those rules apply.

THE TECHNICIST MODEL

In the technicist or rational model, "the planner begins with a set of externally defined goals and, through comprehensive analysis of complex information 'solves' the problem for the proper mix of resources and actions to achieve those goals" (McGinn, Schiefelbein, & Warwick, 1979, p. 218). It promotes through education the effective transmission of skills and technology.

The planner assumes that since knowledge is objective and science is value free, the model applies universally and requires little adaptation to particular contexts or different countries. Decision-making is centralized, top down, and expert driven. Successful implementation means that the plan was followed as written. Evaluation activities, expressed as quantifiable outputs, come at the end of the project cycle and usually do not affect or alter the elements of the plan.

Centralized education systems, international organizations, and ministries of education in countries that demand local compliance with hierarchical administrative structures most frequently use the technicist model. Its use persists, in part, because the model has practical appeal, and many international donor organizations demand compliance to their methodology (Adams, 1991; Farrell, 1997; McGinn, Schiefelbein, & Warwick, 1979).

Manpower Planning

Traditionally, most decisions about resource allocation for vocational education and training have been based on manpower forecasting, the most widely advocated technicist model for macro-level planning. Various survey procedures identify projected needs for trained workers. Data are aggregated at the national level by occupation or industry and are seldom desegregated to the local level. This information identifies shifts in the total rates of employment within industries, along with participation, unemployment, and underemployment rates. Data on the age structure of the labor force allow replacement rates to be calculated, but migration rates are more difficult to project. Manpower and employment data link to educational planning by matching the various occupational categories with levels and kinds of educational attainment (Campbell, 1996).

Despite its wide and continuing use, this approach to resource allocation has substantial limitations. Data generally are too aggregated to be useful and, as previously suggested, projections often are too erratic to use for decision-making (Dougherty, 1989; Method, 1979). International experience shows that projections often fall wide of the mark. In addition, inappropriate data are often collected. Then again, national planning data tend to focus on the modern economic sector, while in many countries considerable job expansion occurs in the informal sector. The planning model used in the modern sector and the occupational structure and staffing patterns of the more highly organized industries tend to be inapplicable as models for small- and medium-sized enterprises.

In highly dynamic economies, such as in the United States, the results are often too static to use. Projections based on a certain point in time do not capture significant and rapid changes spurred on by technology and innovation. Planning at the local level, moreover, is hard to accomplish with any accuracy. In national level projections, aggregated data tend to smooth out anomalies, but at the local level major discontinuities may be inadequately captured and abrupt economic changes may throw forecasts completely off. In some communities, for example, closing one plant drastically alters the economic picture and, hence, the demand for education and training. At the local level, labor markets simply do not function as smoothly and regularly as the manpower projection model implies. Forecasts often are inaccurate or at best misleading for planning purposes. Economic environments are seldom as stable as they are assumed to be, and rarely do changes occur entirely as predicted.

A technical criticism finds the basic assumption of fixed and rigid job structures throughout a particular occupational sector faulty. Individual firms vary greatly in how they recruit, train, and use personnel. The scale of the enterprise, its organizing pattern, the technology used, and the particular work culture contribute to shaping how workers are recruited, trained, and employed. It does not make sense to assume that there is a particular skill mix always associated with a given occupational classification.

Despite its limitations, the apparent technical rationality supporting human capital development makes manpower planning attractive. From the application of the process, education and training specifications emerge that, in turn, establish training targets and, at the program level, instructional objectives, even if the validity of the results is questionable. The means for meeting the objectives can, in turn, be specified. These include curricular requirements; teacher needs; and accompanying materials, supplies, and equipment. Manpower planning provides a sense of security since "objective" data can be pointed to as the basis for making choices. When relevant and reliable data are available, the match is reasonably good and the results can serve as an easily understood basis for making budgetary allocations.

Manpower planning approaches have proven most useful when applied to relatively stable occupational categories and when used for micro-level planning in key industries, special localities and regions, or for special programs. Manpower planning is also most effective when applied to short-term training as a way to adjust programs to address changing market requirements. The consensus on man-

power forecasting today seems to be that desegregated data, analyzed over the short term, are useful for anticipating employment trends, but that aggregated data, projected into the future, are too unreliable to justify the effort. Finally, using manpower planning in combination with other approaches enhances its application.

Manpower planning—most widely applied in centralized, planned economies—assumes that economic growth targets, and hence educational needs, can be estimated with enough accuracy to provide reliable planning guidelines. This is seldom the case. One option, however, would apply manpower planning to a limited number of crucial economic sectors, and thus direct training resources accordingly (Farrell, 1997).

Because of the limitations associated with conventional manpower planning concepts, current thinking shifts the emphasis of planning away from forecasting the number of trained workers needed and toward determining the kind and flow of information required, as well as improving access to that information. Since the market sends signals in the form of job vacancies and surpluses, determining market changes and speeding up the flow of information between training providers and employers is essential. Effectively channeled information better anticipates and articulates the needs of local employers. This approach stands in marked contrast to conventional manpower planning, which emphasizes the formulation of specific training targets. It is process oriented and results in "the gradual molding of the labor force in a direction which is consistent with the general direction of development and which takes due account of the relative costs of different types of skill development" (Dougherty, 1989, p. 5).

Rate-of-Return

Rate-of-return studies are not widely used among the technicist models because they are complex, their methodological flaws are hard to overcome, and the ability to generalize results is questionable. Nevertheless, the general idea that some educational investments yield greater social and individual returns than others is powerful and has shaped decision-making. Some planning security comes from the ability to point to concrete evidence of an educational investment's apparent superior performance. But even without conducting detailed studies, it is still useful to talk in terms of alleged benefits that will likely arise from a particular education and training investment. The use of rate-of-return studies is briefly reviewed here because they still strongly influence planning for vocational and technical education, even though the general concept is more persuasive than the results of individual studies.

In its basic form, rate-of-return compares total educational costs to the expected future earnings of program completers who enter the workforce. It calculates an internal rate-of-return, indicating the relative "profitability," or return, on the investment in relation to alternative programming choices. Programs that show greater potential returns are considered the better investments to make, since more value is returned either to society or to the individual. Both costs and benefits can be considered from the views of social and personal returns. When public money is invested, high social returns in relation to other programming alternatives are taken as the best investment choice.

Planning aims to evaluate the effectiveness of past resource use and then determine how the resources might be used more efficiently in the future. Rate-of-return studies reinforce the attempt to link the development of education and training to economic development, and to maximize economic growth and productivity. Rate-of-return assumes that just the act of attending an educational or training program will add value to an individual's potential to earn. Added value and potential are considered increases in productivity. Thus education receives an economic justification.

This planning perspective also assumes considerable substitutability in the workforce. It basically rejects the segmented labor market theory. One kind of education is considered capable of fulfilling multiple purposes, with individuals prepared to take any one of many work roles. It rejects the notion that a relatively fixed occupational structure exists, determined by technology and organization, and that occupational roles require individuals with a specific type and amount of education. It prefers a general, vocational education supported by strong foundation skills over more specific, in-depth preparation. Some rate-of-return advocates, for example, would direct public financial resources almost solely to elementary and secondary education, leaving specific job preparation to take place within the firm (Psacharopoulas, 1987).

Rate-of-return studies, however, have a number of serious conceptual and methodology shortcomings. They attribute earnings differences between more- and less-educated individuals solely to additional education, even though numerous other factors independent of education—such as socio-economic background, experience, or on-the-job training—also account for earning differentials. They also assume that wages serve as a valid measure of the return on education, when in fact market imperfections make rate-of-return studies a poor measure of productivity. Many elements affect wages, such as union control and market monopoly—education and training is but one. Then again, decisions based on potential monetary returns may not necessarily be a good measure of the worth of future educational and training investments. In other words, rate-of-return does not calculate indirect spillover benefits—such as increased social mobility, improved citizenship, greater family stability, and the development of positive individual attitudes and values—when indeed they may have considerable social and personal worth.

Assigning expenditures to individual programs in a multiple-program environment presents a technical problem. Benefits derive from combined courses in the program, often over an extended period. It is hard to desegregate individual program costs and benefits.

Finally, while rate-of-return analysis provides useful data to assess past program performance and planning decisions, caution must be exercised in using study results to make future program decisions. Results of the immediate past do not necessarily provide a good indication of what actions to take in the present or in the long-term future. This is particularly true in the case of economies experiencing rapid change.

Rate-of-return studies probably are most useful for planning at the micro-level in making decisions within individual firms. For example, is it better to invest in more training or more technology, or a combination of the two? At the firm level, decisions are more purely economic and are based on a limited set of objectives and variables. Rate-of-return studies' greatest value for general and vocational educational planning have been to confirm the crucial importance of basic education, particularly as a key element in shaping a high-skilled workforce. Training systems in Japan, South Korea, Taiwan, Singapore, Hong Kong, and Germany, among others, for example, are built on a firm foundation of general skill development and are distinguished by the high general-skill levels of the population pursuing more specific skill development. The idea that good general education is good vocational education has been instrumental in developing an effective workforce.

Cost-Effectiveness

Cost-effectiveness analysis links in purpose and outcome with rate-of-return studies. Both provide an economic rationale to planning decisions, and both result in identifying specific education and training investments of allegedly higher economic worth. However, cost-effectiveness and its related perspective, cost-benefit analysis, tend to apply at the institution or program level, whereas rate-of-return studies mainly are used for making macro-level national or regional resource allocation decisions. Also, unlike rate-of-return studies, cost-effectiveness analyses consider nonmonetary benefits, such as program completion and placement rates, when calculating the relative investment worth of different educational and training alternatives.

Typical inputs included in cost-effectiveness analyses are the direct and indirect costs of instructors, material, equipment, and physical facilities. Benefits include the level of skill development attained, increased earnings, employment stability, job satisfaction and mobility, as well as returns to society in the form of higher taxable earnings, among other factors. Cost-benefit analysis uses the ratio of benefits-to-cost to project optimal investment decisions. Both benefits and costs are converted to monetary terms and are discounted to present value, considering appropriate interest and inflation rates. But a cost value cannot always be easily assigned to either inputs or benefits. This difficulty is overcome in part by cost-effectiveness analysis (Tsang, 1997).

Cost-effectiveness analysis addresses two aspects of decision-making. One is internal effectiveness, which measures the direct effects of classroom instruction, using standard as well as teacher-made tests. Programs that produce higher student achievement are considered more effective, and hence, better training investments. All other factors assumed equal, students learn more for the amount of money spent.

Another application of cost-effectiveness analysis attempts to assess external effectiveness, the extent to which school or program outcomes actually relate to the economic, social, or political purposes intended. If training, for example, aims to reduce unemployment among a certain group, does this actually happen, or would alternative, less costly means work as well?

Applying cost-effectiveness analyses to vocational and technical education generally has produced mixed results (Dougherty, 1989; Tsang, 1997). Dougherty (1989) suggests that most studies that assess the external effectiveness of education and training alternatives are so flawed methodologically that the results are open to serious question. Their inability to distinguish between training design problems and implementation problems is a major limitation. Program completers may not obtain employment for a number of reasons: training inappropriate to the needs of the labor market (external effects) or training of poor quality (internal effects). Cost-effectiveness studies tend to assume low external effects as the primary cause of low placement rates, although mounting evidence shows that the latter is the real cause (Herschbach, 1989).

Whenever there is a failure to discriminate between the effectiveness of program design and program implementation, considerable policy confusion results. On the one hand, less investment in a particular training alternative may be needed; on the other, greater emphasis on program improvement may be needed. The planner cannot easily determine which is the case. An inability to yield insight into the need for program improvement may present the greatest drawback to cost-effectiveness analysis.

The weakness of technicist planning models in dealing with vague or shifting goals, conflicting values, and an uncertain and changing planning environment, in addition to methodological limitations, has resulted in the search for interactive approaches that consider more directly the implementing context itself. Planning must be more participatory and must consider competing claims on educational and training goals and resources. The political model moves planning in this direction.

THE POLITICAL MODEL

The political model, also known as transactive or incremental model, assumes that personalities, negotiation, and information exchange strongly influence planning outcomes (Warwick, 1980). Planners who do not work at least partly within a political framework often complain that "the politics of personal-ity and manipulation" thwart their efforts (Cohen, Grindle, & Walker, 1985, p. 1216). While many planners attempt to circumvent these conditions, practitioners who use the political model acknowledge that strong, charismatic leaders often control the planning process.

The political model further acknowledges that "the bureaucracy survives and is able to only partly satisfy the major groups, for example, small and large capitalists, unions, political parties, churches, and the military" (McGinn, Schiefelbein, & Warwick, 1979, p. 220). The political model recognizes that due to the uneven distribution of power, democratic or full participation is unlikely, or at least unusual; thus, coalition-building among competing interest groups becomes the preferred way to effect change and achieve reform (Cohen, Grindle, & Walker, 1985). Decision-making in this model emerges from negotiations among competing or opposing groups. Successful implementation is process, rather than product, oriented. The ongoing communication and dialogue among groups is itself a form of implementation.

Social Demand

Planning based on social demand is the most benign form of the political model. While consultation, negotiation, and compromise are usually minimal and passive, key planning decisions, nevertheless, flow from the political context. Simply stated, decisions are made to make one type of educational investment instead of another, based on highly perceived demand. And, as Blaug (1979) suggests, decisions on how to make public expenditures are "only vaguely connected with any objectives that might be described as economic" (p. 365). The forms of social-demand planning used tend to ignore economic growth goals or cost criteria.

Social demand usually translates into a political process: constituency groups express to decision-makers their desire to pursue various educational options. Social and political objectives, such as enhancing educational opportunity, developing national literacy, or creating a "world-class workforce," serve as the purpose or rationale for making financial resource decisions. Education is considered a basic right rather than an investment. Open admission policies are generally followed, based on admission standards and available education and training capacity. When tuition is charged, it is usually kept at a minimum to promote equity and opportunity.

Planners are assigned the simple mandate of setting educational targets, given the limitations on resources and the demand for particular programs. Shifts in programming follow shifts in social perception on the importance of particular school subjects, reactions to political events, and responses to external influences. Recent emphasis on tech prep and school-to-work programs in the United States exemplifies this.

Limits on classroom space, admission standards, accessibility, financing, and institutional capacity are determinants of enrollment. Everything that might determine future enrollments—except purely economic factors—is taken into consideration.

Social-demand planning generally has a very limited (if any) theoretical foundation. Basing curriculum decisions on social demand, however, does not eliminate planning. "Facts" are often amassed to support the political decision to make one kind of educational investment over another. Neutral planners, on the other hand, can use available data to help modify plans and direct implementation along more socially and economically functional lines. Planning data may be used to formulate political, social, and educational goals, and since the social-demand approach is so widely used, this may be one of the most potent uses of planning data. Generally, the following types of data are useful in social planning.

Demographic data—Includes population data by single-year age levels, indicating enrollment trends by age. It is obviously desirable to place more of the new programs in areas that show either growth or stability in potential enrollment.

Stock and flow data—"Stock" data include a count of what exists on a given day in each school year, in contrast to "flow" data that indicate the movement of students and teachers into, within, and out of the system during the year. Information on the stock of students typically includes cross-classification by grade, sex, age, and branch of study. Counts of ethnic groups are often included. Also useful is a count of the proportion of students completing each course, the numbers repeating and withdrawing, as well as the proportion proceeding to different types of education and training at other levels.

Stock and flow data indicate to what extent the capacity of the education and training system is being used, as well as program completion rates. Cross-tabulated with costs, stock and flow data make it possible to calculate program and student costs.

Cost and finance data—The costs of education place real limits on the social-demand approach to planning. Are plans feasible in light of available resources? Certain demands simply cannot be accommodated without additional resources or without shifting resources from one program to another. Data on past capital and recurrent expenditures, along with estimates on additional funds, provide the base for initial decision-making.

Data on the total annual cost of education, broken down by grade level and type of program yields recurring and capital costs per student enrolled. Costs may also vary according to geographic location. Information on the sources of funding should include private and public expenditures.

Manpower and employment data—Existing and potential skill shortages, manpower projections, and other manpower data (usually not collected in sufficient depth to form the full basis of planning) often support social-demand decisions, lending credibility, if not reality, to decisions. Curriculum decisions, moreover, often tie directly to general economic policy decisions. In this area, social-demand planning interfaces with the intent and, to a lesser degree, the methodology of technicist planning perspectives.

Contingency Planning

Contingency planning, as advanced by Rondinelli, Middleton, and Verspoor (1989), rests on the premise that introduced changes "must be appropriate for the socioeconomic environment in which they will be implemented and the value orientations of those who will participate in them" (p. 47). They suggest a four-phase interactive analysis through which successive adjustments are made in planning objectives and program elements to accommodate voices of the various stakeholders. "Project planners," they contend, "must consider the social and cultural values of those who will implement the project, especially where the project will require changes in management processes" (p. 50). While their model contains elements of technicist planning, it nevertheless attempts to also consider the more uncertain and interaction-dependent elements of planning.

The political model is criticized on the grounds of social reproduction theory. While major stakeholder groups may achieve considerable participation, those with the least political influence and voice may, nevertheless, still have very little representation in decision-making. The marginalized and dispossessed remain dispossessed. Birdsall, Bruns, and Sabot (1996), for example, observed that in Brazil the more affluent social groups retained such a firm lock on resources and political control that, even despite reforms, the poor had very little educational opportunity. Attendance, retention, and achievement remained low for the marginalized population. Similarly, even when changes are instituted in vocational and technical education programs to strengthen academic preparation, increase program options, and encourage advanced job preparation, the poorest are still at a disadvantage in the training and job scramble because they remain captive to the constraints of their social and economic class.

THE CONSENSUAL/CRITICAL MODEL

As with the political model, the consensual/critical model assumes an unstable environment in which conditions cannot be predicted or generalized from one context to another, and that "meaningful action presupposes understanding and that legitimate action presupposes agreement" (Adams, 1991, p. 16). In this sense, the consensual/critical model differs from the political, which maintains that full knowledge and participation are neither realistic nor necessary. In the former, however, "communication, not political power, pluralistic bargaining, or expert knowledge," is the key to success (Adams, 1991, p. 16). All stakeholders share decision-making at all points throughout planning and implementation. Although goals are set, they are intended to be modified in an ongoing, formative process. In the same way, evaluation is ongoing and ideally offers concrete learning and training experiences to participants.

Decentralized and nongovernmental organizations in which consensus building is important most commonly use consensual/critical designs, although international donor organizations are becoming increasingly involved in consensual planning because it contributes to sustainable institutional development. According to Brinkerhoff and Goldsmith (1992), sustained institutional development requires bottom-up consensual participation of all stakeholders.

A Planning Framework

Davis (1991) proposes an eight-step framework for workforce planning based on critical theory that builds on decentralized decision-making, stakeholder participation, and information sharing.

1. Identify the planning problem and all stakeholders.
2. Conceptualize and describe the planning

problem or the proposed change from the viewpoints of all stakeholders.

3. Analyze the background and crucial antecedent conditions of the planning problem.

4. Dialogue with participants to develop an understanding of the intersubjective meanings, values, and motives held by all stakeholders with regard to proposed programs or changes.

5. Identify contradictions and inconsistencies between views of the different groups.

6. Design a plan that achieves the proposed change while satisfying the agendas of all stakeholders.

7. Evaluate the plan in a formative, ongoing way.

8. Implement the plan.

This planning framework tries to equalize benefits, empower beneficiaries to make decisions, attend to the historical background of a problem, and encourage communication and dialogue among stakeholders. The framework is influenced by the contingency model of Rondinelli, Middleton, and Verspoor (1990), as well as by the work of Rudqvist (1992) and others regarding participatory development. Coomer's (1985) framework for a critical theory approach to educational evaluation and Comstock's (1982) work on methods for critical research suggest the steps in the conceptual framework.

Davis's (1991) planning framework provides a way to address a number of theoretical and practical concerns. According to critical theory, a problem or a need for change is seen differently from multiple perspectives. Opposing and competing groups naturally conceptualize issues in different ways. While some groups have an investment in maintaining the status quo, others feel limited or constrained by an existing situation. Communication through dialectic, in which opposing viewpoints are expressed, enables stakeholders to understand these multiple perspectives. In a critical approach, the open articulation of the values, motives, and agendas of all stakeholders can achieve such an understanding. Inevitably, such communication leads to conflict.

Conflict, as part of the planning process, is both a positive means of deepening communication and a way to arrive at compromise. Habermas (1970), for example, strongly asserts the necessity for conflict as part of the critical process. "It is [through] the process of argument that we achieve true statements about reality" (p. 113).

Careful analysis of the historical situation at an early stage of planning is important. Such an analysis enables stakeholders to understand the sources and origins of their conflicts. Critical theory maintains that accumulation of quantitative data and establishment of an "objective" hypothesis cannot neutralize historical realities. Instead, the background of a particular educational problem must be acknowledged as integral to the solution of the problem. For example, contemporary implications of ways in which traditional systems have engendered inequities by favoring one class or ethnic group over another can be explored through a historical analysis.

Analyzing the historical background enables participants to understand the intersubjective meanings, values, and motives they all hold. Once these meanings are clarified, the inevitable contradictions and inconsistencies can be approached in a reasonable, dispassionate way.

The actual implementation design occurs relatively late in the planning. The design is thus organic to the entire process rather than imposed from the top down on beneficiaries by planners. In designing the program, planners can address such elements as financing, management, staffing, organizational structure, and instructional resources, in keeping with the values and norms inherent in the critical theory paradigm.

While creating the plan, participants can simultaneously analyze the implementing context to ensure that the design does not overwhelm the resource base. According to Rondinelli, Middleton, and Verspoor (1990), "the gap between proposed reforms and the ability to implement them" tends to widen as implementation designs become more ambitious and complex (p. 4). Planners must match the design of the program with the financial, social, and human realities of the implementing context.

Critical and rationalist models approach the final step, evaluation, differently. Conventional evaluation models (technicist) tend to assume that evaluation is primarily a technical activity in which education produces a product. The plan is seen as the means for realizing the desired ends or product. As will be seen in the subsequent discussion, a critical approach to evaluation addresses underlying values rather than a specific end product.

A Critical Evaluation Perspective

Evaluation is an ethical activity because it implies making choices among alternatives and selecting one of these choices as a basis for action. Actions in turn are grounded in intentions, goals, and aims and are also shaped by experience and by history. An action that has a constructive or beneficial history, on either a social or a personal level, is likely to be positively evaluated. However, as Habermas (1979) pointed out, historical precedent can lull people into performing actions that are apparently beneficial but are in reality harmful or destructive because they reinforce an inequitable system. Thus, the underlying criteria for evaluation are important in determining whether educational outcomes are positively assessed.

Traditional evaluation models in American education, such as the empirical approach designed by Stufflebeam (1973), encourage conformity to a system of specific behaviors and values that reinforce the existing social, economic, and political system. American society, for example, values consumerism, individualism, self-expression, saleable skills, and institutional structures with various controls. Since an educational system reflects social values, activities that perpetuate social values are evaluated positively. Stufflebeam's empirical/analytical model—predicated on cost-effectiveness, efficiency, and objectivity—uses standardized scores to assess the degree to which

students are consumer-oriented and individualistic. The Stufflebeam model does not, however, recognize a political or historical context of education or a holistic approach to human growth and development. The model is also politically conservative, since it maintains the status quo and "provides a view of problem solving that tends to avoid conflict regarding educational issues while relying on existing institutional practices" (Coomer, 1985, p. 69).

Variations of Stufflebeam's evaluation model dominate educational planning in many countries (Adams, 1988; Rondinelli, Middleton, & Verspoor, 1990). Lately, however, it has been acknowledged that many program evaluations are based on criteria that reflect the values of those in authority and not the values of the beneficiaries (Rudqvist, 1992). Because it is important that both the evaluator and the evaluated work toward the same goals, onesided designs are inappropriate for planning education. For example, a program considered "successful" sometimes merely maintains inequitable conditions and upholds the interests of the elite, since it avoids any activities that might lead to change or social conflict (Comstock, 1982).

The term "success" is meaningless if a program is evaluated according to an inappropriate model. A critical approach to evaluation bases success on the (a) degree of substantive change in the status quo, (b) involvement of stakeholders, and (c) extent to which the program can sustain change over time. Analyses of the historical background and the implementing context of the program are important elements in a critical evaluation. Typically, a critical evaluation consists of the following elements:

1. Stakeholder agreement on program goals and on appropriate indicators of progress by all stakeholders.

2. Progress monitoring by beneficiaries and planners.

3. Data sharing among stakeholders.

4. Reevaluation of goals on a periodic basis.

5. Modification of original goals, if necessary.

6. Data utilization by participants in order to improve their situation in a self-managed way (Uphoff, 1992, p. 139).

The precision and quantification of data thus become less important than people's participation in its acquisition and use. In addition to being based on appropriate criteria and using an appropriate model, an effective evaluation should be ongoing and formative, not merely an exercise in which data is gathered and appended to project documentation. Evaluation "should be done in ways that strengthen intended beneficiaries' capacities to help manage project activities and sustain program benefits" (Uphoff, 1992, p. 135). Such approaches have the added benefit of being cost-efficient because "the expenditure helps to build up management capabilities among local communities, rather than just produce information for monitoring" (Uphoff, 1992, p. 135).

DISCUSSION

The consensual/critical perspective is limited to the extent that clear policy prescriptions and program elements seldom emerge from planning. This is particularly true at the macro level. In actual practice, planning is often messy and inconclusive. It is not enough to point out social and economic inequities without some clear idea of what to do about them. Competing claims of participants may prevent the very consensus mandatory for program development. Moreover, the objective of equality and opportunity may so totally overwhelm all other concerns that planners and decision-makers lose sight of the fact that economic goals are still important outcomes of education and training interventions. Lack of efficiency in program design and implementation decreases rather than extends opportunity.

On the other hand, plans for vocational and technical education conceived primarily as a set of technical exercises provide little insight into inherent value conflicts and view planning as a mechanistic, top-down process with little need for understanding the attending education, social, economic, and political environment. Rational planning models have difficulty accommodating value issues and ethical concerns. A major but erroneous assumption is that interventions are "objective," neutral, and unaffected by norms or values. A rationalist concept of efficiency often sacrifices equity concerns.

Ultimately, however, all planning involves value questions about the purpose and goals of education and training. Planning is not exclusively a technical matter, and no neutral or value-free approach to educational planning exists. Differences relating to the particular planning methodology applied are also differences about goals. The particular planning approach applied implicitly or explicitly acts on goal-formation.

As other chapters will show, the conflicting goals of efficiency and equity continue to play out as planners and decision-makers the world over grapple with the challenges of economic sufficiency, globalization, technological change, population explosion, poverty, and opportunity. To be sure, vocational and technical education play important economic and social development roles. But tension exists between efficiency and equity goals, manifest clearly in the three basic planning perspectives: the technicist, political, and consensual/critical models. This chapter has attempted to uncover each perspective's value-based underpinnings.

References

Adams, D. (1988). Extending the educational planning discourse: Conceptual and paradigmatic explorations. *Comparative Education Review, 32*(4), 400-415.

Adams, D. (1990). Analysis without theory is incomplete. *Comparative Education Review, 23*(3), 380-385.

Adams, D. (1991). Planning models and paradigms. In R. V. Carlson & G. Awkerman (Eds.), *Educational planning: Concepts, strategies, practices* (pp. 5-20). New York: Longman.

Adams, D. (1994). Educational planning: Differing models. In T. Husen & T. N. Postlethwaite, *International encyclopedia of education* (2nd ed., pp. 1804-1810). Oxford: Pergamon.

Birdsall, N., Bruns, B., & Sabot, R. H. (1996). Education in Brazil: Playing a bad hand badly. In N. Birdsall & R. H. Sabot (Eds.), *Opportunity foregone education in Brazil* (pp. 7-47). Washington, DC: Johns Hopkins Press.

Blaug, M. (1979). The quality of population in developing countries, with particular reference to education and training. In P. M. Hauser (Ed.), *World population and development* (pp. 361-402). Syracuse, NY: Syracuse University Press.

Brinkerhoff, D. W., & Goldsmith, A. A. (1992). Promoting the sustainability of development institutions: A framework for strategy. *World Development, 20*(3), 369-383.

Campbell, C. P. (1996). Determining the market demand for skilled workers. In C.P. Campbell (Ed.), *Education and training for work: Vol. I. Planning programs* (pp. 1-53). Lancaster, PA: Technomic.

Carter, P. A. (1994). Women's workplace equity: A feminist view. In R. D. Lakes (Ed.), *Critical education for work* (pp. 67-81). Norwood, NJ: Ablex.

Cohen, J. M., Grindle, M. S., & Walker, S. T. (1985). Foreign aid and conditions precedent: Political and bureaucratic dimensions. *World Development, 13*, 1211-1230.

Comstock, D. E. (1982). A method for critical research. In E. Bredo & W. Feinberg (Eds.), *Knowledge and values in social and educational research*. Philadelphia: Temple University Press.

Coomer, D. L. (1985). Critical science as a mode of inquiry: A critical study of educational evaluation theory and practice. *Journal of Vocational Home Economics Education, 3*, 56-77.

Davis, C. (1991). Vocational education project planning in developing countries: A critical theory paradigm. *Journal of Industrial Teacher Education, 28*(3), 35-45.

Davis, R. (1994). Education planning: Models and methods. In T. Husen & T. N. Postlethwaite (Eds.), *International encyclopedia of education* (2nd ed., pp. 1825-1830). Oxford: Pergamon.

Dougherty, C. (1989). *The cost-effectiveness of national training delivery modes: Issues and experience* (Population and Human Resources Department Working Paper Series). Washington, DC: World Bank.

Farrell, J. P. (1975). Reaction to the micro-planning of education: Why it fails, why it survives, and the alternatives. *Comparative Education Review, 19*(2), 202-209.

Farrell, J. P. (1997). A retrospective on educational planning in comparative education. *Comparative Education Review, 41*(3), 277-313.

Giroux, H. A. (1983). Theories of reproduction and resistance in the new sociology of education. *Harvard Educational Review, 53*(3), 257-293.

Gregson, J. A. (1995). The school-to-work movement and youth apprenticeship in the U.S.: Educational reform and democratic renewal? *Journal of Industrial Teacher Education, 32*(3), 7-27.

Habermas, J. (1970). *Knowledge and human interests*. Boston: Beacon Press.

Habermas, J. (1979). *Communication and the evolution of society*. Boston: Beacon Press.

Herschbach, D. R. (1989). *Improving training quality in developing countries: Toward greater instructional efficiency*. Washington, DC: World Bank.

Hudson, B. M. (1979). Comparison of current planning theories: Counterparts and contradictions. *Journal of American Planning Association, 45*(4), 387-406.

Kincheloe, J. L. (1995). *Toil and trouble: Good work, smart workers, and the integration of academic and vocational education*. New York: Peter Lang.

Klees, S. (1991). The economics of education: Is that all there is? *Comparative Education Review, 35*(4), 721-734.

Lakes, R. D. (Ed). (1994). *Critical education for work*. Norwood, NJ: Ablex.

McGinn, N., Schiefelbein, E., & Warwick, D. (1979). Educational planning as political process: Two case studies from Latin America. *Comparative Education Review, 23*(2), 218-239.

Method, F. J. (1979). *The development of technical skills in LDC's*. Washington, DC: Planning Office of the Institute for Scientific and Technological Co-operation.

Psacharopoulas, G. (1985). Returns to education: A further international update and implications. *Journal of Human Resources, 20*(4), 583-604.

Psacharopoulas, G. (1987). To vocationalize or not to vocationalize: That is the curriculum question. *International Review of Education, 33*(2), 187-211.

Richter, L. (1984). Manpower planning in developing countries: Changing approaches and emphases. *International Labour Review, 123*(6), 677-692.

Rondinelli, D. A., Middleton, J., & Verspoor, A. M. (1989). Contingency planning for innovative projects. *Journal of the American Planning Association, 55*(1), 45-56.

Rondinelli, D. A., Middleton, J., & Verspoor, A. M. (1990). *Planning education reforms in developing countries: The contingency approach*. Durham, NC: Duke University Press.

Rudqvist, A. (1992). The Swedish International Development Authority: Experience with popular participation In B. Bhatnagar & A. C. Williams (Eds.), *Participatory development and the World Bank: Potential directions for change* (World Bank Discussion Papers Number 183). Washington, DC: World Bank.

Simon, R. I., Dippo, D., & Schenke, A. (1991). *Learning work: A critical pedagogy of work education*. New York: Bergin and Garvey.

Stufflebeam, D. (1973). An introduction to the PDK book: Education evaluation and decision-making. In B. Worthen & J. Saunders (Eds.), *Education evaluation theory and practice*. Belmont, CA: Wadsworth.

Tsang, M. C. (1997). The cost of vocational training. *International Journal of Manpower, 18*(1/2), 63-89.

Uphoff, N. (1992). Monitoring and evaluating popular participation in World Bank-assisted projects. In

B. Bhatnagar & A. C. Williams (Eds.) *Participatory development and the World Bank: Potential directions for change* (World Bank Discussion Papers Number 183). Washington, DC: World Bank.

Warwick, D. (1980). Integrating planning and implementation: A transactional approach. In R. G. Davis (Ed.), *Planning education for development: Vol. I. Issues and problems in the planning of education in developing countries* (pp. 379-411). Cambridge, MA: Harvard University Press.

2

Women, Education, and Training: Old Challenges in a New Age

By Jeanette Daines, Annette Hartenstein, and Megan Birch

More than a half century ago, in the wake of World War II, signers of the United Nations Charter began the long journey toward closing the gender gap with respect to the status of women and men throughout the world. The Charter expressed belief in human rights and in equality, thereby becoming a catalyst for change in many facets of everyday life. Advocating universal access to education was a critical dimension of the United Nations' efforts to promote peace and progress. Considerable gains were made in the years that followed, resulting in the expansion of educational opportunities in many countries. Nonetheless, these opportunities have been insufficient to overcome persistent gender disparities.

Gender continues to be a strong determinant of education, training, and work opportunities, even though public policy in many countries has encouraged—or expected and depended on—women's participation in the workforce. Cultural patterns differ among the kinds of work roles open to women at any point in time. Societies have evolved from the age of hunting and gathering to agrarian pursuits, through the industrial era, and into the

information/knowledge age with little substantive change in women's work responsibilities and opportunities. In each period, women had responsibilities for production that helped sustain families. However, in most countries, women still do not have broad access to the range of work and education or training opportunities that would enable them to rise above the lower income strata of their culture.

Lack of access for women is a societal problem that results in underdeveloped human resources throughout the world. It also limits a nation's development, for a nation's ability to have a healthy economy directly relates to developing its human resources. This chapter explores some factors that influence work opportunities and conditions for women and suggests ways that they might be addressed.

A PRELUDE TO THE FUTURE

First, as a baseline: The International Labour Office (1998) has well documented the impact of women's labor force participation, and it can be said without equivocation that without women's participation, the global economy would grind to a halt. Throughout the past two decades, women made up most of the world's new labor supply. During this time, women's labor force growth significantly outpaced men's in all regions of the world except Africa, where growth rates were equal. Women's share of the total labor force growth ranges from 40 to almost 80 percent (pp. 139-140). Women clearly have an expanding role in the global economy.

Women's increased participation in the labor force has occurred during a time when rapid technological advances, substantive political and social transitions, and dramatic shifts in the world economy have affected the work situations of both men and women. This is unlikely to change in the foreseeable future. The new millennium promises an escalating spiral of technological and organizational development. Bold innovations in communications lead the way, paced by scientific and technical breakthroughs that result in many creative applications. Correspondingly, political and social change are widespread. Revolution has forced cultural disintegration in many countries, and marked violence and disruption have led to great migrations of people seeking refuge. Fragile economies are shattered—or bolstered—by events occurring in far-distant places. And in all situations, the effects reverberate around the world.

Globalization

Globalization has been described as a "fundamental process of change" that, in an economic sense, integrates the world economy through trade, financial flows, exchange of technology and information, and movement of people throughout the world (Chottepanda, 1998, p. 33). Each contributing factor has created new opportunities and heightened risks and vulnerabilities. The effects of high unemployment and/or recession can be starkly evident, affecting markets and the futures of investors and customers, governments and individuals. Similarly, when unemployment is low, the need for workers with desired but scarce abilities can drive a worldwide search for la-

bor. The resulting organizational adaptations transform the landscape of opportunities for workers in many different places.

Migration

Migration exacerbates the societal effects of globalization. The flow of people to different regions may come in response to a supply-and-demand situation, such as the seasonal har-

Imagine what the world would be like in a developed country such as the United States if women withdrew from the labor market. The total labor force would decline to the point where it would be impossible to sustain current levels of production of goods and services. The economy would shrink, limiting the capacity of the country to participate in the global market. Household incomes would drop and, consequently, there would be fewer purchases of goods and services as these became less affordable. Jobs created in industries that emerged as a result of women's participation in the workforce would likely disappear (e.g., child care services, food services, cleaning services). Fewer vehicles would be needed for transport; travel would be limited; entertainment preferences would change; the media would refocus. Likewise, fewer people would pay taxes that support essential programs and services, contribute to retirement funds that provide future resources, or contribute to charitable causes. Lower revenues would limit government services. Infrastructure maintenance would be jeopardized; office buildings, shopping malls, and many dwellings would be vacated; and so forth.

What would the scenario be like for a developing country?

vesting of crops, but it may also be due to other forces. The many refugees throughout the world attest to the human and societal costs of political unrest and violence. Once uprooted from their homes and countries, individuals and families bear the heavy burdens of making a home in a strange land and finding or developing new ways to provide for their needs. The great diaspora of the 20th century continues into the 21st, challenging countries of origin and countries of relocation to adapt to new human resource configurations.

Aging of the Population

Over the longer term, but on just as significant a scale, aging of the population will profoundly alter the characteristics of the workforce. Declining birth rates and increasing life spans are showing their effects. One analysis (Longman, 1999) indicates that older persons in some countries of the developed world outnumbered youth as early as 2000. Within the next 50 years, more than one out of every five people in the world will be over age 60. The number of persons over 85 will increase sixfold. How will workforce needs and societal obligations to people be met when that occurs? Even if men and women remain in the workforce for more years than they do at present, an eventual decline in the numbers of available workers will result in less productivity.

EFFECTS OF CONTEXT

Conditions such as these are particularly volatile for women new to the labor force. However, the conditions are not new. In the mid-1980s, Cornell University published a report that may help us understand the ways that events then affected women. The report describes the situations of women workers in 15 countries, and includes a chapter by Marion Janjic of the International Labour Office (ILO) that focuses on women in industrialized market economy countries. Janjic (1985) describes a three-pronged evolution that profoundly affected women's employment—particularly since it came at a time when their participa-

tion was rapidly increasing, and when there was also increased concern that women workers have equal opportunity and treatment. First, Janjic recognizes that economic slowdown and recession resulted in rising unemployment for both men and women. Second, she notes that the use of advanced technologies began to change the occupational structure and shrink labor demand, particularly in sectors that had employed greater numbers of women. Finally, she points out that labor-intensive industries with low skill requirements had shifted to developing countries.

All three factors increased competition that placed women at a disadvantage because of their concentration in certain occupations, generally low skills, and relative lack of mobility. The suggested educational response was to help women understand the importance of acquiring new skills to broaden their occupational options and increase job specialization. Janjic (1985) concludes by noting that women's employment remained precarious—even though their rights to full employment were recognized—because cultural and institutional supports were insufficient to permit them to exercise those rights, and because the division of work kept them in subordinate positions within the labor market. Her admonition is that women must be made conscious of their need to adapt their skills to the requirements of postindustrialized society. Now, 15 years later, similar conditions still prevail. In fact, they may have intensified as a result of the world economy's increasing globalization.

Within the current landscape, women workers continue to be especially vulnerable. Again, the International Labour Office (1998) explains that the rapid pace of technological progress in production work has resulted in greater job insecurity for women. The need for highly skilled workers has increased, while the demand for workers with low skills or limited, rudimentary knowledge has decreased. When technological and organizational restructuring do result in more employment opportunities for women, they tend to be for relatively low-skilled jobs offering poor wages and benefits. Likewise, the increase in part-time or temporary work has resulted in more opportunities and has created more flexibility but most often in poorer quality employment. The ILO's report also notes that public sector downsizing and privatization have severely affected women workers. In many countries, more women than men are employed in the public sector, where working conditions and wages tend to be better than in the private sector. Consequently, when jobs in the public sector are cut, women are disproportionately affected (pp. 141-142).

Given the conditions of uncertainty that confront women in their work lives, access becomes a critically important factor. Access to education and training, information, and technology remain the main strategies for advancing human life and society. Advocating these approaches assumes that education, technical training, and lifelong learning are of equal importance as integral parts of an ongoing curriculum. The historic model for providing this curriculum rests on formal education, beginning with preschool and primary school, and progressing to secondary and tertiary education. This is complemented (or in some situations, replaced) by informal education, which uses a variety of approaches to provide learning opportunities within communities.

However, girls and women have difficulty obtaining access within all of these venues. According to the International Labour Office (1998), inequalities persist throughout the following areas:

• Access to formal education—Unequal enrollments of males and females are most evident in developing countries and persist at all educational levels. However, in developing countries, female participation in postsecondary education is beginning to equal or surpass that of males (p. 147).

• Access to vocational training—Education and training systems reinforce gender-based occupational segregation in the workforce, thereby limiting access to a wide range of occupations. With half the world's workers in occupations where at least 80 percent of the workforce is of the same gender, women's opportunities are severely curtailed because there exist seven times as many male-dominated occupations as female-dominated ones. Male-dominated occupations are perceived as having greater value and are typically characterized by higher pay, higher status, and more advancement opportunities (p. 150).

• Access to work-based training—Discrimination in employer-provided training especially affects women. Employers are less likely to invest in initial or further training for women because of their higher rates of job-leaving due to family responsibilities and because they may be part-time or temporary workers (p. 152).

• Access to lifelong learning—Lifelong learning opportunities tend to be most available to those who already work in high-level jobs. Women working in lower skilled or less secure employment could be disadvantaged in obtaining lifelong learning opportunities (p. 153).

• Access to training programs for the unemployed—These programs may underrepresent women when (a) women are not registered as unemployed, (b) the training programs lack such related support provisions as child care, or (c) male-focused occupations are targeted (p. 154).

• Access to new technology training—Skill development in such areas as information and communications technology is critical if women are to progress. However, this area also presents more opportunities for men (p. 156).

BARRIERS TO EFFECTING CHANGE

True and lasting success toward meeting the educational and employability needs of girls and women requires a strategic, integrated approach. Such an approach includes creating enabling policy and a supportive institutional environment; accommodating cultural beliefs; educating parents and communities about the benefits of education; improving the quality, access, and relevance of education and training; and enhancing employability by linking women more effectively with work opportunities. The challenge facing vocational and technical educators is how to do this, given existing cultural, economic, and political barriers. These gender barriers include the (a) historical roles of men and women, (b) inequitable allocation of resources, (c) underlying structures of power and authority, (d) cultural and family constraints, (e) poverty, (f) curriculum limitations, and (g) inaccessible delivery structures.

Far from being gender-neutral, past international development initiatives mainly focused on males as the key participants. Subsequently, international and national approaches to education and training, whether formal or informal, reflect bias toward preparing boys and men for traditionally male occupations. Historically, the importance of female roles often went unrecognized. When it was recognized, it also reflected a gender-specific orientation.

Too few resources are devoted to basic services for women. In 1997, the United Nations (1997a) estimated that $6 billion was spent for basic education worldwide, compared with $780 billion for military spending. Making basic education a priority is not easy. In countries where the culture requires separating pupils by sex, schools for girls are often fewer and less accessible. Countries must make tough choices related to allocating scarce resources. Often, choices may be made between primary schools and higher education institutions, when the reality is that both types of institutions need support. Some governments are beginning to spend more on primary and secondary education, but higher education is still more heavily subsidized relative to other tiers (United Nations, 1998, p. 37). Public spending reflects the beliefs, values, and priorities of the power group(s) in a country. These may be deeply ingrained.

Discrimination against girls and women persists because of cultural and religious patterns that include early marriages and pregnancies; inadequate, gender-biased communications; sexual harassment; and heavy domestic responsibilities that start at an early age. Even when women do achieve a level of education similar to men, they may not use it to the extent men do.

Families—especially poor families—prefer to educate boys because they have more income potential for the family. In low-income countries, most of women's work takes the form of unpaid activities—much of the nonmarket work performed in all societies remains statistically invisible. Women work longer hours than men in most countries and often carry a disproportionate burden of coping with family matters and poverty.

Despite improvements in access to education, the quality of education that girls receive suffers because of biases that persist in teaching materials and the curriculum. General education lacks career orientation. When girls and women receive vocational training, they train for a narrow niche of stereotyped occupations considered "appropriate and suitable" but which have low market value and limited employment prospects.

Deficiencies prevail even in training programs organized to help women. For example, most women live dispersed in rural areas, but vocational and technical institutions are concentrated in urban areas or in a few provinces or districts. Even when institutions are located in rural areas, women lack information about program offerings. Long commuting distances or cultural traditions that isolate women from public observation prevent or inhibit travel. In addition, women may not possess necessary entry requirements or qualifications, such as a secondary school certificate or math and science knowledge. Fees and costs of training may be prohibitive, or the time required to complete a program may make it too hard to reconcile domestic responsibilities and training. Finally, there may be a lack of accommodations or facilities for women (United Nations, 1997b).

INTERNATIONAL AGENDAS FOR WOMEN

Given the significant worldwide barriers to

access and change, it may help to recognize several declarations that encourage further action for women. In addition to the initial support provided by the United Nations Charter, a significant consensus on an international agenda for women's development has emerged via such world policy arenas as the World Conference on Education for All in 1990, the Copenhagen Declaration and Programme of Action of the United Nations World Summit for Social Development in 1995, and the Beijing Platform. The ground-breaking agreements from these venues included the following commitments:

- Eradicate absolute poverty by a target date to be set by each country.
- Support full employment as a policy goal.
- Achieve equality and equity between men and women.
- Attain universal and equitable access to education.

The World Conference on Education for All in 1990 resulted in an agreement to increase the scope and quality of primary schooling and to expand adult education. Ending gender inequalities and increasing enrollments and the performance of girls were among the agreement's priorities (United Nations, 1997a, p. 108). Likewise, the Beijing Platform recognized the importance of education and training for women and girls, both as a human right and as an essential tool for improving equality. This agenda called for eradicating women's illiteracy; improving women's access to vocational education, science and technology education, and continuing education; developing nondiscriminatory education and training; allocating sufficient resources to monitor the implementation of educational reforms; and promoting lifelong training for girls and women (United Nations, 1997c, pp. 10-21).

In addition to these legacies, the United Nations Educational, Scientific, and Cultural Organization (UNESCO) World Conference on Higher Education (1998) adopted a declaration containing specifically targeted provisions within its "new vision" portion. In addition to equity of access, Article 4 on "Enhancing participation and promoting the role of women" included the following assertions:

(a) Although significant progress has been achieved to enhance the access of women to higher education, various socioeconomic, cultural and political obstacles continue in many places in the world to impede their full access and effective integration. To overcome them remains an urgent priority in the renewal process for ensuring an equitable and nondiscriminatory system of higher education based on the principle of merit.
(b) Further efforts are required to eliminate all gender stereotyping in higher education, to consider gender aspects in different disciplines and to consolidate women's participation at all levels and in all disciplines, in which they are underrepresented and, in particular, to enhance their active involvement in decision-making.
(c) Gender studies (women's studies) should be promoted as a field of knowledge, strategic for the transformation of higher education and society.
(d) Efforts should be made to eliminate political and social barriers whereby women are underrepresented and in particular to enhance their active involvement at policy and decision-making levels within higher education and society. (p. 6)

ANOTHER AGENDA FOR CHANGE

Vocational educators have long prided themselves on providing relevant, practical learning experiences targeted toward developing competence for work. The roots of vocational education were firmly planted in the belief that meaningful work has importance for individuals and for society—that is, the work of individuals contributes to the well-being of society. Vocational education's liberating purpose sought to help individuals acquire the knowledge and skills necessary to successfully participate in the economic sector, freeing them from dependency. With the progression of the industrial age and its concern for efficiency, policymakers and vocational educators have emphasized the importance of matching the skills of the labor force with the needs of the labor market over individual development and fulfillment through meaningful work.

At this point, however, the prudent thing to do to prepare for the new millennium may be to propose an agenda for vocational/technical education that revisits the need to provide for individual development as well as the need to serve society. For example, an agenda that focuses on education and training for women might highlight such actions as the following:

1. *Support and actively contribute to the further development of basic education and literacy programs.* Significant gains have been made in improving access to formal education for girls and women, although considerable variation exists. At the primary levels, about 22 percent of the world's primary-school-age children are out of school. In developing countries, about 20 percent of the children do not go beyond fifth grade. More than two-thirds of the world's children who never go to school, or who drop out before completing primary school, are girls (United States Agency for International Development, 1996/97, pp. 1, 4). At postsecondary levels, female enrollments equal or surpass those of males in a number of developed countries. In developing countries, however, enrollments of females in postsecondary education continue to lag (International Labour Office [ILO], 1998, p. 147).

2. *Examine practices that may contribute to gender-related socialization patterns leading to*

• There has been broad progress toward literacy, but the literacy gap between men and women is still growing. In 1995, 597 million women were illiterate as compared with 352 million men.

• A great literacy deficit remains among adult women that will persist well into the 21st century, especially in such rural areas as sub-Saharan Africa, and southern and western Asia.

• Illiteracy rates have dropped, yet the number of illiterate girls and women has increased from 543 million in 1970 to 597 million in 1985. The increase was less for boys and men.

• Girls' school enrollments in primary and secondary schools now equal boys' in most developed countries, as well as Latin America and the Caribbean.

• More women now enroll in colleges and universities, but there are wide disparities among countries, ranging from enrollments nearly equal to that of men (in developed countries, and some in Southern Africa, Latin America, and the Caribbean) to fewer than 30 women per 100 men in sub-Saharan African and southern Asian countries (United Nations, 1991, pp. 45-46).

segregated occupations. Do we engage in practices that inadvertently perpetuate stereotypes we want to eliminate? As Pehu, Avotie, and Lasonen (1997) note in the report of their study of training needs for entrepreneurial leadership for women,

[I]nternal constraints that hold both men and women back from making nontraditional vocational and professional choices are constructed in gender-related socialization processes and shaped by structural forces (for example, the gender system). The purpose of socialization processes is to make us individuals that are both able and willing to play traditional gender roles. The other side of this coin is, naturally, that such processes also tend to make us individuals of the kind that do not have the skills necessary for or interest in making nontraditional choices. (p. 213)

Perhaps educators underestimate their role in this process. Rather than thinking "gender differences are biological," they need to consider a broader view: gender differences derive from a complex interaction of biological, cultural, psychological, and environmental factors.

3. *Develop strategies that effectively engage and sustain individuals in nontraditional occupations.* These strategies might necessarily begin in early education, extending through and beyond an individual's formal education into lifelong learning. Consequently, several arrays of strategies will be needed—for example, those that cause a person to consider possibilities and define them broadly, those that offer alternative instructional approaches, and those that feature finding-the-job and on-the-job support. These strategies will be most effective if they evolve with community participation and support.

Other important questions concern the way that work in nontraditional occupations is valued. What assumptions drive wages down when more women become involved? What information could an educational setting provide that would help workers assess the potential value of their work?

Another dimension involves assigning emerging occupations to one gender or another. What can be done to resist such tendencies? For example, the International Labour Office (1998) notes that occupations in information

technology risk becoming male-dominated (p. 156). What are the reasons for such developments? Unless women and girls participate fully in cyberspace, they will face a new kind of exclusion from society.

In many countries, women now enroll in postsecondary education programs to a much greater degree than ever before. Their interests extend to areas of study nontraditional for them. How can their involvements be sustained?

4. *Emphasize programs that meet the needs of the knowledge age.* Basic education and literacy are fundamental to other gains but are insufficient for the knowledge age. A wide gap exists between basic literacy and the sophisticated, entrepreneurial abilities currently needed. Effective education and training for

- More women in college programs now enroll in male-dominated fields, having reached a ratio of 1 to 2 in developed regions, Latin America, and the Caribbean by 1984. In Africa, Asia, and the Pacific, however, the ratio remains 1 to 5.
- Except for Africa, women have made rapid gains in advanced training for law and business. By 1984, enrollments of men and women in these fields were nearly equal within developed regions, Latin America, and the Caribbean.
- In all regions, women increased their representation in advanced science and engineering programs by about half.
- The proportion of women primary school teachers also increased everywhere, but with wide regional differences. Men outnumber women in secondary school teaching in all regions except Latin America and the Caribbean, where they are equal (United Nations, 1991, pp. 47-48).

girls and women must meet the educational needs of the knowledge society. In the 21st century, all individuals will need entrepreneurial life skills in order to succeed in a world where traditional safety nets may have disappeared. They must be able to (a) assess their own talents and abilities to determine how these match workplace needs; (b) sell their abilities in a way that gives them access to opportunities; (c) convince others that they are competent, trustworthy, and committed; and (d) create relationships that build group effectiveness and lead to future opportunities. Also, they must be effective in creating and sustaining—or disengaging from—partnerships that may be cross-cultural in nature. Finally, entrepreneurial learners must be able to assess the happenings of the world around them and use this knowledge toward planning for the future (Daines, 1993, p. 18).

But, in the future, work also will increasingly take place within a collaborative context. The United Nations 1992 World Economic Survey, for example, emphasizes that "[t]he complex and cumulative nature of contemporary technical progress, as well as the amount and quality of information and knowledge required to innovate, make modern entrepreneurship more of a collective effort than an individual one" (ILO, 1998, p. 147). Barriers to the full participation of women will impede team effort.

5. *Establish partnerships to build commitment, extend resources, and improve effectiveness.* Among the most beneficial partnerships that could be developed would be one that unites academic and vocational interests within the educational environment. This could help address gender disparities by building respect for different kinds of knowledge and skills. Learning would connect to the real-world experiences of individuals and, consequently, would be interesting to consider. Integrating these dimensions to educate the whole person could result in new ideas about work, the kind of preparation needed for certain kinds of work, and the effects of making particular choices. Certainly other essential partnerships involve different sectors within a community. They should be viewed from the perspective of being mutually beneficial and collaborative.

6. *Develop a multifaceted approach.* This idea simply involves using more than one strategy or designing a system of strategies to address the problem. For example, the U.S. Agency for International Development (1997) uses six major interventions to address gender issues, including (a) awareness raising and promotional/advocacy campaigns, (b) career information and counseling services, (c) professional development, (d) mentors, (e) work-based learning, and (f) parental involvement (p. 25). Another multifaceted approach would focus on policy, programs, innovative delivery structures and systems, outcomes, and other dimensions.

CURRICULA AS AN EDUCATIONAL RESOURCE

The nature of these challenges requires educators to consider using curriculum models that can address complex issues. This section describes situated curricula and introduces practical reasoning as examples to consider. Both cases involve constructing meanings within a cultural context and questioning conventional instructional perceptions. Situated curricula and practical reasoning aim to reconstruct the learning environment rather than reproduce the existing learning and work culture, with the expectation that this reconstruction will contribute to changing the vocational aspirations of young women, as well as young men.

Situated Curricula

A "situated curriculum" features a pedagogy based on feminist theory (Brady, 1995; Haraway, 1991) that challenges students and teachers to understand that the positions one is allowed to occupy, because of larger systems of dominance and privilege, limit one's perceptions. As a result, a situated curriculum challenges teachers and students to acknowledge, negotiate, and metamorphose systems of dominance by searching for connections to see from multiple perspectives and thereby recover power as learners and future workers. At the same time, students learn to become responsible and accountable whenever they hold positions of authority, as can be the case in many working situations.

By visualizing the world in this way, "a person's view is always constructed and stitched together imperfectly, and therefore able to join one another to see together without claiming to be one another" (Haraway, 1991). In order to develop this understanding, a pedagogy must sustain multiple purposes, allow for shifts in organization, use problems as a basis for instruction, and recognize the potential of classroom practice to act as direct theory in which teachers and students become powerful agents in their own working lives.

Sustaining multiple purposes. A feminist pedagogy for vocational education would sustain multiple purposes. Instead of maintaining only one goal (i.e., to get a job to make money), the concept of work would be addressed holistically by examining diverse, conditional, and/or overlapping ways to work and reasons for working. Multiple purposes would emerge, whereby different students, schools, and communities could focus on the larger purpose of providing all students with practical skills, space, and possibility in order to emerge from vocational education/training as critical, engaged participants of the working world. Educators cannot count on a one-size-fits-all mentality in forming a purpose or rely on what they think is the desired purpose. Rather, there must be an intense local analysis and evaluation of how communities and individual students are positioned between vocational need and desire. "It requires all involved, teachers, students, parents, community members to become active participants in working through fears, misunderstanding, and conflict" (Brady, 1995). Women as well as men would come together to voice ideas and concerns relating to work and work training. Across communities, students would experience a vocational education that could both resemble and differ from the vocational education experi-

enced by students in neighboring towns. In this way, there would be multiple purposes to education.

Allowing shifts in organization. Multiple purposes also could be sustained within communities and among students. That is, a student may have a different reason for enrolling in a particular class than another student in the same class, or a student could have more than one reason for enrolling in a program. To accommodate this need, vocational education would change in structure to allow for shifts in organization.

Shifts in organization would also require grappling with such dichotomies as vocational/academic track, classroom/real world, teacher/student, worker/employer, women's work/men's work, and paid/unpaid labor. Since accepting dichotomies legitimizes or naturalizes them to the extent that one person may be placed in a more powerful position than another, analyzing the ways that terms have been historically constructed and used in relationship to each other may help clarify the ways they have been used to justify power positions.

Situated curricula would combat dichotomies as both a strategy and a goal in mapping new relationships between students and the working world. One way to do this is by shifting organization to accommodate the many roles that people fulfill within cultural systems of power relationships and work responsibilities. For vocational education, this would mean restructuring by asking the following types of questions.

• What counts as work training?
• What skills should be taught?
• What courses should be included?
• Where should training occur—in school? On the job?
• What counts as work?
• What results are sought?

Envisioning a shifting organization would allow students to position themselves in and out of school, mapping programs with skills and choices that consider both vocational need and desire.

Being problem-focused, contextualized, and contradictory. Here again in situated curricula, a perception of multiple purposes calls for an analysis and evaluation of vocational need and desire. For example, if women study subjects and seek jobs that have traditionally been men's purview, there may be, on the one hand, more money for women to support families; yet there may also be more cases of sexual harassment. A need for more money and a desire for access to a specific working role directly conflict with the need and desire for a harassment-free working environment. By allowing for multiple purposes defined by communities and by shifting organization, this conflict could be recognized.

Using classroom practice as direct theory. Classroom practice has the potential to become a place where teachers and students become powerful agents in their own working lives. Because the working world is dynamic rather than static, it makes little sense to effect a curriculum that prescribes specific skills and goals to attain. To be consistent, teachers and students must engage in an ongoing critical analysis of recommended definitions of content.

At the same time, vocational educators must recognize their own teaching as located and positioned. Feminist educator Jeanne Brady (1995) describes four ways in which teachers can act as intellectuals:

> First, it highlights the importance of teachers recognizing the role that they play in constructing political subjects. . . . Secondly, a feminist notion of engaged intellectual . . . points to addressing how the specificity of one's own context can be addressed in terms of its strengths and weaknesses. . . . Thirdly, it is imperative that the issue of authority be addressed as both a moral and political question. Fourthly, the notion of engaged intellectual . . . draws from the feminist emphasis on building alliances, developing new forms of solidarity, and organizing collectively. (p. 99)

Brady (1995) challenges teachers to recognize and act responsibly with the authority, power, and influence that come from teaching.

Practical Reasoning

In many respects, situated curricula resemble approaches based on practical reasoning, which evolved as a way to address problems of home and family. "The essence of practical reasoning is the reflective deliberative process used by individuals and groups when faced with uncertainty about what actions to take" (Laster, 1998, p. 53). It focuses on particular real-life situations that emerge through one's interactions with society; it involves a value component that includes examining the effects of one's decisions on others; and it develops shared meanings related to the case in point. Because it is situated, and because each situation has multiple layers of context, it is impossible to generalize what is right to do across situations (Rettig, 1998, p. 103).

Practical reasoning—defined as a "skilled intellectual and social process of inquiry used in addressing and answering practical questions" (as quoted in Fedje, 1998)—is

• Used for complex, continuing human concerns that are never completely solved.

• Reflected through four interdependent categories of questions (context, valued ends, means, consequences) requiring conscious, deliberate examination.

• Manifested in specific everyday examples.

• Dialogical, seeking with others to clarify and challenge ideas and define continuing concerns more clearly.

• Dependent upon critical and creative thinking skills.

• Used to establish the moral defensibility of goals and means (Fedji, 1998, p. 30).

In a teaching/learning situation that involves practical reasoning, the teacher and student are both learners. They identify the important questions together and determine how to approach them. As they engage in thoughtful examination and construction of meanings related to the question considered, development occurs, enabling participants to explore other dimensions. The resulting framework guides further action.

SUMMARY

Although education and training are essential to development in the knowledge age, women continue to experience unequal access despite increasingly high participation in the world's labor force. Globalization and other factors contribute to the uncertainties and disparities inherent in women's work situations. Systemic barriers persist despite consensus on the need for substantive change. True and lasting success toward meeting the education and employment needs of girls and women requires creating a discrimination-free and enabling environment. An aggressive agenda would examine education and training reforms in the following areas: basic education, current practices (for stereotyping), nontraditional occupations, knowledge-age programs, partnerships, and multifaceted approaches. Curriculum models that address context from different perspectives may help improve the effectiveness of education and training.

References

Brady, J. (1995). *Schooling young children: A feminist pedagogy for liberatory learning.* Albany, NY: State University of New York.

Chottepanda, M. (1998). Workforce shortage issues: A national and global perspective. In Economic Resource Group, *1998 Economic report to the governor* (pp. 33-44). St. Paul, MN: Author.

Daines, J. (1993). *Preparing the work force for the 21st century: Postsecondary education in the midst of paradigm shift* (The Leadership Academy Monograph Series). St. Paul, MN: University of Minnesota College of Education.

Fedje, C. (1998). Helping learners develop their practical reasoning capacities. In R. Thomas & J. Laster (Eds.), *Family and consumer sciences teacher education: Yearbook 18. Inquiry into thinking* (pp. 29-44). Peoria, IL: American Association of Family and Consumer Sciences and Glencoe/McGraw-Hill.

Haraway, D. (1991). *Simians, cyborgs and women: The reinvention of nature.* London: Routledge.

International Labour Office [ILO]. (1998). Women and training in the global economy. In *World employment report 1998-99: Employability in the global economy—How training matters* (pp. 139-162). Geneva, Switzerland: Author.

Janjic, M. (1985). Women's work in industrialized countries: An overview from the perspective of the International Labor Organization. In J. Farley (Ed.), *Women workers in fifteen countries* (pp. 1-12). Ithaca, NY: Industrial and Labor Relations Press, Cornell University.

Laster, J. (1998). Assessment of practical reasoning. In R. Thomas & J. Laster (Eds.), *Family and consumer sciences teacher education: Yearbook 18. Inquiry into thinking* (pp. 47-74). Peoria, IL: American Association of Family and Consumer Sciences and Glencoe/McGraw-Hill.

Longman, P. (1999, March 1). The world turns gray: How global aging will challenge the world's economic well-being. *U.S. News & World Report, 126,* 30-39.

Pehu, E., Avotie, L., & Lasonen, J. (1997). Training needs in entrepreneurial leadership for women: Cases from north and south. In J. Lasonen (Ed.), *IVETA '97 conference proceedings: The challenges for the 21st century for vocational education and training* (pp. 212-218). Helsinki, Finland: Institute for Educational Research, University of Jyväskylä.

Rettig, K. (1998). Families as contexts for thinking. In R. Thomas & J. Laster (Eds.), *Family and consumer sciences teacher education: Yearbook 18. Inquiry into thinking* (pp. 101-128). Peoria, IL: American Association of Family and Consumer Sciences and Glencoe/McGraw-Hill.

United Nations. (1991). *The world's women 1970-1990: Trends and statistics* (Social Statistics and Indicators, Series K, No. 8). New York: Author.

United Nations. (1997a). *Human development report.* New York: Author.

United Nations. (1997b). *Commission on the status of women: Report on the forty-first session.* New York: Author.

United Nations. (1997c). *Guidelines: Women in Asia.* New York: Author.

United Nations. (1998). *Human development report.* New York: Author.

United Nations Educational, Scientific, and Cultural Organization World Conference on Higher Education. (1998, October 9). *World declaration on higher education for the twenty-first century: Vision and action.* Available: www.unesco.org/education/educ/prog/wche/declaration_eng.html

United States Agency for International Development [USAID]. (1996/97). *Girls' and womens' education: A USAID initiative underway in gender action.* Washington, DC: U.S. Office of Women in Development, USAID.

United States Agency for International Development. (1997). *Human capacity development in the 21st century.* Washington, DC: Author.

Women, Education, and Training: Old Challenges in a New Age

3

Education and Training Partnerships: An Enabling Framework

By Sharon Coursey

Partnerships are an appealing concept. They have considerable potential for linking services and resources: schools and training organizations unite with other social partners into collaborative relationships to organize, fund, and conduct workforce preparation activities. Combining resources reduces costs, and equally important, service delivery directly involves the various stakeholders. Stronger articulation results. Within the education and training community, one of the best ways to reshape the overall design and conduct of workforce preparation is to strengthen the links among business, labor, education, community groups, and the government at all levels.

The concept of education and training partnerships is not new. In the past two decades, however, considerably more emphasis has been placed on the collaborative advantages that may derive from partnerships. Although the concept once was primarily the province of the business community, a growing international consensus exists that partnerships can stimulate reform within and between business, education, and human services. Based on a study of public/private training partnerships in 14

countries, Mitchell (1998) concludes that many countries are developing new types of partnerships because they are seen as "strategic" in the sense that "they can have a significant impact on the development of skilled manpower and on social and economic development" (p. 10).

As governments and organizations struggle over how to best garner needed resources to address the challenges of globalization and complex social problems, the use of partnerships is seen as a viable strategy. They can create opportunities for collective learning and action, overcome scarcity, reduce costs, and spread financial burdens (Kantor, 1994; Pease & Copa, 1994; Raben, 1992; Saranson & Lorentz, 1998).

The first part of this chapter explores the underlying conditions that promote partnerships and presents a brief review of literature on the topic. It points to the limitations of existing approaches to partnerships, specifically as they relate to partnering between business and education. The second part offers a more encompassing framework for enabling partnerships, a framework that takes more than functions and structures into account and requires that we give at least proportional consideration to understanding human behaviors and interactions that can facilitate or impede the success of partnerships.

CONDITIONS GIVING RISE TO PARTNERSHIPS

Society is undergoing a transformation that affects all spheres of economic, social, and political life. The combined forces of globalization and rapid technological change drive this transformation, particularly those innovations in information and communication technologies that force companies to become more competitive (Gibbs, Hedge, & Clough, 1991; Stern, Bailey, & Merritt, 1996). At the same time, deregulation and the liberalization of international markets are leading to the dismantling of trade barriers, new multilateral trade agreements, and trade groupings (Mitchell, 1998).

In light of these circumstances, organizations face challenges that require them to transform internal structures, create new types of organizations and methods of work, and reconstruct their relationships with the external environment. A more "learning-intensive economy" is changing the connections between education and work as employment becomes increasingly fluid, occupational boundaries blur, and larger numbers of jobs become temporary or transient. The new economy requires the workforce to be differently educated and higher skilled, creating preparation challenges too complex and resource intensive for any single player to address (Stern, Bailey, & Merritt, 1996).

Addressing the challenge of workforce preparation has driven the proliferation of partnership efforts between business and education in the past decade. The resources and comparative advantages among and between organizations, as well as across sectors, are being enlisted for the mutual benefit of the various partners on behalf of those who are served. Some researchers optimistically suggest that these partnerships may ultimately help reconcile differences between business and education. The partnerships are viewed as potent tools for education, training, and re-tooling the workforce. Efforts have resulted in an increasingly wide array of partnership types and forms but also, unfortunately, in a mixed record of successes and failures.

INFORMATION ON PARTNERSHIPS

There has been no dearth of guidance and recommendations for establishing effective partnerships. To a great extent, much advice emanates from the business sector, advice shaped largely by experiences in corporate partnering and cooperative efforts. The information on partnerships tends to fall into two categories: (a) that which addresses the necessary functional components or essential features of a partnership and (b) that which emphasizes the importance of structural and technical conditions that enable partnerships. Admittedly, the literature does not divide as neatly as indicated here, and some overlap exists between the categories.

Functional Components

Research and popular literature alike are dense with normative advice and replete with theoretical frameworks that advance certain functional components that will likely produce effective partnerships (Pease & Copa, 1994; Raben, 1992). They emphasize relational properties and the organizing features fundamental to successful partnering. Authors repeatedly mention the following features as essential to establishing partnerships with solid foundations.

• *Unity of purpose and mutually compatible goals*—Many authors logically suggest that a partnership be based on a shared sense of an existing problem or opportunity, and the ability to see that collaborative efforts will likely make a difference.

• *Commitment of members*—Commitment to a partnership must be broadly based. It cannot function successfully or sustain itself if only a few individuals who see its promise and potential try to make it work.

• *Commitment of resources*—Partners must know what resources each has to offer and be willing to deploy their capital, facilities, human resources, and so forth, to partnership requirements.

• *Exchange of information*—Partners must communicate frequently and willingly supply each other with information on problems, successes, and any concerns that emerge.

• *Trust and respect among and between partners*—This is quite possibly the most frequently cited feature of successful partnerships.

The literature suggests that establishing partnerships is a natural process of employers and educators uniting, aligned in their sense of mission goals and willing to commit their respective resources and expertise in the interest of shared outcomes and purpose. It is hard to argue with the logic and importance of shared intent, commitment, and outcomes. However, the literature does not offer tangible advice on how to attain this or how to deal with complex interactions that stem from competing motives, perspectives, and values, and those that preclude trust, shared purpose, and overt commitments from materializing in the first place.

Structures for Enabling Partnerships

Proponents rightfully point out that productive partnerships require structure (Pease & Copa, 1994). Authors and experts who address structure emphasize the importance of policy frameworks; supportive and coherent organizational design; delineation of roles, responsibilities, and performance expectations; as well as the need for planning, funding, and evaluation mechanisms to be in place (Gibbs, Hedge, & Clough, 1991; Raben, 1992; Saranson & Lorentz, 1998). They view structure as a critical strategy for overcoming barriers in partnerships. Examples include

• Formalizing structures and processes for stakeholder involvement.

• Developing internal procedures for identifying priorities and projects.

• Preparing position descriptions and performance expectations.

• Establishing mechanisms for documenting progress and success/failure.

• Accounting for costs and benefits.

• Providing partners with opportunities to maximize their respective interests and structuring adequate incentives to evoke cooperation.

The purposes underlying these structures may vary but generally they allow for (a) clarifying different priorities to ensure that people know their roles and duties in relation to the partnership and (b) an orderly, well-managed process that allows the partnership to progress toward its objectives. Authors of this advice, to their credit, caution against partners having illusions about easily achieving their purpose. However, their adherence to the notion that well-designed structures and systems adequately ensure against misunderstandings and potential failure may be overly optimistic.

WHERE DO FUNCTION AND STRUCTURE LEAVE US?

As with the functional components identified earlier, the logic and importance of structure as a facilitative mechanism is not without merit. Structures are essential and pave the way for orderly and organized workings within a partnership, whether in workforce development or other joint endeavors. Notwithstanding all of the advice from experts, however, pundits and researchers alike admit that, despite their prevalence and potential, partnerships flounder and fail at least as often, if not more often, than they succeed (Gibbs, Hedge, & Clough, 1991; Kantor, 1994; Raben, 1992; Saranson & Lorentz, 1998).

Partnerships between education and business have not been immune to this failure (Grubb, 1989). This phenomenon is not unique to the United States; it is most prevalent in countries that lack traditions of (a) employer participation in the education and training of youth and (b) centralized decision-making among social partners, as can be seen in more successful partnerships such as in Germany and Denmark (Olsen, 1997; Stern, Bailey, & Merritt, 1996, p. 39).

Collaboration between public and private sectors is not a habitual mode of relationship (Gibbs, Hedge, & Clough, 1991). In the absence of the unifying form that social partnerships provide, differences in values, motivation, and beliefs inevitably surface, posing unique challenges to joint endeavors. On-going antagonisms and misunderstandings more aptly characterize many of the interactions and relationships between business and education (Grubb, 1989). Gibbs, Hedge, and Clough (1991) write that, "Within the galaxy of education-business partnership groups and organizations there is, on the one hand, rhetoric of collaboration and cooperation, and on the other hand, a high degree of paranoia in partnership work, often focused on survival and power" (p. 52). It is unlikely that clear functions and sound structures can adequately reconcile these conditions. It is therefore necessary to move beyond function and structure.

REFOCUSING ON EXPERIENCES AND PERSPECTIVES

One of the single-most important understandings that has emerged from failed efforts during the past decade is that productive partnerships emphasize substantive interface and interactions between partners (Bodinger deUriarte, 1994; Gibbs, Hedge, & Clough, 1991). Promoters of functional and structural approaches tend to overlook that education and business are both "complex sub-systems comprised of people within a society which is itself a complex socio-technical and cultural system" (Woolhouse, 1991, p. 9). Individually and collectively, the two sectors have different values, experiences, and perspectives that long preceded partnering efforts and that subsequently shape human interactions. They influence receptivity and willingness to partner; how problems and opportunities are viewed; how goals, resources, and expertise are defined; and the choices made about structure and approach. Successful partnering requires (a) a better understanding of one another's experiences and differing perspectives and (b) learning to bridge these differences through new forms of interaction.

Understanding Education's Views of Business

The education sector tends to see itself as having broader and more encompassing social objectives than the business sector. Many educators believe that businesses are preoccupied with their survival and with ensuring they have an adequate supply of workers, and that they care little about or do not value the intellectual growth and development of students. They tend to view business as a self-interested institution, with a mind and intent singularly focused on "no-holds-barred" profitability (Harrison & Bluestone, 1988).

Educators understandably question the motivation and commitment of corporate leaders who consistently attack their credibility and the quality of their work. Some are unwilling to ignore what they see as businesses' efforts to eschew genuine social responsibilities. The lack of commitment in supporting their own workforce's development has been duly documented (Harrison & Bluestone, 1988; Olsen, 1997).

Involving the business community in education raises moral and ethical issues for many educators, and educational institutions are genuinely and rightfully concerned about motivation, undue influences, and the prospects of exploitation (Gibbs, Hedge, & Clough, 1991; Pease & Copa, 1994).

Understanding Business's Views of Education

On the other hand, the business sector tends to view education and educators as resistant to change and unwilling to embrace the realities and demands of the new economy. They view the education system, including colleges and universities, as overly bureaucratized, insufficiently accountable, and out of touch with everyday realities and economic demands. Members of the business community have spearheaded efforts to restructure schools and curriculum. They have been determined in their efforts to bring educational institutions into the 21st century and have enjoyed both popular and political support in these efforts.

The business sector's ascendancy to power in American educational matters during the 1980s, and its subsequent influence on educational policy, remains a source of frustration and misunderstanding to some in the education community. Business effectively framed the economic downturns of the 1970s and 1980s in the U.S. as problems of an inadequate education system and poor teaching (Harrison & Bluestone, 1988) leading to increased scrutiny and demands for accountability at all levels.

The sting of this critique, and the subsequent perceived infringement on professionalism and autonomy, have not been forgotten by many educators and impinge on their comfort with and enthusiasm for partnering. The beliefs of educators, as well as others, that the business sector escaped unscathed for the extent to which its own strategies and lack of acumen contributed to the country's economic and competitiveness problems further exacerbate this situation (Harrison & Bluestone, 1988).

PARTNERSHIPS ARE COMPLEX UNDERTAKINGS

Personal experiences and points of view form part of the legacy that professionals in business and education bring to partnership building. Historical experiences inform their interactions and shape their diverse perceptions about the purposes of education and work; workforce development; and each other's missions, roles, interests, and power. Understandably, according to Woolhouse (1991),

motives of partners will be mixed and are not necessarily consistent or compatible. Agendas will be of an infinite variety and may not constitute an effective means of conciliating the problems they were intended to address. (p. 9)

Thus, partnering as a process must be recognized for its complexity. It requires much more than merely attending to functional and structural dimensions to address the tensions that surface in the face of the perceived threats to autonomy and mission, threats that understandably emerge in such a change effort as building a partnership (Gibbs, Hedge, & Clough, 1991; Kantor, 1994; Raben, 1992; Saranson & Lorentz, 1998; Wilson, 1992). These experiences and the meanings individuals ascribe to them constitute an extraordinary challenge to doing the complex work of collaborative interaction and interdependence that partnering requires. And particularly, for workforce development with its complex web of private and public institutions and oft-competing and paradoxical economic and social considerations, one cannot expect to partner meaningfully and productively without deeply rooted conflicts arising. Prospective partners must be prepared to allow for substantive exchanges and interactions on these matters.

CONNECTING THE HUMAN ELEMENT TO OTHER CONSIDERATIONS

Moving away from the suspicion and distrust that emerge from these histories toward substantive forms of interaction requires that prospective partners honestly examine their respective motivations for forming a partnership. What is the impetus? Is it forced or imposed? Is one's real interest to dominate or direct? Does one partner plan to use what may be its greater leverage and power to coerce cooperation? Do all prospective partners see and believe that a legitimate and appropriate role exists for others, and that the prospect exists for creating greater value and impact than either enterprise could create alone?

Successfully implementing and institutionalizing any partnership will unlikely occur where perceptions of relative social (and professional) status are unequal or defined in terms of one or more organizations dominating or parenting the other, or of one being more right than the other (Bodinger deUriarte, 1994, p. 2).

In her study on role appropriateness in education-business partnerships, Bodinger deUriarte (1994) suggests that

> [b]eneath the structures, roles and resources, participants in partnerships operated from one of two perspectives which were found to effect the implementation, interorganizational interaction, and sustainability of the effort. The one perspective viewed the relationship as a "social contract," based on pluralist conceptions of social structures, while the second perspective was paternalistic, and based on a hierarchical conception of stratification. (p. 22)

The pluralist perspective of the interactionist model recognizes that people do not share the same world of meaning and believes that this is an acceptable feature of social reality. The pluralist ideal in interaction is a "balance of power, in a heterogeneous setting, earmarked by a variety of interests" (Bodinger deUriarte, 1994, p. 2). Engaged in pluralist efforts, individuals (and groups) create a balance of power that makes room for a variety of interests and forges structure based on negotiations.

Pluralist partnerships will likelier take on forms that consist of divisions of labor between organizations and take into account the respective assets and expertise of the various partners. Each partner brings valuable resources to the endeavor and has legitimate, respected, and complementary roles and responsibilities to carry out. Together the partners create synergistic value that neither might establish on its own.

A paternalistic perspective, on the other hand, sees one partner as dominant and recognizes one world of meanings as primary, wiser, or more developed than the other. The paternalism manifests itself in more highly stratified organizational structures and interactions. The meanings, goals, and aspirations of the primary partner comprise those that the partnership forms around. The primary partner holds an inflated sense of importance as the one with the most critical expertise. Primary partners set the partnership's tone and direction, and their organization is distinguished by its role as leader (Bodinger deUriarte, 1994).

It is easy to envision how, in the case between those partnering in the education and business sectors, paternalist-oriented interactions would do little to foster trust or diffuse suspicions. Inevitably, individuals (and members of their respective groups), revert to retrospective meaning-making. Past experiences and long memories dominate the tone of interactions in the relationship, manifesting themselves in both subtle and perceptible routines and blocking behaviors that can undermine prospects for any type of long-term collaboration or forging of new understandings.

The horizontal methods of communication and collaborative decision-making embedded in the pluralist perspective support a less-stratified partnership, one where substantive interactions and exchanges, different interests and interpretations can more freely surface. Pluralist approaches will likelier afford business and education partners the opportunities to shed some of the constraints that their histories and long memories can impose and, in the long term, strengthen the prospects for an

TABLE 1—ENABLING FUNCTIONAL, STRUCTURAL, AND INTERACTIONAL CONSIDERATIONS FOR PARTNERSHIPS

Functional considerations	Structural considerations	Interactional considerations
Shared, unified purpose	• Formalized structures and processes for gathering stakeholder input • Policy infrastructure in place for supporting collaboration	• Set agendas jointly • Create shared purpose by jointly identifying stakeholders • Inform the partnership's purpose with stakeholder interactions • Consider stakeholders in broad terms and include, for example, equity groups and unions
Mutually compatible and agreed-upon goals and outcomes	• Strategic planning systems and goal-setting activities • Decentralized governance structures that allow for responsiveness to local/regional needs and conditions	• Create opportunities to discuss partners' interpretations of purpose and motivations • Partners individually identify goals and interests, then exchange these and identify compatible and competing interests as well as ways they can be accommodated • Discuss concerns and pitfalls rising from partners' different values and experience
Equitable commitments from the partnering entities	• Written agreements that identify the resource commitments (monetary and other) • Transparent plans and time tables for deploying resources • Understanding and agreement on joint budgeting/funding approaches and other resource matters	• Identify (discuss and negotiate) both monetary and non-monetary resources that partners commit • Exchange views about what each partner sees as their own and each others' assets and liabilities • Discuss how the partnership enhances assets and resources, and the mutually beneficial value created by the partnership
Complementary roles and responsibilities	• Appropriate roles and divisions of labor • Clarity in performance expectations, new positions, and position descriptions • Incentives and rewards • Training and support for new and/or substantially different tasks and roles	• Develop various ways to build understanding and learn more about other partners' work and activities— for example, cross-training and cross-organizational exchanges— and involve people at all levels in the respective partner organizations • Collaboratively create new, different, and/or amended roles and expectations with those likely to be affected internally

Note: Information presented in this table draws upon the works of Bodinger deUriarte (1994); Gibbs, Hedge, and Clough (1991); Pease and Copa (1994); and Saranson and Lorentz (1998).

Workforce Preparation: An International Perspective

TABLE 1—ENABLING FUNCTIONAL, STRUCTURAL, AND INTERACTIONAL CONSIDERATIONS FOR PARTNERSHIPS (CONTINUED)

Functional considerations	Structural considerations	Interactional considerations
Supportive exchanges of information	• Communication systems and meeting schedules for formal exchanges • Mechanisms for documenting and disseminating information about activities as well as successes, failures, problems, etc. • Agreements to establish new or use existing infrastructure of boards, advisory groups, civic associations, etc.	• Engage cross-organizational teams to research what's working and what's not • Create stability in partner organizations during initial phases of transition • Address concerns about job change and loss • Create forums for exchanging and airing concerns

enduring partnership. Bodinger-deUriarte's (1994) insights are well-grounded in interactionist theory in sociology. They are also consistent with what those who research and work in the fields of organizational change and transition have come to appreciate about the importance and consideration that must be given to the perspectives underpinning individual actions (Kanter, 1989; Wilson, 1992). The pluralist view helps connect the human element in partnerships to functional and structural considerations.

Table 1 presents a conceptual framework for incorporating functional, structural, and interactional considerations into partnerships. The first column lists five essential functional considerations that must be in place for partnerships to operate. The second column details the structural considerations and mechanisms that facilitate operating and/or implementing the partnership; and the third column provides examples of how interactions might be conducted from the pluralist perspective.

Structures and process informed by a pluralist perspective emphasize joint and equitable interactions. Goals are, in fact, shared and jointly determined following sufficient input and dialogue about each partner's views of problems and opportunities. The interests of one partner do not dominate the agenda. Room exists for multiple interests to emerge and for partners to integrate respective concerns about efficiency and equity, just to name one example.

Local participation forms the cornerstone of the partnership. Stakeholders are identified broadly, and legitimate processes are put in place for using that input in planning and decision-making. Each partner's assets and liabilities, as well as how partners see them, comprise a part of the discussion about resources. Written covenants identify the partners' commitments to each other and to the effort.

Prospective partners must also recognize the diverse needs and interests of the members of their respective organizations. Partnering may have unsettling internal effects. It may be perceived as a threat to autonomy or as forcing unpalatable alterations of missions and customary roles. Approaching these as "acceptable interpretations" and understandable occurrences versus dismissing them as unreasonable or unfounded is critical for cultivating the broad internal commitment necessary to support the partnership.

A pluralist perspective, in sum, facilitates collaboration and allows for a substantive and respectful exchange of views. It must logically reside at the heart of any genuine partnership effort and reinforce the prospects for successful outcomes by joining complementary and compatible strengths, assets, and access. Despite the time-consuming effort and extent of negotiation and compromise required in the pluralist world, institutions increasingly appear to be adopting its logic, successfully establishing partnerships where substantive interactions between and among partners occur. Sustainability as well as impressive accomplishments result. Partnerships emerging between the education and business sectors show that failure is not by any means inevitable.

CONCLUSION

Partnerships are potent tools for workforce and economic development. Successful partnering efforts require attention to the functional and structural aspects of the partnership, as well as to the tremendously complex human beings who must work to make it succeed. Partnering that encourages genuine collaboration and is informed by a pluralist philosophy will likelier produce successful business-education outcomes.

Successful partnerships increasingly prevail and will continue to be possible if the two sectors can grow in their appreciation of the understandings and discipline that collaboration requires. To the extent that they can do so, their communities will reap the associated benefits of these collective efforts.

References

Bodinger deUriarte, C. (1994). *Business-education partnerships: The impact of role appropriateness.* Washington, DC: U.S. Department of Education.

Gibbs, B., Hedge, R., & Clough, E. (Eds.) (1991). *The reality of partnerships: Developing education and business relationships.* London: Longman.

Grubb, N. (1989). *The developing vocational education and training system: Partnerships and customized training.* Washington, DC: National Center for Research in Vocational Education, Office of Vocational and Adult Education, U.S. Department of Education.

Harrison, B., & Bluestone, B. (1988). *The great U-turn.* New York: Basic Books.

Kanter, R. M. (1989). *When giants learn to dance: Mastering the challenges of strategy, management and careers in the 1990's.* New York: Simon and Schuster.

Kantor, S. L. (1994). Training for customized training: Learning to teach the fully employed learner in the workplace. In S.L. Kantor (Ed.), *A practical guide to conducting customized work force training.* San Francisco: Jossey-Bass.

Mitchell, A. G. (1998). *Strategic training partnerships between the state and enterprises.* Geneva, Switzerland: International Labour Office.

Olsen, L. (1997). *The school-to-work revolution: How employers and educators are joining forces to prepare tomorrow's skilled workforce.* Reading, MA: Addison-Wesley.

Pease, V., & Copa, G. H. (1994). Partnerships in the school-to-work transition. In A. J. Paulter (Ed.), *High school to employment transitions: Contemporary issues* (pp. 243-256). Ann Arbor, MI: Prakken.

Raben, C. S. (1992). Building strategic partnerships: Creating and managing effective joint ventures. In D. Nadler, M. Gerstein, R. Shaw, and Associates (Eds.), *Organizational architecture: Designs for changing organizations* (pp. 81-109). San Francisco: Jossey-Bass.

Saranson, S., & Lorentz, E. (1998). *Crossing boundaries: Collaboration, coordination and the redefinition of resources.* San Francisco: Jossey-Bass.

Stern, D., Bailey, T., & Merritt, D. (1996). *School to work: Policy insights from recent international developments.* Berkeley, CA: University of California at Berkeley, National Center for Research in Vocational Education.

Wilson, D. C. (1992). *A strategy of change: Concepts and controversies in the management of change.* New York: Routledge.

Woolhouse, J. (1991). Partnership principles. In B. Gibbs, R. Hedge, & E. Clough (Eds.), *The reality of partnerships: Developing education and business relationships* (pp. 3-23). London: Longman.

4

Education, Training, and the Economy

By Stephanie Young

Whatever arguments may rage over the nature and purpose of general education, vocational education and training (VET) is unequivocally directed toward making available within the workforce the knowledge, skills, and motivation necessary to efficiently produce and distribute goods and services. In such a role, VET underpins a national aim to establish a sturdy and growing competitive economy that supports the attainment of long-term social and political goals. That synthesis of ideology and material forces that shape a nation's economic and industrial policies determines the principles by which the state, business, and individual trainees divide the costs of such vocational education and training.

VET policies can be characterized within a continuum that defines the economic boundaries of the state. At one extreme is the command economy typified by the U.S.S.R. before 1989, where centralized, coercive state planning controls most economic activity. At the other extreme is the neoliberal model epitomized by Hayekian laissez-faire economics in which the resolute absence of state interference unites with democracy, defined as "a utilitarian de-vice for safeguarding internal peace and individual freedom" (Hayek, 1967, p. 194).

In the command economy, the state is the sole provider of all general and vocational education. At the opposite extreme, the need to share basic knowledge about the operation of democratic institutions justifies state funding—but not state monopoly—of general education. At this extreme, no case for state funding of VET exists, since it is said to provide clear private benefits to the individual.

The United Kingdom (U.K.) of the 1960s exemplified a mixed economy set roughly at the mid-point of the continuum. Government intervention at the micro- and macroeconomic levels sought to restore national economic fortunes. Corporatist policies involving national and local government, trade unions, employers, and educationalists for the first time assumed a role in VET. However, by the late 1970s a new political strategy challenged the foundations of the mixed economy with a sustained program of action that promoted

a certain distinctive set of practices, ideas and institutional reforms, which constituted a very important new way of thinking about how rules and processes, norms and habits could be inculcated and regulations put in place that would alter the conduct of others. (Hall, 1993, p. 14)

This new managerialism so embedded the incentive, coordinating, and choice-enhancing effects of markets in the political culture that the onus of proof was unavoidably placed on those who argued for a wider set of considerations. As a result, VET policy was reoriented to emphasize the responsibilities of the individual and the employer, although government retained a role in specifying standards and in easing organizational frictions and institutional barriers.

The U.K.'s renewal of market ideology was not isolated but part of an international process. The world-wide deceleration in economic activity during the decade from the mid-1970s was the product of a number of successive economic shocks—the Bretton Woods collapse in 1971, oil price increases in 1973 and 1979, increasing inflation throughout the 1970s, and biting recessions in 1974-75 and 1980-82—that triggered a new and intense international reorganization of production aimed at restoring levels of profitability. The intensification of international competition and capital mobility forced those countries organizing for participation in economic growth to remove barriers to the free operation of market forces.

The spectacular growth of such developing economies as Singapore and Taiwan occurred within the market framework and provided an object lesson to other countries seeking to emulate their success. On the other hand, the dramatic collapse of the Soviet economy and the visible economic contrasts between such politically splintered countries as North and South Korea and East and West Germany sounded the death-knell of the centrally planned economy. Nevertheless, such political

and economic changes have not seen an end to significant state involvement in VET.

Postmodern capitalism has propagated the market as the supreme, implacable force that ensures economic growth through its ability to maximize benefits. It is represented as a morally meritorious guiding principle leading inescapably to globalization, technological change, labor market deregulation, and flexible employment, as well as unstable job tenure, unemployment, and intermittent financial crises. The pervasiveness of market rhetoric extends to the domain of individual consciousness, depoliticizing the human condition, as a new self-interested responsibility for personal economic success vindicated by market rationality weakens the collective responsibilities and entitlements of traditional social ties. Thus, those who first struggled against the system, the industrial working class, are absorbed into it.

Nevertheless, in a world of international competition, advantage in one area creates favorable conditions for advantage in another, so that the market favors those countries with market power. Thus, in failing or developing economies, or where particular sectors are floundering in successful economies, policymakers are led to consider how far the state should intervene to achieve the desired objective of improving industrial and commercial performance. The world openly acknowledges the reality of market failure and provides a "respectable" basis for state intervention in designing and operating national and local economic policies. While the moral standards of the market remain intact, they lead us to reappraise the balance between public and private investment in VET.

SELF-INVESTMENT IN TRAINING

Economic analysis of VET policy starts with the notion of *human capital*, defined by Rosen (1989) as the "the productive capacity of human beings as income producing agents in an economy" (p. 136). In recent years, the economic principles underpinning material capital have been extended to analyze the problems surrounding improvement in the stock of skills and productive knowledge of the individual.

VET is thus viewed as investing in the augmentation of human capital. As with any investment, a positive return is expected and someone has to foot the bill. The individual learner retains ownership of the skill, regardless of who pays for the investment, so that an employer must pay the higher salary that the superior skill commands, or risk poaching by a competitor. Thus, since only the employee can fully trap the financial benefits of training, he or she should bear its full cost. Nevertheless, where a firm leads in implementing new technology that necessitates its employees developing new skills, it is generally prepared to pay for training, including it in the evaluation of the costs and benefits of the material investment.

The techniques of investment appraisal involve discounting, whereby the financial net benefits of future events are converted to present values using the rate of interest at which funds may be obtained. The interest rate that would make the present value of future net benefits zero is the rate of return on the investment. That rate of return will diminish with each successive round of investment, but investment in training will continue to be profitable until the marginal rate of return equals the rate at which the individual can borrow money to finance the training cost. That is, the optimal level of investment by the individual occurs when the individual's private discount rate equals the rate of return on the self-investment.

The individual, intent on self-investment, must obtain funds by relinquishing some current consumption or by borrowing. Those who could most benefit from training—unskilled workers with low incomes—may have little room to reduce consumption, so that borrowing is their only alternative. However, the uncertain promise of a future increase in earnings is not collateral for the lender, and the transaction costs of small loans are high, so that borrowing may be impossible or subject to interest rates inflated to account for the lending risk involved. Nevertheless, labor is not homogeneous. Some people are better placed to achieve optimal training levels—the young because of the longer payback period, the able because superior learning ability means lower investment costs, and the wealthy because funds need not be borrowed. In addition, people may form incorrect perceptions of the benefits and costs of training, especially where a strongly progressive system of personal taxation exists.

Furthermore, there may be many other impediments: a lack of awareness of the opportunities for learning, misrepresentation or misperception of labor market signals, avoidance of the risks of training failure or the burden of debt, an absence of motivation or ability, restrictive labor practices or other barriers to entry, racial or gender discrimination, inadequate early schooling, or a bias toward academic education. Thus, collectively, individuals will undertake less than the optimal level of investment in training, and economic decline—or at best stagnation—inevitably results.

Collective action may remedy such market failures. Government, acting in the interest of society as a whole, may borrow at rates below market rates because it benefits from the advantages of diversification and risk-pooling. Thus, the government's social discount rate[1] is lower than the private discount rate, so that the optimal level of training will be greater than that where the private discount rate is applied. (See Diagram 1 on following page.)

[1] *The choice of discount rates for public sector investment remains a theoretical matter unresolved among economists. However, in practice, the rate is significantly less than the private discount rate.*

DIAGRAM 1—PRIVATE/PUBLIC OPTIMAL INVESTMENT

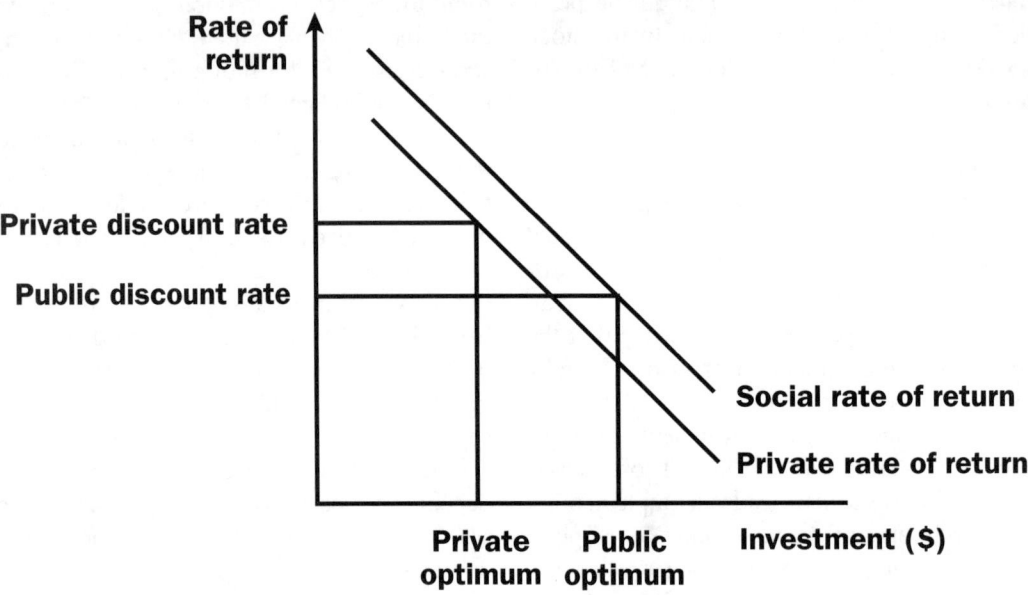

GOVERNMENT SUPPORT

Although rigid adherents to the market philosophy value minimal government intervention on the grounds that private administrative ineptitude and self-interest are preferable to bureaucratic excess and political self-interest, few disagree on the need for some level of regulation that establishes law and order, moderates destructive and damaging outcomes, or promotes social goals. On such grounds, public financial support to attain optimal levels of investment in VET may take many forms, ranging from full or partial provision of fees to easier borrowing through subsidized interest rates or delayed repayments.

Where the deterrent to training is not wholly monetary but rather relates to motivational, informational, or risk-averse factors, governments may seek to introduce such measures as vocational counseling services and reverse discrimination to counteract market failure. Such a system emphasizes universal access, common standards, and purposeful learning that recognize VET as a social investment rather than an investment in the individual. The aim is not to stifle enterprise and initiative but to remedy the inherent inefficiency and threat to quality arising from divergent goals pursued by self-interested business firms, learners, and educationalists.

Business firms see VET as a means to enhance productivity and profitability, while individual learners seek credentials as a route to improved income and social esteem. Meanwhile, the institutions of education and training—left to judge the balance between acquiring general cognitive abilities and practical skills, personal development and inculcation of the work ethic, tend to drift toward solutions that ensure continued budget allocations. In such an arena, only government has the power to enforce VET standards of quality and ensure that each member of the working population receives equal opportunity to continuously develop work skills in a competitive labor market while, at the same time, maintaining an efficient allocation of resources. Understanding the theoretical justification for collective action in providing VET dispels the intrinsic fatalism of the dictum "You can't buck the market" and encourages a willingness to design and develop VET policy that confronts the practical problems of acquiring and maintaining skills in a competitive labor market.

LABOR MARKETS

In the analysis of skills acquisition in a competitive labor market, VET has been categorized as *firm-specific,* where skills are specific to a particular employer, or *general,* where skills transfer between employers. Firms may willingly bear the cost of the former, but do so for the latter only where they will not be financially disadvantaged. This skill categorization has been equated with the notion of the internal labor market and the occupational labor market.

In any occupational labor market (OLM), a pool of workers exists who have achieved certified levels of performance in a standardized mix of skills that may be matched to specified job descriptions. The worker may achieve entry to the OLM by completing an approved course of training within a firm as an employee or before entry to the employment market at a school or college where the individual and/or the state provides funding. A firm offering employment training, as in apprenticeship, pays a lower wage rate that reflects the value of the apprentice until training is completed, so that, effectively, the employee shares the cost of training. Similarly, since college-based training provides insufficient work-based experience, it may also necessitate lower rates of pay in the early years of employment. Nevertheless, the fear by skilled workers of "cheap labor" trainee substitution may limit the scope for wage differentials, so that a firm never completely escapes training costs.

There are a number of difficulties in maintaining OLMs. First, "free-riders" may poach employees (attract skilled workers away from their employers by offering a higher wage) without contributing to training costs or economize on training costs by failing to maintain standards. Second, the system is inflexible in adjusting to increases in demand as well as costly and cumbersome in adapting to technical change. Third, discrete occupational identity provides a basis for collective bargaining that may give rise to entry barriers, job demarcation, dislocation of production, and wage-push inflation. Institutional regulation that depends essentially on the power and authority of state intervention in market operations may mitigate such disadvantages. However, employers will always be under pressure to insulate themselves from market forces by internalizing the labor market within the boundary of the firm.

In internal labor markets (ILMs), firms operate manpower policies deliberately designed to minimize labor turnover. Such firms may be either public or private but tend to be large and can therefore obtain economies of scale in the delivery of training. Ideally, employees are appointed (hired) on the basis of their undeveloped abilities and on the firms' perceived need to maintain job flexibility together with high production standards, especially in quality, design, and technical superiority. Labor market competition is thus set aside in favor of internally controlled pay, working conditions, job allocation, and a large measure of job security. Progression within the firm is balanced between seniority and individual appraisal. Training is highly specific to the firm and based on a mixture of on-the-job training and classroom instruction, where required. The firm pays for training, captures the benefits, and is thus the sole judge of the quantity and quality of instruction.

Where ILMs dominate the industrial structure, the threat of poaching is low since an influx of workers from outside a firm will destabilize the internal system of rewards. The ILM concept was used originally to explain high-skill formation using on-the-job training as commonly organized in Asia. However, it also applies to truncated ILMs that encompass relatively low-skill operations with distinctly limited promotional opportunities.

Training in ILMs is thus a private good insofar as the firm retains control over the investment. OLM training, on the other hand, is

DIAGRAM 2—MULTIPLE EQUILIBRIA: LOW/HIGH SKILLS

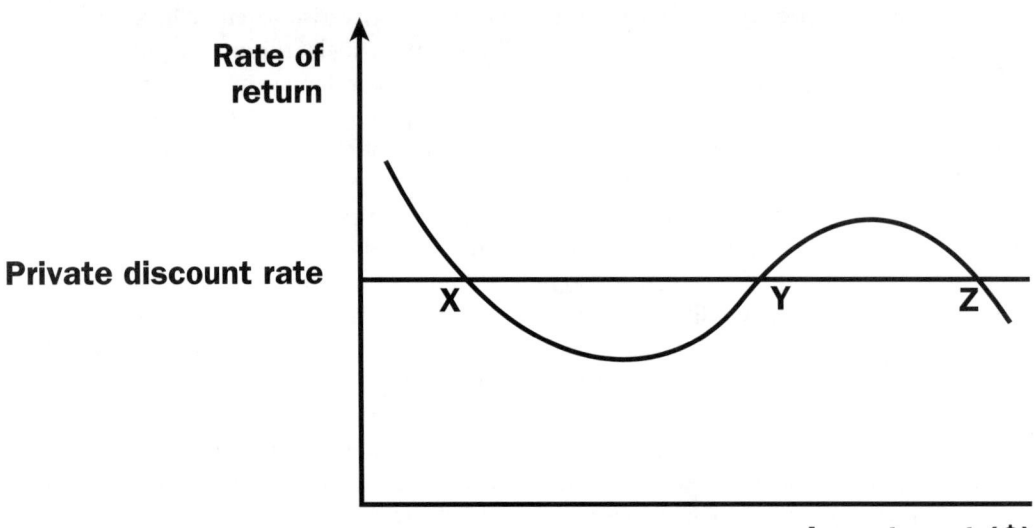

a public good in that, once training has been paid for, all employers have access to the income streams that may derive from the investment. The simultaneous existence of ILMs and OLMs in a national economy implies that an undifferentiated economy-wide state training policy will not likely wholly succeed.

TRAINING INVESTMENT AND THE ECONOMY

The VET policies' need for diversity, to reflect labor market structure, does nothing to compensate for another type of market failure associated with the under-provision of VET, where widespread beneficial effects (social benefits, or what economists call *externalities*) originate from the scale of investment.

In Diagram 2, point X appears to be the socially optimal level of training since, with additional training, the marginal rate of return becomes negative. However, with continued training investment, the skilled labor pool increases to point Y, where the consolidated acquisition of new skills again provides positive returns until point Z is reached. Such a case conforms to the dynamic equilibrium model of training proposed by Finegold and Soskice

(1988) where there is either a (a) high-skill/high-wage economy or (b) low-skill/low-wage economy with an ever-present possibility of moving on toward higher skills.

The low-skill/low-wage economy is associated with misperceiving the costs and benefits of upskilling as a result of an overemphasis on short-term, profit-maximizing outcomes and a reluctance to adopt remedial intervention. On the other hand, the high-skill/high-wage economy is characterized by a sustained state-generated policy that seeks continuous improvements in competitive advantage through material and human investment. The availability of high skills is believed to shape market demand for labor. When workers have only low skills, employers use technology to de-skill production, whereas "an educated skilled labor force broadens rather than forecloses choice in the competitive development and application of technologies" (Cohen & Zysman, 1987, p. 228). In both cases, the attained skill equilibrium achieves a bounded stability fortified by many societal factors, so that the gap in economic wealth between the two models widens. As a result, a low-skill/low-wage economy can become locked in a self-perpetuating predicament of relative economic decline remedied only by the state using its power and authority to design a strategic intervention to reverse the descent.

The nature of intervention is not homogeneous, for although adherence to market principles and market failure in the provision of VET occurs everywhere, countries have developed distinctly different systems in foundation education and training for young people as well as training in the adult labor market. These differences are attributed to variety in the historical circumstances of industrialization where formative influences on developing institutions have remarkably persisted, hindering change by constantly reformulating the practices and ideas that held sway during the early years of transition.

INDUSTRIAL GROWTH

In the first half of the 19th century, Britain was the world's only industrialized nation. Its industrialization was accomplished without centrally funded state education and without the control or direction of government. "The paid officials of the state were few in number, . . . placemen . . . too incompetent and corrupt to administer anything. The idea that . . . [they] could tell businessmen what to do was laughable. The demand for economic liberty was irresistible" (Kemp, 1993, p. 94). Britain's success was built on an empire that provided raw materials and captive markets. State assistance commonly propelled the industrializing countries of continental Europe in their struggle to compete, especially Germany and France, where a strong tradition of bureaucratic intervention existed. In the case of the U.S.A., access to markets and territory did not hinder industrial growth. The American Civil War in the 1860s provided an immense stimulus to industrialize. After the war, the pace of growth increased, with expansion aided significantly by the Fourteenth Amendment to the U.S. Constitution, which treated corporations as persons—which meant that state governments were powerless to intervene in the operations of business.[2] In the absence of institutional restraint in the pursuit of profits, large corporations thrived and, as they did, so did the whole American economy, to the extent that by 1913 its combined output equaled one-third of world output—only slightly less than that of Britain, Germany, and France combined.

Also in the mid-1800s in Japan, the Meiji regime overthrew a system that had lasted 250 years. A new paternalistic regime emphasizing nationalism and patriotism deliberately set out to industrialize, adopting the institutions of the West—private property and capitalist enterprise—as it built by regulation a modern industrial economy complete with banking system. As the fruits of the policy were sold off (in today's parlance, *privatized*) in the 1880s, the state continued to exert a controlling influence on developing industries.

Newly industrialized countries, such as Singapore and Taiwan, entering the capitalist market system in the 1960s, rigorously pursued a course of authoritarian nationalism, limiting individual freedoms as they endeavored to achieve collective goals. General and vocational education were institutionalized within a seamless unit to be harnessed to the current and future needs of an internationally competitive productive system where investment is force-fed by a protected banking and finance system.

VOCATIONAL SYSTEMS AND POLICIES

In each country mentioned, the institutional inheritance of the transition from agrarian to industrial society continues its effect on today's VET system. A good example of this is the dual system pioneered by Germany long ago. To-

[2]*Representative John Bingham, who also wrote the due process clause, later admitted that he had phrased it "word for word and clause by clause" to protect the rights of private property owners and corporations (Hunt, 1990).*

day, young people between the ages of 16 and 18 who cannot continue academic education, or who prefer hands-on occupational training, enter an apprenticeship that includes a mixture of school-based education and work. The system guarantees high-status vocational qualifications recognized throughout Europe. The full cost of the school-based element is borne by the government, while employers absorb the workplace component of this dual system. (For detailed information, see Chapter 8—Germany's Vocational Training/Apprenticeship System.)

The dual system is lauded for its consensual cooperation. However, problems have surfaced in recent years:

• The system is cumbersome in the face of rapidly changing technology.

• The essential employer support is increasingly withheld as international competition grows and poaching becomes a means of cost-cutting.

• The system is unresponsive to a supply/demand balance, in that rising youth unemployment and government pressure have led employers to replace apprentices who pass their final exam with new, beginning apprentices, rather than hiring the graduates (journeymen), thereby frustrating long-term secure employment and efficient production objectives.

More common is a multiplicity of state-directed systems with varying degrees of financial support, compulsion, enforcement of standards, and employer involvement. These state-directed systems also vary in the degree to which general and vocational education integrate with state industrial policy.

France, Sweden, and Singapore have centralized state systems that resort to general levies that support VET. However, while France and Sweden have developed a tripartite corporatist approach, Singapore has eschewed involving trade unions. Japan, Italy, Taiwan, and Korea also exclude trade unions but operate decentralized systems that depend heavily on employer involvement. Generally in Asian capi-

talist economies, state-business relationships dominate VET policies, whereas European policies are likelier to include labor representation.

Both the U.K. and the U.S.A. have major VET systems that are largely market-based. In both countries, concern over the growth of unemployment and a "culture of dependency" generated by the welfare system have chiefly propelled direct state assistance for training. However, in the U.S., although there appears to be consensus on the need for VET reform, action remains at the local level, since policy disagreements and state rights render federal initiatives ineffective. Nevertheless, many continue to argue for centralized direction. Brand (1998) shows that "a major report by the U.S. General Accounting Office tallied 154 VET programs valued at $25 billion, at 14 agencies [in the belief that] vocational education programs should be consolidated [by the federal authorities] with funding going to states and localities in a more flexible manner" (p. 150). Current U.K. policy funds technical and further education colleges but emphasizes the importance of decentralization when it restricts its direct efforts to exhorting partnerships between the state, employers, and individuals, while allotting funds to local enterprise groups to coordinate VET allocation in local markets.

In VET literature, the policies of the U.S.A. and the U.K. tend to draw severe criticism because the free-market approach—which emphasizes short-term rather than long-term training, and allocative rather than productive efficiency—cannot meet the following six requirements for high-skill formation, as suggested by Ashton and Green (1996):

1. A ruling elite committed to a high level of skill formation and an innovative use of the productive system.

2. The open availability of a solid foundation education that only the state can fund.

3. The commitment of employers to high skills.

4. Institutional arrangements, the substance of state-regulated industrial policy, that must

encourage employers to relinquish the opportunism of market behavior in favor of a stable long-term, cumulative approach to training.

5. Employees who stay with employers long enough that employers can recoup the cost of their training.

6. Skills acquired at work underpinned by theoretical knowledge, in the belief that such a practice stimulates innovation.

The authoritarian organization of the internal labor markets of the Asian "tiger economies" are said to embody these requirements. However, nothing inherent in the configuration of actions and attitudes excludes the possibility of attaining high skills through comparatively restricted interventionist policies, such as those of the U.K. or the U.S.A., policies that seek to provide structures of incentives aimed at balancing competing interests. The critical question is not whether the state should intervene in the provision of VET, but by how much it should intervene and what the nature of that intervention should be. Economic prosperity is the prize.

During the last two decades, parallel growth in the acceptance of market forces and a willingness to approve political regulation signals the recognition of the conflict between individual rights and public goals in the drive toward economic success. Politics is forced on stage, compelled to play an active role in developing VET policies. Failure to accept responsibility for maintaining an educated and skilled workforce will have the sure consequence of long-term economic decline.

References

Ashton, D., & Green, F. (1996). *Education, training and the global economy.* Cheltenham, England: Edward Elgar.

Brand, B. (1998). The process of change in vocational education and training in the United States of America. In I. Finlay, S. Niven, & S. Young (Eds.), *Changing vocational education and training* (pp. 137-155). London: Routledge.

Cohen, S. S., & Zysman, J. (1987). *Manufacturing matters: The myth of the post-industrial economy.* New York: Basic Books.

Finegold, D., & Soskice, D. (1988, Autumn). The failure of training in Britain: Analysis and prescription. *Oxford Review of Economic Policy, 4*(3), 21-53.

Hall, S. (1993, November 26). Thatcherism today. *New Statesman and Society,* pp. 14-16.

Hayek, F. (1967). *Studies in philosophy, politics and economics.* London: Routledge.

Hunt, E. K. (1990). *Property and prophets: The evolution of economic institutions and ideologies.* New York: Harper and Row.

Kemp, T. (1993). *Historical patterns of industrialisation.* London: Longman.

Rosen, S. (1989). Human capital. In J. Eatwell, M. Milgate, & P. Newman (Eds.), *The new Palgrave: Social economics* (pp. 136-155). London: Macmillan Press.

5

Workforce Certification

By Dennis R. Herschbach and Clifton P. Campbell

Completers of vocational education and training (VET) programs enter a workplace filled with the uncertainty of rapid and pervasive change. Economic competition, coupled with the integration of global markets, challenges conventional assumptions about skill formation and employability, as well as job security and stability. At the same time, rapid and on-going technological developments place additional demands on work preparation, while new forms of work organization change the relationship of individuals to employers and to each other. Many workers today face a more complex and demanding workplace than before.

Historically, certification has been valued as a way to assure that individuals have proficiency in job-related knowledge and skills to perform job tasks. In today's workplace, certification continues to confer the recognition of competence, but it also plays an important role in accommodating change. Certification systems are effective means through which changing labor market requirements are incorporated into education and training programs. At a time of intense global economic competition, rapid technological development, and altering forms of work and work organization, certification systems provide an essential link between workforce preparation and the changing nature of work.

Certification systems are particularly important in countries undergoing a rapid transformation of their workforce. Individual proficiency in traditional knowledge and skills can be assessed and maintained, and at the same time, standards can be established for those parts of the education and training system undergoing change. Standards provide an essential guideline for charting labor market development.

This chapter examines the basic concepts, issues, and terminology surrounding certification systems. A discussion on how certification systems work and the roles of major participants is followed by an examination of how a certification system is developed and implemented. Selected international practices are presented throughout the chapter to show the importance of the link between economic development, education and training, and certification. The chapter ends with case studies drawn from developed as well as developing countries. They reveal how workforce certification has been used in eight different countries to resolve policy and operational issues.

OVERVIEW

Certification systems take many forms; however, all have the same primary purpose. Certification assesses the knowledge and skill qualifications of individuals to verify that they have met predetermined requirements and can competently perform in a particular craft, trade, or profession (occupation). Hamm (1996) asserted that certification denotes professional or legal rights to practice an occupation. Furthermore, certification helps define work roles that, in turn, influence the content of VET courses and programs designed to prepare individuals for workforce entrance. Thus, certification plays a powerful role. In contrast to diplomas or degrees awarded on completion of prescribed course work, certificates are highly valued as evidence of individual proficiency.

Certification tests mirror, as much as possible, actual work requirements. Successful certification programs adjust assessments as work requirements change and involve employers to assure that certified individuals are indeed proficient in the requisite knowledge and skills. Certification contributes to the development and delivery of high-quality instruction. Through the certification system, detailed information on knowledge and skill requirements and graduates' test results can be fed back into the instructional development and revision process, providing an important check on both internal and external program effectiveness. From the results of certification tests, it is possible to ascertain whether courses/programs deliver the right content and whether learning is occurring. Curriculum and instruction can then be changed accordingly. Certification also encourages the development of a workforce preparation framework that links different forms and levels of education and training into a coherent whole responsive to labor market requirements.

Government's role in certification systems includes approving and monitoring certification bodies as well as ensuring control against unfair practices and corrupt behavior. The certification process should, however, be free from undue governmental influence. Common practice gives certifying bodies, rather than government, responsibility for administering the process. Certifying bodies include trade and professional associations, worker or employer groups, and so forth. The government may grant certification authority or it can be assumed without official authorization.

Subject matter experts generally identify and revise standards, while tests and measurements specialists develop, review, and revise tests (qualifying examinations). A procedure is established for administering tests, as well as analyzing results, providing feedback, and issuing certificates. Certification can be only as good as the standards used, however. Consequently, the development and revision of standards is a critical task. Since the standards themselves emerge from the workplace, they must keep current with it.

CONCEPTS AND TERMINOLOGY

One of the traditional uses of certification is to determine whether VET graduates can proficiently perform job tasks. However, certification has expanded to include other forms of education and training, since diploma and degree requirements do not necessarily reflect labor market requirements. In addition, certification is increasingly used to assess upgrading, updating, and retraining—in fact, in the near future, this may be its most frequent use.

Certification can also play a role in articulating national skill development efforts. The output of alternative routes to skill development, such as secondary and postsecondary VET, apprenticeship and on-the-job training and retraining, as well as experiential learning and self-study, can be united. In some occupations, candidates take qualifying examinations when they are deemed ready—they need not complete any specific training program and may, in fact, acquire the necessary knowledge and skills through a combination of training approaches. With certification, employers have a benchmark on which to judge job-applicant qualifications. This reduces hiring costs, while increasing certified workers' marketability. When different kinds and levels of VET produce uneven results, certification becomes even more important.

A Check on Relevance

Usefulness in establishing instructional relevance is an important contribution of a certification program. Effective certification is grounded in actual work requirements. Program development starts by identifying the knowledge and skill requirements of competent workers, whether they are craftsmen, technicians, engineers, or other professionals. Once these requirements are identified, they become the foundation on which tests are developed to assess individual proficiency. VET courses and programs also base their instruction on knowledge and skill requirements—otherwise their graduates could not score well on certification tests. Moreover, they will not succeed in the workplace, unless training and certification relate closely to work requirements.

When a strong relationship exists between the knowledge and skills taught and workplace requirements, the course/program is considered highly relevant. VET programs that lack external relevance are a poor training investment and should be substantially reformed or eliminated. Certification tests provide one of the best ways to check on course/program relevance. However, the certification tests must be current and comprehensive and effectively measure actual job task performance.

Countries such as Singapore and Taiwan that are restructuring their economies face the challenge of retraining workers to meet technological developments. At each stage, planning mechanisms take into account changing economic development priorities and resulting workforce requirements. As a result, the education and training system must make relatively rapid instructional changes, which are kept in focus with feedback from employers and the results of certification tests.

A Check on Quality

Certification provides an important check on instructional quality. Students can perform poorly on a certification test for various reasons. Perhaps the instructor lacked expertise in the knowledge and skills to be taught or delivered the wrong content. In some cases, the right content may be poorly taught. Poor instruction can arise from a lack of appropriate tools, equipment, or materials; inadequate classroom management; low student motivation, and so forth. Unsatisfactory test results should lead to a check on instructional relevance and quality. This is one of the more powerful, yet often overlooked, uses of the certification process.

It is useful at this point to examine the relationship between certification, diploma or degree, and accreditation programs as ways to assess individual competence and judge program quality.

Certification

The idea of assessing and recognizing occupational/job skill qualifications dates from the craft guilds of medieval Europe. Then, as now, individuals are judged qualified (competent) to engage in an occupation or job after passing the test. Consequently, as previously indicated, the test must be based on job requirements rather than on a theoretically or conceptually defined body of knowledge. Successful and respected certification bodies link tests closely to workplace performance requirements.

Government agencies finance and administer some certification programs. More commonly, however, nongovernmental bodies that have an interest in protecting and furthering the status of an occupation, and the individuals engaged in it, design, develop, and administer certification programs. Worldwide, these bodies include trade and professional associations/societies; worker or employer groups; certifying and licensing agencies; independent organizations; and so forth. In general, the certifying body is separate from the education and training system that supports or delivers the VET. Separation ensures a higher level of objectivity.

Diploma or Degree

Diploma and degree programs are based on set requirements, including number of credit hours and completion of specific courses. The diploma or degree is granted upon successful completion of a formally established program in a field of study, often with little or no direct relationship to specific job requirements. By contrast, certification linked directly to job requirements characterizes nondegree VET.

An accredited institution[1] may award an individual a diploma or degree, with a specialization in an occupation or profession, but that person may then have to pass a certification (licensing) test to work at (practice) the occupation. For example, a student may graduate from a diploma or degree nursing program at an accredited college or university but be ineligible for employment as a nurse until he or she has passed a certification (licensing) test. In some occupations, a breadth of supervised work experiences is required before a graduate can take the certification test.

Accreditation

Accreditation is a process by which an independent association, society, agency, or organization recognizes an educational program or institution. Accredited programs may certify graduates because the accreditation standards and process seem rigorous enough to ensure the development of appropriate work skills. Accreditation, however, is granted to programs, not individuals.

A strong combination unites an accreditation agency that assesses the quality and substance of VET programs with a certification body that assesses the competence of individual graduates. Many countries follow this practice.

ATTENDING CONSTRAINTS

In rapidly developing economies, the tasks that make up a job and the way they are performed change so often that it is hard to stay abreast of changes, not to mention incorporate them into instructional courses/programs. Identifying and maintaining current job tasks and their standards of proficient performance is labor-intensive and costly, and it requires both time and expertise. Unless job task standards are kept current, however, the certification system quickly grows outdated and dysfunctional. An outdated certification system can hinder economic development and individual advancement because it locks VET into outdated skills.

All certification systems face this problem. It is not enough to develop and implement a system; resources must also be allocated to maintain it. The scope of an initial certification system should not exceed the ability to maintain up-to-date standards through available human and financial resources.

A sound certification system also requires a strong VET system. It does little good to have a well-functioning certification system if the quality of training is so poor that individuals do not learn what they need in order to demonstrate proficient performance. As suggested, feedback from certification test results provides a good indication of both the internal and external effectiveness of VET. This information is crucial to maintaining course/program relevance and quality. However, if a systematic way to feed this corrective information back into the instructional system does not exist, it is difficult to establish and maintain the necessary links between certification and instruction. Many countries have little or no linkage between certification and instruction; consequently, the benefits that one can provide as a check on the other are lost. Full value is not gained from the certification investment.

An advantage of administering certification

---

[1] *In this chapter, the word* institution *refers to a school, center, academy, institute, or college.*

through worker or employer groups is that the costs are more equally shared, although employers pass costs on to consumers in the form of higher-priced products and services. Even the governments of wealthier, industrialized countries do not want to bear all the costs of certification. However, if too great a percentage of the costs are passed on to users, they will likely consider the system unduly expensive and resist using it. The problem is particularly acute in low-income countries already making high educational and training investments.

One obvious cost-containment strategy limits the extent of the government-financed certification system. For example, the government might cover only those occupations that impact directly on health and public safety. Another way to reduce costs is to certify journeymen who successfully complete a final apprenticeship exam that includes both knowledge and performance (skill) components. This alternative is not completely satisfactory, however, since there could be a breakdown or disagreement as to what job tasks and standards of proficiency ought to be included in the tests when they are not developed or administered by an independent certification body.

PROGRAMS AND MARKETS

Academic and vocational-technical institutions commonly conduct certification programs, but the workplace can also offer them. Workplace-based programs tend to be more realistic and cost less. Also, their instruction concentrates on the knowledge and skills required; the time period is condensed; scheduling is flexible; actual equipment is used; and testing takes place in the work environment. Many countries have a mix of formal and workplace-based certification programs.

Delivering Certification Training

It is generally agreed that there are three distinct approaches to delivering certification training. The first approach best serves traditional occupations. Here, consensus exists regarding the knowledge, skills, and experiences necessary for proficient performance, and requirements are somewhat stable. Training for traditional occupations is typically associated with VET programs conducted at formal education and training institutions.

A second delivery approach is favored for upgrading, updating, or retraining in occupations experiencing substantial technological changes. Formal programs often prove irrelevant or ineffective in this situation because they may not have access to new knowledge and/or the latest technology. Employers using the technology, working through trade groups, professional boards, or agencies, can usually better address certification requirements through short-term, concentrated training that includes practical experience.

The third delivery approach works well for interdisciplinary fields. Some emerging technologies are not based in a traditional occupation but rather cut across a number of work classifications; many integrate academic and practical learning. Essential skills are rapidly changing and there may be little agreement about what constitutes core knowledge and skills. It may be necessary to recruit and train instructors who can provide interdisciplinary training. Formal education and training programs often prove unsuitable for offering this type of certification training because they cannot readily accommodate technological change. In such situations, certification can link to leading-edge firms using emerging technology in an integrated way.

There is, of course, the possibility of combining the strengths of formal and workplace-based training. For example, academic and theoretical instruction could be provided by a formal institution and applied training offered through work experience at a firm using the latest technology.

Types of Training Markets

Colardyn (1994) links certification to three types of training markets. In the case of formal vocational and technical education, certification tends to be knowledge based. Formal, institution-based programs can best provide instruction that develops a foundation on which specific skill training can build.

Formal institutions in many countries offer more generic, academic, and theoretical instruction. They realize that technological change and global economic competition require a workforce that possesses good knowledge-based skills. However, in such cases certification may have to combine with work experience, occurring only after sufficient and specific practical experience is gained.

The nonformal sector is a second training market. Certification is competency-based and related to specific job skills. Employers and unions usually participate as partners in identifying requirements. Certification is based on success in criterion-referenced performance tests that mirror actual work requirements.

The third market is the commercial sector, consisting of profit-making institutions and enterprises that provide highly specialized, tailored training. Often privately financed, they show flexibility in adjusting to market demand. Course completion would be a part of the certification requirement.

Records of Acquired Skills

There is a trend in some countries to recognize skills acquired throughout an individual's life and in different learning contexts. France uses assessment centers that record each individual's previously acquired skills and relevant learning experiences. As more training and skills are acquired, they are added to the record. Individuals use their records in negotiating employment, work assignments, or additional training.

The United Kingdom and Australia are trying to link formal certification and learning through work experience at different occupational levels (Drake, 1991). Professional councils recognize skills acquired through experiential learning. Providers of formal education and training award certification taking previous work experience into account. Parties that have a stake in training and work (public authorities, educators and trainers, and unions) have a representative on the council.

COMPONENTS OF A CERTIFICATION SYSTEM

The certification process embraces three organizational elements. At the government level, there is an agency responsible for certification. Accreditation and certification functions may link together because they both bear on the relevance and quality of education and training. Major functions of the government agency include granting authority to certification bodies; monitoring processes; and addressing issues of discrimination, corruption, and so forth.

A second element involves the certifying body that identifies and validates standards, develops and administers certification tests, and records/reports results. The certifying body also establishes and maintains links with the government agency responsible for certification and the training providers.

Providers of education and training services make up the third element. They include formal public institutions, private institutions and enterprises, and trade or professional associations.

Government's Role

When issued by a government, certificates are legal instruments that convey the right to practice a craft, trade, or profession (occupation). Trade associations; professional organizations; worker, employer, or independent groups; and others issue certificates as well. However, these certificates do not carry legal authority unless it has been granted by the government. Certificates are licenses to practice, ensuring that individuals have at least the minimum competencies required by the occupation. Certificates may be granted for a lifetime, but recertification is generally required and plays a particularly important role for hazardous occupations and those undergoing change.

The first step in developing a certification system is to secure authority from the appropriate legal entity. There is a fine line between constructive authority and authority that is so specifically defined that it prevents appropriate modification of the requirements and hinders flexible management, administration, and effective regulation. Authorizing statutes must devolve considerable decision-making responsibility and authority to the certifying bodies responsible for administering the system. This is crucial because a certifying body must be able to adapt to change—otherwise, the certification itself will retard innovation and economic development.

The second step identifies or creates the appropriate administrative body to develop, implement, monitor, and upgrade the certification system. In most countries, government plays a role in creating the body but does not administer the certification program. Since government agencies, in both market-driven and planned economies, tend to be inflexible and remote from business and industry, their decision-making proves unresponsive.

The granting of certification authority generally happens through an application-and-approval process that considers the qualifications of the requesting body; stipulates requirements, such as tripartite membership; and outlines the relationship between the body, government, and education and training providers. The requesting body also must demonstrate that it (a) represents the occupation and (b) can develop and administer a certification program. Approval, often in the form of a charter, is usually for a stipulated period.

Government specialists often work with the certifying body to develop certification standards and assessment procedures. They may also monitor the administering and scoring of certification tests. The government itself may even issue the certificates.

Furthermore, the government ensures that the certification process is free from any discriminatory practices and barriers that could restrict access and progression. The process should be free from age and other restrictions, unless legally required, and ought to include an appeals system for resolving disputes.

Different government ministries, departments, or agencies have responsibility for a range of education and training activities. However, the accreditation and certification function should be independent of the education and training function. An agency removed from program operations should preferably conduct certification to protect the integrity of the certification process and enable the agency to work without pressure or undue influence from within government.

A common practice is to set up a certification board that has government representation but whose members largely come from outside government and include appropriate representation from businesses that are not government contractors and workers. Nongovernment experts contracted by the board actually determine certification standards. These individuals represent the particular occupation under consideration, not the government.

Education and training programs are typically spread throughout government organizations, so it is generally impossible to combine all certification functions under one agency or department. What is important, however, is to maintain vertical integration and articulation. Both education and training programs should come under the same certifying authority. For example, if the ministries of education and labor run similar VET programs for youth and adults, respectively, they both should fall under the same certification body in order to establish and maintain articulation between different occupational levels, as well as education and training programs.

Certifying Bodies

As mentioned earlier in this chapter, certification is controlled by government, trade, professional, worker, employer, or independent agencies, associations, societies, organizations, boards, and so forth, that are also concerned with the maintenance of standards and quality within occupations. The idea is that organizations closely connected with an occupation are in the best position to determine which knowledge and skills are critical. It is in their best interests to maintain quality and assure that only qualified individuals practice the occupation. Those taking the certification examination usually pay a fee. As a result, the certification process is at least partly self-supporting. The organization typically funds the remaining costs.

Certification bodies should include balanced representation from the particular craft, trade, or professional group. They should concentrate on setting policy and overseeing administration, not on managing the certification process. A professional staff has responsibility for the certification process, including developing, validating, administering, and updating certification tests.

Development of certification standards has crucial importance. Standards statements stipulate all important knowledge and skills that individuals must master to perform successfully on the job. Developing certification standards is no easy task, since work requirements vary among establishments and change over time. There are job and task analysis techniques that address this function, but standard setting is judgmental, and, ultimately, the wisdom, experience, and ability of the standard setters determines the validity of the standard. As a result, it is crucial to use experts well versed in actual workplace requirements.

The certification body must involve itself in setting standards, but it does not identify the actual standards. Experts in job and task analysis, as well as subject matter experts, typically perform that function. Also, identifying and verifying standards must occur continuously to accommodate workplace changes.

Independent of identifying and verifying standards is developing assessment instruments/tests. Professional staff performs this function under the certification body's guidance. Subject matter experts work with test and evaluation specialists to develop test items for each identified standard. The items are then field tested to determine both their validity and usability. Administering certification tests for the first time uncovers unanticipated problems.

The final function, test administration, commonly uses specialists (not instructors) who are experts in the occupation. Staff members of the certification body can select, train, coordinate, and ensure the competence of the external assessors. Assessor performance is also periodically evaluated. Complete records of the certification process must be kept, including reports of visits and advisory activities, reports to the awarding body, recommendations for improvements to assessment practices, tests, and records verifications (Cotton, 1995).

Service Providers

Education and training services are provided in a number of ways. Formal secondary-level vocational and technical education programs are the main provider of preemployment training. Typically, however, these programs prepare only about 10 percent of the workforce. The majority of skilled workers receive their training in other ways, including through apprenticeships; specialized public, private, and military institutions; adult education programs; courses offered through trade associations and worker groups; job-specific training by employers; and certification and diploma courses conducted by two- and four-year colleges. There are, of course, exceptions. South Korea, for example, trains roughly half of its skilled workforce through government-sponsored three-year vocational high schools and one-year training institutes (Stacy & Duc, 1994). Japan provides job-specific training mainly at the workplace (Alexander, 1993).

Nevertheless, dynamic and diverse economies have a variety of approaches to deliver VET. Each addresses particular audiences and specific labor market needs. As labor market forces interact, demand and trained supply achieve a rough balance. See the previous heading, Delivering Certification Training, for additional information.

Government-sponsored VET programs typically respond slowly to the requirements of new technology and changing economic conditions. Employer- and work-based education and training are more responsive, and typically lead the way in accommodating change (International Labour Office, 1987). For these reasons, the most effective certification programs structure themselves to accommodate a range of service providers. Accordingly, they do not focus on a particular institutional form or program, but rather assess performance in the specific occupation, regardless of how individuals acquired their competency.

School-based instruction. For several reasons, in many countries the trend in school-based vocational and technical education is away from job-specific preparation to generic instruction. First, this approach costs less. It is expensive to house, equip, and operate specialized training programs. In addition, pervasive technological change requires large reinvestments in job-specific tools and equipment. Second, and perhaps most important, increased generic training may be the most functional initial preparation to provide for economic restructuring and technological development. Third, individuals perform better in the labor market when they possess a solid grounding in generic skills, including related academic and technical knowledge. Not only can they acquire job-specific skills quickly, but they can also undergo upgrading, updating, and retraining as work requirements change.

Non-school-based instruction. Non-school-based providers of job-specific instruction are gaining importance in many countries. These providers may serve an industrial sector or concentrate on a particular occupation. In the United States and Canada, the International Brotherhood of Electrical Workers (union) and the National Electrical Contractors Association (employer organization) together formed a National Joint Apprenticeship and Training Committee (NJATC) for the electrical industry. Every year in more than 300 locations across North America, the NJATC trains some 40,000 apprentices, and more than 50,000 journeymen upgrade and update their skills.

Journeymen who are graduates of the NJATC National Training Institute or technical representatives of companies teach courses in new technology, procedures, and products. Participants who demonstrate proficiency after completing standards-based courses are certified. Once certified, they may install, connect, or maintain the technology/product. The NJATC invests approximately $80 million a year in training, money that comes from employers and the union (agreed to through collective bargaining), not from public taxes (S. D. Anderson, personal communication, September 23, 1999).

Employers worldwide do a considerable amount of training. In the U.K., for example, employer-provided training accounts for 70 percent of training for skilled and semiskilled workers. The training qualifies individuals for internal job advancement, but also commonly leads to certification approved by a government agency.

Most employer-based training occurs in-house, with employers designing and presenting the courses. In Japan, for example, 88 percent of new workers and 75 percent of experienced workers received their initial job-specific training from their employing firm. For managers and supervisors, the amount is 65 percent (Stacy & Duc, 1994).

Employers also outsource training to contractors and consultants. In this way, they do not have to maintain their own specialized personnel. Small employers often find it more cost effective to rely on outside training firms. In addition, for-profit training firms can quickly address new market needs and develop training to meet particular requirements.

Equipment manufacturers/suppliers, software developers, and others play an important training role. Where new technology is involved, the manufacturer or supplier may have expertise that is simply not available from any other source. For example, equipment suppliers train approximately 18 percent of Japan's blue-collar workers (Cairncross & Dore, 1990).

Training agreements between employers and public or private education and training institutions are common. In the U.S., for example, employers contract with secondary and postsecondary vocational and technical institutions to provide employee training. Depending on scheduled training periods, day, evening, or adjunct faculty are used, often giving them an opportunity to earn additional income. Public technical and community colleges and postsecondary institutes in the U.S. and Canada are major trainers of adults through continuing education courses and programs. In the state of Maryland, for example, Toyota and Ford both contract with Catonsville Community College to provide technician training. The companies keep the college instructors updated, equip their instructional facilities, and evaluate the training. This arrangement proves cost effective for the companies, and provides for up-to-date instruction that uses modern tools and equipment. At the same time, participants meet certification qualifications.

CERTIFICATION ASSESSMENT

The development of a certification system cannot be separated from the larger policy questions concerning the knowledge and skills to be taught and the institutional forms to be used. This education and training framework addresses certification. The source of all content, however, must be work requirements.

Work involves applying a variety of skills. Those who make certification assessments tend to measure primarily the knowledge (also called *cognitive*) components of work because written (paper-and-pencil) tests can readily assess cognitive skills. However, if certification is limited to the measurement of cognitive skills, it is conceived too narrowly. To be sure, work involves cognitive skills, but it also involves psychomotor job skills—the particular techniques and processes applied to work.

Cognitive Skills

Cognitive behavior relates to the knowledge and intellectual abilities involved in performing a job. Very little job activity can be carried out without grounding in a cognitive structure. Some job tasks require complex levels of cognitive skills, such as when diagnosing an engine malfunction without sophisticated test equipment. This is especially true in emerging technological fields and cannot be overlooked when designing instruction. Unless instructors recognize the requirement for cognitive behavior and design instruction accordingly, students cannot be expected to adequately perform job tasks.

Proficiency in basic academic skills establishes the foundation for successful psychomotor skill development. As the technology incorporated into work becomes more complex, academic skill requirements tend to increase. Many students in developing countries do not now possess high enough basic skill levels to enable them to profit from VET, either in school or at the workplace.

Jobs that require significant cognitive skills are probably best learned in formal courses and programs. In a similar way, the academic skill component of many jobs is best learned in a classroom or laboratory environment. An institution is also the best site for assessing cognitive skills.

Psychomotor Skills

Some jobs consist primarily of psychomotor skills, such as manipulating machinery and equipment. In general, psychomotor skills are best learned and assessed within the work setting. Becoming proficient often requires relatively long practice periods using the machinery and equipment of production. Combinations of classroom instruction and work experience often provide the best results, with classroom instruction focused on cognitive skills and familiarization with manipulative skills, while supervised work experience brings the trainee to required proficiency levels.

Formal VET provides more generic skills

training. The individual attains the skills necessary to gain entry-level employment, but requires additional specific training either just before, or at the time of, employment. The instruction itself is less costly because large groups learn common skills, making efficient use of available resources.

Usually, a certification body is created to coordinate job and task analysis efforts and the development of criterion-referenced performance tests. In most cases, this body includes tripartite representation: government, employers, and workers. In the U.K., a National Lead Body was established for every occupational area. Each lead body works under the auspices of the National Council for Vocational Qualifications (Cotton, 1995).

Because certification tests represent only a sample of what is important to know and do to perform satisfactorily in the workplace, the sample must represent the knowledge and skills required for proficient job performance. Furthermore, it is important to have an understanding of the particular "mix of skills" presented in an instructional program. As previously suggested, there are many different ways to configure an instructional program. Depending on the resources available, student background, and the availability of alternatives, judgments must be made concerning the content of the necessary skill profile.

Some countries have a layered certification system representing a multi-dimensional education and training system. This makes it possible to accommodate different skill levels and student backgrounds while, at the same time, accommodating a range of proficiency levels. Individual proficiency in traditional knowledge and skills can be assessed and maintained, for example, while the skill requirements for emerging technologies are also addressed.

MEASURING PERFORMANCE

Next to determining which knowledge and skills to train and identifying their accompanying conditions and standards, the most important procedure is developing tests that measure proficiency. A certification system that does not measure job-relevant knowledge and skills is dysfunctional and usually not worth the investment of resources. However, the tests used to measure performance must also be sound.

Poorly developed tests produce disappointing results. They may have low content validity, and no one knows just what is being measured. Tests must measure the right skills, and they must do it accurately.

Norm-Referenced Measurement

Traditional methods of assessment, based on what is termed *norm-referenced testing*, compare examinees to each other and place them in rank order or on a normal distribution curve. Arbitrary pass marks are specified, and a predetermined number or percentage of passes may be established; thus, examinees compete against each other. The level of pass established, however, usually does not directly relate to performance levels required in the workplace. High pass marks mean that the tested examinees did better than others, but it does not mean they can perform proficiently on the job. Norm-referenced tests are useful for comparing the performance of one examinee against another and for assigning grades. They are less useful for assessing the ability to perform in the work setting (Bott, 1996).

Criterion-Referenced Measures

In contrast to norm-referenced measurement, criterion-referenced measures are based on absolute standards. The number of examinees receiving high or low scores and their relative ranking are irrelevant. What is important is that the examinee demonstrate proficient job task performance. Criterion-referenced assessment is also termed *competency-based* or *performance-based* assessment.

Criterion-referenced tests derive from job tasks and provide the most direct, complete, and realistic method of testing ability to perform tasks under workplace requirements. As a result, they are developed and used for tasks considered essential to proficient job performance.

The task statement, conditions, and standards of these tests mirror actual on-the-job task performance and clearly distinguish whether or how well examinees can perform. Ideally, a criterion-referenced test evaluates task proficiency using actual equipment under realistic work conditions and standards. These tests keep both instruction and certification consistent with job requirements (Campbell, 1993).

Observation of Workplace Performance

One of the best ways to determine the competence of individuals is to observe their performance in the workplace. This is termed *natural observation*, and is an especially important assessment method to use when upgrading and updating experienced workers. It is only necessary to observe the new skills, but it is important that the observation be carried out in the context of total job performance. To be most effective, the observation must be planned and structured in accordance with the following procedure:

1. Develop an assessment plan that identifies the job task(s) and task elements/steps (competencies), the conditions under which they will be performed, and the performance/proficiency standards.

2. Prepare an observation checklist(s) and structured interview questionnaire.

3. Observe performance unobtrusively and record performance results on the checklist. The assessor should not make suggestions, provide information, or help the worker except as necessary to prevent injury and/or equipment damage.

4. Interview the worker before, during, or after performance to assess related knowledge, reasons behind practical procedures, and so forth.

5. Decide whether the worker performed the task(s) and task elements/steps proficiently and was knowledgeable in the theory behind practical procedures. Other factors should not

be taken into consideration when making a judgment. Feedback should be specific, constructive, and given promptly after the performance. If the worker's performance did not meet proficiency standards, the worker must be told what has to be done to attain the standard(s).

6. Maintain complete and accurate records, including observation checklist(s), an account of the structured interview, and feedback provided on the performance.

Simulation

When evidence of job task proficiency is critical and performance cannot be observed in the actual workplace, or when the test environment cannot adequately duplicate the conditions and standards of the workplace, a substitute approach must be developed. Devising a testing situation that resembles task performance on the job is one of the most challenging aspects of test development.

Simulation is a viable option for testing job task skill and knowledge. This is a testing situation that re-creates, with as much fidelity as possible, the conditions encountered in the actual workplace. An imitation of the entire environment—considering, for example, facilities, weather conditions, equipment, sounds, and smells—is critical in quality simulation. The closer the simulation resembles workplace conditions, the better.

When deciding whether to use simulation, consider the following factors: (a) the effect on productivity, and so forth, when the actual facilities and equipment are used for testing; (b) potential danger to examinees or damage to equipment; (c) the cost of materials, supplies, equipment, and so forth used under workplace conditions; (d) the effects of reduced physical fidelity; and (e) the efficiency of simulation (Campbell, 1993).

Practical Tests

Practical tests measure ability to perform job tasks using actual tools and equipment under real or closely simulated work conditions and actual workplace standards. They measure a product, process, or both. The end product is the most obvious output of job task performance, since it is observable and can be physically examined. The other output is the completion of procedural steps (process). Occasionally, the process itself may leave no record. The skills involved (for example, in safe driving) can best be evaluated by direct observation of performance. In certain cases, both product and process must be examined as task output. Many tests evaluate processes that result in products to provide feedback on process errors that affect the end product.

The processes or procedures in performing a job task may be critical to ensuring personnel safety or preventing damage to tools or equipment. For example, a driver arrives at destination B from point A as required by the task. But, in the process, the driver might have violated traffic laws and safety regulations or even caused an accident. In such a case, product evaluation alone would be inadequate.

Practical tests measure the same factors—product, process, or both—used as a basis for the job task standard. It may be necessary, however, to incorporate some form of simulation, such as using a cardiopulmonary resuscitation (CPR) mannequin instead of a real person in performing mouth-to-mouth resuscitation (Campbell, 1993).

Written Tests

Assessing cognitive performance tends to be overemphasized because of the comparative ease of constructing, administering, and scoring such tests. There is a tendency to measure unimportant information for the same reason. Assessing cognitive information has an important place in the certification process, but it is only one kind of assessment and should not be used when inappropriate. Cognitive tests tend to include short-answer and multiple-choice items. Drawings, and objects such as hand tools and machine parts, may also be used for identification and other types of written items.

Portfolios and Profiles

Certification aims to communicate an assessment of an individual's competency to interested parties. The assessment summarizes the individual's performance. In more conventional assessments, the information takes the form of quantitative indicators, such as test scores, percentages, and so forth. Furthermore, the information provided takes a form determined by the examining authority, which may not be useful to potential employers. For these reasons, supplemental and/or alternative ways of reporting descriptive information are advocated.

Portfolios have a long record of use in art and architecture. Portfolios present samples of an individual's work along with background information including any awards received. Photographs, videotapes, or audio tapes may also be used to display and describe the work.

Profiles provide a more complete and valid assessment of performance through multiple measures, using a variety of reporting formats: checklists of skills mastered; test results; instructor appraisals; records of practical work completed; assessments of self-reliance, cooperativeness, punctuality, reliability, and ability to work with others; and course grades. More than one assessor is involved and the profile is generated over the length of the training in an attempt to assess all relevant aspects of performance.

BUILDING BLOCKS OF A CERTIFICATION SYSTEM

Certification systems vary between countries, reflecting how government agencies are organized and operate, as well as the characteristics of their education and training systems. Nevertheless, there are six common functions and requirements for an effective certification system:

1. Constitute the foundation of the certification system. Define the roles and functions of government, certifying bodies, and service providers. However, avoid constructing the legal framework so rigidly that adapting to change will prove difficult.

2. Establish or select a government agency free of internal and external pressure and interference. Important functions of this agency include granting certification authority, monitoring the development of standards and proficiency tests, administering tests, and maintaining links with certifying bodies as well as education and training service providers. The government agency also ensures that the certification process is fairly administered and is free of discrimination and corruption.

3. Establish or approve certifying bodies, including trade, professional, worker, or employer groups; government agencies; a particular industry; or independent organizations. The certifying body sets policy; administers the program; and oversees identifying standards, developing assessment instruments, and administering examinations. The more effective certification bodies include broad-based representation from employer and worker groups.

4. Select a procedure for identifying standards based on work requirements. This is crucial—the validity of the certification process rests on the validity of the standards.

5. Develop certification tests and a process for administering them. There should be a feedback loop through which information on test results is provided to education and training institutions that use it to make curriculum and instructional change.

6. Establish a process for internal and external verification. This is a major function of the government agency and it guards both the integrity and validity of the certification process. Develop a process for revising, upgrading, and validating standards.

SELECTED CASE STUDIES

Certification systems vary significantly among different countries. The following examples illustrate their different uses and how they relate to education and training. They also show different approaches to resolving policy and operational issues. The examples are drawn from developed (U.S.A., Japan, U.K., and Germany) and developing (Jordan, Honduras, Singapore, and Taiwan) countries, and include both successes and disappointments. The use of education and training as an economic development tool stands out in the case studies. Both planned and market-based economies look to certification as a means of maintaining quality and regulating the supply and demand of skilled workers.

Certification in the United States of America

The United States has a highly decentralized, loosely coordinated, locally administered, mixed public-private system of education and training. Its economy is large, diverse, and dynamic, and has many regional economies, each responding to different market forces, and each experiencing different training-related needs. Public VET is primarily provided through local comprehensive and specialized vocational/technical secondary schools and two-year technical/community colleges. Postsecondary, private, profit-making schools also offer vocational and technical training in a host of occupations. Unions and employers run apprenticeship programs. Employers conduct extensive further and upgrade training, either directly or contracted through private training firms. Total funds budgeted for formal training in 1998 by U.S. employers was $60.7 billion ("Industry Report 1998," p. 45). Many trade, worker, and professional organizations also offer training. How does certification occur in such a diverse, multilayered system of workforce preparation?

How the system works. First, the training organization—whether a public or private institution, union or employer apprenticeship, training contractor, or trade association—provides learning experiences in preparation for certification tests but does not participate directly in certification. An outside certifying body customarily does this. Individuals can prepare for certification in many different ways, the common element being the test itself and not the particular institutional form through which training is provided.

Government agencies, primarily at the state but also at the national and local levels, administer certification tests and grant licenses in selected occupations, often hazardous ones requiring a high level of proficiency or impacting directly on public safety and services. In some occupations, a specialized certifying body directly associated with the occupation grants certification. The state delegates this authority or, in some cases, the certificate has professional, but no legal, basis. It is a professional advantage for individuals to gain certification, but most occupations require no licensure.

The individual organization generally issues national certification based on high quality, tightly controlled certification tests financed wholly or in part by examination fees. These examinations establish the job level and may reflect regional occupational differences. In some cases, the individual states in turn grant a license to practice the occupation based on the recommendation of the particular certifying body. The individual applies directly to the state and pays a fee. Before doing this, however, the state must accredit the certifying body.

There are also regional certifying bodies. When individuals move into a different region, they must apply for certification through the new regional body. Additional training and/or work experience may be required along with another proficiency test.

An accreditation process checks program quality and the substance of the education and training institution. Independent or state accreditation agencies grant accreditation to programs and institutions. During the accreditation process, instructional relevance and effectiveness are examined. In the case of private vocational and technical institutions, job placement and certification pass rates figure heavily into the decision to grant approval.

The approach to certification in the U.S.A. reflects the diversity of the economy as well as the variation characterizing the educational and training systems through which individuals are prepared for work. In the United States,

government alone cannot adequately implement a comprehensive certification system. It would simply be too costly and unresponsive to market forces. A mixed public-private certification system better accommodates the diverse and changing labor market requirements of regional, state, and local economies. In addition, a considerable amount of the cost shifts to those who use and benefit from certification: the employers and workers.

Certification in Japan

Training policy and practice in Japan differs sharply from most other Asian countries. First, the emphasis is on building a strong general education foundation in the elementary and secondary school years for all students, in the belief that vocational/technical training must rest on a foundation of academic accomplishment.

General high schools, special training schools, and vocational training centers offer specific training, but the emphasis remains on foundation skills (Alexander, 1993). Consequently, formal educational qualifications are the most important prerequisite for employment in a leading company or a prestigious government bureaucracy. Those who have earned formal education qualifications generally succeed in employer-conducted training.

Secondary school and university graduates often enter employment at full salary, even though they typically undergo a year of on- and off-the-job training. Older employees act as trainers and supervisors and pass on their specific knowledge and skills. Courses within and outside the company supplement this training.

The Ministry of Labor establishes training and performance standards in individual specializations for recognized in-company and outside-company vocational training. The training period, content, and materials are regulated; nevertheless, each company tailors its training to specific requirements. Most training is application-related in narrowly defined, single activities. Upgrading and updating training are the major way that workers acquire new skills.

The state maintains a standards and qualification system, with employer and training associations playing a supporting but minor role. Rather than intervene directly in job preparation, the state influences skill development, at a relatively modest cost, through the qualification system. Employees in technical fields take tests to establish their qualifications. In order to maintain their certificate or license, some take periodic recertification tests. Large firms have their own qualification examinations, although individuals who demonstrate sufficient proficiency can take state-administered tests.

Diplomas and graduation certificates in Japan have high value because of the social status associated with achievement, but within the corporate culture found in larger firms there is less need for an outside certification system. The functions of training, quality control, and advancement are carried out primarily by a company to maximize the potential of its employees. Employees accept this system because they perceive the cultural climate of the company as promoting their personal welfare. For further information on how skilled workers in Japan are trained and certified, see Chapter 14—How the Japanese Prepare for Work.

Certification in the United Kingdom

External examinations and certification assessment in the United Kingdom date back to the founding of City and Guilds in the 19th century. City and Guilds is an independent vocational testing and certification organization that was originally financed by the City of London for its livery companies. It has extended its certification services internationally and now has representation in more than 100 countries.

A multi-layered organization. To unify certification in vocational and technical occupations, the National Council for Vocational Qualifications (NCVQ) was established in 1986. The result is a national coordinating and monitoring body for vocational qualifications with local involvement. For different occupational areas, *lead bodies* are constituted to formulate proficiency standards. Lead bodies represent their sectors of employment, including small and leading-edge employers. These employment-led organizations develop, maintain, and improve national standards of performance, codified as National Vocational Qualifications (NVQs) for each occupational area. Each set of NVQs reflects a clear structure, a set of mandatory units that forms the major part of the qualifications, clear progression from one occupational level to the next, and comparability between NVQs in similar occupational areas.

Lead bodies work with awarding bodies in forming and structuring certification tests. Awarding bodies take responsibility for assessment and verification. Sanctioned by the NCVQ, they may represent professional or trade organizations, worker groups, and so forth. The awarding bodies appoint and train external assessors to administer the certification tests. Assessors are specialists in their respective occupational areas. In addition, external verifiers, appointed and trained to check the overall quality of education and training programs, also approve the form and content of the tests and other forms of assessment, agree to changes in the assessment process, check student/trainee progress, oversee testing, and monitor the overall assessment process. They form the link between the awarding body and the NVQ center. External verifiers also check the quality and consistency of assessors' judgments, provide feedback, resolve disputes, and interpret rules and regulations.

A recognized local center run by an internal verifier controls certification awards. Each center maintains links with the lead body, the awarding body, and the NCVQ. The internal verifier maintains the quality and fairness of the assessment and assures that the required standards are met. Each center must maintain an effective management system, provide sufficient resources to adequately conduct the assessment process, and provide adequate arrangements and resources for quality assurance. The focus of control is at local centers (Cotton, 1995).

Main points. In sum, then, lead bodies formulate standards. An NVQ assessor carries out assessment. NVQ internal and external verifiers carry out verifications. An awarding body approves each center. Awarding bodies review external verifier reports and center procedures with respect to assessment, verification, and equal opportunity, and report to the NCVQ. NCVQ officers and their representatives participate in accreditation-monitoring activities, visit awarding bodies, approve centers, check documentation, and monitor the assessment process.

The certification process established through the NCVQ illustrates a government-led system that incorporates private sector contributions and participation. In addition, the decision-making process is flexible and open enough to bring into its fold different participant groups. Decisions about standards are made at the worker and enterprise levels.

Certification in Germany

Germany has a long and respected tradition of workforce preparation rooted in the craft guilds of the middle ages. In our time, the dual system of apprenticeship training represents this tradition. The dual system combines instruction in part-time public vocational schools with workplace training and practice. For details on how the system works, see Chapter 8—Germany's Vocational Training/Apprenticeship System.

Young adults enter the German labor market principally through apprenticeships. At any one time, about 70 percent of a given age cohort is participating in the dual system. Access is not tied to specific school-leaving qualifications. After completing 9 school years, or 10 in those states that extended full-time schooling, students can enter training for any

government-recognized skilled occupation, as long as they find an appropriate apprenticeship placement. Applicants who cannot find a placement to their liking can either enroll in full-time, in-school vocational training, or take a job that does not require initial training (Haskell, 1993).

Training regulations. Workplace training for each government-recognized skilled occupation is implemented according to a training regulation. These regulations specify the knowledge and skills to be acquired, general training plan, and examination requirements. They ensure a nationwide uniform level of training for all apprentices in a skilled occupation. Among other things, training regulations guarantee mutual recognition and acceptance of qualifications, thereby facilitating maximum employability and job mobility.

Responsibilities of chambers. Chambers are self-governing, not-for-profit organizations constituted under public law and organized at the regional, state, and national levels. Private sector enterprises must belong to a chamber. There are different chambers for occupational specializations, but the most important are the Chambers of Industry and Commerce and the Chambers of Crafts. In other countries, government authorities would exercise some of the powers of the chambers. For example, chambers regulate and supervise apprenticeship training, as well as administer journeyman and master craftsman tests (Vocational Training Act of 1969, § 46).

Under provisions of the Vocational Training Act, each chamber must have a vocational training committee. Committee membership must consist of representatives from employers' organizations, unions, and part-time vocational schools (nonvoting members).

Apprenticeship tests. The Vocational Training Act requires apprentices to take both an interim and a final test. The interim test is administered at about the midpoint of an apprenticeship period. It reveals progress and identifies problems so that corrective action can be taken. The final test, taken at the end of the training period, determines whether the required qualifications have been acquired. The training regulations for each recognized skilled occupation specify examination requirements.

To conduct the tests, chambers establish examination committees (boards) for each occupation, consisting of at least three members, with an equal representation of employers and employees, and at least one teacher from a part-time vocational school (Vocational Training Act of 1969). Committee members must be recognized as experts in the skilled occupation being examined.

The chamber's vocational training committee issues rules for administering the final examination. These rules stipulate conditions of admission, form(s) of the tests, evaluation criteria, consequences of breaches of the rules, and so forth.

The crafts, trades, and industrial occupations test apprentices in both knowledge and skills. A written test measures occupational knowledge and theory. In addition, economics, social studies, language skills, and mathematics are tested at the part-time vocational school. A comprehensive performance test follows written tests. While performance tests vary according to the skilled occupation, in the crafts, trades, and industrial occupations, they call for the production of a workpiece or the submission of a work sample (*The Dual System*, 1988).

Apprentices who pass all parts of their final examination are awarded a certificate that confers journeyman status and a description of the occupation for which they qualified (printed in German, English, and French) ("Trilingual 'business card'" 1997). The certificate exists to show that the qualifications for a specific skilled occupation have been acquired. The certificate serves as a portable credential that can travel within and across enterprises. It is the basis for employment as a journeyman, career advancement, and geographic mobility. All member states in the European Union recognize the journeyman certificate. It is also required for admission to master craftsman and technician programs as well as other further training courses and programs leading to supervisory certificates or to engineering training in Germany (*Dual Vocational Training*, 1988, p. 9).

Those apprentices who do not perform satisfactorily in both parts of the final examination can be reexamined. The Vocational Training Act stipulates that the final examination may be taken twice. Generally, the examination committee encourages an unsuccessful apprentice to try again later. When the problem is an inability to meet proficiency standards in performing skills, and the fault is thought to owe to inadequate training, the examination committee arranges for remediation.

In spite of the precautions taken and special efforts to help those who fail their initial final exam, some apprentices fail the second time as well and do not become journeymen. Nevertheless, they are not complete failures. A skills ID card (performance certificate) documents what these apprentices did learn during the training period. This card serves as evidence of acquired skills that helps former apprentices in their job search or provides a head start in any future attempt to obtain occupational qualifications (Kloas, 1997).

Chamber oversight. Chambers employ training advisors (counselors) to ensure that training is provided in accordance with regulations. These counselors visit enterprises to monitor training progress. Poor exam results may also trigger a counselor's visit. When counselors first become aware of a problem, they discuss it with the trainers or their manager. In most instances, this is sufficient; however, if corrective action is not taken, the chamber sends an official letter. As a last resort, the chamber can (a) send apprentices to an interfirm training center (at the employer's expense) for supplementary instruction, (b) rotate apprentices among several enterprises, or (c) move apprentices to another enterprise.

Union works councils also play a role in the control of apprenticeship training. They have rights of co-determination in implementing and supervising training within the enterprise. In large enterprises, subcommittees enforce legal requirements. However, small- and medium-sized enterprises often have no workplace representation and, therefore, lack control and supervision by works counselors (LaFlamme, Basset, & Michlin, 1993).

Jordan

Apprenticeship as conducted by the Vocational Training Corporation (VTC) in Jordan is the most comprehensive application of the dual training system in a developing country. Like its German model, it combines formal instruction with on-the-job training and practice. In large enterprises, formal instruction also occurs at the workplace. This reduces government costs since the enterprise provides instructors and all supporting materials (Herschbach, 1993).

A number of factors contribute directly to the effectiveness of the VTC. A high degree of cooperation between the VTC and employers results in part because the line between public and private sectors is not sharply drawn. The Jordanian government has extensive shareholdings in many private sector enterprises; thus, its own self-interests and the economy in general are served by an effective VTC. In the case of Jordan, which closely coordinates economic policy with training policy, centralized authority and control contribute to training relevance, effectiveness, and efficiency. Unfortunately, the number and quality of off-site training facilities is inadequate, and the related instruction is often of low quality.

The VTC has not succeeded in correcting labor market imbalances. Ideally, potential training sites and job placements should equal openings. In fact, a sizable number of trainees are placed with a single enterprise, and few are employed when they graduate.

Compounding the employment problem is the lack of an effective certification system. Certificates are granted on the basis of program completion, not demonstrated competency, as measured by written and practical tests. The fact that an individual completes the training cycle does not evidence performance capability. Potential employers have no way to judge the knowledge and skills of job candidates, since no set of uniform standards exists by which to gauge proficient performance.

Honduras

The Advisory Council for Human Resource Development (Centro Asesor para el Desarrolo de Recursos Humanos de Honduras—CADERH) was established to address private sector training needs. Employers experienced the lack of a skilled workforce as a major limitation. Moreover, low levels of cost-effectiveness, poor communication with employers, and the absence of effective systems for identifying training needs and monitoring results characterize existing vocational/technical training. Of particular concern was Instituto Nacional de Formacion Profesional (INFOP), a semi-autonomous training system financed by the private sector through a payroll tax. Issues of concern to employers included high overhead expenses, a lack of instructional relevance and quality, and poor coordination.

Although they were paying the bill for INFOP, employers had little influence over the way training was delivered or in establishing standards for its quality. As an alternative, CADERH, a private sector training organization, was developed (Herschbach, Hays, & Evans, 1992). Membership dues and income generated through training and certification services finance this organization of approximately 300 employers. CADERH has a full-time executive director and three departments: Vocational Training and Testing, In-Plant Training Needs Analysis and Programs, and Multimedia and Instructional Materials Production.

The certification system. Because the quality of education and training throughout Honduras is uneven, and since it is hard to determine the qualifications of job applicants, CADERH set out to develop a national certification system. Volunteer craft and trade committees composed of employers, highly skilled workers, and vocational instructors formed to define standards for each occupation. These standards guided the development of sets of specific performance objectives and assessment items. Employers and skilled workers validate the objectives and assessment items that form the basis for developing certification tests representative of the different skill levels in each occupation. These tests certify the competence of VET graduates, screen job candidates, and evaluate employees. The standards developed for each occupation also guide the development of competency-based instructional materials.

Constraints. While instructional materials development and in-plant training activities showed marked success, certification has not succeeded as well for a number of reasons. First, examinees who lack literacy and numeracy skills find the certification tests too difficult and the performance standards too high, which reinforces the crucial importance of sound basic education and adequate technical training.

Second, identifying and validating standards, and constructing and validating objectives and test items were so labor-intensive, complex, time-consuming, and expensive that the process could not be completed. Revisions in some occupations were needed before the certification tests were validated. CADERH simply had insufficient resources to keep up with development requirements. Consequently, development requirements and the need to continually revise standards, objectives, and assessment instruments should not be underestimated. Finally, employers and individual participants were reluctant to pay the high testing fees necessitated by development costs and the small user populations. To approach cost-effectiveness, a certification system must be used with a large population.

Singapore

Many western industrial countries developed educational and training systems with little consideration of each other or economic demands. This is not so among some of the newly industrializing economies of Asia. Singapore is perhaps the best example. Education and training here are linked with each other and to economic development policy (Ashton & Sung, 1997).

Stages of development. Significant changes have been made in Singapore's education and training to address policy requirements at different stages of economic development, enabling the country to sustain growth by moving from low-value-added to high-value-added production, without experiencing crippling shortages of skilled workers.

Such a highly coordinated system requires an effective certification system. It is essential to be able to judge with a high degree of assurance whether required skill levels are achieved. Because education and training so closely link to industrial growth, performance deficiencies directly influence the achievement of national economic development targets.

Linking with development. At each stage of economic development, education and training objectives closely link with workplace skill requirements. Consequently, the education and training system has had to make significant, relatively rapid programming changes based on the assessment of student/trainee competencies and feedback from employers.

The Ministry of Trade and Industry (MTI) is the key government player. Through its Economic Development Board, it establishes industrial development and education and training targets. Other ministries and government agencies feed information to the MTI. Employers provide input about their skill needs, and education and training institutions supply information about student achievement. This information is used to identify and set national educational and training targets.

The Council for Professional and Technical Education translates national targets into specific targets for each of the formal education and training institutions and organizations responsible for workforce preparation. The Singapore Productivity and Standards Board

(SPSB) sets targets for on-the-job training. In combination, the targets established by the Council as well as the SPSB comprise a representative set of education and training targets that correspond with workforce requirements projected by the economic development plan. The output of the educational and training system is gauged against these targets.

Educational planning is not left to market forces but rather is based on rationally defined economic development targets. The state must ensure not only approximate equilibrium between the supply of and projected demand for skilled workers but also a level of education and training that reflects the qualitative requirements of development.

Taiwan

Like Singapore, Taiwan uses education and training to complement national economic development policy. However, Taiwan applies a more basic approach to realigning education and training priorities.

The ratio of vocational to academic education is altered to adjust output to changed industrial targets. In the 1960s, for example, the ratio of vocational schools to academic high schools was 2:3. As the economy shifted toward higher-value production in the 1980s, the ratio also changed, becoming 7:3. During the recent phase of development, the government changed the ratio again, to 3:2. The current objective aims to reduce the number of vocational school completers while increasing the output of academic students to accommodate projections for high-technology industrial development (Ashton & Sung, 1997).

Considerable social demand for academic education exists but, by controlling academic placements, vocational education becomes a viable option for many capable young people. Industry is thus assured a supply of skilled workers from both the vocational and academic tracks, but at the same time a close link exists with the demands of the economy at different development stages. The state, in a real sense, creates the demand for the kinds and quantity of skills in the economy as a whole as economic targets realign.

Three major demands are placed on the qualifying and certification system. First, it must reflect the particular skill mix required by industry in terms of the quantity of training, representative occupational levels, and quality, requiring close coordination with industry. Second, there must be a relatively short response time to changing skill requirements; therefore, the system must be flexible and efficient. And third, it must reflect the new training priorities embedded in the higher level technologies and higher value-added production.

The Council for Economic Planning and Development (CEPD) acts as the coordinating mechanism, formulating industrial strategy and bringing other ministries into line with the economic objectives. As in the case of Singapore, the economic arm of the government is the major influence on the education and training system. CEPD must ensure that education and training targets are realized. Folded within CEPD is the Manpower Development Committee, which oversees the implementation of education and training policy. Taiwan's economic development policy rests on a continuous flow of educated and trained personnel into its economic system to address current and projected requirements.

References

Alexander, P. J. (1993). *The German dual training system in Japan.* Tokyo: German Chamber of Industry and Commerce in Japan.

Ashton, D. N., & Sung, J. (1997). Education, skill formation and economic development: The Singaporean approach. In A. H. Halsey, H. Lauder, P. Brown, & A. M. Wells, *Education, culture, economy and society* (pp. 207-218). Oxford, England: Oxford University Press.

Bott, P. A. (1996). *Testing and assessment in occupational and technical education.* Boston: Allyn and Bacon.

Cairncross, D., & Dore, R. (1990). *Employee training in Japan* (Report submitted to the Industrial, Technological and Employment Program, Office of Technological Assessment). Washington, DC: United States Congress.

Campbell, C. P. (1993). Manipulative performance tests. In L. G. Duenk (Ed.), *Improving vocational curriculum* (pp. 173-202). South Holland, IL: Goodheart-Willcox.

Colardyn, D. (1994). Certification in adult education. In T. Husen & T. N. Postlethwaite (Eds.), *International encyclopedia of education* (2nd ed., pp. 662-665). Oxford, England: Pergamon.

Cotton, J. (1995). *The theory of assessment.* London: Kogan Page.

Drake, K. (1991). Recent developments of continuing professional education (United Kingdom's report to OECD). In Office for Economic Cooperation and Development (Ed.), *Higher education and employment.* Paris: Office for Economic Cooperation and Development.

The dual system: Vocational training in the Federal Republic of Germany. (1988). Bonn, Germany: Association of German Chambers of Industry and Commerce.

Dual vocational training in the Federal Republic of Germany. (1988). Bonn, Germany: Deutscher Industrie-und Handelstag.

Hamm, M. S. (1996). What are the building blocks of good certification and accreditation programs? In M. A. Pare (Ed.), *Certification and accreditation program directory.* New York: Gale Research.

Haskell, R. W. (1993). The dual system: Admission criteria, progression and evaluation. In C. P. Campbell & R. B. Armstrong (Eds.), *Workforce development in the Federal Republic of Germany* (pp. 56-77). Pittsburg, KS: Press International.

Herschbach, D. R. (1993). *Financing vocational education and training in developing countries* (Training Discussion Paper). Geneva, Switzerland: International Labour Office.

Herschbach, D. R., Hays, F. B., & Evans, D. P. (1992). *Vocational education and training: A review of experience.* Washington, DC: United States Agency for International Development.

Industry report 1998: A snapshot of employer-sponsored training in the United States. (1998, October). *Training Magazine, 35*, 43-45.

International Labour Office. (1987). *Training and retraining—Implications of technological change.* Geneva, Switzerland: Author.

Kloas, P. W. (1997). *Modularsierung in der beruflichen bildung [Modularity in vocational education].* Bielefeld, Germany: Bertelsmann-Verlag.

Laflamme, G., Basset, C., & Michlin, P. (Eds.). (1993). *Vocational training: International perspectives.* Turin, Italy: International Labour Organization, Turin Centre.

Stacy, N., & Duc, L. T. (1994). Adult education and training markets. In T. Husen & T. N. Postlethwaite (Eds.), *International encyclopedia of education* (2nd ed., pp. 103-111). Oxford, England: Pergamon.

Trilingual "business card" gives dual vocational training graduates a stronger profile. (1997, February). *CEDEFOP Info*, p. 14.

Vocational Training Act of 1969. (1986). Bonn, Germany: Federal Ministry of Education, Science, Research and Technology.

6

Financing Workforce Preparation Programs

By Dennis R. Herschbach and Vladimir Gasskov

Adequate financial resources are essential to the development and maintenance of workforce preparation programs. Without sustained, adequate financing, it is difficult to provide high-quality services. Inadequate financing inevitably results in poor programming over the long term.

Financing presents a major challenge to policymakers and planners. Education and training budgets are stagnant or declining in many countries, while heavy demands are being placed on education, including work preparation programs. Formal programs provided through public institutions find themselves particularly hard pressed, although adequate financing presents a problem for privately operated programs as well. Vocational and technical education (VTE) is expensive to provide. Administrators, pressed to balance budgets, often opt to cut vocational programs in favor of subjects that cost less, or they increase enrollments to reduce unit costs. Resources for program development and maintenance are often kept at a marginal level. As a consequence, many institutions face a decline in the number, quality, and relevance of the VTE programs

they offer. This results in fewer individuals receiving meaningful workforce preparation.

VTE provided through the private sector in many countries also is insufficient and underfinanced. When employers face budget constraints, training is often the first area to be reduced or eliminated. Some governments have used special incentive schemes to elicit greater employer participation in human resource development. Others have engaged in co-financing schemes, or have formulated partnerships with joint responsibility for public and private training services (Gasskov, 1994). There is no optimal way to finance workforce preparation. There are ways, however, to mobilize diverse financial resources to extend opportunity and enhance the quality of workforce preparation programs.

This chapter sets out, first, to examine the various ways of financing workforce preparation and related policy issues. We should no longer assume that government can or will continue to cover a high proportion of the overall cost of vocational and technical education. Quite simply, too many competing demands for public resources exist. To maintain financial resources at a sufficient level to ensure program quality, we must implement alternative ways of financing VTE and make better use of existing resources. However, complex policy issues are involved, relative to the respective roles of public and private financing

Second, we examine the immediate constraints associated with various ways of financing VTE, along with key conditions that contribute to sound financing. Different financing alternatives have conflicting impacts on policy, programs, and people. There also are limitations that impact the way to best use funds. Some of these limitations are at the policy level; others relate to the kind of training that should be provided, the constituency served, and program implementation. Any search for alternative ways to finance work preparation must be pursued within the boundaries of the accompanying conditions (Herschbach, 1993).

Third, and finally, we present selected examples of financing alternatives, drawing from our international experience. Country examples are interwoven with the financing discussion. Different countries pursue different paths to the financing of their workforce preparation systems, and we can learn much from how they address financing issues.

CRITICAL CONDITIONS

Distinctions between workforce preparation systems are not so much about the end purpose of instruction as they are a reflection of the organization and financing of education and training. Local communities in the United States (U.S.), and to a lesser extent Britain, for example, finance the major portion of elementary and secondary education, including vocational and technical education, while the federal government assumes major responsibility for financing training of the unemployed, the poor, and the displaced. In the U.S., the private sector invests considerable sums in training, but usually on firm-specific initiatives that are independent of public programs. Employers in Germany and Japan, by contrast, accept the

obligation to contribute to broad-based employment preparation for all. In Singapore, the education and training system is highly centralized and government directed, including the generation and distribution of resources for VTE. Both general tax revenues and funds from specific taxes levied on firms go to support public and private forms of education and training.

In Brazil and Colombia, vocational training authorities supported through payroll taxes constitute the main approach to workforce training, while France has an extremely diversified training service delivery system based on a combination of publicly supported, preservice training; enterprise-financed in-service training; client fees; and contracted services. In many countries, however, the distinction between public and private blurs as policymakers question their nation's capacity to continue providing social services and search for new collaborative ways to finance education and training (Ashton & Green, 1996; Gasskov, 1994; Herschbach, 1993).

What is the optimal financing mix? A number of crucial conditions surround the answer to this question, regardless of the funding stream. Prudent policy and planning decisions are based on an understanding of both the opportunities and constraints associated with the various financing approaches. From the standpoint of implementing and maintaining VTE programs, there are at least six conditions that should be considered when making policy decisions: (a) adequacy, (b) stability of resources, (c) resource balance, (d) equity and equality, (e) responsiveness, and (f) administrative complexity (Herschbach, 1993; Jordan & Lyons, 1992; Monk & Brent, 1997). We examine these conditions under the following headings.

Adequacy of Financing

Obviously, one of the most important conditions is the adequacy of financing. As implied earlier, without adequate resources, workforce preparation programs cannot operate at a level of quality that justifies even limited expenditures. However, in both developed and developing countries, social demand tends to drive program expansion, regardless of whether sufficient funding exists to maintain program quality at a level high enough to justify the investment. Both individual and social returns are marginal. This suggests that, for quality to be maintained, program expansion must stay within the boundaries of available financing. Ironically, as basic educational opportunity is extended, and as greater numbers of individuals aspire to a higher standard of living, public demand increases for more advanced education and training, including opportunities to pursue higher-level vocational and technical education.

Decisions to initiate programs must be based on, among other factors, a realistic assessment of the funding level that can be expected over the long term. Educational costs generally fall into two basic categories: capital and recurrent expenditures. Of the two, capital expenditures are easier to predict and measure. They also have a physical presence in the form of facilities, machinery, and equipment. For capital expenditures, the condition of adequacy is usually met. Decisions are not generally made to establish new schools or programs without the availability of sufficient resources to support initial capital costs.

However, in the long term, the level of recurrent financial support is crucial to a program's ability to maintain quality. A lack of adequate resources impacts most directly on recurrent expenses. Programs fail unless adequate funding exists to support minimal levels of recurrent expenses such as equipment, machinery, and building maintenance; instructional resources; program development; and staffing.

Resource Stability

The development and maintenance of vocational and technical education and training systems require a stable funding source over a substantial period of time. VTE systems need a relatively long time to fully mature (Dougherty, 1989; Middleton & Demsky, 1988). Administrators and planners have to know that they can count on a reliable source of revenue to meet annual fixed operational costs as well as anticipated increases. Revenue sources that produce a consistent funding stream from year to year are obviously preferable over less predictable ones.

Between all financing alternatives, however, there are trade-offs. Some alternatives, for example, are highly responsive to economic shifts, and thus are less stable, but they may have potential to generate substantially higher revenue. Income and sales taxes are examples discussed in more detail later. Property taxes, by contrast, are more stable but, in some communities, they have limited capacity to generate sufficient resources.

The capacity of income revenue streams to fluctuate with economic shifts is termed *elasticity*. Private financing generally has a higher level of elasticity than public financing. The elasticity associated with private financing is less detrimental to programming because of the firms' ability to phase programs in and out in response to changed revenue. Publicly supported institutional training, on the other hand, is considerably less flexible because of embedded fixed costs, extended programming, and long-term funding obligations. It is almost impossible for public institutions to quickly eliminate or shift programming, or to reduce or redeploy permanent staff. Highly elastic sources of financing are not as suitable for public training situations.

Balanced Resource Allocation

Different funding sources are unequal in their ability to collect and use resources. When there are substantial differences in the economic base among the various funding sources, horizontal imbalance results. Some schools, for example, have more financial resources available simply because of their location in areas of greater wealth, where there is greater tax revenue. The ability of different geographic locations to raise revenue may vary significantly and, unless funds are redistributed, unequal access, opportunity, and services will result. In centralized government systems, such as in France or Singapore, equalization can be achieved more easily than in federal systems. Taxes can be collected centrally and distributed proportionately across all jurisdictions. In decentralized systems, such as the one found in the United States, horizontal balance is difficult to achieve (Hinchliffe, 1987, 1989).

Vertical imbalance occurs when the amount of financial resources controlled by a higher organizational level is significantly disproportionate to the amount available to lower levels. While different organizational levels may have different resource needs, the allocation of resources, nevertheless, should be proportional to the relative needs at each level. However, because higher organizational levels have more power over the collection and allocation of resources, those resources may be disproportionately distributed.

Central governments usually control the most gainful sources of revenue. Not only do they have more efficient ways to collect taxes, but the taxation forms used have the potential to generate high levels of revenue. State, regional, and local governments, on the other hand, tend to have less powerful ways of generating income and, unless there is some form of revenue sharing with the central government, sufficient levels of public resources may not be available. The U.S. is a case in point. In recent years, the federal government has tended to delegate social responsibilities to the states, yet the full resource streams do not accompany the increased responsibilities. States and localities are left with added social and financial obligations, but no new revenue. Until equitable solutions are found, social services, including education, will continue to face severe financial constraints. Vertical imbalance has contributed in the U.S. to inadequate financial resources to support education and training programs.

Vertical imbalance applies to governments as well as to organizational and institutional levels. In school systems, for example, the central administrative office may consume a disproportionately high percentage of resources simply because of its ability to secure a greater share of available funds. Those who control budgeting tend not to deny themselves, regardless of needs elsewhere. For example, one problem experienced in national training agencies supported through payroll levies, such as the Servicio Nacional de Aprendizagem (SENA) scheme in Colombia, is high administrative and management costs, due, in part, to overly expanded administrative structures (Herschbach, 1993). Funds are absorbed in administrative costs to the detriment of program quality and development. Direct VTE services are usually delivered by lower organizational levels, but these may be the very levels that have the most-limited resources.

Regarding the private sector, considerable imbalance exists among firms. Large companies have the financial capacity to develop and maintain training within the firm. Small firms generally do not. The phenomenon of *poaching*, where one firm hires away trained employees from another, arises at least in part from resource imbalance. Firms poor in training resources attempt to benefit from the training investments of others.

One way to mediate this problem is through training provided by associations, boards, and so forth, serving a complete industry. All firms within the industry, regardless of size, contribute proportionally to a fund, and then all have access to training and trained personnel. One example of this practice is the Construction Industry Training Board which has operated successfully for many years in the United Kingdom.

Equity and Equality

The enhancement of equity has traditionally served as justification for the public financing of education. Publicly supported vocational and technical education, in particular, often provides opportunities to students who would otherwise have limited educational and employment prospects (Cohen & Geske, 1990; Dougherty & Tan, 1997; Psacharopoulas & Woodhall, 1985). However, concepts of equity and equality are complex. The means of raising revenue to finance education must be equitable. At the same time, the use of resources must be fair.

Equality is linked to equity, but achieving equality requires a more deliberate allocation of resources than is usually achieved. Achieving equality often implies the equal distribution of resources among unequal recipients (Cohen & Geske, 1990; Monk & Brent, 1997). However, resources may be fairly, but not equally, distributed if greater resources are required to overcome unequal opportunity (vertical equity). Providing the same amount of financial support does not necessarily produce comparable results for the poor and disadvantaged. In many cases, they need additional resources.

Vocational and technical education can play a major role in promoting equal opportunity among the poor and disadvantaged, but substantial resources are needed. Such instruction is costly, but to promote equality, an even greater taxpayer resource commitment may be required. Whether this can be achieved is highly questionable. In any case, in making decisions on how best to finance work preparation programs, the conditions of equity and equality require full consideration.

A major rationale for public funding of education is that governments can collect and distribute resources in a way that ensures the greatest public benefit. In some countries, moreover, government plays a major role in the mobilization of private financial resources to support vocational and technical education and training (Gasskov, 1994). All ways of raising revenue, however, are not summarily equitable.

Responsiveness

In the case of workforce preparation programs, the condition of responsiveness has importance. The particular ways of financing VTE must permit a reasonable amount of programming flexibility to accommodate not only changing economic and demographic conditions, but also changing labor market requirements. Planners may face rapid enrollment increases or decreases, more demand for bilingual or special education/training, or significant shifts in programming to accommodate both student interests and labor market demand. While some inertia may arise from administrative and organizational factors, the particular way that funds are raised and used can also contribute to institutional inflexibility.

In some countries, enhancing the role of market forces has become a major strategy for improving the responsiveness of VTE systems (Atchoarena, 1998). Efforts are being made to encourage competition among public and private education and training providers, and to promote more flexible use of funds. In the United Kingdom, for example, the Training Credit Initiative encourages public training institutions to accommodate market demand. Public funds go directly to students, rather than to individual training institutions. Students may choose which institutions and programs they will attend, and training providers generate revenue according to their ability to attract students (Gasskov, 1994).

The need for responsiveness, however, must be balanced with stability of funding. One should not come at the expense of the other. Changes in the funding mix also should not result in a reduction in overall financial support.

Administrative Complexity

All ways of financing VTE involve administrative costs. Consequently, the best means is the least complex and costly, administratively. Individuals and/or companies must comply with tax requirements easily and at low cost. As compliance becomes more complex, not only are collection expenses higher but the incidence of evasion increases. Compliance must be predictable and dependable. Moreover, high administrative costs subtract from the amount of funding available to support actual programming.

FOCUS OF REVIEW

Next, we will examine three fundamental ways to finance workforce preparation programs: general public tax revenues; enterprise-financing, either directly or through special earmarked taxes and subsidies; and user fees. Most countries use combinations of these sources. This reduces dependency on any one, and contributes to revenue generation and stability.

Financing through Public Funds

Approximately 4 percent of the U.S. gross national product is spent annually on public elementary and secondary education alone. Education generally represents the largest single category of state and local government expenditures, and revenues are raised from multiple sources. Four general tax bases are used for raising revenue: wealth, income, consumption, and privilege (Swanson & King, 1991). Each has a different impact on the government's ability to fund VTE and address issues of effectiveness, equity, opportunity, and quality.

Generating public resources. Taxes on real estate, personal property, or accumulated assets at the time of death are kinds of wealth taxes. Wealth taxes, in the form of real estate property taxes, continue to be the single most important form of raising revenue for local schools in the United States. Approximately 47 percent of school income at the local level is raised through property taxes. Property tax revenues tend to be fairly stable since property assessments, on which the taxes are based, stay reasonably constant from year to year. Thus, fairly accurate projections can be made of future revenue. Property taxes also experience relatively little decline during periods of economic downturn. The large yield and predictability of revenues facilitate planning, budgeting, and program development.

However, wealth taxes can be an inequitable form of financing. Wealth is not distributed equally across local communities; consequently, their abilities to finance education prove unequal. Considerable horizontal imbalance may exist. Until governments find a way to redistribute funds centrally, unequal access, opportunity, and services will continue. This has direct implications for vocational and technical education. The greatest need for workforce preparation programs often exists in the poorest communities, but these are the very communities that lack the wealth, and hence the ability, to raise sufficient revenue to support such programs.

States may compensate for unequal wealth by granting aid to less wealthy jurisdictions through "equalization" formulas. In the United States, a considerable part of both state and federal funding to support local education goes to equalize differences in revenue-generating capacity between communities. Based on full-time equivalent student enrollment, a specified fund amount is allocated so that all local schools will have at least a basic level of support. To compensate for differences in taxable wealth, additional funds go to less affluent communities. Some states also allocate funds to different categories of programs, such as high-cost vocational and technical education.

Generally speaking, the use of both federal and state funds attempts to correct for differences in wealth and horizontal imbalance, and to encourage certain kinds of vocational and technical education. Nevertheless, equity is difficult to achieve in practice for political, legal, and practical reasons. Those that have more tend to get more. Within individual states, and between states, wide variation exists in the mixture of local, state, and federal revenues (Johns, Morphet, & Alexander, 1983).

The income tax is an important source of revenue for governments because of its large yield. Wages and salaries, corporate earnings, and investment income each year generate enormous revenues for government at all levels. Income taxes are generally hard to evade and easy to collect, and they keep pace with rising wages and economic growth. The considerable elasticity of income taxes, however, suggests that they are not a stable form of taxation. In addition, since income taxes are such an essential part of government financing at all levels and competition for government financial support is so intense, only limited amounts of revenue are available to support schools. In the United States, for example, federal and state support for vocational and technical education is important, but it is almost totally based on income tax revenue, which continues to be an underutilized, secondary source of support (Thompson, Wood, & Honeyman, 1994).

Consumption taxes are yet another source of financing for public services, including schools. In many European countries, value-added taxes (VAT) on goods and services constitute a major source of national income. Similarly, in the United States, sales taxes have been the single most important source of income at the state level. In some countries that have poorly developed income and property tax systems, excise taxes and customs duties constitute a major source of government revenue. Needless to say, consumption taxes are highly elastic, are considered highly regressive, and reflect the economic conditions of a country.

Privilege taxes in the form of license and user fees constitute a relatively small revenue source in relation to wealth, income, and consumption taxes and, although they cannot be ignored as a source of government funds, their impact on adequacy of income, stability, and equity is not clear. They are probably negligible with regard to school financing.

Use of public funds. Public general purpose funds from tax revenues are usually allocated annually to schools on a per-student or unit basis. They are easy to administer because funds come from a central source and the amount can be anticipated. Capital building and equipment costs are usually administered separately from operational funds through a central support agency and distributed for spe-

cific purposes, such as building and equipping a new facility, rather than by a set annual amount.

When funds for operations are allocated on a per-student or unit basis, they usually do not account for variation in need, capacity, or performance. Administrative convenience comes at the expense of responsiveness to local variation. This can lead to inequity, particularly when only a portion of financial needs are funded by the central authority. Wealthier communities have considerably more funding by virtue of their larger tax base. When the state funds a high share of program costs, greater equity can be achieved, but overall resources may be limited because of the general demand on state resources.

Increased central funding may also mean increased central control and, therefore, loss of local flexibility. The resulting vocational and technical education is apt to be less responsive to unique local conditions (Herschbach, 1993).

When funds are allocated on the basis of enrollment, programs have less incentive to strive for instructional quality. A set amount of funding is allocated per student or unit, regardless of instructional performance. The tendency is to maximize enrollment at the expense of qualifications and achievement, and to minimize direct classroom instructional expenditures. There also is less incentive to respond to either student or labor market needs.

Alternatively, funds may be allocated on the basis of student performance, judged by achievement and program completion. There is greater incentive to maintain relevant, high-quality programming, particularly when performance is judged against external criteria, such as job placement or examinations. However, there may be less opportunity, and thus equity, because the programs' tendency is to select only those applicants with the highest performance potential. Nevertheless, under conditions of limited resources, allocation of funds on the basis of program performance and completion may prove the best alternative.

If the primary objective is to expand vocational and technical education opportunity, funding on the basis of enrollment is appropriate. If the objective is performance and responsiveness, the best choice is funding by completion and external evaluation. There is also a middle ground, however, in which a foundation grant based on student enrollment is combined with an additional allocation per program completer (Cohen & Geske, 1990). This combination assures a degree of equity and quality. In any case, regardless of the method of public funding allocation, it is critical to have a stable and adequate source.

Enterprise-Based Financing

In most countries, a large part of education and training for work is financed through private means. In the United States, for example, more than $60 billion dollars annually is spent on company training, although most of it goes to management and high-skill training. A considerable amount of on-the-job training also is conducted, but we have no reliable cost estimate. Employers train because it is required by law (compliance training) and less costly than recruiting workers from the open market. They also train to fill crucial skill needs and to shape the skill profile of their internal workforce. Employers also provide training to develop a work culture that embodies the concept of long-term career development. The best example is in Japan's corporate training—employees build corporate loyalty through participation in lifelong training, progressing to higher job responsibilities and pay throughout their careers.

In many countries, however, enterprise financing extends to education and training initiatives designed to raise the general level of training beyond that voluntarily undertaken by individual employers. There are four basic approaches. A revenue-generating levy scheme in the form of an earmarked payroll tax is used to support a national training agency. This is the method of choice for financing nonformal VTE in most Latin American, some Caribbean, and more than 30 other countries. A widely applied variation is the levy-grant scheme. Firms that elect to start or expand training programs receive grants from a fund established through payroll contributions. A more recent alternative is the use of tax rebates or credits to encourage firms to provide training. Singapore probably provides the best example. Firms that engage in training for high-wage, high-value-added production, in turn, receive tax credits. The German dual system, the Industrial Social Fund in the Netherlands, and the French training tax scheme are other examples that use a combination of public and private financing (Dougherty & Tan, 1997; Gasskov, 1994, 1998; Whalley & Ziderman, 1990).

Regardless of its form, enterprise-financed training cannot be assumed to substitute completely for public financing. Generally, preemployment preparation can best be provided through publicly financed programs, since employers prefer to fund specific skill training associated directly with their firm. Enterprise financing can be viewed as a way to complement, rather than replace, public funding. Nevertheless, an effective combination is achieved, with public financing providing the foundation programs for more specific enterprise-based training.

The earmarked payroll tax. The most common alternative to the use of general government funds to support work preparation programs is the earmarked payroll tax. Typically, a tax ranging from 1 to 2 percent of gross payroll is levied on firms. In some cases, smaller firms may be exempt and larger ones may pay more. Government collects and disperses revenue but does not conduct training. Government commonly uses the levy income to support the development and maintenance of an independent national training agency responsive to participating firms (Ducci, 1991).

Training services take many forms: apprenticeship, in-firm, institutional, short-term, long-term, or any combination. The SENA schemes in Brazil, for example, make extensive use of established training centers, while SENA in Colombia has a system of regional on- and off-the-job training, using combinations of center- and workplace-based training. In Denmark, the levy fund finances training for employed workers. Japan finances small-firm training through a revenue-generating levy scheme (Gasskov, 1994).

Revenue-generating levy schemes generally meet the condition of financial adequacy. The payroll levy is a sheltered, earmarked tax. It represents a large resource pool outside normal government channels. However, because the levy produces a relatively large, unallocated amount of revenue, governments may try to divert resources to nontraining activities. This poaching of funds can become a source of contention as employers and workers unwillingly finance other social services with revenue intended to support their own, immediate training needs. Also, the accumulation of surpluses may encourage the growth of large, top-heavy training bureaucracies and the tolerance of ineffective, high-cost training programs (Dougherty & Tan, 1997).

Levy schemes basically meet the condition of funding stability. The revenues tend to be reasonably stable, subject, of course, to economic fluctuations. As economic activity picks up and payrolls increase, the resulting levy revenues also increase. Conversely, when economic activity declines, so do revenues. If one assumes, however, that training needs roughly mirror economic activity, then as more income is generated through expanded payrolls, increased training activity can be supported.

Lag time between revenue collection and the delivery of training can be a problem. In the case of long-term training, considerable time may elapse between immediate need, available financing, and training completion. Maintaining a reserve fund contributes significantly to moderating the influence of economic fluctuations. In the case of short-term, specialized training, lag time generally does not present a major problem.

Payroll levies are a form of benefit tax. The costs of training are borne by the enterprise and the employee, but both profit from a more highly trained and productive workforce. For this reason, they are, in theory at least, considered equitable. However, firms with greater numbers of employees may pay a larger share of the tax without receiving more services in return, and some firms may already have a highly trained workforce. Payroll size is only indirectly linked with training requirements. On the other hand, small employers, as a group, tend to benefit less from training because, over the long term, they have difficulty retaining employees.

Considerable evidence also suggests that at least a portion of the cost falls on workers in the form of lower wages (Whalley & Ziderman, 1990). For this reason, younger workers profit more because of the greater potential for advancement and earnings over an extended working life.

Although earmarked payroll taxes may appear, at a glance, to be a good approximation of benefit-related taxation, this can be deceptive. Services are not always received in proportion to the taxes paid by both firms and individuals. The condition of equity may be only partly realized and is seriously impaired when government diverts funds to other uses. Dougherty and Tan (1997) suggested that, to eliminate severe inequities, tax rates should be adjusted to take into consideration the types of workers employed and the accompanying training requirements.

Levy-grant scheme. In many countries, the payroll tax goes primarily to support a grant scheme. This is its newest and most widespread use. Firms that start or expand training programs receive grants, the amount depending on the kind, level, and scope of training. The grants are issued from a specially established fund on a cost-incurred basis or to support the establishment of training programs. However, grants awarded do not closely reflect a firm's levy contribution since they are allocated on the basis of the actual training conducted. The grant scheme is a redistribution of funds to firms that train (Gasskov, 1998).

Singapore uses the payroll tax as a mechanism to restructure its labor force. Through the Skills Development Fund, established in 1979, firms receive grants as an incentive to promote skill development in strategic, high-skilled, high-wage fields. Firms are encouraged to invest in training so that they can pursue high-value-added production. Funding to support training comes through a levy assessed primarily on low-wage employment. The expectation is that not only will the wage level rise, but that firms will perceive investments in human resource development as important as capital investments. The higher-skilled workforce that results can then play a lead role in Singapore's economic restructuring (Ashton & Green, 1996).

In Sweden, employers and unions voluntarily established the Employment Security Fund without government intervention. The Fund provides training to unemployed workers or individuals threatened by changing technology, potential factory closures, or production change. In addition, new companies, or companies moving into new areas of product development and production, can receive grants for up to 80 percent of their training cost (Ashton & Green, 1996; Gasskov, 1994, 1998).

Common practice is to award grants on a cost-sharing basis to develop a commitment on the part of firms to engage in meaningful training. The assumption is that since the firm also contributes, the training commitment will be taken more seriously. Firms that lack sufficient resources, however, may not have to match funds. Levies are not refundable to firms that do not train.

Special provisions often are made to promote training for small firms. The Social Development Fund in Singapore, for example, contributes substantial financing to 16 industry-based training centers for small- and medium-sized firms. In addition, grants of 50 to 70 percent of training charges are provided to enable participants from individual firms to attend approved public training courses. Finally, grants are awarded to offset the cost of external consultants to conduct training needs assessments and develop training plans (Gasskov, 1994).

Levy-exemption schemes. Exemption schemes enable firms to reduce their levy obligation by a certain percentage of the cost of the training they provide, through either in-firm training or outside contracting. Participating firms are exempted, in France for example, from part of the training tax. In some countries, including Belgium, Chile, Korea, and Pakistan, training costs are deductible from various taxes as an alternative, or in addition to the payroll tax.

A variation of the levy-exemption is to grant rebates to firms that train (Whalley & Ziderman, 1990; Gasskov 1998). However, exemption schemes are less cumbersome administratively because taxes do not have to be collected first and refunded later.

Exemption and rebate schemes tend to encourage firms to develop training capacity in-house. It is to their advantage to train on a continuing basis. A disadvantage of the exemption/rebate schemes, in general, is that without enforceable guidelines, firms may conduct all kinds of training activities, regardless of whether they are needed, just to qualify for the tax benefit. The high, and in some cases prohibitive, administrative cost of drawing up and establishing an approved training plan, however, discourages this practice. Smaller firms, in particular, tend not to participate in rebate schemes unless special provisions are made (Dougherty & Tan, 1997).

The levy-grant and -exemption schemes generally meet the conditions of adequacy and stability of resources. Because of their use, an increase in company-provided training has occurred in various countries. However, the incidence of training by small firms continues to lag. Resource allocation is not balanced; firms that have more resources benefit the most. The upgrading of older and disadvantaged workers probably has not occurred at the rate envisioned, and training has tended to be concentrated in higher skill occupations, contrary to some countries' objective of upgrading lower-paid, unskilled workers. This points to the policy dilemma of attempting to achieve responsiveness and greater equity at the same time (Dougherty & Tan, 1997; Gasskov, 1998; Whalley & Ziderman, 1990).

Combining enterprise and public financing. At any one time, 60 to 70 percent of the young people of a given age cohort participate in the German dual training system. In its most basic form, the system combines instruction in public vocational schools with training and experience at the workplace. For one or two days each week, apprentices attend public vocational education classes; the remainder of the week is spent on the job. Programs are two to four years in length, after which those who pass a final examination receive a journeyman's certificate. Graduates may take a job or continue to other levels of education or training. See Chapter 8—Germany's Vocational Training/Apprenticeship System, for detailed information.

The dual system is perhaps the best-known example of joint financing between government and employers. School costs are funded by the state through tax revenue. The federal and regional governments' annual outlay is relatively large, amounting to about 1.6 percent of gross domestic product (GDP). Participating firms defray the costs of in-firm training, including the cost of materials and equipment. Employers must absorb the hidden costs associated with training, such as lower productivity on the part of experienced workers charged with instructing apprentices, breakage and waste of materials, and the cost of processing and management. Apprentices also help support the cost of their training by accepting lower wages than they could earn in unskilled work (Herschbach, 1993).

When the supply of potential apprentices exceeds available training openings, the state may provide funds that enable firms to absorb the cost of additional training. In addition, to compensate for imbalances between demand and opportunity, training shops funded by the state are established in larger firms. At the same time, external training centers are funded through user fees, levies on firms, worker groups, and public subsidies.

In the Netherlands, employer organizations and trade unions are active in supporting training for their particular sector. Through collective agreements, Industrial Social Funds (ISFs) were set up voluntarily without government intervention, and participating employers must pay levies. Needs assessment, advisory services, apprenticeship programs, skills upgrading, and training for the unemployed are among the activities financed though ISFs. In addition to support for training and training-related activities, ISFs provide a variety of other services, including support activities for employer organizations and unions. Levies are kept relatively low (0.7 percent on the average) and are used to finance roughly two-thirds of program costs, with the remainder supplied through public grants. ISFs also actively seek additional private and public funds (Veeken, 1994).

The Dutch government contributes mainly in the form of subsidy funds, administered by boards comprised of employer and union representatives. ISF and board membership often overlap. The major use of the combined levy-based and government funding is to target training to priorities. Overall, only about 20 percent of training is financed through such a combination. The remaining 80 percent is financed directly by individual employers (Veeken, 1994).

Subsidy funds are used to promote sectoral training targeted to specific activities. Separate National Apprenticeship Boards, funded through the Ministry of Education, provide training in sectors that lack Industrial Social Funds.

France has the most comprehensive system of financing. Employer contributions fund about 60 percent of all VTE expenditures. The remainder is financed through public funds.

Employer contributions come from two compulsory payroll levies: an *apprenticeship tax* that supports public and private VTE institutions, including apprenticeship centers, and a training tax used to support employee training and retraining.

The apprenticeship tax consists of 0.6 percent of a company's wage bill, of which 0.1 percent is reserved by the French government for training young adults between the ages of 16 and 25. The remaining 0.5 percent is administered by regional councils and local organizations. Employers, however, can be exempt from the tax if they show that they have spent an amount at least equal to the tax bill on authorized training. Employers meet their training obligation, in one of four ways, by

• Accepting apprentices or offering in-plant courses.

• Paying fees directly to external institutions to provide courses.

• Bestowing their assessment on a specific training institution or association, even though no direct services are received in return.

• Paying the tax directly to the government.

Not surprisingly, little of the tax goes to the government, since employers tend to provide their own training or support outside training institutions. Considerable competition has been generated among training institutions that seek funding from employers (Bas, 1994).

The compulsory training tax, which applies to all firms with 10 or more employees, constitutes 1.5 percent of a company's total wage bill. Employers can use 0.8 percent of this to conduct their own inhouse training, or they can contract for training services to be provided inside or outside their firm. Of the remaining 0.7 percent, 0.3 percent goes to fund government training programs for youth seeking their first job, and 0.15 percent is allocated for paid training leave (Bas, 1994). Employers with fewer than 10 employees are exempt from the levy, and they are not eligible for training benefits. Overall, the training levy has stimulated training activities. However, large enterprises tend to invest more heavily in training and even spend beyond the obligated amount, while smaller employers tend to invest less (Bas, 1994).

General tax revenues support both public and private secondary-level preemployment preparation. The government's financial outlay is large, totaling 1.5 percent of GDP. Almost everyone in France has the opportunity to pursue training of one type or another. This provides newcomers to the labor force with a basic foundation of general and technical skills on which more focused enterprise-based training can be structured.

Funding combinations generally provide good examples of benefit-related financing. Those who pay the costs also tend to receive the greatest benefits. For this reason, they are considered the most equitable forms of financing. They generate high levels of resources, are balanced schemes, and are responsive. They may be complex to administer, however, such as in the case of France.

In terms of policy, financing combinations provide an effective use of government funds, since just a partial contribution can produce considerable leverage and services. In a period of limited public resources, diversification of financing may be the only reasonable option for extending and maintaining quality education and training services. Yet the single greatest barrier to the use of multiple sources of financing may be existing practices. New ways of raising revenue require new working relationships between social partners, and to a large degree, the delegation of authority and responsibility. Policy must nourish the conditions that make collaboration among organizations possible.

Financing through User Fees

The use of fees to pay at least a part of education and training costs is a well-established practice in some countries. In Japan, for example, fees make up as much as 30 percent of the support for general and vocational secondary education. As the limits to public financing grow more evident, interest in user fees has expanded. Public financing of elementary and secondary education can be readily justified because the social benefits are thought to accrue to all of society. However, in the case of more specialized education and training, such as VTE, it can be argued that fees should be applied because a highly select group profits most. The benefit principle that those who profit should pay is evoked to justify charging fees (Wurzburg, 1998).

Even in countries like the United States, which has a long tradition of public funding of a broad range of education programs, there is a discernable change in public perception. More vocational and technical education is being shifted to the technical and community college level where students pay at least part of the educational costs. As charter schools and vouchers shift public funds to support mainly programs of academic preparation, public funding for VTE at the secondary level is becoming even more uncertain.

The most common practice is to use fees to support only a portion of the costs, with the remaining revenue generated through a combination of other sources. There are limits to the level of fees that can be charged, and hence potential income, and fees tend not to be a stable source of income. By using multiple revenue sources, these limitations to the use of fees alone are partly countered.

In the case of short-term training programs, fees generally can be relied upon to fund a large proportion, if not all, of instructional costs because the relative amount is within a range that can be reasonably afforded by individuals. This is particularly true in high-tech, high-wage occupational fields and less true in low-wage fields. Individuals are willing to make the personal investment because of the potential return from high-wage jobs.

Extensive, formal preservice programs prove more difficult to finance through fees. The program may lead to inconclusive results, so individuals are less willing to make a heavy financial commitment over a relatively long period of time, even if they can afford to do so,

when job placement is uncertain. Program length and the relatively high cost tend to discourage enrollment—especially if there are no alternative sources of support available, such as grants or loans. If the training is conducted by an employers' association or by specific companies that offer high job prospects, potential employees may be more willing to shoulder the high training cost.

The influence of fee level. In general, fees alone cannot be relied on to fund large amounts of the operational costs of long-term (lasting a year or more), preemployment VTE programs without a reduction in quality. Also, fees generally cannot fund capital costs. Since fees tend to be a relatively unstable source of revenue, they should not be relied on to fund a high proportion of fixed, direct recurrent costs.

At first glance, the potential to generate more income through high fees may seem a viable option, but the impact on programming and enrollment may be detrimental. To continue to attract students, institutions have to limit program offerings to high-skilled, high-wage occupations that coincide with the career aspirations of the more affluent. This skews the program mix, so that many skill areas do not receive adequate attention. Chile's efforts toward self-financed VTE schemes, for example, resulted in the phasing out of a number of vocational/technical education programs. This was due to the institutions' tendency to gravitate toward low-cost, high-appeal programs with greater potential to generate considerable funds through fees, even though job placement prospects were low (Ducci, 1991).

In Jordan, the extensive two-year community college system is divided about evenly between private, fee-charging institutions and publicly supported schools. The private institutions are distinguished by programs that require a low capital investment and generate a high rate of return, whereas publicly supported community colleges offer primarily high-cost, low-enrollment programs (Herschbach, Reinhart, Darcy, & Sanguinetty, 1985).

High fees also may be inequitable. Less-affluent students are excluded from preparing for occupations that have high employment prospects but high enrollment fees. Enrollment disparities that already exist between more-affluent and lower-income groups are reinforced. The relative impact of fees, moreover, tends to vary across income levels; evidence suggests that the effects of this disparity are felt most among the very poor (Gertler & Glewwe, 1989). If too-heavy reliance is placed on fees to support courses and programs, one very real consequence is to discourage enrollment of the very students who could profit most from training opportunity but who cannot afford the required investment in their future welfare.

Low fee level. Even in the absence of adequate funding from other sources, a low fee level can have a negative impact. Only limited instructional offerings can be provided, and program quality suffers. The incentive to respond to student interests also is lessened, and the students themselves may be less selective or appreciative of the opportunity they have.

Economic theory suggests that charging training fees can actually enhance efficiency and quality. Students are more cautious and pragmatic about their potential job preparation options when they have to pay a substantial part of their training costs. They are generally unwilling to invest in programs perceived to be of marginal benefit. Over time, the marketplace acts as a screening and selection mechanism, with less-desirable programs eliminated and strong ones expanded. When fees are too low, this self-correcting mechanism does not work (Psacharopoulas & Woodhall, 1985).

Some governments try to regulate fee level in the name of equity and opportunity. James (1987) observed, however, that this practice can have unforeseen consequences. If fees are kept too near market value, a downgrading of quality usually results. It becomes difficult for fee-charging schools to meet expenses or make a profit without reducing instructional costs.

Incentives to expand programs also are removed. Keeping fees below costs may result in a serious downgrading of instruction.

Governments sometimes regulate fees expecting to increase opportunity for the less affluent. However, this may prove counterproductive. The removal of incentives for expansion may result in less, rather than more, VTE capacity, and, hence, less enrollment opportunity. Competition for limited placements is usually won by more-affluent students (James, 1987).

Optimal uses of fees. If the policy is to expand VTE opportunity, a combination of fees and government subsidies is effective. Fee levels are established and enforced by the government with a view to enhancing opportunity and equity. At the same time, subsidies are provided at a level sufficient to ensure program quality and encourage expansion. The combination of fees and subsidies enables schools to maintain quality and build new programs (and, in the case of proprietary institutions, to make a profit), while keeping the fee level low enough not to exclude the less affluent. In cases of extreme poverty, scholarships, grants, or loans can be used.

One way to counter the issue of equity is to adjust fee level according to the ability to pay. The Educational Foundation of Montes Claros, in Brazil, for example, receives no government funding for the 2,400 students annually served through its day and evening training courses. It relies heavily on fees to support programs, with assessments ranging from 30 to 70 percent of training costs, depending on family income. The remaining revenue comes from a combination of industry-sponsored scholarships, contributions from donors, and the sale of services (Gomes, 1991).

Bas (1989) suggested that, in select industries, it may be more cost-effective to finance trainers rather than organized formal training programs, through user fees. The fees can be used to pay stipends to master workers who, in turn, provide training within the firm itself. Income from fees is used to offset the cost of the additional responsibilities associated with providing in-firm training.

The joint apprenticeship model. The joint apprenticeship model in the United States provides an example of self-financing through wage contributions negotiated between unions and employers. Apprentices and journeymen (union members) contribute a percentage of their hourly wages to support centers and other forms of training under the administration of local joint apprenticeship councils (committees) and a national committee comprised of worker and employer representatives. The councils/committees and their employees are responsible for curriculum; training facilities; instruction; instructional materials; standards, rules, and regulations, and their enforcement; instructor training; and oversight of training. Neither employers nor government contribute directly (Herschbach, 1993).

The training contribution is a form of benefit levy. Apprentices pay for their own training, which leads to good jobs and high wages. Journeymen continue to pay into the training fund because their contributions during their apprenticeships did not fully cover the training they received. They realize the benefit early, but pay later. The apprentices' contribution is counterbalanced by training-wage increases throughout the apprenticeship and a high starting salary on apprenticeship completion.

The joint apprenticeship model has several positive characteristics. Although contributions from the levy go to the National Joint Apprenticeship and Training Committee, local councils/committees control local funding and training. The local training councils have autonomy over who they train and who does the training, while working within the framework of their national organization and federal apprenticeship regulations. This assures a certain level of quality, allows training flexibility, maintains relatively low administrative and training costs, and presents incentives to use funds effectively. While the federal government does not directly contribute to training costs, it does retain a voice in regulating and monitoring

training. The method of financing is considered equitable since those who profit most pay the costs.

Apprenticeship training of the type discussed is limited in the United States for a number of reasons. The approach described is most commonly found in the crafts and trades (carpenters, electricians, sheet metal workers, etc.) that have a tradition of organized apprenticeship training.

DISCUSSION

Financing presents a major challenge to policymakers and planners the world over. While public education and training budgets are stagnant or declining in many countries, there are heavy demands for VTE. For this reason, in virtually all countries, greater emphasis is being placed on diversifying revenue sources for both public and private workforce preparation programs and using collaborative arrangements that share resources. This involves new ways of providing education and training services, as well as new relationships between the public and private sectors, schools and employers, and community participants.

The various ways of financing have different effects on policies, programs, and people. This chapter examined some of the more important issues surrounding the financing of VTE. A number of crucial conditions associated with the various funding streams have been identified and discussed. Financing decisions must be made with a clear understanding of the potential as well as constraints associated with different revenue sources.

There are strong arguments for the public financing of workforce preparation programs (Cohen & Geske, 1990; Dougherty & Tan, 1997), but these depend on the kind and quality of programming provided, and on whether issues of adequacy, resource stability and balance, equity and equality, responsiveness, and administrative effectiveness are satisfactorily addressed. In a climate of competition for public resources, VTE policymakers must make clear to the educational public not only the social and economic benefits that accrue to individuals and society at large, but they must also demonstrate the ability to sustain quality programming. Decisions about the use of public funds ultimately are judgments about what is fair, possible, and effective, and consequently these decisions relate to resource use.

References

Ashton, D., & Green, F. (1996). *Education, training and the global economy.* Cheltenham, England: Edward Elgar.

Atchoarena, D. (1998). The alternatives for the financing of vocational training: The example of emerging countries in Latin America. *Vocational Training European Journal, 13*(1), 56-66.

Bas, D. (1989). *Training in the informal sector. Does it pay?* (Discussion paper no. 33E). Geneva, Switzerland: International Labour Office.

Bas, D. (1994). The French system. In V. Gasskov (Ed.), *Alternative schemes of financing training* (pp. 86-108). Geneva, Switzerland: International Labour Office.

Cohen, E., & Geske, T. G. (1990). *The economics of education* (3rd ed.). Oxford, England: Pergamon Press.

Dougherty, C. (1989). *The cost-effectiveness of national training systems in developing countries.* Washington, DC: The World Bank.

Dougherty, C., & Tan, J.-P. (1997). Financing training: Issues and options. *International Journal of Manpower, 18*(1/2), 29-62.

Ducci, M. A. (1991). *Financing of vocational education in Latin America* (Discussion paper no. 71). Geneva, Switzerland: International Training Policies Branch, International Labour Office.

Gasskov, V. (Ed.) (1994). *Alternative schemes of financing training.* Geneva, Switzerland: International Labour Office.

Gasskov, V (1998). Levies, leave and collective agreements incentives for enterprises and individuals to invest in training. *Vocational Training European Journal, 13*(1), 27-36.

Gertler, P., & Glewwe, P. (1989). *The willingness to pay for education in developing countries: Evidence from rural Peru* (LSMS working paper no. 54). Washington, DC: The World Bank.

Gomes, C. A. (1991). *Alternatives in vocational education finance: An example of participation by employers in Brazil* (Discussion paper no. 69). Geneva, Switzerland: International Labour Office.

Herschbach, D. R. (1993). *Financing vocational education and training in developing countries* (Discussion paper no. 111). Geneva, Switzerland: Training Policies Branch, International Labour Office.

Herschbach, D. R., Reinhart, B. A., Darcy, R. L., & Sanguinetty, J. A. (1985). *Linking training and employment: A case study of training systems in Jordan.* Washington, DC: The World Bank.

Hinchliffe, K. (1987). *Federal finance, fiscal imbalance, and educational inequality* (Discussion paper, Educational and training series report no. EDT72). Washington, DC: The World Bank.

Hinchliffe, K. (1989). Focus on federal-state relations in educational finance. *Comparative Education Review, 33*(4), 437-488.

James, E. (1987). The public/private discussion of responsibility for education. An international comparison. *Economics of Education Review, 6*(1), 1-14.

Johns, R. L., Morphet, E. L., & Alexander, K. (1983). *The economics and financing of education.* Englewood Cliffs, NJ: Prentice-Hall.

Jordan, K. F., & Lyons, T. S. (1992). *Financing public education in an era of change.* Bloomington, IN: Phi Delta Kappa.

Middleton, J., & Demsky, T. (1988). *Changing patterns in vocational education* (Policy, planning, and research working papers). Washington, DC: The World Bank.

Monk, D. H., & Brent, B. O. (1997). *Raising money for education.* Thousand Oaks, CA: Corwin Press.

Psacharopoulos, G., & Woodhall, M. (1985). *Education for development.* New York: Oxford Press.

Swanson, A. D., & King, R. A. (1991). *School finance: Its economics and politics.* New York: Longman.

Thompson, D. C., Wood, R. C., & Honeyman, D. S. (1994). *Fiscal leadership for schools.* New York: Longman.

Veeken, N. (1994). Industrial social fund in the Netherlands. In V. Gasskov (Ed.), *Alternative schemes of financing training* (pp. 108-113). Geneva, Switzerland: International Labour Office.

Whalley, J., & Ziderman, A. (1990). Financing training in developing countries: The role of payroll taxes. *Economics of Education Review, 9*(4), 377-387.

Wurzburg, G. (1998). Issues in financing vocational education and training in the EU. *Vocational Training European Journal, 13*(1), 22-26.

Part II: Case Studies of Selected Country Practices

Introduction

Work preparation is a diverse enterprise. It includes various forms of public and private education and training, ranging from prevocational, exploratory instruction to general foundation programs, apprenticeships, and short-term courses designed for specific skill preparation. Instruction takes place in public schools, special vocational centers, at the workplace, within both school and work locations, and in colleges and centers of advanced training. Instruction ranges from the almost purely manual to the highly complex and abstract, and it can vary in duration from hours to months or even years. The different modes of education and training for work, moreover, require significantly different conditions for successful implementation. And certain kinds of program interventions work better for addressing the respective employment requirements of one constituency population rather than another.

There is practically universal consensus, however, that education and training contribute substantially to social and economic welfare. Indeed, they constitute a crucial element in the international competitive economy, even though there is less agreement on the particular form that workforce preparation programming should take. This is because education and training systems respond to, and take on the characteristics of, the political, social, economic, and institutional systems of which they are a part. Thus, it is important to distinguish between the basic, fundamental forms of education and training and the specific conditions within countries that impact the implementa-

tion and use of these forms. It is not enough to speak of apprenticeship training or national vocational training agencies, for example, without also probing the differences, often subtle, embedded in the various applications that individual countries make of what appear on the surface to be similar education and training modes. This is the value of a comparative study, such as is found in the cases presented here. Both similarities and differences are explicated.

Accordingly, the 10 chapters in Part II have two main objectives. The first is to acquaint the reader with the structural and functional characteristics of education and training systems designed to prepare individuals for work. How are programs organized, financed, operated, and evaluated? What user groups attend, and how are participants selected? What kinds of instruction are offered, and how? What kinds of linkages exist between constituency groups? What are the roles of the public and private sectors? These, and other questions, are important. At a time when significant international interest in workforce preparation exists, it is useful to know how professionals in other countries address the challenges of preparing individuals for work.

A second objective, however, involves developing an understanding of the more subtle, crucial differences grounded in distinctive education and training traditions. Value positions on access and opportunity, individuality, conformity and control, and competency and efficiency, for example, affect in often powerful ways how specific countries apply program structures and functions. Moreover, the form of a particular country's political and economic system impacts directly its use of education and training. On closer examination, what appear on the surface to be program similarities mask real and crucial underlying value differences. These differences often set individual country practices apart. Understanding them helps to make sense out of similar, yet distinctive, applications of education and training interventions.

The first five chapters in Part II focus on vocational education and training in Europe. In Chapter 7, Lasonen and Rauhala examine preparation for work in the Nordic countries (Denmark, Iceland, Finland, Norway, and Sweden). They draw attention to how a historical democratic tradition contributes to shaping the education and training system. Freedom of choice, social inclusion, opportunity, and equity are major social objectives that condition the organizing and financing of education and training, admission policy, and articulation between institutions. While the workforce preparation systems in Nordic countries have contributed to high economic productivity and efficiency, the countries have not sacrificed social goals. Indeed, they have recently shown considerable interest in achieving "parity of esteem" among academic and work programs.

Chapter 8 discusses the highly regarded and recognized German dual apprenticeship system. The authors point out the key elements in the German model: constructive collaboration between social partners, the articulation of school-based and on-the-job preparation, and a qualification and certification system grounded in actual work requirements.

The next chapter, by Streumer, outlines attempts in the Netherlands to link the formal vocational education and training system more closely with work. This involves closing the status gap between academic and vocational education, forming closer collaborative working relationships with business and industry, broadening curricula, and strengthening the national qualifications systems. The reforms outlined are embedded in human capital for-

mation objectives, and contrast with reform efforts in the Nordic countries.

In the chapter by Niven, "Vocational Education and Training Policies and Practice in the United Kingdom," attention goes to the modular system of instruction designed in Scotland to serve vocational preparation and continuing education objectives. Niven also discusses the National Vocational Qualifications system in the United Kingdom. This case study provides a good example of the attempt to design and implement vocational certification on a national scale.

Gleeson, in the entry on vocational education and training in Ireland, discusses the tension between achieving equity while also addressing economic development concerns. While Ireland has a robust economy, high unemployment and the lack of opportunity continue to present complex education, training, and social problems.

Chapter 12 examines the concept of national training agencies, and attention turns to the Latin American region, where training agencies are being tested as international competition, technological change, and social pressures place new demands on workforce preparation systems. Changes that training agencies are trying to institute in response to reform efforts are discussed along with constraints that continue to limit the agencies' effectiveness. Newer and contrasting forms of national training agencies in other countries are also examined.

In a brief chapter, "Combining School and Work: New Pathways for Learning in Australia," Athanasou highlights trends toward integrating academic and vocational/technical instruction, closer school/employer collaboration, and the use of alternative forms of workforce preparation.

The final three chapters focus on the Asian region, where the link between education and training and economic development policy is often both strong and deliberate. Chapter 14, "How the Japanese Prepare for Work," explores how Japan's education and training system in a comprehensive sense prepares citizens for work. Japan can be considered a "learning society," with all of its institutional forms, from kindergarten to university, focused on achievement and moral development and, ultimately, on preparation for and employment in the workforce. Government has an important role, but it serves more as a facilitator, rather than as a major provider of services. Parents, community leaders, worker groups, and business and industry all play a part in developing a workforce with the highest educational levels found in any country. To the Japanese, good vocational education is good general education preparation, grounded in moral responsibility.

Ashton and Sung, in Chapter 15, suggest that Singapore reflects a new approach to skills formation in which the state plays an active role in setting targets and in linking the output of the education and training systems directly to economic development policy.

Singapore thus pursues economic development and education and training objectives in concert, which requires a flexible workforce preparation system that can make significant and relatively rapid programming changes in response to changing development priorities. Articulation becomes a major policy objective, requiring strong state intervention to keep worker groups, employers, and providers of education and training services working in harmony.

In the final chapter, on vocational education and training in Laos, Lamoureux draws attention to the complexities of establishing a workforce preparation system in a low-income, human-resource-deficient, developing country. Although Laos has structural and functional elements of education and training similar to those found in developed countries, implementation problems are extremely complex, and are compounded by the on-going transformation from a command, to a market-based, economy.

7

Vocational Education and Training in the Nordic Countries

By Johanna Lasonen and Pentti Rauhala

The Nordic countries—Denmark, Iceland, Finland, Norway, and Sweden—have much in common. They resemble each other in their natural conditions, language (except Finland), culture, and history. They are historically peasant societies, which has led to deep-seated democratic attitudes and a profound appreciation of the freedom and equality of the individual. These five countries are nationally and religiously homogenous societies, with the exception of Sweden, which has an immigrant population of a million, most of whom come from other Nordic countries. Their religious homogeneity stems from the fact that, since the Reformation, nearly 90 percent of the Nordic population have been Lutherans. Socially and politically, the Nordic countries are very stable, having no national or other conflicts since World War II.

The Nordic countries are often called "welfare societies" because the population receives free education, health care, and social welfare services. Due to these and other public sector obligations, the Nordic countries' tax rates are among the highest in the world. During the last few years, this has caused economic prob-

lems because it does not seem feasible to continue such extensive public services. Nevertheless, the Nordic countries have among the highest rates of gross national product per capita in the world. Their economic growth has been steady and continuous. They were industrialized in the nineteenth century and are today among the more prominent information societies, with high levels of information technology. For example, the last few years have seen a change in the bulk of Finnish exports from traditional paper and metal products to electronics, mobile phones, and other information technology products. Overall, the Nordic societies are modern and open-minded.

The Nordic countries are among the northernmost inhabited parts of the world. They have relatively large land masses and small populations. Sweden has the largest population, with 8.7 million inhabitants. Finland and Denmark each have populations of about 5 million; Norway, 4.2 million; and Iceland, 262,000. The low population density results in small schools and high costs for realizing geographical equality.

Finland was a province of Sweden until

1809, when Russia annexed it. Russian rule lasted until 1917, when Finland became an independent republic. Finland has a Swedish-speaking minority that has a high degree of cultural and educational autonomy. Norway was united with Denmark from 1380 to 1814, and later with Sweden (1814–1905) before gaining independence in 1905. Iceland, which was also united with Denmark in 1380, gained independence in 1944. Today, Denmark, Norway, and Sweden are monarchies with deep historical roots, while Finland and Iceland are republics. Denmark, Finland, and Sweden are members of the European Union (EU), and Iceland, Norway, and Denmark are members of the North Atlantic Treaty Organization (NATO).

Cultural and economic cooperation between Nordic countries is close. As early as the 1950s, they established a passport union and a common labor market. These early arrangements are losing some of their importance since the EU has also created a common labor market and is in the process of establishing a passport union that will cover the whole of the EU. Finally, the Nordic countries' common cultural and legislative heritage has led to closely parallel educational structures and ideas.

VOCATIONAL EDUCATION IN DENMARK

A leading principle of the Danish educational system is freedom of choice. The state provides educational opportunities, but individuals are free to choose between alternative forms of education.

Upper secondary education in Denmark can be divided into general upper secondary education (three years between ages 16 and 19) and vocational upper secondary education (up to four years between ages 16 and 20). Initial vocational training attracts two-thirds of a typical age group. It is provided in three main forms after the completion of lower secondary education: (a) basic vocational education and training, (b) higher commercial courses, and (c) higher technical courses. Practical training

is conducted in a firm (business/industry), while theoretical education is given in school. In this respect, Denmark's approach differs from that of Finland, Norway, and Sweden, where vocational education is primarily school based.

The predominant feature in Danish vocational education is the central role of employers and organized labor. These social partners are involved at the national, regional, and school levels. They are responsible for modernizing training schemes and for delivering the work experience component of vocational programs. They also exert considerable influence on the programs' school-based components. The structure and content of programs, the allocation of time between school-based instruction and practical training, and forms of assessment are decided by the Ministry of Education and the social partners in 85 committees that represent different industries.

The main responsibility for vocational education lies with the Ministry of Education and the social partners. On the national level, the Council for Vocational Education serves as an advisory body. Vocational schools are self-governing and administered by a board and head teacher. At the school level, education and training committees play a role in the interaction between schools and on-the-job training. Private schools must follow public school standards.

The state subsidizes both public and private education. Private schools can obtain 85 percent state funding, whereas public schools receive 100 percent. A total annual grant consists of teaching grants based on the number of active students and fixed grants to cover joint expenditures, allocated as a single block grant. This type of financing, where state subsidies are based on the average national costs of vocational education, rather than the actual costs of a given school, is common to all Nordic countries. It is important to add that a school can earn extra income by offering special courses and selling know-how (European Education Information Network [EURYDICE] &

European Center for the Development of Vocational Training [CEDEFOP], 1995).

There are two routes to vocational education and training in Denmark: a school-based route and a practical training route. Students who choose the school-based route (more than 75 percent in 1991) normally start with a 20-week period at school. During this period, vocational guidance, workshop instruction, and optional subjects are provided. Afterward, students select their vocational program.

Those who select practical training spend the first 20 weeks in a firm. They must have a training contract. Trainees receive pay throughout their education and training period, partly subsidized by allocations from a collective employers' levy fund intended to cover wage costs while trainees attend school.

School-based and practical training routes merge at the start of the second school period, during which students complete the same education and training. About one-sixth of the total teaching time is devoted to optional subjects and about two-thirds to practical training in firms. One feature of Danish vocational education and training policy is that youth training programs are not a "dead end," but rather provide opportunities for continued training.

Technical and commercial schools offer three-year programs in higher technical and commercial education to 16-year-old students. They qualify pupils not only for employment but also for university programs, advanced commercial schools, and engineering diploma courses. Students can gain admittance to technical and commercial schools directly from a lower secondary school. It is also possible to switch from basic vocational education courses to higher technical and commercial courses.

In vocational higher education, there are two-year programs that lead to technician qualifications, as well as three- to four-year intermediate programs that lead to engineering qualifications, a social work diploma, and so forth. Admittance to such programs requires completion of upper secondary education. There is also a well-organized vocational adult education program with courses in vocational schools and adult education centers.

VOCATIONAL EDUCATION IN ICELAND

The basic principle guiding education in Iceland is an equal opportunity for everyone to acquire education, irrespective of gender, economic status, place of residence, and cultural or social background. In the 1970s, general and vocational education were combined into a single comprehensive system and practical and academic education were given equal status. Credits obtained in one institution can be transferred to others.

Approximately 85 percent of the pupils who complete primary and secondary education enter the upper secondary school. The various types of upper secondary school are (a) grammar schools, which offer a four-year academic program leading to matriculation and giving the right to apply for admission to university; (b) comprehensive schools, which provide academic courses comparable to those of grammar schools; (c) industrial-vocational schools; (d) vocational training comparable to that offered by industrial-vocational schools; and (e) specialized vocational schools, which train students for specific occupations.

At the upper secondary stage, vocational education lasts three to four years. There are three alternative routes:

• An apprenticeship contract with a master craftsman.

• One year of basic academic and practical study at a vocational school or a comprehensive school, followed by an apprenticeship contract.

• One year of basic academic and practical study, followed by another year of specialized academic and practical study at a vocational school or comprehensive school, followed by an apprenticeship contract.

In this respect, the Icelandic and Danish vocational education systems resemble each other, while differing from the systems in Finland, Norway, and Sweden.

In Iceland, as in other Nordic countries, standardized tests do not play an important role in student selection. All students have access to enrollment in some form of vocational education and training at the upper secondary level. Access to higher education, however, is regulated by student preference, grade point average, advancement level and combination of courses previously taken, and admissions examinations.

The administration of upper secondary education in Iceland is centralized. There is no regional or local administration and the social partners do not participate. This is no doubt due to Iceland's small population. Education is organized within the public sector and there are only a few private schools. Vocational education is financed by the state and local authorities (EURYDICE & CEDEFOP, 1995).

VOCATIONAL EDUCATION IN FINLAND

The main goal of Finnish educational policy is to offer equal educational opportunities to all citizens, regardless of their place of residence, economic status, mother tongue, or gender. More than 90 percent of those leaving the nine-year comprehensive school continue their studies in general upper secondary school or in a vocational institution. The network of general and vocational upper secondary schools covers the entire country. Vocational education is mainly school based, although the proportion of apprenticeship training will increase to 20 percent by the year 2001. A measure intended to improve connections between school-based education and working life stipulates that, by the year 2000, all vocational education will comprise three-year programs and will include a minimum of one-half year of workplace training.

There are historical reasons for the Finnish system of vocational education being school-based. Finland was a predominantly agricultural country until just after World War II. Then, its industrialization was one of the most rapid in Europe. As a result, industries needed workers who lived in rural areas, where opportunities for apprenticeship training did not exist. As a consequence, vocational schools were founded throughout the country so that young people could acquire, in their home area, the required knowledge and skills. This system proved an efficient approach to fulfilling the fast-growing demand for skilled workers. Information technology is now Finland's most important industrial sector and vocational education programs are increasing the number of people trained to meet workforce requirements.

Upper secondary education, which caters to 16- to 19-year-olds, is divided into two pathways: (a) three-year general upper secondary education that leads to the Matriculation Examination (attracting 60 percent of the age group), and (b) two- to three-year vocational education (attracting 40 percent of the age group). Vocational education is based either on the nine-year comprehensive school or on the Matriculation Examination, taken after 12 years of school attendance. A student can combine studies at both the general upper secondary school and the vocational school in a single examination and still take the Matriculation Examination alongside a vocational qualification. However, this practice is not common because of the academic demands it places on the student.

The social partners' influence on vocational education has been increasing. On a national level, there are now 30 advisory education and training committees that include representatives of the social partners. The committees work with the Ministry of Education in every educational sector. They handle such matters as national curriculum principles in different vocational fields and questions involved in the structure of examinations.

Apprenticeship

As previously stated, Finland is increasing its provision of apprenticeship training, which by law is linked with vocational schools. Apprentices receive their theoretical education in a vocational school during course periods and their practical training at a workplace. The length of training is two to four years, during which apprentices are paid a trainee's wage. After completing their training, apprentices take an examination and a skills test.

Higher Vocational Education

In 1992, a Finnish equivalent to the polytechnic institute was established. These AMK (Finnish *ammattikorkeakoulu*, meaning literally "vocational higher education") institutions conduct programs lasting three and a half years. Admission is based on the Matriculation Examination or three years of vocational education. This system replaced the former vocational colleges, which offered programs that last two to four years after the completion of basic vocational education or the Matriculation Examination. AMK institutions represent the nonuniversity sector of higher education. They are more practically oriented and train experts for the new labor market. The goal is that about 35 percent of the 16-to-19-year-old age group receive higher vocational education and about 20 percent receive university education. The larger percentage for higher vocational education arises from changes in Finnish business that have resulted in a labor market demand for high-tech professions. In particular, there is an acute shortage of experts in information technology.

In the past, the Finnish vocational school network was maintained by the state. Now, however, nearly all state-owned vocational schools have been transferred to local authorities. Furthermore, an increasing number of AMK institutions are being maintained by joint stock companies whose shareholders are mostly local authorities. About 20 percent of vocational schools are private establishments, among them some AMK institutions, but they have the same form of financing as institutions maintained by the public sector. The state provides a lump sum based on the number of students in the given educational sector. It then collects from local authorities a share of the vocational education costs based on the population of each municipality, which amounts to 43 percent of the total expenditure.

Adult Education

Adult education is available at all levels of the educational system. It is financed by government, employers, and students. Vocational education for the unemployed, as well as adult education, are state-financed. Adult education related to current employment is mostly financed by employers. Adult education centers are operated by municipal or private bodies located throughout the country. Their activities are largely concentrated on employment training. In the 1990s, Finnish unemployment rates were among the highest in Europe, in spite of rapid economic growth. As a consequence, adult education serves an important purpose.

Adult education is also provided in vocational schools and AMK institutions, which introduced skills-based examinations open to all adults. These exams measure occupational skills regardless of how they were acquired. The aim of this program is to raise the educational level of the adult population and to install a national quality-assurance system covering the whole field of adult vocational education (National Board of Education, 1996).

The link between testing and labor market requirements is established and maintained by educational committees at the national level and by examination committees at the local level. The content of skills-based examinations is decided by national education committees and then approved by local examination committees. Committee members are elected by employer, employee, teacher, and principal organizations.

VOCATIONAL EDUCATION IN NORWAY

The overall objective of Norwegian education is to provide equal opportunities to all citizens irrespective of their place of residence; economic, social, or cultural background; or gender. Attention is focused on the quality of education, preparing youth for the information society, environmental education, and intensifying the teaching of foreign languages.

Upper secondary education, which follows nine years in a comprehensive school, is organized in a single school facility. In this regard, the school systems of Norway and Sweden are alike and differ from those of Iceland, Denmark, and Finland, where general upper secondary education and vocational education take place in separate schools. Upper secondary school lasts three years and is divided into 10 study fields consisting of a general studies program and nine vocational programs titled (a) aesthetics, (b) agriculture and rural, (c) commercial and clerical, (d) fishing trade, (e) home economics, (f) maritime, (g) physical, (h) social services and health, and (i) technical and industrial. About 45 percent of 16-year-olds enroll in the general studies program, and this percentage is rising. All study fields have essentially the same structure: a foundation course (one to two years), advanced courses (one to two years), and shorter courses. The foundation course combines general and vocational subjects. After completing the foundation course, students choose either an academic or a vocational track for advanced courses. The norm is two years of vocational training in an upper secondary school followed by a period of practical training in industry.

The apprenticeship training system is based on close cooperation between schools and employers. It consists of a combination of school-based training and practical apprenticeship (Andersen, 1996). Apprentices can attend an apprenticeship school one day per week and receive workplace training four days per week. Early in the 1990s, the number of apprentices was about 10 percent of the total number of people enrolled in upper secondary school.

Regional authorities have responsibility for guaranteeing at least three years of initial training, either through school-based provisions or through combinations of school-based provi-

sion and apprenticeship. The most-favored model in policy debates has been a combination of two-year school-based education followed by a two-year apprenticeship. The social partners actively cooperate in reforming the public education system. They have emphasized that vocational education and training pathways must be open for progression to both employment and higher education (Kämäräinen, 1995).

Technical colleges offer two-year courses to students who already have trade skills or practical work experience and who have completed their upper secondary education. Students who pass the technical college examination receive a vocational certificate, which also qualifies them for further technical studies.

There are two main higher education sectors: university and college. Nonuniversity institutions of higher education offer programs that last one to four years. Longer courses and graduate programs of up to six years have also been introduced at some institutions. Most programs are oriented toward specific professions, including teaching, engineering, administration, automated data processing, health occupations, and so forth.

All public and, to a certain extent, private education and training is subsidized by the central government. Counties provide the upper secondary schools. A central government grant covers 40 percent of the costs; 50 percent is covered by taxation; and 10 percent is charged in fees. There are only a few private schools (5 percent), which also charge fees. Public funding for private schools can be from 75 to 85 percent of the costs. County authorities receive state subsidies as a lump sum that they allocate for education, culture, and health services (EURYDICE & CEDEFOP, 1995).

Contact with the social partners is maintained through a system of meetings and ad hoc committees for areas not covered by agreements. The main associations of employers and employees have a key role in apprenticeship administration and the development of apprenticeship training programs.

VOCATIONAL EDUCATION IN SWEDEN

A fundamental principle of the Swedish educational system is that everyone must have access to equivalent education, regardless of their ethnic or social background or place of residence. The right to a place in upper secondary education is prescribed by law. In addition to initial education and training, adult education has a long history in Sweden, and further and continuing education options are available in many different forms. Private upper secondary schools exist in Sweden, but they attract only a small percentage of the students.

In 1970, the various types of schools for academic and vocational education were amalgamated into a single type of comprehensive upper secondary school. Norway followed this example later, but in Denmark, Iceland, and Finland, academic and vocational education are still delivered through separate institutions. The Swedish practice may arise from the very strong emphasis that Swedish society puts on social equality.

More than 95 percent of compulsory-school leavers continue their studies at the upper secondary level. Most programs are provided in schools under municipal responsibility. Studies in agriculture, forestry, horticulture, and certain caring occupations, however, are delivered in schools run by county administrative boards. The upper secondary school is organized into 16 study programs, each of three years' duration. Two programs prepare students for university studies, while 14 are vocational and have at least 15 percent of students' time spent in workplace training. Apart from this, it is also possible to have a custom-designed or individual program.

Sweden also has apprenticeship training programs, which combine training organized by employers with education in the upper secondary school. In adult education, there are labor market education centers where unemployed people receive employment education. This resembles the Finnish adult education system. Swedish vocational education also has nonuniversity higher institutions, mainly in the health care field. Programs vary between two and five and a half years in length.

Municipalities have responsibility for maintaining upper secondary schools. Nearly half the costs are covered by state subsidies, with the balance coming from local authorities. Subsidies received by the municipalities are not earmarked, which allows local authorities to organize school activities as they wish, as long as national goals are achieved. Schools and social partners cooperate through joint vocational committees responsible for the vocational study lines of upper secondary schools.

NORDIC UPPER SECONDARY EDUCATION STRATEGIES

The educational policies followed in the Nordic countries have a number of common features:

• A shared aim of educating the entire age cohort.

• Free education and extensive student welfare benefits.

• An ambition of making general and vocational education equal in status in an effort to promote equality among students.

• Educational administration that evolved from a centralized system into a decentralized system, resulting in a high degree of school autonomy along with a national assessment system.

• Vocational higher education provided mainly by the state, with the exception of Finnish AMK institutions.

• Linkages between education and work.

In addition to these six features, local authorities have responsibility for education and training, with only a few private schools. They receive generous government subsidies, without "set-asides/earmarking," to help meet expenditures.

There are also differences among the Nordic countries:

• The influence of labor market organizations varies, from greatest in Denmark to least in Norway.

• Sweden and Norway have a combined general and vocational secondary level, while elsewhere general and vocational education are provided separately.

• Alternating periods of school-based instruction with practical learning and work experience in enterprises are emphasized in Danish, Norwegian, and Finnish vocational education and training.

Comparisons and Contrasts

Further discussion of Nordic vocational education and training in this chapter focuses on the upper secondary level (mainly ages 16 to 19), which covers initial vocational education in a school-based system. As an educational stage, it is significant for young people because it qualifies them for further or higher education and/or employment.

The aims of vocational education reforms undertaken in the Nordic countries during the 1990s were to (a) increase equality by guaranteeing all students a place in upper secondary education, (b) raise the reputation of vocational education, and (c) enhance student motivation by increasing flexibility and student choice. All the Nordic countries integrated vocational education into their educational system. Their main purpose was to modernize secondary education. Further purposes of reforms involved making academic competencies available to vocational students (and, to some degree, providing vocational competencies to academic students), thus improving their chances of launching successful working careers. The reforms have also been a response by the countries to the changing demands of work life and society.

To create a unified vocational and academic upper secondary education system, Norway and Sweden established comprehensive schools. Notwithstanding the effort, there is a clear division between programs. Sweden, for example, has 2 programs for university studies and 14 vocationally oriented programs.

Norway's Reform-94 gives vocational students an opportunity to gain a double qualification—that is, a vocational qualification certificate as well as access to higher education for students in certain programs. The Norwegian and Swedish reforms ideally presuppose combined schools that offer both academic and vocational programs. Increasingly, this is becoming reality.

A common feature in the upper secondary education of both Norway and Sweden is their compulsory core courses—a step toward a more comprehensive upper secondary school. Cooperation with people in working life, emphasized in the reforms, will probably influence not only the content of various subjects but also school culture as a whole. The practices of working life will thus fundamentally change school traditions. The freedom of choice given to students, teachers, head teachers, and local authorities will make school operations more market-oriented (Lasonen, 1996; Lasonen & Young, 1998).

In Finland and Denmark, vocational and general education are separate paths, and there have been no attempts to integrate them. Instead, the Finnish are experimenting with youth education being run in 16 localities, while national vocational education reform projects aim to reinforce the strengths and identities of the two separate educational tracks by offering students alternative programs. The main focus of the Finnish reform is the introduction of horizontal flexibility between vocational and academic pathways. This involves (a) making the curricula more flexible by increasing freedom of choice, (b) giving students more autonomy by allowing them to combine studies from both vocational and academic upper secondary schools, and (c) organizing cooperation between vocational and academic institutions. Cooperation at the local level includes collaboration between the staff and teachers to prepare a selection of courses open to students of both institutions. Finnish students may organize their programs to take a general or vocational qualification or both. A secondary focus is the introduction of vertical flexibility by increasing the number of pathways that give access to higher education.

In Denmark, general and vocational education are similarly two parallel subsystems of upper secondary education. Furthermore, vocational education distinguishes clearly between school-based and apprenticeship-based alternatives. In the early 1990s, the two alternative approaches for initial vocational education and training were merged into one basic model which provided a unified curricular framework both for trainees with an apprenticeship contract and for students in vocational schools.

In modern working life, there are two conflicting trends. One focuses on broad-based skills, while the other recognizes increased demands for specialization. The Nordic countries responded to this problem by making educational programs broad based, increasing the number of academic subjects, and leaving specialization to the workplaces. To improve the students' practical skills, the amount of training was increased. Research concerning employer demands shows that the importance of general abilities has increased as workplace requirements changed. This means that cooperative and communication skills, for example, are becoming more important, even in vocational education. Thus, vocational education and training also aims to provide general/core skills, competencies, and qualifications. In addition, the Nordic educational systems are flexible, allowing various access routes and transitions between study lines.

Teacher Preparation

Teacher training was reformed in Finland and Norway in the 1990s by the introduction, in some teacher training colleges, of one-year qualifying programs common to vocational and academic teachers. The Norwegian reform is more radical and comprehensive than the Finnish one. Teacher in-service training in support of the reforms is being implemented mainly on the basis of local interest and funding. Popular in-service training topics include new working and teaching methods, project work, interdisciplinary approaches, and new evaluation methods.

Training for vocational teachers is provided at occupational or professional colleges, and teacher training for general/academic teachers is delivered at universities (CEDEFOP, 1997). One-year teacher training programs for vocational teachers qualify them for both vocational and general education. Prerequisites for student teachers include an advanced occupational diploma or degree, or a university degree plus practical experience at the skill and management levels in enterprises. In Finland, vocational teacher training colleges were suspended and their mission transferred to the AMK institutions (polytechnics or professional colleges) in 1998.

Enhanced Authority

In their attempts to prevent inequality resulting from educational choices, Nordic countries have adopted similar approaches to promoting parity of esteem between vocational and academic education. On the whole, 85 to 90 percent of each age cohort in the Nordic countries that leave compulsory education immediately continue their education at either the general upper secondary school or a vocational school. Student progression is promoted (a) by lowering barriers between different types of school and different levels of the educational system; (b) vertically, by increasing student opportunities to find a pathway that enables them to continue in further or higher education and by allowing them to take studies offered by higher education institutions as a part of their upper secondary program; and (c) horizontally, by allowing them to combine vocational and academic studies at different institutions.

In Finland, the extended student choice introduced into the curricula increases vocational students' opportunities to gain access to higher education by including more theoretical subjects in their programs. Academic students can study vocational subjects along with their primarily academic studies. Vocational and academic programs are acknowledged as equivalent and students are credited for parallel or earlier studies in other upper secondary institutions.

Reform-94 in Norway tried to increase the attractiveness of vocational education through an improved structure of vocational study lines, including a commitment on the part of business and industry to create better apprenticeship programs. The reform also enabled vocational students to gain access to higher education. In the Swedish upper secondary school, all students study core subjects that give them general qualifications for entering higher education. Students may choose the same courses, regardless of their study program.

Compared with the other countries, Denmark and Iceland offer a broader range of alternative ways to acquire work-based vocational training. This is made possible by cooperation between schools and enterprises. For example, upper secondary education encourages sharing areas of teaching and knowledge across different pathways, combining different types of knowledge within the broadened range of student choice, and incorporating increased flexibility into curricula.

The principle of social inclusion has been a leading goal of Nordic educational and social policy. All students between the ages of 16 and 19 are included in upper secondary education, which reflects the goal of full integration. The curriculum principles introduced by legislation allow flexible arrangements that can be used to encourage different types of learners, including students with special needs. Increased student choice regarding courses and schools gives both high and low achievers a wide field within which they can construct study programs. This has created a new demand for education competencies among teachers in the upper secondary school system. The curriculum emphasizes that schools must support all students' development according to their interests and abilities.

References

Andersen, K. (1996). Norwegian upper secondary reforms in academic/general and vocational education in the 1990s. In J. Lasonen (Ed.), *Reforming upper secondary education in Europe: The Leonardo da Vinci Project Post-16 strategies* (Publication Series B92. Theory into Practice, pp. 171-185). Jyväskylä, Finland: University of Jyväskylä, Institute for Educational Research.

European Center for the Development of Vocational Training [CEDEFOP]. (1990). *The role of social partners in vocational education and training including continuing education and training* (Summaries of the Reports of the Member States of the European Community). Luxembourg: Office for Official Publications of the European Communities.

European Center for the Development of Vocational Training [CEDEFOP]. (1997). *Teachers and trainers in vocational education and training* (Volume: Denmark, Finland, Iceland, Norway, and Sweden). Luxembourg: Office for Official Publications of the European Communities.

European Education Information Network [EURYDICE], & European Center for the Development of Vocational Training [CEDEFOP]. (1995). *Structures of the education and initial training systems in the European Union* (2nd ed.). Brussels, Belgium: Author.

Kämäräinen, P. (1995). Reforms in the vocational education and training systems of the Nordic countries. *European Journal of Vocational Training, 1*(4), 37-45.

Kivinen, O., Rinne, R., Järvinen, M-R., Koivisto, J., & Laakso, T. (1995). *Koulutuksen säätelyjärjestelmät Euroopassa* [Systems of educational regulation in Europe]. Julkaisupaikka, Finland: National Board of Education of Finland & Research Unit for Sociology of Education, University of Turku.

Lasonen, J. (Ed.). (1996). *Reforming upper secondary education in Europe: The Leonardo da Vinci Project Post-16 strategies* (Publication Series B92. Theory into Practice). Jyväskylä, Finland: University of Jyväskylä, Institute for Educational Research.

Lasonen, J., & Young, M. (Eds.). (1998). *Strategies for achieving parity of esteem in European upper secondary education.* Jyväskylä, Finland: University of Jyväskylä, Institute for Educational Research.

National Board of Education. (1996). *The development of education 1994-1996* (National report of Finland). Helsinki, Finland: Author.

Nielsen, S., & Svendsen, S. (1999). Reforms in upper secondary education in Denmark. In M. L. Stenström (Ed.), *Reflections on Post-16 strategies in European countries* (pp. 51-61). Jyväskylä, Finland: University of Jyväskylä, Institute for Educational Research.

Njerve, I., & Sandvik, O. (1997). Training upper secondary school teachers: The combined initial teacher training experiment in Agder College. In J. Lasonen (Ed.), *IVETA 97 conference proceedings. The challenges of the 21st century for vocational education and training* (pp. 282-290). Jyväskylä, Finland: University of Jyväskylä, Institute for Educational Research.

Numminen, U., Lampinen O., Mykkänen, T., & Blom, H. (1997). *Nuorisoasteen koulutuskokeilut ja ammattikorkeakoulukokeilut. Raportti 7. Kokeiluvuodet 1991-1996 ja lukuvuosi 1995-1996* [Experiments in youth education and in polytechnical education. Report 7. Years 1991-1996 of the experiment and school year 1995-1996]. Helsinki, Finland: Ministry of Education.

8

Germany's Vocational Training/ Apprenticeship System

By Clifton P. Campbell and Hermann Diedrich

The apprenticeship[1] system in Germany is based on cooperation between government, employers, and organized labor (unions), and between the organizations that conduct the training, enterprises and vocational schools. It is a relevant, effective, and efficient system of initial vocational training that gives young adults instruction and experience, on and off the job, in the practical and theoretical aspects of a skilled occupation.

Under Germany's apprenticeship system (also known as the dual system), young adults are simultaneously apprentices in an enterprise and students at a vocational school (*Berufsschule*). The federal states (*Lander*) have responsibility for the *Berufsschulen*. Authority for the on-the-job part of this training is at the national level; therefore, framework conditions are standardized across the country.

School attendance is compulsory in Ger-many from age 7 until age 18. After completing 9 school years, or 10 in those states where full-time schooling is extended, students may attend their remaining years (to age 18) on a part-time basis. Since the mission of the *Berufsschule* is to complement apprenticeship training, part-time attendance continues until the training period is completed, even if the apprentice is older than 18.

Apprentices are generally occupied at a production facility or service enterprise three or four days out of a five-day work week. In addition, they attend the *Berufsschule* for 480 hours each school year. Up to 12 hours of classes are scheduled for a maximum of two days per week. Lengthier periods, called *block-releases*, may run for a week or more.

The decision on whether to use the day- or block-release approach is made regionally by *Berufsschule* representatives and local training

[1]*Apprenticeship has been the traditional method of training skilled workers in Germany since the days of the craft guild system in the Middle Ages. Reforms have adapted craft and trade apprenticeship to a wide range of occupations and added a school-based component to progressive on-the-job training conducted by a master craftsman with the necessary personal and vocational aptitude.*

employers or their representatives (e. g., the guilds serve as representatives for 127 different occupations under the Chamber of Crafts). Given the host of variables, it is easy to see why different organizational and scheduling approaches exist within and between states.

BERUFSSCHULE

The *Berufsschule* provides occupation-related training and general education. Most of these part-time public vocational schools specialize in trade and industry, commerce, farming, or home economics. Some have more than one specialization.

Since 1972, the national government and the *Lander* have held coordinating sessions to draw up the *Berufsschule* curricula. Currently, two-thirds of the instruction focuses on technology, math, drafting, and other subjects that complement and supplement the practical training received in the workplace. The remaining one-third of instruction consists of general education courses in economics, social science, religion/ethics, sports, and English (as a foreign language). The findings of a study titled "Obligatory Foreign Language Learning in Vocational Schools," which were made public in 1998, pointed out that appropriate language skills improve career prospects. This shows that there is also a supportive link between general education courses and the occupation-related training provided at a *Berufsschule*.

The qualifications required to teach a general education course include eight semesters of study, a year's training in a practical specialist field, and a two-year period of teacher training. Instructors for technical and vocational courses, which also include workshop learning experiences, must have completed an apprenticeship. Then, they go on to a *Fachschule* (specialized technical college). Before taking a teaching position, potential instructors participate in a teacher training program (Oehler, 1998, pp. 20, 21, & 23).

The *Berufsschulen* are the weaker part of the training partnership. Try though they do, the *Berufsschulen* have a difficult time coordinating and integrating instruction with on-the-job learning experiences. The apprentices that make up large classes come from many enterprises, all with different product mixes and production processes. Coordinating the learning of job skills with formal instruction in school is problematic. Consequently, larger enterprises tend to provide their own in-house theoretical and related training.

BASIS FOR APPRENTICESHIP TRAINING
Training Act

The Vocational Training Act of 1969 governs apprenticeship training conducted by employers. It is classified as labor and economic legislation, not education legislation. Consequently, it does not apply to vocational training provided (a) in *Berufsschulen* controlled by state laws, (b) under employment contracts regulated by public law, or (c) on board merchant ships covered by the Law of the Flag Act.

The 1969 Act stipulates that people under 18 years of age can receive training only in those apprenticeable occupations recognized by the national government. This restriction prevents training of short duration with a narrow range of content that would limit an individual's job mobility and further training opportunities (Laflamme, Basset, & Michlin, 1993; *Vocational Training in the Dual System*, 1992).

Enterprise Training

Employers are entitled (not required) to take on and train apprentices. Nevertheless, the German Industry and Trade Advisory Board for Vocational Training reported that about 450,000 large, medium, and small enterprises made the necessary effort to meet qualification requirements so that they could exercise this entitlement. Reasons for this voluntary participation are provided later in this chapter under the heading Why Train Apprentices.

The following breakdown shows the percent of involvement in apprenticeship training by size of enterprise:

- 94 percent of all large enterprises (more than 500 employees).
- 68 percent of all enterprises with 50 to 499 employees.
- 47 percent of all enterprises with 10 to 49 employees.
- 36 percent of all small enterprises (5 to 9 employees).

It is also important to note that more than 60 percent of the enterprises in Germany have a workforce of fewer than 5 employees. Those registered under the Chamber of Crafts, including the self-employed, are owned or managed by a master craftsman *(Meister)*. As a result, they are entitled to take on apprentices. Unfortunately, only about 38 percent of these enterprises do so *(Berufsbildungsbericht, 1997)*. By and large, the smaller the enterprise, the less likely it is to engage in apprenticeship training. Small enterprises view the training and management requirements as too expensive and time consuming. The thought is that they can, and probably at less expense, go into the labor market and hire the journeymen they need. Those employers do not see training as being in their economic self-interest beyond informal on-the-job training of new employees.

Specialization in a product, process, or service, as well as continuous technological developments, makes it difficult for small- and medium-sized enterprises to ensure that apprentices acquire all the knowledge and skills specified in the relevant training regulations. As a result, workshops and inter-firm training centers are commonly used to augment workplace training.

Workshops. Large enterprises typically have workshops in which apprentices receive their initial training. Here, apprentices (a) undergo systematic instruction in complex skills, (b) operate complicated equipment for the first time, and (c) practice and receive tutoring before taking examinations. Small enterprises often pay for their apprentices to attend such workshops to acquire required skills that are not performed in their workplace.

Inter-firm training centers. The concept for the promotion of inter-firm training centers was adopted by the Federal Parliament in 1988. By 1994, about 600 centers had been established, with a total capacity of nearly 77,000 training places. In the new states (after reunification), the national government funded an additional 10,000 training places at 47 locations as part of the economic restructuring process (Arnold & Much, 1997, p. 34).

From a legal point of view, inter-firm training centers are part of the workplace training effort and come under national vocational training legislation and regulations. Their purposes are to (a) compensate for any workplace training deficiencies, (b) provide structured training in those required skills that cannot be adequately learned on the job, and (c) supplement and broaden workplace training. Inter-firm training often focuses on recent technological developments that may not yet be fully applied in all workplaces. Most inter-firm training centers are operated by chambers and guilds. However, local organizations (municipalities, rural districts, etc.), employers, unions, occupational associations, and churches also operate centers.

Public funds (subsidies from national and state governments) provide for approximately 90 percent of the cost of building and equipping a center. The remainder comes from the organization that operates the center. Operating costs usually come from contributions made by enterprises that send apprentices for training. However, guilds and some other organizations that operate centers have arranged for a training levy that is paid by all enterprises, even those that do not train apprentices. Apart from this, the national and state governments provide subsidies to help cover some operational costs.

Apprenticeship Contract

The training relationship is established by an apprenticeship contract that is distinguished in both legal and business practice from an employment contract. Apprenticeship contracts must conform with provisions of the Vocational Training Act of 1969. Section 4 of the Act specifies that as soon as the vocational training (apprenticeship) contract has been agreed on, and before training starts, the training employer must set out the following essential details in writing:

• Skilled occupation for which the apprentice is to be trained, as well as the nature, syllabus, timetable, examination requirements, and purpose of the training.

• Starting date and length of training (training period).

• Training to be done outside the enterprise (e. g., in an inter-firm training center, or a workshop in a different enterprise).

• Length of the normal working/training day.

• Length of the probationary period.

• Amount of wages and manner of payment.

• Amount of leave (vacation periods).

• Provisions governing contract termination (*Vocational Training Act of 1969*, § 4).

The training employer and the trainee/apprentice (or the trainee's parents, in the case of a minor) sign the contract. Afterward, a copy is given to the apprentice and the original is registered with the training employer's regional chamber (Raggatt, 1988, p. 169).

Training period. Apprenticeships last from two to three-and-a-half years, depending on the complexity of the skilled occupation for which the apprentice is training. Of the 373 skilled occupations recognized for training, only 33 involve a two-year apprenticeship period. Both the apprenticeship contract and the training regulations for the skilled occupation being pursued specify the length of the training period. Since 1991, gifted apprentices have been allowed to shorten their obligatory training period. They have also been offered special programs, funded by the Federal Ministry of Education, Science, Research and Technology. These programs are intended to improve their vocational and personal abilities.

Contract termination. During the probationary period (one to three months), either party can terminate an apprenticeship contract without specifying the reason. After the probationary period expires, the contract is binding (Munch, 1986, p. 73). Nevertheless, approximately 25 percent of all apprenticeship contracts are terminated prematurely. The reasons, in order of frequency, are the apprentice's (a) desire for training in a different skilled occupation, (b) wish to be trained in a different enterprise, (c) desire to give up apprenticeship training, or (d) unsatisfactory workplace performance. Of apprenticeship contracts terminated in 1995, 46 percent were in their first year, 28 percent in the second year, and 26 percent in the last year and a half (*Berufsbildungsbericht*, 1997, pp. 56-57).

Workplace Responsibilities

According to the Vocational Training Act of 1969, training employers must:

• Ensure that the apprentice receives the knowledge and skills necessary to attain training objectives.

• Ensure that the apprentice acquires the necessary work experience.

• Provide the tools, materials, equipment, supplies, and so forth necessary for training and examinations.

• Divide the course of training according to a schedule and a curriculum and prepare a training plan.

• Train the apprentice or appoint a qualified trainer to do so.

• Allow time off for the apprentice to attend a *Berufsschule* and take exams. Persons providing training are also obliged to care for the apprentice's safety and to promote their character (*Vocational Training Act of 1969*, § 6).

The apprenticeship operates as a mentoring program, with apprentices acquiring direct knowledge of working life and maturing under the guidance of a caring, yet demanding trainer. This transforming experience is thought to build character and self-esteem along with skills (Nothdurft, 1989, p. 33). As a result, apprenticeships not only prepare young people for a skilled occupation but also support their transition to adulthood.

Training Regulations

Workplace training for each of the 373 government-recognized skilled occupations is implemented according to training regulations. These regulations are issued by the ministry responsible for the occupation, with the approval of the Federal Ministry of Education, Science, Research and Technology, which has responsibility for coordination.

Training regulations are binding as legal directives for workplace-based apprenticeship training. They are developed to ensure a nationwide uniform level of training for all apprentices in a given skilled occupation. Among other things, training regulations guarantee mutual recognition of qualifications, facilitate job mobility for completers (journeymen), and establish a uniform foundation for further training.

All training regulations specify, as a minimum, the (a) designation (name) of the skilled occupation, (b) length of training (training period), (c) knowledge and skills to be acquired, (d) general training plan (guidelines regarding the structure and schedule for acquiring the knowledge and skills), (e) requirement for apprentices to keep a report book, and (f) examination requirements (*Vocational Training in the Dual System*, 1992, p. 14). The apprenticeship contract and training plan include other important details of the apprenticeship arrangement.

Revision procedure. As technology, work organization, and employer requirements change, training regulations also need to change. There is a procedure for the development of training regulations for both new and reorganized occupations. It involves (a) employers' associations, (b) unions, (c) appropriate federal ministries, and the (d) Federal Institute of Vocational Training (BIBB).

When employers' associations (chambers,

at the national level), guilds, or unions determine that a training regulation is outdated, the revision procedure is instituted. Legally, the appropriate federal minister for the skilled occupation also has responsibility for the revision. In most cases, this is the Minister of Economic Affairs. The BIBB gets involved when (a) the case is difficult, (b) the regulation has not been revised for some time, (c) related occupations are to be revised simultaneously, (d) sufficient information is not available on the occupations to be revised, or (e) employers and unions have different opinions on proposed revisions.

The BIBB not only cooperates with employers, unions, and federal ministries, but also seeks advice from committees of experts representing different occupational groups. In their discussions, which are often difficult and protracted, the committees consider the widely differing conditions that exist throughout the nation and their impact on training regulations (*Dual Vocational Training*, 1988, p. 7).

Since BIBB pledged, in the early 1970s, not to issue new regulations unless they are acceptable to both employers and unions, the social partners must strike a balance between their interests. The procedure described here includes involvement and compromise and has been used successfully to develop new regulations and to abolish those for obsolete occupations.

Between 1969 when the Vocational Training Act went into effect and 1993, more than 250 training regulations were revised. In 1996-97 alone, more than 60 new regulations were issued. Seventeen of these were for completely new occupations. Despite all of these changes, regulations for roughly 90 of today's 373 government-recognized skilled occupations are now being upgraded. Once a new regulation is issued, it is coordinated with the *Berufsschule* curricula in each *Lander* (Oehler, 1998, pp. 20 & 21).

Recently issued training regulations go beyond addressing the acquisition of knowledge and skills and call for apprentices to practice independent planning, execution, and quality control functions, as well as to demonstrate their ability to work cooperatively in groups (*Vocational Training in the Dual System*, 1992, p. 16). Since 1996, a description (profile) of each occupation has been published, in English and French as well as German, along with the regulation.

Problematic procedure. The protracted procedure for developing and revising training regulations ensures representation of the social partners and a high level of congruence with existing work requirements. But, it is hard to stay abreast of changing work requirements in cutting-edge technological fields precisely because of the extensive nature of the consultation process and the need for compromise. "Finalized" regulations are often issued just as new technological developments appear. This does not present a problem in traditional occupations, particularly the crafts and trades, because of their relatively slow, selective, and limited pace of technological change. In other occupations, however, where change is common, training can rapidly grow outdated. The recent concerted effort to develop and revise training regulations indicates the scope of the struggle to stay current. "The large number of officially-defined jobs, with their officially-recognized syllabuses," Pritchard (1992) observed, "can all too quickly become obsolescent, despite continuing attempts to modernize content and to broaden each job's range" (p. 138). The problem is particularly acute in the newly emerging high-tech fields that cut across occupations.

CHAMBERS AND GUILDS
Chambers

Chambers are autonomous (self-governing), not-for-profit organizations constituted under public law. They are organized at the regional, state, and national levels. Private sector enterprises must belong to a chamber and pay the appropriate fees. In addition to a membership fee, chambers charge for registering apprenticeship contracts and conducting examinations.

There are different chambers for different occupational specializations, but the most important are the 83 Chambers of Industry and Commerce and the 59 Chambers of Crafts (*Ausbildung und Beruf*, 1994). Some enterprises belong to both a Chamber of Industry and Commerce and a Chamber of Crafts because of the kinds of work and training they are involved in. In such cases, membership fees are apportioned according to the amount of business done in the specializations covered by each chamber.

Some of the powers of the chambers are generally exercised by government authorities in other countries. They issue licenses, work permits, and certificates of origin; arbitrate disputes between members; reconcile customer complaints; and promote members' products and services through trade fairs, exhibitions, publicity campaigns, and so forth. Chambers are legally entitled to express their views in a variety of governmental forums from the local to the national level; hence, they testify at hearings and lobby to influence legislation on economic, customs, environmental, transportation, tax, education, and training matters. Apart from providing these important services, chambers have responsibility for recruiting apprentices and regulating, as well as supervising, apprenticeship training in accordance with the Vocational Training Act. Small- and medium-sized enterprises are the principal beneficiaries of these services.

Role as a competent body. Chambers of Industry and Commerce, Crafts (Handicrafts), Agriculture, Home Management (Economics), Maritime Shipping, and Public (Civil) Service, as well as Veterinarians, Lawyers and Notaries, Business and Tax Consultants, General Medical Councils, Protestant Churches (recognized as public corporations), and the Catholic Church (at the Diocese level) are identified by the Federal Ministry of Education, Science, Research and Technology as competent bodies charged with

• Determining whether enterprises and individuals have the qualifications needed to train apprentices.

- Maintaining a register of trainers.
- Advising and providing assistance to enterprises on training matters.
- Maintaining a register of apprenticeship contracts.
- Serving as an information-and-complaints office for apprentices.
- Administering journeyman and master craftsman exams (*Vocational Training Act of 1969*, § 46).

Other training-related activities performed by chambers in their role as competent bodies include (a) preparing initiatives for revising training regulations, (b) establishing and operating inter-firm training centers, (c) operating master craftsman schools and craft/trade academies, and (d) conducting further training and retraining courses.

Vocational training committee. The Vocational Training Act of 1969 requires each chamber to have a training committee. Committee membership consists of six representatives from each of three groups: (a) employers' organizations, (b) local unions and independent workers' associations, and (c) *Berufsschulen*. The committee chair changes annually, alternating between an employer and employee representative. *Berufsschule* representatives serve in an advisory capacity and are not entitled to vote (Krekeler, 1986, pp. 18 & 19). In addition to making recommendations to the chamber, the vocational training committee is responsible for the statutory regulations that deal with implementing apprenticeship training (*Vocational Training in the Dual System*, 1992, p. 35).

Approval to train. As mentioned previously, employers may take on and train apprentices only if they are qualified according to the regulations and can fulfill two conditions. First, they must be able to provide state-of-the-art (a) facilities; (b) equipment, tools, and so forth; and (c) production or service work necessary for training and practice in the prescribed knowledge and skills. Second, the employer and trainers must satisfy the necessary personal and technical aptitude requirements.

Because the quality of instruction is affected by a trainer's competence, decisions on who may train are controlled by official qualification requirements. Master craftsmen (*Meisters*), whose course of study and examinations attended to both vocational and pedagogical competence, are entitled to train apprentices. Since enactment of the Instructor Suitability Order in 1972, those who have the necessary personal aptitude (respectability) and who can meet the following four technical aptitude requirements, are also entitled to train apprentices.

- Be at least 24 years of age.
- Be a journeyman in the skilled occupation in which training is being given or, alternatively, pass a final exam at a German higher education institute. The requirement to train the crafts and trades includes both a journeyman's certificate and a passing grade on the final exam at a German institution of higher education (e. g., master craftsmen's college).
- Have adequate and appropriate practical experience in the skilled occupation. A minimum of three years' experience is specified for training the crafts and trades.
- Pass an examination on the (a) basic issues and legal foundations of apprenticeship training and (b) planning and implementation of apprenticeship training (Krekeler, 1986; Raggatt, 1988).

The names of those who qualify are added to the register of trainers kept by the chamber. Training apprentices is considered a prestigious activity for experienced journeymen. Consequently, they are highly motivated to become registered trainers.

The suitability of an employer to offer apprenticeship contracts is determined by a chamber based on whether the conditions discussed under this heading are met. Furthermore, even after an employer and individual training provider(s) are approved, the chamber monitors continuous compliance with all conditions.

Apprenticeship exams. The Vocational Training Act of 1969 requires apprentices to take both an interim and a final examination. The interim exam reveals progress made toward attaining knowledge and skills and identifies problems to allow for corrective action. The interim exam is administered near the midpoint of an apprenticeship period.

The final exam, taken at the end of the training period, determines whether an apprentice has acquired the required qualifications. Examination requirements are specified in the training regulations for each recognized skilled occupation. Apprentices receive a copy of the appropriate regulation along with their apprenticeship contract.

To conduct the exams, the responsible chambers establish examination committees (boards) for each occupation,[2] consisting of at least three members, with an equal representation of employers and employees, and at least one *Berufsschule* teacher (*Vocational Training Act of 1969*). Committee members, whether journeymen or master craftsmen, must be recognized as experts in the skilled occupation being examined. Employee representatives are customarily journeymen, while employer representatives are often master craftsmen who have become managers within an enterprise.

Rules to be observed in administering the final examination are issued by the chamber's vocational training committee. These rules stipulate (a) conditions of admission (from the Vocational Training Act of 1969), (b) form of the examination, (c) evaluation criteria, (d) consequences of breaches of the rules, and (e) possibility of repeating the exam.

In the crafts, trades, and industrial occupa-

TABLE 1—FINAL EXAM RESULTS FOR OCCUPATIONAL SPECIALIZATIONS BY CHAMBER IN 1995

Chamber responsible for occupational specializations	Final Examinations		
	Number repeating	Total number taking	Percentage who passed
Industry and commerce	29,876	308,918	95.7
Crafts (handicrafts)	21,854	179,911	91.6
Agriculture, horticulture, forestry	1,150	12,540	95.7
Public (civil) service	1,747	29,615	97.1
Liberal professions[1]	4,047	53,546	92.8
Home management (economics)	727	7,830	96.1
Maritime shipping	3	144	99.3
Total for all occupational specializations	59,404	592,504	94.3

Note: [1] Occupational specializations trained under the supervision of the liberal professions include (a) law clerks, trained by lawyers; (b) medical receptionists, trained by physicians; and (c) draftsmen, trained by architects.

Adapted from: *Berufsbildungsbericht* (1997), p. 60.

[2] *According to the Association of German Chambers of Industry and Commerce, their 83 regional chambers alone conduct 360,000 final examinations annually, involving 20,000 examination committees.*

tions, apprentices are tested in both knowledge and skills. Skills tests call for the production of a workpiece or the submission of a work sample (Raggatt, 1988; *The Dual System*, 1988). The examinations for a large number of skilled occupations are uniform throughout the country and are therefore taken on the same day. In other occupations, several chambers or all the chambers in a state collaborate in developing the exam.

As shown in Table 1 (page 114), the percent of apprentices who passed final examinations in 1995 ranged from a high of 99.3 percent for occupational specializations under the Chamber of Maritime Shipping to a low of 91.6 percent for occupational specializations under the Chamber of Crafts. The total rate of success for all 373 skilled occupations was 94.3 percent.

Certificates and skills cards. Apprentices who pass all parts of their final exam are awarded a certificate, printed in German, English, and French, that confers journeyman status. They also receive a trilingual description of the occupation for which they qualified ("*Trilingual 'Business Card'*", 1997). The main purpose of the certificate is to show that the apprentice has acquired the qualifications for a specific skilled occupation. The certificate serves as a portable credential that can travel within and across enterprises. It is the basis for employment as a journeyman, career advancement, and geographic mobility (across Europe). All European Union (member states) recognize the journeyman certificate. Germany requires it for admission to master craftsman and technician programs as well as other further training courses and programs that lead to supervisory certificates or to engineering training (*Dual Vocational Training*, 1988, p. 9).

Apprentices who do not perform satisfactorily in both parts of the final exam can be reexamined. The Vocational Training Act stipulates that people can take the final exam twice. Generally, the examination committee encourages an unsuccessful apprentice to continue the apprenticeship and to take the exam again later.

During the past five years, nearly half of those who failed in their first attempt took the exam a second time. When the problem is a lack of proficiency in performing skills and the fault is thought to be inadequate training, members of the examination committee have been known to take apprentices into their enterprises for remediation.

In spite of all the precautions taken, and the special efforts to help those who fail their first exam, some apprentices are unsuccessful the second time as well and do not become journeymen. Nevertheless, they are obviously not complete failures. To recognize what these apprentices did succeed in learning during the training period, a study for BIBB recommended the use of a "skills ID card." This personal skills card/certificate would provide documented evidence of acquired manipulative skills and achievements that could help in a job search or provide a head start in any future attempt to obtain occupational qualifications (Kloas, 1997).

Oversight and assistance. Chambers provide assistance to enterprises on training-related problems. This includes information on the skilled occupations to be considered, how to structure the training, equipment needs, the use of instructional materials and training aids, relationships with apprentices, and educational as well as legal questions.

Chambers employ training advisors (counselors) to ensure that training is provided in accordance with regulations. These counselors visit enterprises to monitor training progress and to ensure that apprentices are neither exploited as cheap labor nor displacing journeymen workers. Poor examination results may also trigger a counselor's visit.

When counselors first learn of a training problem, they discuss it with the trainers or their manager. Usually, this intervention is sufficient; however, if corrective action is not taken, the chamber will send an official letter. As a last resort, the chamber can (a) send apprentices to an inter-firm training center (at the employer's expense) for supplementary instruction, (b) rotate apprentices among several enterprises, or (c) move apprentices to another enterprise. In extreme cases, the chamber may even revoke the enterprise's entitlement to take on new apprentices (Laflamme et al., 1993; Raggatt, 1988).

Union works councils can also play a role in the control of apprenticeship training. They have rights of co-determination in implementing and supervising training within an enterprise. In large enterprises, subcommittees enforce legal requirements. However, in small- and medium-sized enterprises, workplace representation often does not exist and, as a result, control and supervision by works counselors and shop stewards is often lacking (Laflamme et al., 1993, p. 231).

Guilds

Guilds (*Innungen*) are associations of master craftsmen in a particular craft or trade (bricklayer, electrician, etc.) in a defined geographic region. Like chambers, they are constituted under public law and organized at the regional, state, and national levels. In addition to their compulsory membership in a Chamber of Crafts, business owners, including self-employed master craftsmen, may voluntarily join a guild. Approximately 80 percent of the self-employed master craftsmen who are members of a Chamber of Crafts also belong to a guild.

What guild members have in common is (a) ownership of a business, (b) master craftsman status in a particular craft or trade, and (c) an interest in influencing training and qualifications in that craft or trade.

Guilds deal with matters of importance to small businesses and provide members with benefits such as group insurance. However, their principal concerns involve cooperating with Chambers of Crafts and caring for the professional and moral training of apprentices

while they are on the job, at the inter-firm training center, or in the *Berufsschule*. Activities performed in cooperation with Chambers include (a) providing input on revisions to training regulations, (b) preparing and registering apprenticeship contracts, (c) serving on examination committees for apprenticeship exams (both interim and final) and master craftsman exams, and (d) providing expert advice on craft-related issues.

Like chambers, guilds operate inter-firm training centers. These centers provide apprentice, master craftsman, and further training as well as retraining for redundant workers. Guilds also lobby, monitor legislation, and conduct public relations campaigns on behalf of their craft or trade.

FINANCING THE DUAL SYSTEM
Sources of Funding

The German apprenticeship system exemplifies collaborative and benefit-related financing. Support comes from different sources: national, state, and regional government; employers; worker groups; and apprentices. At the national level, the Federal Ministry of Education, Science, Research and Technology; the Federal Institute for Employment; and the Federal Ministry of Economic Affairs contribute to the support of (a) inter-firm training centers, (b) pilot projects, and (c) access to training for targeted groups, such as redundant workers. They also provide grants to talented apprentices and to those with special needs.

State and regional governments budget public funds to build, maintain, and operate *Berufsschulen*. The cost of this school-based instruction, including teachers' salaries, facilities, equipment and materials, as well as administrative and other expenses, was DM 9.3 billion (about US$6.1 billion[3]) in 1991 (Thiele, 1994).

[3]*Deutsche Marks (Germany's national currency) were converted to United States dollars at the 31 December 1991 exchange rate as reported in the 1 January 1992 issue of* The Wall Street Journal. *The 1991 rate was used so that readers can compare the Deutsche Mark amounts cited in the text with dollar amounts for the same time period.*

Training employers voluntarily pay the greatest share of apprenticeship costs. This contrasts with other countries where government (taxpayers) bears the total cost of initial vocational training. Peter Thiele (1994) "reported":

> Overall, the country's expenditures on initial vocational training (without the public administration sector) total to approximately DM 36.7 billion. . . . [T]wo-thirds [of this] is paid by employers. (p. 135)

German enterprises that engage in the apprenticeship system invest an average 2 to 3 percent of their wage bill on training.

Organized labor, which is deeply involved in vocational training policy and legislation, and supports the dual system in nearly all of its particulars, suggests that the approach to financing apprenticeship training ought to be modified—though still be funded largely by employers. Labor representatives feel that, if all employers had to contribute to a national training fund, more would find it in their economic self-interest to take on and train apprentices. In any

event, organized labor agrees with its social partner (employers) that they, not government, need to have the lead.

Costs

The Federal Institute of Vocational Training reported that the total cost for an apprenticeship, across all recognized skilled occupations, was approximately DM 29,573 (about US $19,520[3]) in 1991. As shown on Table 2, this amount consisted of: (a) 48.8 percent—apprenticeship wages; (b) 39.4 percent—salaries for trainers; (c) 3.5 percent—facilities, tools, equipment, materials, and supplies; and (d) 8.3

TABLE 2—COSTS OF APPRENTICESHIP TRAINING IN SKILLED OCCUPATIONS UNDER THE CHAMBER OF INDUSTRY AND COMMERCE AND CHAMBER OF CRAFTS IN 1991

Classification of costs	All recognized skilled occupations		Chamber of industry and commerce		Chamber of crafts	
	DM	%	DM	%	DM	%
Apprenticeship wages	14,435	48.8	15,930	50.1	11,324	45.5
Trainers' salaries	11,652	39.4	12,019	37.8	10,890	43.8
Facilities, equipment, etc.	1,048	3.5	1,236	3.9	656	2.6
Miscellaneous costs[2]	2,438	8.3	2,639	8.2	2,019	8.1
Total costs	29,573	100.0	31,824	100.0	24,889	100.0

Note:
[1] The sum of 2,438 DM for miscellaneous costs is made up of the following:

1,241 DM training-related administrative costs
568 DM costs for inter-firm training
247 DM fees/charges by the chamber (registration of apprenticeship contract, interim and final exams)
140 DM instructional materials (books, handouts, etc.)
110 DM purchase and laundry of work clothes
132 DM miscellaneous personal costs

Adapted from: *Berufsbildung in Wissenschaft und Praxis* (3/1994), p. 3-11.

percent—administrative and other miscellaneous costs. Table 2 also shows the breakdown by amount and percent for those occupational specializations under the Chamber of Industry and Commerce and those under the Chamber of Crafts. It is interesting to note that the average gross training expenditure per apprentice for skilled occupations under the Chamber of Industry and Commerce was DM 31,824, whereas under the Chamber of Crafts it was DM 24,889, or DM 6,935 (about US$4,577[3]) less.

The costs of training vary among skilled occupations, but also between the years of an apprenticeship. This is because the value of the apprentices' productive work differs dramatically between occupations and increases from year to year. Thiele reported in 1994 that the highest wages (earnings) from apprenticeship were by occupations in the food, printing, and wood-processing sectors, where they accounted for more than 50 percent of gross training costs. Thiele also pointed out that earnings in the crafts and trades occupations, in general, amounted to less than half of employers' training costs. By comparison, apprenticeship earnings accounted for less than 30 percent of costs for occupations in the chemical, banking, and insurance sectors.

The costs and benefits of training are shared by apprentices and employers, and somewhat by the government. Apprentices contribute to cost savings by accepting lower wages during training and benefit by gaining the means to earn considerably more once they become journeymen. Employers accept the lower initial output of apprentices, pay for the training, and benefit in a host of ways (many of the benefits are identified later in this chapter under the heading Why Train Apprentices) (Middleton, Ziderman, & Van Adams, 1991, p. 8; Siebert, 1985). The government accepts lower tax payments, allowing enterprises to deduct their training costs from profits before taxes, and contributes to Berufsschule costs because of perceived benefits to society: reduced youth unemployment and a more highly skilled workforce.

Wages

An important ingredient in the success of the dual system is the low apprenticeship wage, which favorably affects employers' training costs and, consequently, their willingness to offer apprenticeships. Apprenticeship wage guidelines are provided by the Vocational Training Act of 1969. Wages vary greatly by skilled occupation, location (state), and labor market factors, but they must be raised at least annually, according to the apprentice's training progress. Actual wage amounts are based, in part, on minimum levels fixed nationally by collective bargaining agreements between employers and unions.

Since apprenticeship is legitimately distinguished from employment, apprentices are viewed more as trainees than as workers. As a result, their low wages do not violate the norms of fair pay, especially since apprentices (a) are not likely to be as productive as regular workers and (b) must be given time off, with pay, to attend a Berufsschule and to take both an interim and final examination. These circumstances, along with assurances of quality training, induce unions to accept the practice of low apprenticeship wages.

A typical 18-year-old apprentice receives about 33 percent of the entry-level skilled worker wage, less than that earned by unskilled workers (Laflamme et al., 1993, p. 238). The highest wages are paid to skilled occupations in the public administration sector and the lowest to those in the crafts and agricultural sectors. However, in the building (construction) occupations, where there is a shortage of workers, apprentices generally receive up to 51 percent of a journeyman's earnings in the last year of the apprenticeship.

Despite comparatively low wages, apprenticeship is popular with both young adults and their parents. They view the apprenticeship as training in knowledge and skills that is costly to provide but, once acquired, transferable across a range of employers. For this reason, it makes economic sense for graduate apprentices (journeymen), as sellers of the knowledge and skills, to help pay for its development by accepting lower wages during the apprenticeship period (Siebert, 1985).

WHY TRAIN APPRENTICES

There are so many employers in so many different industries with varying business conditions and interests that caution is in order when generalizing about why they train apprentices. Nevertheless, it is widely accepted that employers conduct apprenticeship training so that they will have a qualified workforce in the future. They understand that their investment will produce dividends of higher productivity and increased profitability. Further, it is vital to their long-term economic success and international competitiveness. Employers also recognize the public good associated with this investment.

In spite of the risk of losing apprentices along with the training investment to higher-paying competitors when the apprentices become journeymen, enterprises voluntarily participate in apprenticeship training for the following reasons:

• They want to retain control over the goals and structure of apprenticeship, as well as over the selection, training, and testing of apprentices. Interference or regulatory intervention by government is viewed as a hindrance to participation and therefore must be avoided.

• They are free to offer apprenticeship contracts to the applicants they select and in occupations they wish to train.

• They don't have to pay apprentices as much as they pay skilled or unskilled workers. Nevertheless, an enterprise that wants to retain skilled workers after their apprenticeship offers reasonable wages during the training period.

• Apprentices' productive work over the total training period reduces training costs.

• Training expenditures can be deducted from profits before taxes.

• Participating enterprises receive preference in the awarding of government contracts for construction as well as goods and services.

• A highly skilled and adaptable workforce can enhance the quality and efficiency of product development and is more versatile in production, maintenance, and service tasks.

• They can evaluate apprentices under work conditions before they make a job offer. This reduces the risks and costs in recruiting employees. By training their own apprentices, enterprises are assured of the skills, personal characteristics, and safe practices of those they choose to hire.

• Workplace training (a) increases personal satisfaction, (b) promotes morale, and (c) contributes to a sense of loyalty to the enterprise and a commitment to its long-term prospects.

There is a historic tradition of apprenticeship, and cultural roots support the training of young adults on the job. Enterprises also provide training out of a sense of their social responsibility to take care of the younger generation. Offering apprenticeships leads to good standing in the community, which, as a result of a trained and informed citizenry, can hope for a more serene democratic life.

A CLOSING THOUGHT

Germany is renowned worldwide for the quality and scope of its initial vocational training (apprenticeship) system. Apprenticeship, which combines instruction in theory with training and practice on the job, is generally accepted as the best way to prepare skilled workers. The approach works brilliantly in a growing economy, and well in a healthy one, but problems surface during economic downturns. In the first place, there must be an approximate balance between aspiring apprentices and available training places. During difficult economic times, there may not be enough placements, and even available ones may be in inappropriate occupations or with undesirable training employers. Even in a healthy economy, the system has an over-preponderance of apprentices in craft and service occupations because this is where most placements are, even though the occupational aspirations of apprentices may lie elsewhere.

A compounding dilemma is that local and regional disparities exist in the availability of training places. There may be a mismatch between the number of eligible and interested students, the areas where they reside, and the number/type of enterprises participating in apprenticeship training.

A second related problem is collaboration. The dual system depends on collaborative relationships among the various social partners. The collaborative and contractual relationships between employers and unions are particularly crucial. As long as a nonadversarial relationship prevails, these partners can cooperate. In the past, employers have resisted attempts by unions to control the process of skill formation and certification—it has only been in the last 50 years that a climate of social cooperation has prevailed. Some attribute this to healthy economic times (Ashton & Green, 1996). As the German economy experiences stress, the climate of collaboration so essential to the functioning of the dual system also undergoes stress.

Nevertheless, the apprenticeship system has continued to produce a skilled workforce unequaled elsewhere in Europe. It is based on strong, lower-level basic education, as well as coordination and collaboration among the social partners. National labor and economic legislation imposes the framework, while chambers, relevant government agencies, and unions negotiate the substance of the training. As Europe moves further into its economic and political union, Germany's system continues to be the model that other countries emulate.

References

Arnold, E., & Much, J. (1997). *Questions and answers on the dual system of vocational training in Germany*. Bonn, Germany: Federal Ministry of Education, Science, Research and Technology.

Ashton, D., & Green, F. (1996). *Education, training and the global economy*. Cheltenham, England: Edward Elgar.

Ausbildung und beruf (Training and occupation). (1994). Bonn, Germany: Federal Ministry of Education, Science, Research and Technology.

Berufsbildung in Wissenschaft und Praxis [Vocational training in science and practice]. (1994). Berlin, Germany: Federal Institute for Vocational Education.

Berufsbildungsbericht (Vocational training report). (1997). Bonn, Germany: Federal Ministry of Education, Science, Research and Technology.

The dual system: Vocational training in the Federal Republic of Germany. (1988). Bonn, Germany: Association of German Chambers of Industry and Commerce.

Dual vocational training in the Federal Republic of Germany. (1988). Bonn, Germany: Deutscher Industrie-und Handelstag.

Kloas, P. W. (1997). *Modularsierung in der Beruflichen Bildung* [Modularity in vocational education]. Bielefeld, Germany: Bertelsmann-Verlag.

Krekeler, N. (1986). *Learning for the working world: Vocational training in the Federal Republic of Germany* (Monograph No. BW Nr. 3-4e). Bonn, Germany: Inter Nationes.

Laflamme, G., Basset, C., & Michlin, P. (Eds.). (1993). *Vocational training: International perspectives*. Turin, Italy: International Labour Organization, Turin Centre.

Middleton, J., Ziderman, A., & Van Adams, A. (1991). *Vocational and technical education and training*. Washington, DC: The International Bank for Reconstruction and Development/The World Bank.

Munch, J. (1986). *Vocational training in the Federal Republic of Germany*. Berlin, Germany: European Centre for the Development of Vocational Training.

Nothdurft, W. E. (1989). *Schoolworks: Reinventing public schools to create the workforce of the future*. Washington, DC: The Brookings Institution.

Oehler, E. (1998). *The school system in the Federal Republic of Germany* (Monograph—Education and Science 1/98). Bonn, Germany: Inter Nationes.

Pritchard, R. M. O. (1992). The German dual system: Educational utopia? *Comparative Education, 28*(2), 131-143.

Raggatt, P. (1988). Quality control in the dual system of West Germany. *Oxford Review of Education, 14*(2), 163-186.

Siebert, W. S. (1985). Development in the economics of human capital. In D. Carline, C. Pissarides, W. S. Siebert, & P. Sloane (Eds.), *Labour economics*. London: Longman.

Thiele, P. (1994). Financing the German dual system. In V. Gasskov (Ed.), *Alternative schemes of financing training* (pp. 132-137). Geneva, Switzerland: International Labour Office.

Trilingual "business card" gives dual vocational training graduates a stronger profile. (1997, February). *CEDEFOP Info*, p. 14.

Vocational training act of 1969. (1986). Bonn, Germany: Federal Ministry of Education, Science, Research and Technology.

Vocational training in the dual system: In the Federal Republic of Germany. (1992). Bonn, Germany: Federal Ministry of Education, Science, Research and Technology.

Author note: This chapter synthesizes English- and German-language literature that describe how the dual system of apprenticeship training prepares youth for skilled occupations. Thanks to a collaborative research grant from the North Atlantic Treaty Organization, the authors also (a) interviewed experts in the public and private sectors, (b) visited both inter-firm training centers and *Berufsschulen*, and (c) observed training activities, firsthand, at a host of enterprises.

9

Vocational Education and Training Practices in the Netherlands

By Jan N. Streumer

In addition to changes in technology, the economy, demography, culture, and politics have all greatly impacted the workplace. As a result, vocational education and training (VET) programs in the Netherlands have sought to prepare more flexible workers, since this would reduce labor market friction in terms of quality as well as demand and supply. VET must also respond with flexibility to contextual factors that put pressure on and impact school-to-work transition. This flexibility can be put into operation through three system factors: input, process, and output (Nijhof & Streumer, 1994).

The responsiveness of the system as a whole leads to *input* decisions, which create new interfaces between the labor market and schools and demand new qualification and certification structures. The second category, *process* decisions, transforms the traditional education system into one that is flexible and highly individualized in terms of entry and learning conditions, with modular-structured curricula and new learning/instruction technologies. Both teachers and students are encouraged to develop new *outputs,* including so-called ge-

neric skills, key qualifications, and transferable skills. The main assumption related to flexibility is *transferability*, the competence or ability to apply skills in new situations (Nijhof & Streumer, 1995).

This chapter describes the evolution and current status of vocational education and training in the Netherlands. A number of organizational and curricular measures have been integrated into the formal education system to link education and the labor market in a positive way. One could argue that, by 1997, this linkage no longer presented a major problem. This was due in part to the work of the Wagner and Rauwenhoff Committees, both of which recommended increasing the influence of business and industry in the VET system. This would take place notably through joint initiatives of schools and employers, to align education with the labor process. Government policy agreed entirely with this recommendation.

This chapter also focuses on several key areas, including VET policy in the Netherlands; the current delivery system, with attention to recent innovations; the status of efforts to improve the transition from school to work; and related research findings. In addition, several issues are discussed: the need for a transparent VET system and for broad occupational training to give (potential) employees ample opportunity to adapt to new situations.

VOCATIONAL EDUCATION AND TRAINING POLICY

Responsiveness of the Dutch education system's vocational sector to changes in the labor market cannot be easily understood without clarification of the relationship between general education and vocational streams within that system (Ministry of Education and Science, 1993). The relationship has evolved over 20 years to the point where general and vocational education are currently regarded as complementary components of a single, coherent whole with a common purpose. Up until the early 1980s, opinions were heavily influenced by the ideal of equal opportunities. The aim was to reduce differences between general and vocational education as much as possible. However, more recently, interest has centered on employment opportunities and the need to meet a demand for qualifications.

The first period of thinking saw interest concentrated on opportunities for mobility within the educational system. Heavy emphasis went to the principle that vocational education should not be a dead end—it should offer students at least some of the same opportunities as general education. The second, and more recent, period is linked to the economic crisis of the 1980s in the Netherlands. Themes that dominated related to the need to find a solution to the problem of youth unemployment and the desire to tailor content and qualifications to match changes in the country's economic structure. This meant that vocational education had to become more specific. In doing so, it played an important role in managing a more direct relationship between education and the labor market.

Vocational education differs from general education in its degree of orientation toward particular sectors of the labor market. It emphasizes applied knowledge rather than theory. General education is increasingly considered a transitional form of education that leaves more options for further study and careers. The range of later occupational practice is much more limited in vocational education, which is consequently considered more a form of final education (Ministry of Education and Science, 1993).

Vocational education became a major theme in the economic and social debate beginning in the early 1980s. As a result of several stimuli, including the Wagner Committee report, business and industry gained influence. The report recommended the creation of central as well as sectoral consultative bodies. The involvement and influence of business and industry in these bodies was acquired in exchange for assurance of an adequate supply of practical training and work experience placements.

In 1990, the Rauwenhoff Committee expanded on the concept of shared responsibility. Based on this committee's work, agreements were made between employers, worker organizations, and the government on

• Achieving starting qualifications by all, at a level comparable to the primary level of apprenticeship.

• Developing a national qualification structure and an attainment target for each occupation by tripartite consultative bodies.

• Joint initiatives between schools and enterprises which are, according to Dercksen and Van Lieshout (1993), the most important means of gearing education to the labor process.

• The integral dualization of vocational education (e. g., the apprenticeship system).

The Commissie Dualisering (1993) questioned whether dualization would help to ensure that courses at all levels of vocational education respond flexibly to industry needs. Dercksen and Van Lieshout (1993) noted that selective dualization currently exists, that further dualization possibilities are being examined, and that the principle of integral dualization was rejected.

Another stimulus for business and industry involvement was the Manpower Service Act introduced in January 1991. A key section of this Act relates to the formulation of an administrative, financial, and statutory framework within which central government and the social partners (employers and unions) can jointly implement broad national employment policies. The aims include the preservation and expansion of employment and an adequate supply of skilled workers. The general national policy outline is then interpreted and implemented at regional levels. One of the main tasks of the employment-strategy framework is to promote training (e. g., training for those seeking work). In this way, it is hoped the various training programs will be harmonized and focused on actual labor market needs (Ministry of Education and Science, 1993).

THE DELIVERY SYSTEM

VET courses and programs are presently offered (a) at prevocational education schools, (b) at senior secondary vocational education schools, (c) within the apprenticeship system, (d) at vocational colleges and universities, and (e) at a broad range of institutions for adult/continuing education.

Prevocational Education

In 1993, the government introduced a form of full-time basic education, *Voorbereidend Beroepsonderwijs* (VBO), which replaced the first two years of all types of secondary education, including junior secondary vocational education. The first two years of the four-year VBO are devoted mainly to general subjects, whereas the last two years are vocationally oriented, with students choosing from up to 16 vocational options.

Senior Secondary Vocational Education

Following immediately after VBO or junior general secondary education, *Middelbaar* *Beroepsonderwijs* (MBO) lasts a maximum of four years. It provides VET for middle-management positions in industry, service companies, and government. A large-scale innovation was introduced within MBO, the so-called SVM operation (sector formation and innovation of senior secondary vocational education). Apart from trying to increase program efficiency by reducing dropout rates and improving student progress, SVM fosters the relationship between education and the labor market.

A practical training (i. e., internship) period is required in every MBO program. It lasts approximately 200 days, usually during the student's third year of study. The practical training component amounts to 20 to 35 percent of the total program, whereas in apprenticeship, the practical component ranges from 60 to 80 percent. With the exception of requirements for duration, content, and form, there are no set guidelines for the internship contract.

During the 1980s, demand for senior secondary vocational education increased. In 1991, the number of MBO students stabilized at approximately 350,000, having nearly doubled since 1980. Students who pass the MBO final examination and acquire a diploma may set up practice as an independent entrepreneur in any country of the European Union. Recently, MBO schools have been merged, along with the apprenticeship system and several types of adult education, into regional training centers.

Apprenticeship System

There are approximately 400 apprenticeable occupations in the Netherlands. VBO completion, along with additional requirements, including specific subjects and examination levels, is generally required for admission. Apprenticeships include one or two days a week at school, while practical training takes place in an in-company training program for the rest of the week. Students work on the basis of a labor agreement. The primary training program (initial course) within the apprenticeship lasts two years, whereas the secondary training program (continuation course) takes one additional year. After receiving a certificate for the secondary training level, a student may continue on to the tertiary level.

In 1993, the apprenticeship bodies merged with MBO consultative bodies to form national bodies for vocational education. These national bodies have responsibility for the quality of the "output" of secondary vocational education and the apprenticeship system. They also have responsibility for defining the attainment targets for both delivery approaches and for setting and monitoring examinations.

As should be expected, trends in apprenticeship participation are related to economic conditions. The higher the level of industrial activity, the more apprenticeships businesses offer. In times of economic recession, businesses offer fewer apprenticeships. Enrollment in the apprenticeship system was approximately 150,000 students in 1996, up substantially from 100,000 in 1986.

Higher Vocational Education

For admission to one of the 70 *Hoger Beroepsonderwijs* (HBO) programs, a student needs at least an MBO diploma, or a diploma of senior general secondary education. As is true of other vocational education delivery approaches, HBOs have gained a large measure of autonomy. Colleges can now design and adapt their own curricula in conformance with labor market needs. The increased freedom changed relationships with the business community: Each HBO college now has responsibility for setting its own attainment targets. Most, however, set targets in consultation with advisory councils. HBO education aims at the development of knowledge and skills relevant to workplace requirements. A full-time HBO course of study takes four years. Those who successfully complete all requirements earn a bachelor's degree. For occupations with more demanding requirements, second-phase postgraduate courses of variable duration are available.

The HBO curriculum includes an internship with a company or institution so that students can gain practical work experience. This is frequently their introduction to actual working practice. During the internship, students receive an expense allowance. Practical training ranges from 15 to 25 percent of the total program. In addition, there are a number of part-time HBO courses, where the practical training constitutes up to 50 percent of the content. When students work at least 20 hours a week in a job relevant to their course, the phrase *concurrency education* is used.

Another HBO innovation used to improve the transition to work is called *cooperative learning* (co-op), in which each four- and six-month period of learning is followed by an equivalent period of work. The first year consists of theory. Students prepare for their working period (and, consequently, the labor market) through labor market orientation and application training.

Universities

Admission to university study requires a preuniversity diploma, an HBO certificate, or a passing score in a colloquium doctum (a test that replaces a diploma/certificate). Some university courses include a practical training period or internship of several months during the first phase (four years) of study. A second phase of study (two to four years), with specialized courses in a dual-learning scheme, is offered to medical and law students, as well as to assistants or researchers in training. The time students spend on the job ranges from 75 to 100 percent.

Adult/Continuing Education

Although neither adult basic education nor adult general secondary education directly prepare people for the labor market, either can be a prerequisite for admission to a vocational program. Vocationally oriented programs function in three ways. First, as an intermediary support for general vocational or job-specific training, they can be important for starting or changing a career. Second, they can give adults another chance to get qualified. Third, they may contribute to greater participation in the labor market. Vocational education for adults includes the apprenticeship system, part-time secondary vocational education, and specific training (e.g., courses with the National or Regional Employment Agency). Present policy is to introduce retraining and refresher courses in order to (a) align education with the labor market and (b) use the existing education infrastructure for the benefit of both the employed and the unemployed (Dercksen & Van Lieshout, 1993).

Responsibilities for adult/continuing education have been decentralized. Training courses are now developed, coordinated, and tested at a regional level, and their content is partially determined by regional labor market requirements. In addition, existing educational facilities and manpower services cooperate extensively with other organizations concerned with education and employment (Ministry of Education and Science, 1988). Table 1 lists the various delivery approaches in the Dutch VET system and indicates the practical-training proportions for each.

FEATURES OF PRACTICAL TRAINING OPTIONS

The features of work-based training are determined by the work that students perform. Frietman (1990) distinguished five types of practical training, gradually decreasing in their connection to actual labor: (a) on-the-job training in one company; (b) on-the-job training, with rotation among several companies; (c) on-the-job training in one company, in combination with off-the-job training; (d) on-the-job training, with rotation among several companies and in combination with off-the-job training; and (e) off-the-job training. According to the Commissie Dualisering (1993), examples of on-the-job training directly linked to the primary production process in a company are found in apprenticeship training and sometimes in part-time MBO or HBO. Practical training separated from actual production processes can be organized in company-owned schools or training centers that involve students in producing goods and services for sale. This form of on-the-job training is sometimes also found in the apprenticeship system. Practical training in off-the-job "pseudo-companies" is carried out in company-owned schools, training centers owned by vocational education bodies, school-based enterprises, and so forth.

Simulated practical training places are well suited for occupations/jobs with high safety and ethical requirements. A simulated environ-

TABLE 1—PROPORTION OF PRACTICAL TRAINING BY VOCATIONAL DELIVERY APPROACH

Delivery approach	Proportion of practical training
Apprenticeship system	60 to 80 percent (3-4 days per week)
Senior secondary vocational education (MBO)	20 to 35 percent (internship)
Higher vocational education (HBO)	15 to 25 percent (internship) in full-time HBO Up to 50 percent in part-time HBO
University courses	10 percent in first phase (4 years) 75 to 100 percent in second (2 to 4 years)
Adult/continuing education	Variable, but with strong emphasis on practical work

ment may work better in cases involving complex, time-consuming, or high-risk/-liability tasks. When a student needs training related to preventing problems or dealing with emergencies that cannot be provided in a real setting under real work conditions without possible equipment damage or personal injury, simulation is the best approach. Simulated training places also have the advantage of being less sensitive to economic fluctuations (Commissie Dualisering, 1993).

Student practical training most often takes place through learning-by-doing in one company. Students may rotate between several establishments belonging to one company or between several companies within an industrial sector. The apprenticeship system uses the workplace most intensively to fulfill the practical training component. Another possibility, sometimes classified as work-based learning, involves the use of trainee workshops set up by firms under the supervision of an experienced employee/practical teacher (Moerkamp, Onstenk, Dronkers, & Felix, 1993).

Frietman (1990) found that a nontraditional form of the apprenticeship system's practical component (i. e., completely off-the-job training) takes place most frequently in the commercial and metal/electrical sectors. In the commercial sector, students often train in a

TABLE 2—PRACTICAL TRAINING ARRANGEMENTS BY TRAINING ENVIRONMENT

Training environment	Practical training arrangements		
	Labor contract (apprenticeship)	Learning contract (apprenticeship or part-time MBO/HBO)	Internship contract (full-time MBO/HBO)
On-the-job (directly involved in primary process)	• Company	• Company	• Company
Off-the-job (separated from primary process)	• Company-owned schools or practical training centers • Practical training centers owned by national bodies for vocational education • Branch-owned practical training centers • Company-owned schools	• Company-owned schools (in apprenticeship system) • Practical training centers owned by national bodies for vocational education • Branch-owned practical training centers	• Company
Simulated situations	• Practical training centers owned by national bodies for vocational education	• Practical training centers owned by national bodies for vocational education • Centers for vocational adult education • School-based enterprises	• School-based enterprises

Adapted from: Commissie Dualisering (1993).

Vocational Education and Training Practices in the Netherlands school-based enterprise. The metal/electrical sector sometimes uses a temporary off-the-job workplace until a student finds a suitable traineeship in a company. In most sectors, however, traditional on-the-job training dominates.

Nevertheless, the Commissie Dualisering (1993) reported that combinations of practical training environments exist. Some students spend four days a week in a company and attend school one day a week (4-1 combination). The school may be company owned, with practical training at an employer's organization-owned training facility, or a regular vocational institute. Another possibility is for students to spend two days a week in a company, two days in a regional practical training center, and one day in school (2-2-1 combination).

Table 2 shows the most frequently occurring practical training arrangements for apprenticeship, part-time MBO and HBO, and full-time MBO and HBO, by type of training environment. Approximately 75 percent of apprentices have labor contracts, with part-time employee status. The remainder have learning contracts that describe in detail the responsibilities of both the company and the student/apprentice concerning the learning process.

RESEARCH FINDINGS

Most studies that deal with the transition from school to work have been quantitative. Many were directed at the number of participants who found jobs after completing a course (*gross return*), but little attention has been paid to whether participants found the jobs because of the course they followed (*net return*) (Gelderblom & Hammink, 1991).

Meesters (1992) conducted research on the labor market position of certain levels of vocational education. A noteworthy conclusion was that the labor market position of MBO graduates generally relates to their pre-education. In general, students who complete MBO after junior general secondary education have better labor market prospects than those who complete their MBO after a prevocational education course.

The labor market prospects for holders of apprenticeship (journeyman) certificates are actually better than for students with MBO qualifications (Ministry of Education and Science, 1993; Moerkamp et al., 1993). One possible explanation for this is that most apprenticeship students take jobs in the companies in which they train (Frietman, 1990). Frietman also found that 90 percent of students were employed immediately after completing their courses. About two-thirds obtained work directly linked to the sector in which they trained, which gives an indication of the qualitative link between the course and the labor market.

According to Frietman (1990) and Moerkamp and others (1993), the chances of employment in the company in which students' apprenticeship takes place depend on whether they have a labor contract. A student can often continue employment and be offered a new labor contract, or has a priority if there is a job vacancy. If the apprenticeship takes place without a labor contract, which usually implies that the student does not perform the practical training within a company, he or she has less likelihood of future employment. Frietman (1990) also found that students who completed their practical training off the job more often got jobs that differed from their initial training—in another sector, for example. It is remarkable that in the long run (after about five years), the character of practical training in an apprenticeship no longer really influences the position held in the labor market. Where internships are concerned (in MBO and HBO), the prospect of future employment in a student's internship company is less clear. However, the internship remains an important path through which senior secondary (MBO) and higher vocational (HBO) education students enter the labor market (Moerkamp et al., 1993).

Qualitative research has focused on design of the practical training component of apprenticeships/internships, the appreciation of practical work by students, and the number of practical training positions available. Nieuwenhuis and Onstenk (1994) considered the conditions under which the workplace can be a powerful learning environment. They cautiously suggested that qualifications in the technical domain are best gained off the job until students' skills are sufficiently routinized. Sociocognitive qualifications are complex, vocation-oriented, problem-solving skills and can best be learned in on-the-job situations, preceded by or in combination with complex off-the-job learning situations. Further, the researchers recommend providing variety in practical training situations.

As far as the design of internships in MBO, on the basis of a considerable amount of empirical research, De Vries (1988) distinguished between school-centered and labor-oriented internships, and recommended the latter, noting that internship, as part of initial vocational education, should be considered a first career step. De Vries stressed the importance of continuing or recurrent education during a working life.

Frietman (1990) focused on the differences between on-the-job and off-the-job training with regard to both learning effects and student opinions. He found that students considered on-the-job training the form of education that had the least possibility for actual learning and that paid the least attention to theoretical subjects. They felt, however, that the more training takes place on the job, the more they appreciate it with regard to their later work. Thus, on one hand, training linked to real work is appreciated, but on the other hand, students think they learn less from it. These results seem to be in conflict, which points to a need for improved on-the-job training procedures.

To examine the possibilities for extension of dualization of MBO, Moerkamp and others (1993) investigated company opinions toward dualization for this school type. Most companies appeared to have a rather positive attitude. They favored a practical training period of at least six months in the same company,

and learning and internship contracts rather than labor contracts. Although the current number of practical training positions suffices for the number of students applying for them, the increase in dualization will require more positions.

It appears that some companies do not provide any practical training positions. Obstacles cited related to company internal affairs, such as lack of possibilities to support the student and too much work pressure. The most serious problems for practical training positions mentioned were financial and economic: a lack of vacant posts and limited training budget. These problems held for internships as well as apprenticeships. Nevertheless, the Ministry of Education and Science signed a covenant with the umbrella organization of the national bodies for VET to increase the number of practical training positions by 3,000 to 5,000 places on a yearly basis (Leerlingwezen, 1996).

DISCUSSION

In the Netherlands, there is a strong tendency to decentralize responsibilities for the relationship between VET and the labor market. The central government stimulates cooperation between companies and educational institutions at both the national and regional levels to help students face the transition from school to work. All regulations and developments aim at adjusting VET to the changing requirements of the labor market and work structure.

One problem that receives considerable attention is the lack of transparency in the vocational education supply (Dercksen & Van Lieshout, 1993). Public and private training institutes offer a wide array of training programs for potential workers, including both the employed and the unemployed. But program content and educational value are often unclear. A national qualification structure, including formal and nonformal VET, could stimulate student/trainee motivation to participate in VET programs and thereby contribute to their mobility. Such a system, which is under development, rests on the contention that a more transparent education and training supply can lead to more efficient learning schemes and paths.

With the establishment of a national qualification structure, we should see improvement in the possibilities for moving between schools at the same level of advancement and for advancing to higher levels (Streumer, 1993). A more transparent education and training supply will thus increase the efficiency of learning schemes and paths. Aside from a national qualification structure, the newly formed regional training centers, including the apprenticeship system, senior secondary vocational education, and parts of adult/continuing education, will play an important role in making the educational supply more transparent and more responsive to the needs of individual students.

Since a wide range of options exists between broad occupational orientation and specific job-oriented training, VET programs can vary in concert with their vocational orientation. Nieuwenhuis and Onstenk (1994), as well as Nijhof and Streumer (1994), observed shifts in qualification requirements from narrowly defined, domain-specific qualifications toward a combination of these domain-specific qualifications and generic, broadly applicable qualifications. Nijhof and Streumer (1994) concluded that students will increasingly need career preparation that includes lifelong learning, as acquisition of specific factual knowledge and skills becomes less appropriate.

In general, companies can select employees with certain qualifications by using two strategies. First, they can adopt a recruitment strategy that bases employee selection primarily on job-specific qualifications. Second, they can use a training strategy that aims to select employees with broad occupational skills who need further job-specific training to upgrade their potential. This implies that companies are increasingly becoming financially responsible not only for their employees' specific job training but also for their ongoing performance improvement. VET will increasingly need to deliver generic knowledge, skills, and attitudes that are broadly applicable and transferable and that enable students to adjust to new situations in the workplace and also in private life.

References

Commissie Dualisering. (1993). *Beroepsvorming langs vele wegen* [Many roads lead to occupational training]. Zoetermeer, Netherlands: Ministry of Education and Science.

Dercksen, W. J., & Van Lieshout, H., assisted by Kamps, H., & Wijnands, Y. (1993). *Beroepsgewijs onderwijs. Ontwikkelingen en dilemma's in de aansluiting van onderwijs en arbeid* [Developments and dilemmas in the link between education and work]. The Hague, Netherlands: SDU Uitgeverij.

De Vries, B. (1988). *Het leven en de leer. Een studie naar de verbinding van leren en werken in de stage* [A study of the links between theory and practice in internships]. Nijmegen, Netherlands: Institute for Applied and Social Sciences.

Frietman, J. (1990). *De kwaliteit van de praktijkcomponent in het leerlingwezen* [The quality of the practical component in the apprenticeship system]. Nijmegen, Netherlands: Institute for Applied and Social Sciences.

Gelderblom, A., & Hammink, A. C. H. (1991). *Rendement in de volwasseneneducatie* [Output of adult education]. Utrecht, Netherlands: RVE/Advisory Center for Adult Education.

Leerlingwezen na daling nu stabiel [Number of apprentices after decline stable now]. (1996, September 18), *NRC/Handelsblad*.

Meesters, M. J. (1992). *Loopbanen in het onderwijs en op de arbeidsmarkt. Verticale en horizontale differentiatie en het voortgezet onderwijs: Oorzaken en gevolgen voor de arbeidsmarkt positie van Nederlandse jongeren* [Careers in education and the labor market]. Nijmegen, Netherlands: Institute for Applied and Social Sciences.

Ministry of Education and Science. (1988). *The Dutch education system*. Zoetermeer, Netherlands: Author.

Ministry of Education and Science. (1993). The changing role of vocational and technical education and training. In Office for Economic Cooperation and Development (Ed.), (1994), *Vocational training in the Netherlands: Reform and innovation*. Paris: Office for Economic Cooperation and Development.

Moerkamp, T., Onstenk, T., Dronkers, J., & Felix, C. (1993). *Kwaliteit en beschikbaarheid van leerarbeidsplaatsen voor MBO en leerlingwezen* [Quality and availability of training employment positions for senior secondary vocational education and the apprenticeship system]. Amsterdam: SCO-Kohnstamm Institute.

Nieuwenhuis, L., & Onstenk, J. (1994). Werkend leren in opleiding en beroep: De werkpiek als krachtige leeromgeving [The workplace as an influential learning situation]. *Comenius, 14,* 198-219.

Nijhof, W. J., & Streumer, J. N. (1994). Flexibility in vocational education and training: Introduction. In *Flexibility in training and vocational education.* Utrecht, Netherlands: Lemma B. V.

Nijhof, W. J., & Streumer, J. N. (1995). *Verbreed beroepsonderwijs* [Broadening VET]. De Lier, Netherlands: Academic Book Center.

Streumer, J. (1993). *Recognition of skills and co-investment: A study on behalf of FORCE* (Report on the Netherlands). Enschede, Netherlands: University of Twente, OCTO Research Center.

Streumer, J. N., & Feteris, A. (1994). CNC machining and flexible production automation. In Office for Economic Cooperation and Development (Ed.), *Vocational training in the Netherlands: Reform and innovation.* Paris: Office for Economic Cooperation and Development.

10

Vocational Education and Training Policies and Practice in the United Kingdom

By Stuart M. Niven

"Revolution, not evolution" was heralded in vocational education in Scotland following the Scottish Education Department's (1983) publication of *16-18's in Scotland: An Action Plan*. With this publication, the Scottish modular curriculum for technical/vocational education was born. The birth was a closely kept secret, however. An earlier publication, *16 to 18's in Scotland: The First Two Years of Post-Compulsory Education* (Scottish Education Department, 1979), had sought the views of schools, colleges, national examination boards, curriculum development agencies, and others, regarding possible new directions for educational provisions for this age group. Although many suggestions were put forth, there was no unanimity as to the best direction for future development (Niven, 1982). Thus, the 1983 publication, which became known as "The Action Plan," took educators and others by surprise.

Not only did the Action Plan propose radical changes, but it advised that they should proceed swiftly. The Plan provided details regarding how to establish an educational framework that would embrace everyone in the 16- to 18-year-old age group while serving adults as well (Scottish Education Department, 1983). As the Action Plan's ideas for wider application of postcompulsory education gained acceptance, it was renamed "16+ in Scotland." The renaming brought with it a comprehensive scheme for lifelong learning, although it was not described in that way at the time.

The Plan's aims were laudable, pointing out the need to prepare each individual for a rapidly changing society by (a) providing experience in applying knowledge, ability, and motivation to adapt to new challenges; (b) developing individual talents and interests; and (c) instilling an awareness of responsibility within the community. The intent was to express these aims in a new curriculum that included a continuation of the development of literacy and numeracy; experience in the world of work and the community; specialist, industrial, and social (including moral and religious) studies; and informal concerns, including education for leisure and independent study. The curriculum structure had a breadth which could accommodate all that was to follow in the development of non-advanced further education, including vocational/technical courses, such as the Scottish National Certificate Modules (SNCMs[1]) (Scottish Qualifications Authority, 1997b) and, later, Scottish Higher National Units (SHNUs) (Scottish Qualifications Authority, 1997a). As it evolved, the curriculum was markedly influenced by the needs of industry. It is outcome oriented and requires students to exhibit competence in relation to National Standards. The SNCMs and SHNUs have become the building blocks for courses that lead to Scottish Vocational Qualifications.

Just two years from the launch of the Action Plan, the new modular curriculum was in place and offering a complement of more than 1,700 modules. This was an exciting era for vocational/technical education in Scotland. For the first time, schools and colleges could offer vocational courses that led to a recognized award, the Scottish National Certificate. In addition, every successfully completed module was endorsed on the Certificate.

At first, the Scottish Education Department drove implementation of the Action Plan, but the Scottish Council for Vocational Education (SCOTVEC) quickly took over in 1984, following its succession to the Scottish Technical Education Council and the Scottish Business Education Council. SCOTVEC became the main agency in Scotland for technical and business qualifications below the university-degree level. In 1997, a new body, the Scottish Qualifications Authority (SQA) formed in a merger of SCOTVEC and the Scottish Certificate of Education Examinations Board (SCEEB). The SQA is now the sole awarding body for Scottish National Certificates and Scottish Higher National Certificates and Diplomas.

THE MODULAR CURRICULUM

The modules and units within the Scottish curriculum framework for technical and vocational education and training consist of 40 hours of study. Double and triple modules (80

and 120 hours, respectively) are also admissible, though they are used much less frequently. Each module has a unique *module descriptor* that has the following four features:

• A statement of learning outcomes—What learners should know and be able to do as a consequence of completed courses, including knowledge, skills, and attitudes.

• A range statement—Description of the content/context relating to the learning outcomes, including subject matter and processes.

• Learning and teaching methods—Suggested approaches that would enable students to acquire the competence necessary to attain the outcomes.

• Assessment procedures—Performance criteria by which student success (or failure) is determined.

Module Descriptor Guidelines, issued by the Scottish Office Education Department (1983) confessed to the inevitability of a level of arbitrariness and idiosyncrasy in the authoring of descriptors. Early attempts at generating descriptors involved more art than science. Experience has shown that some subjects lend themselves more readily to descriptor treatment than others, but persistent redrafting has improved even the most challenging ones.

In the delivery of modules, the learning outcomes and performance criteria defined by the descriptors are sacrosanct and are the targets to be attained. However, the individual teacher must decide what specific learning experiences and content will lead to performance mastery. Appendix B provides an abbreviated module descriptor (learning outcomes and performance criteria).

Shortly after implementation of the Action Plan in Scotland, its underpinning philosophy spread to other countries in the United Kingdom (U. K.), where the examining bodies followed SCOTVEC's example and introduced modular curricula.

"16+ Scotland" introduced another con-

[1]See Appendix A, page 143, for a list of the acronyms used in this chapter, and their meanings.

cept—competence—into the jargon of technical/vocational education and training in Scotland. It subsequently came to occupy a very special place in the vocabulary of vocational/ technical education throughout the U. K. (Mansell, 1986). Exactly what is to be understood by competence is still a matter of dispute, and the argument between pro-competence and anti-competence factions rumbles on.

OCCUPATIONAL STANDARDS

While vocational/technical education was being overhauled, parallel developments were underway in industrial training. A 1981 government paper, *A New Training Initiative: A Programme for Action*, proposed sweeping changes in youth training programs and in lifelong learning opportunities for adults to enable them to retrain or keep pace with developments. Attention was drawn to the need for development of standards of craft competence, and it was recommended that standards be put in place for all occupations by 1985. Colleges and industry were urged to collaborate in producing work-related programs that included actual work experience or, failing that, simulated work experience. Further, the proposal recommended making provision for assessment of prior learning and job aptitude as well as enhancement of basic skills, numeracy, literacy, and communication (Manpower Services Commission, 1981). Successive Ministers of Education, Employment, and Industry through the following decade did not deviate from a belief in the principles embodied in such programs.

By 1986, government had grown even more penetrating with its idea of standards of competence (including both skills mastery and knowledge) for all occupations, and regarding vocational qualifications (VQs) based on these standards. The National Council for Vocational Qualifications (NCVQ) was formed to "promote, develop, implement and monitor a comprehensive system of vocational qualifications" in England, Wales, and Northern Ireland. SCOTVEC, by now the SQA, was charged to fulfill the same function in Scotland. The respective qualifications, which are based on exactly the same competency standards, are known as National Vocational Qualifications (NVQs) and Scottish Vocational Qualifications (SVQs).

Competence is a wide concept that embodies the ability to transfer skills and knowledge to new situations within an occupational area. "It encompasses organisation and planning of work, innovation and coping with non-routine activities. It includes those qualities of personal effectiveness that are required in the workplace to deal with co-workers, managers and customers" (Department for Education and Employment [DfEE], 1994, p. 11). This is more an insightful statement than a definition, but it is compatible with the process of disaggregation of competence adopted for the specification of national standards.

This disaggregation, or breakdown, is first into Units of Competence and, ultimately, at another level of analysis, into Elements of Competence. Elements can be assessed against specific performance criteria and equate to learning outcomes in the context of the SQA modular curriculum discussed earlier. An Element of Competence and its associated performance criteria constitute a Standard. Standards are accompanied by range indicators that list the Element's applications—that is, the purposes for which achievement of the Element of Competence is required. Standards are also accompanied by statements about the kind and quality of the evidence to be judged against the performance criteria. In all, there are four stages of analysis for an occupation:
- Areas of Competence
- Key Roles
- Units of Competence
- Elements of Competence

Appendix C is an example of the four stages, drawn from the training and development field. The stages shown constitute the national standards for training and development, as devised by the Training and Development Lead Body (TDLB) (1992).

INDUSTRY LEAD BODIES

Although the overall responsibility for the framework of national standards and the vocational qualifications based on these standards lies with the NCVQ and the SQA, the Industry Lead Body (ILB) devises and sets the standards for the particular occupational area. Government policy stipulates that all occupations should be characterized by standards and that these standards must relate specifically to the workplace. As a consequence, it is not surprising that ILBs comprise mainly industry and business representatives from employer organizations, trade unions, professional bodies, and trade associations. Technical and vocational education and training (TVET) providers are also represented, but they are in the minority. The Department for Education and Employment (DfEE) has a central role in determining the membership of the ILBs, but, because Scotland has separate arrangements for TVET, DfEE always discusses these matters with its Scottish Office counterpart.

Lead bodies are gradually being replaced by National Training Organisations (NTOs). At their peak, there were more than 140 ILBs and the number was increasing as more industries entered the national standards framework.

Individual lead bodies have large memberships. For example, the Advice, Guidance, Counseling and Psychotherapy Lead Body has more than 60 members. The Care and Health segment has 21 member categories, including the Royal College of Nursing, the Royal College of Psychiatrists, and the Carers National Association. Table 1 provides examples of other lead bodies and their occupational areas.

VOCATIONAL QUALIFICATIONS

Having looked at standards and standard setting, the next step in coming to terms with TVET in the United Kingdom involves understanding the structure of vocational qualifications. As discussed previously, the National Council for Vocational Qualifications and the Scottish Qualifications Authority collaborate to ensure that their separate provisions are com-

TABLE 1—EXAMPLES OF INDUSTRY LEAD BODIES AND THEIR OCCUPATIONAL AREAS

Lead body	Occupational area
British Polymer Training Association	Manufacturing
Construction Industry Training Board	Construction (building trades, etc.)
Distributive Occupational Standards Council	Providing goods and services
Engineering Training Authority	Engineering
Industry Lead Body for Amenity Horticulture	Tending animals, plants, and land
Institute of Business Counselors	Providing business services
Offshore Petroleum Industry Training Organization	Extracting and providing natural resources
Rail Industry Training Council	Transportation
Screen Printing Association	Communicating and entertaining
Security Industry Training Organization Limited	Providing health, social care, and protective services
Training and Development Lead Body	Developing knowledge and skills

patible. To this end, in 1990, NCVQ and SCOTVEC (now the SQA) reached an agreement that announced the compatibility of their qualifications, thereby ensuring the acceptance of both throughout the U. K.

Vocational qualifications are available at five levels that are described in terms of competence and included in the documentation for national standards.

Level 1—Competence in the performance of a range of varied work activities, most of which are routine and predictable.

Level 2—Competence in a range of varied work activities, performed in a variety of contexts. Some activities are complex and/or nonroutine, and there is some individual responsibility or autonomy. Collaboration with others, perhaps through membership in a work group or team, may be required.

Level 3—Competence in a broad range of varied work activities, performed in a wide variety of contexts, most of which are complex and/or nonroutine. There is considerable responsibility and autonomy, and control or guidance of others is often required.

Level 4—Competence in a broad range of complex, technical, or professional work activities performed in a wide variety of contexts and with a substantial degree of personal responsibility and autonomy. Responsibility for the work of others and the allocation of resources is often necessary.

Level 5—Competence that involves the application of a significant range of fundamental principles and complex techniques across a wide and often unpredictable variety of contexts. Very substantial personal autonomy and responsibility for the work of others and the allocation of substantial resources feature strongly, as do personal accountability for analysis and diagnosis, design, planning, execution, and evaluation (National Council for Vocational Qualifications [NCVQ], 1996).

The descriptions have been refined over the years, and they are guidelines, as distinct from prescriptions. The TDLB (1992), for example, defined Levels 3 and 4 vocational qualifica-

tions in the area of Training and Development as follows:

Level 3—Deliver training specified and designed by others, assess the outcomes of that training, and, from identified learning needs, design training that facilitates learning and meets objectives at operational level.

Level 4—Design, deliver, manage, and evaluate training and development programs and learning experiences to meet individual and organizational objectives.

From the descriptions and specifications above, it is clear that the primary purpose of NVQs and SVQs is to attest competence in occupational settings (i.e., ability to perform in the workplace). This, however, is not the main focus of National Certificate, Diploma, and Degree programs. Any attempt to equate or relate vocational qualifications at different levels with education awards of such bodies as the SQA, City and Guilds of London Institute (CGLI), Business and Technical Education Council (BTEC), Royal Society of Arts (RSA), and universities is frustrated by the different purposes of their several kinds of qualifications and awards. In Scotland, where the SQA has a dual role as accreditation agency and awarding body, there is even more confusion. The confusion over vocational qualifications is further compounded by the existence of Records of Education and Training (RETs). RETs are lifelong records of achievement of SQA Units and Modules which are issued upon their successful completion. Every unit or module achieved, regardless of when, is logged in an RET (NCVQ, 1996).

GENERAL VOCATIONAL QUALIFICATIONS

The complex of vocational qualifications has been enlarged by the introduction of General Vocational Qualifications (GVQs) or, more specifically, General Scottish Vocational Qualifications (GSVQs) and General National Vocational Qualifications (GNVQs). First mentioned in the white papers *Education and Training for the 21st Century* (Crown Office,

1991b) and *Access Opportunity: A Strategy for Education and Training* (Crown Office, 1991a), GVQ programs were piloted in 1992 and are now widely available throughout the United Kingdom. In Scotland, for example, GSVQs are available at levels 2 and 3 in 10 broad categories (Gunning, 1994): arts and social sciences, business administration, care, design, hospitality, information technology, land-based industries, leisure and tourism, science, and technology.

Courses leading to the award of GVQs are preemployment programs suitable for full-time students in colleges and, in some instances, for those in schools. They are intended to provide a broad preparation for employment as well as an accepted route to higher-level qualifications, including higher education. GNVQs are awarded by CGLI, BTEC, and the RSA; GSVQs are awarded by the SQA. These qualifications have been accorded equal standing to academic qualifications at the same level. In addition, they articulate with occupation-specific vocational qualifications so that progression can be made quickly and effectively from general to occupation-specific qualifications upon entry to employment.

Vocational qualifications programs, and in particular GVQs, take a core-plus-options form. In each program, provision is made for the development of core skills: (a) information technology, (b) literacy, (c) numeracy, (d) problem-solving, and (e) personal and social development. Where core skills are concerned, the SQA's practice differs from that of the CGLI, BTEC, and RSA. In the Scottish model, all GSVQs have modules in communication, numeracy, information technology, problem solving, and personal and interpersonal skills. In GNVQs, on the other hand, only communication, application of numbers, and information technology are compulsory, while units in personal skills, working with others, improving one's own learning, and performance are optional. GSVQs conform to the nomenclature of levels prescribed for GVQs and are available at levels 1, 2, and 3. The corresponding GNVQ levels are titled Foundation, Intermediate, and Advanced (Scottish Vocational Education Council, 1994).

In England, there is a fortuitous correlation between vocational and academic qualifications at the various levels. For example, Advanced GNVQs equate to "A-levels," the Advanced Level award achievable at the end of English secondary education. This has been referred to as the "gold standard" of academic education and is designed primarily to attest fitness for entry into higher education. There are no exact equivalencies, however, between vocational qualifications for specific occupations and academic qualifications, nor is there parity of esteem.

The prevailing view is that the academic is still superior to the vocational. This is no different in the U. K. than in other developed countries, despite higher-education students seeing their courses offer a route into jobs or professions. In such circumstances, there is an indistinct line between what might be perceived as academic and what is vocational. In Scotland, the latest curriculum reform, referred to as "Higher Still," hopes to bring a close to the academic/vocational divide (Scottish Office Education and Industry Department, 1994). Meanwhile, in England, differing proposals espoused by the Dearing Committee (School Curriculum and Assessment Authority [SCAA], 1996) and the Kennedy Report (DfEE, 1997) will no doubt determine the outcome. Regardless of the result, A-levels will likely remain a cornerstone of the English education system.

REVIEWING THE NATIONAL PROVISION FOR VOCATIONAL QUALIFICATIONS

The complexities of the entire vocational qualifications system in the U. K. have undergone almost continuous review and critical analysis. The arguments about the limitations—real or imagined—and the practicability of competency-based systems and provision show no signs of abating.

Although Her Majesty's (HM) Inspectorate, the arm of Scotland's civil service that has responsibility for monitoring educational standards, played a major role in devising and implementing the 16+ Action Plan, the Inspectorate was the first to effect a systematic appraisal of the new National Certificate vocational curriculum in 1991. The findings, as reported in *Six Years On*, were based on an inspection of more than one-third of Scotland's colleges during the period 1988 to 1990. The education provision for 13 occupational areas was involved: art and design, business administration and distribution, caring, communication, computing, construction, engineering, hairdressing and beauty therapy, hotel and catering, physical education and recreation, personal and social development, modern languages, and music (Her Majesty's Inspectors of Schools, 1991).

The report praised colleges for opening new opportunities in areas such as physical education, music, media studies, and the performing arts. It also complimented lecturers for adapting well to the new challenges of making professional judgments of student performance in relation to national standards, where assessment had previously been mainly by externally set final examinations (Her Majesty's Inspectors of Schools, 1991).

On the negative side, the new modular curriculum was criticized on the grounds that some programs lacked coherence. More specifically, regarding coherence, the report stated,

It was argued in the Action Plan, and reiterated in many quarters since, that students require to develop certain broad competences or core skills which will prepare them to be flexible and adaptable in a rapidly changing employment market. While examples were found of programmes with a strong emphasis on problem solving, communication, and interpersonal skills, such good practice was attributable to effective teaching or programme design by individuals rather than being a characteristic of the system. The national Certificate would benefit from a more coherent core skills strategy in which SCOTVEC, national curriculum and staff development agencies and further education college lecturers all have a role to play. (Her Majesty's Inspectors of Schools, 1991, p. 3)

This theme will be pursued further as VQs and GVQs evolve. Issues concerning teaching, learning, and assessment were central to the inspections, but deficiencies and dissatisfactions with national standards and the modular national curriculum were not clearly identified. The findings did reveal, however, that student performance was consistently assessed to national standards, although many staff still lacked confidence in the system.

Subsequent reports have been less flattering, especially one submitted by Gordon Beaumont (1996b), which pointed to a need for more than cosmetic revisions to many facets of the VQ system. A few weeks after his first report, Beaumont (1996a) further wrote that his principal aim was to retain the essential characteristics of NVQs and SVQs, while making them more accessible and user-friendly. He recommended changing the form and structure of standards, simplifying the language, and removing unnecessary bureaucracy. Beaumont provided more than 80 specific recommendations for action, each amply backed by evidence gleaned from a comprehensive research exercise conducted by the NCVQ and SCOTVEC under the supervision of an advisory group that he chaired (Scottish Vocational Education Council [SVEC] 1996).

The research showed that, for example, while a significant majority of employers believe VQs have enhanced workforce flexibility, others consider them too narrow, reflecting the needs of only a few individual employers in an occupational area rather than those of the area's overall workforce. Examples were found of standards based on obsolete practice, amid widespread concern about the apparent failure to assess the knowledge which underpins competence. Further research revealed difficulties in grammatical construction of the standards and qualifications and revisions in the wake of Beaumont's revelations have attempted to remove inappropriate vocabulary and jargon and address sentence structure (SVEC, 1996).

Although Beaumont's work uncovered weaknesses and deficiencies, it also revealed widespread support for the concept of competence-based standards and their application to VQs. Indeed, one important outcome was another definition of competence: "The ability to apply knowledge, understanding, and skills in performing to standards required in employment, including solving problems and meeting changing demands" (Beaumont, 1996b, p. 12).

The place of standards-based VQs sought by Beaumont seems secure, given the government's continuing commitment to the National Targets for Education and Training adopted in 1993. In England, the targets are specified in terms of NVQs and relate to foundation learning and lifetime learning targets. The National Advisory Council for Education and Training Targets (NACETT) monitors progress toward the attainment of the targets.

The Advisory Scottish Council for Education and Training Targets (ASCETT) (1997) has taken a slightly different approach by setting the following "Targets for 2000" for a "Competitive Scotland":

• By age 19, 85 percent of young people to attain SVQ/GSVQ Level II, 5 Standard Grades (1-3), or the equivalent.

• By age 21, 70 percent of young people to attain SVQ/GSVQ Level III, 3 Highers (A-C), or the equivalent.

• Sixty percent of the workforce to be quali-

fied to at least SVQ/GSVQ Level III, 3 Highers (A-C), or the equivalent.

• Thirty percent of the workforce to have a vocational, management, or academic qualification to at least SVQ Level IV or its equivalent.

• Seventy percent of all organizations employing 200 or more employees, 35 percent of those employing 50 or more, and 15 percent of those employing fewer than 50 to be recognized as "Investors in People."

For purposes of the targets, Standard Grade and Higher Grade Examination passes of the SCEEB are considered equivalent to SCOTVEC qualifications. Standard Grade Examinations are taken at the conclusion of compulsory education in Scotland. Higher Grade Examinations are taken mainly after a further period of one to two years of secondary education, but they may be taken later.

The NACETT training targets were set high, but after study, the Paul Hamlyn Foundation claimed that they do not go far enough. In light of past numbers of successful completers of training programs, the National Commission on Education (1993) doubted the likelihood of attaining even the existing targets. Given that only 51 percent of 16- to 24-year-olds were qualified to NVQ Level II in 1991, with a growth rate of only 1 to 2 percent each year thereafter, the prospect of reaching 80 percent within the target period is remote. The chances of reaching the NVQ Level III target are also gloomy.

ASCETT (1997) reported that Scotland is making better progress toward the targets, but that organization, too, holds little promise of achieving all targets. Closing the gaps between the 1995 position and year 2000 targets would require an annual growth rate of 2.1 percent for Target 1, 3.1 percent for Target 2, and 2.6 percent for Target 3, none of which were reached for the first two years of the five-year span. ASCETT (1995) sought advice on how best to achieve the targets, but against a backdrop of national budget cuts for training and education, only efficiency gains in the deployment of resources, including education/training providers, could produce the targets. The providers had already reached their limits of "achieving more with less," making target attainment unlikely. A further hindering factor has been the disappointing completion rates for young people in training.

Despite the government's intention, announced as early as 1981 and later reinforced, that all occupations should be included in the framework of national standards, none of the first targets set for education and training referred to levels higher than 3 (Manpower Services Commission, 1981). However, in 1995, ASCETT (1995) set a target at level 4 to promote activity toward meeting the demand for higher levels of technical, professional, and managerial qualifications. These higher-level qualifications lie mainly in the sphere of the professions.

For a variety of reasons, the professions have been slow to show an interest in national standards and have not been pushed. Professional organizations, associations, institutes, and councils, either by statute or habit, serve as the guardians of professional standards and, in this regard, enjoy a large measure of autonomy. They are not employer led, as are the ILBs, occupational standards councils, or national training organizations that have recently superseded them. Professional organizations have actually declined membership in such other bodies.

In parallel with the Beaumont review discussed earlier, the DfEE (1995) circulated a consultation paper, *A Vision for Higher Level Vocational Qualifications*, seeking the views of professions, higher and further education institutions, statutory bodies, lead bodies, and award-granting bodies regarding the extension of the VQ system into higher levels (4 and 5). DfEE asked specifically for indications of interest relating to the (a) achievement of a cohesive framework for vocational qualifications at the higher levels; (b) actual structure of vocational qualifications, including matters regarding knowledge and values; and

(c) assessment, quality assurance, and benefits that could accrue to the United Kingdom from establishing a complete NVQ/SVQ framework.

Early 1996 saw the circulation of a digest of responses to the Vision document as well as a series of seminars that brought together interested parties. Although the consultation process was painstaking and thorough, it proved inconclusive. Respondents believed vocational education and training to be vitally important but lacked understanding or agreement, or perhaps were merely confused, about the nature of the vocational system and its relationship to requirements for professional registration with a statutory body or professional organization. Some respondents considered the VQ framework something of a mystery, and many of the respondents mentioned that further information was needed, despite the fact that a system for levels 1 through 4 had been in place for a decade. Although there were some reservations on matters of detail, a majority favored extending the provision to levels 4 and 5. A requirement for working partnerships among all stakeholders—employers, professionals, and further and higher education—was thought important, but how to best achieve the partnership remained a controversial issue (DfEE, 1997).

Assessment within the VQ framework was another cause for concern. Respondents from the higher education sector commented that "knowledge must be treated holistically . . . [claiming that] it was neither feasible, nor desirable, at these levels to relate items of knowledge to particular elements of competence" (DfEE, 1997). Obviously, a problem exists related to individual understanding of the meanings of terms, similar to what Beaumont encountered in the evaluation of the top 100 VQs. Respondents further pointed to the issue of who should set standards and thereafter monitor their application—Occupational Standards Councils (now National Standards Organisations) or professional bodies with statutory powers.

NEW PLANS AND ORGANIZATIONS

A new government in mid-1996, with a new political party in power, initiated a major review of education and training arrangements. As a result, separate departments for education and employment and training matters, which had failed to work well, were merged into a single Department for Education and Employment (DfEE). Within the Scottish Office, a new combined Education and Industry Department (SOEID) was formed. In addition, three special committees formed to investigate aspects of education and training and recommend improvements:

• The Dearing Committee, supplemented in Scotland by the Garrick Committee, reported on higher education.

• The Kennedy Committee, appointed by the Further Education Funding Council, looked into the provision for further education.

• The National Advisory Group for Continuing Education and Lifelong Learning, set up by the Secretary of State for Education and Employment and chaired by Bob Fryer, gave advice on an array of matters related to adult learning.

Dearing's committee focused on the need to (a) enhance the financial resources devoted to higher education, to enable expansion to continue, thereby making the participation levels sought by government attainable; and (b) promote teaching excellence in universities and colleges of higher learning. It further proposed that any future expansion should be at the subdegree level (SCAA, 1996).

Kennedy and her committee argued that the future prosperity of the country depended on the quality of its education provision and, more specifically, on further education, namely technical/vocational education and training. Her committee argued that ways should be found to widen participation in further education (DfEE, 1997).

Fryer was directed to examine the findings of the Dearing and Kennedy committees and,

thereafter, to advise on measures that could be undertaken to extend lifelong and workplace learning opportunities to those who had previously been excluded, but whose participation could benefit them and the wider community (National Advisory Group for Continuing Education and Lifelong Learning [NAGCELL], 1998).

Legislation based on the early phases of the review is progressing in the form of the Teaching and Higher Education Bill. Among the proposals issued in connection with the legislation is the introduction of a requirement, recommended by the Dearing Committee, that students contribute to their course tuition fees. Some fear that such a requirement would severely disadvantage students from socially deprived areas. Further-education colleges worry that it would markedly affect their enrollment. Historically, colleges have provided access to students with backgrounds not conducive to "going to university." Many people believe that many such students would be unwilling to saddle themselves with substantial loans to finance their studies.

While these developments are being considered for further and higher education, the new DfEE has been enunciating its aims and objectives. The DfEE's aims are to "enable everyone, through the best possible opportunities in education, training, and work, to enjoy a fulfilling life, to have a stake in society, and to contribute to Britain's competitiveness in the twenty-first century." Its objectives are to:

• Ensure that all young people reach 16 years of age with the highest standards of basic skills and a secure foundation for lifelong learning, work, and citizenship.

• Encourage people to continue throughout their lives to develop their knowledge, skills, and understanding and to improve their employability in the job market.

• Help people who have no job to gain work.

• Promote equality of opportunity in education and training and at work, including tackling issues of social exclusion, deprivation, and underachievement (DfEE, 1998b).

It remains to be seen how much of the education and training infrastructure will remain intact as the government seeks to attain these objectives. Already, a network of National Training Organisations is being put into place to provide strategic support. In April 1998, responsibility for the national standards moved from the DfEE to the Qualifications and Curriculum Authority and the Scottish Qualifications Authority (DfEE, 1998b).

A second, more-far-reaching phase of the education and training review is now underway. DfEE (1998a) published and disseminated a green paper, *The Learning Age*, as a means of consulting on (a) possible directions for the future of education and (b) the need, already identified by the government, for a new strategy for lifelong learning. This particular paper was not distributed in Scotland, but another one, specifically related to Scotland, is said to be forthcoming. Britain's Prime Minister, The Right Honorable Tony Blair, echoing Kennedy and her committee, introduced the newest document with the view that "education is the best economy policy [Britain has]."

References

Advisory Scottish Council for Education and Training Targets. (1995). *World class Scotland: Education and training targets for a competitive Scotland.* Glasgow, Scotland: Author.

Advisory Scottish Council for Education and Training Targets. (1997). *Annual report.* Glasgow, Scotland: Author.

Beaumont, G. (1996a). *Review.* Glasgow, Scotland: Scottish Vocational Education Council (Scottish Qualifications Authority).

Beaumont, G. (1996b). *Review of 100 NVQs and SVQs.* London: Crown Office.

Crown Office. (1991a). *Access opportunity: A strategy for education and training.* Sheffield, England: Author.

Crown Office. (1991b). *Education and training for the 21st century.* Sheffield, England: Author.

Department for Education and Employment. (1994). *Competence and assessment* (Compendium No. 3). London: Crown Office.

Department for Education and Employment. (1995). *A vision for higher level vocational qualifications.* London: Crown Office.

Department for Education and Employment. (1997). *Learning works: Widening participation in further education* (The Kennedy report). London: Crown Office.

Department for Education and Employment. (1998a). *The learning age* (Green paper). London: Crown Office.

Department for Education and Employment. (1998b). *Learning and working together* (Prospectus). London: Crown Office.

Gunning, D. (1994). *General SVQs: Evolution, not revolution.* Glasgow, Scotland: Scottish Vocational Education Council (Scottish Qualifications Authority).

Her Majesty's Inspectors of Schools. (1991). *Six years on.* Edinburgh, Scotland: Her Majesty's Stationery Office.

Manpower Services Commission. (1981). *A new training initiative: A programme for action.* London: Author.

Mansell, J. (1986). RVQ: A recognition of change. *Coombe Lodge Report, 18*(9), 236-237.

National Advisory Group for Continuing Education and Lifelong Learning. (1998). *Learning for the twenty-first century* (The Fryer report). London: Author.

National Commission on Education. (1993). *Learning to succeed* (Report of the Paul Hamlyn Foundation). Oxford, England: Heinemann.

National Council for Vocational Qualifications. (1996). *National standards.* Sheffield, England: Crown Office.

Niven, S. M. (1982). *Vocational education in Scotland.* Glasgow, Scotland: Jordanhill College of Education.

School Curriculum and Assessment Authority. (1996). *The national curriculum and its assessment* (The Dearing report). London: Author.

Scottish Education Department. (1979). *16 to 18's in Scotland: The first two years of post-compulsory education.* Edinburgh, Scotland: Author.

Scottish Education Department. (1983). *16-18's in Scotland: An action plan.* Edinburgh, Scotland: Author.

Scottish Office Education and Industry Department. (1994). *Higher still.* Edinburgh, Scotland: Author.

Scottish Office Education Department. (1983). *Module descriptor guidelines.* Edinburgh, Scotland: Author.

Scottish Qualifications Authority. (1997a). *Catalogue of higher national units.* Glasgow, Scotland: Author.

Scottish Qualifications Authority. (1997b). *Catalogue of national certificate modules.* Glasgow, Scotland: Author.

Scottish Vocational Education Council (Scottish Qualifications Authority). (1994). *Specifications for GSVQs.* Glasgow, Scotland: Author.

Scottish Vocational Education Council. (1996). *Review of 100 NVQs/SVQs—A report on the findings of NCVQ/SCOTVEC.* (1996). Glasgow, Scotland: Author.

Training and Development Lead Body. (1992). *National standards for training and development.* Sheffield, England: Crown Office.

Appendix A—List of Acronyms

ASCETT   Advisory Scottish Council for Education and Training Targets

BTEC   Business and Technical Education Council

CGLI   City and Guilds of London Institute

DfEE   Department for Education and Employment

GVQ   General Vocational Qualification

GNVQ   General National Vocational Qualification

GSVQ   General Scottish Vocational Qualification

HM   Her Majesty's

ILB   Industry Lead Body

NACETT   National Advisory Council for Education and Training Targets

NAGCELL   National Advisory Group for Continuing Education and Lifelong Learning

NCE   National Commission on Education

NCVQ   National Council for Vocational Qualifications

NTO   National Training Organization

NVQ   National Vocational Qualification

RET   Record of Education and Training

RSA   Royal Society of Arts

SCAA   Scottish Curriculum and Assessment Authority

SCEEB   Scottish Certificate of Education Examinations Board

SCOTVEC   Scottish Council for Vocational Education

SNCM   Scottish National Certificate Module

SOEID   Scottish Office Education and Industry Department

SQA   Scottish Qualifications Authority

SVQ   Scottish Vocational Qualification

TDLB   Training and Development Lead Body

TVET   Technical and vocational education and training

VQ   Vocational Qualification

Appendix B—Sample Module Descriptor

Module Title
Stringed Instruments: Manufacture of Components

Learning Outcomes
The candidate should:
1. Manufacture jigs and templates.
2. Manufacture instrument neck and fingerboard.
3. Prepare instrument front.
4. Prepare instrument back.
5. Prepare and bind instrument sides.

Performance Criteria for Learning Outcome 1
1.1 Instruments are correctly cut.
1.2 Instrument mold is correctly manufactured.
1.3 Jigs are produced according to accepted workshop procedures.

Adapted from: Scottish Qualifications Authority (1997b).

Appendix C—Stages of Analysis for the Field of Training and Development

Stage 1: Areas of Competence
At the first level of analysis of the field of training and development, five Areas are defined:
A. Identify training and development needs.
B. Design training and development strategies and plans.
C. Provide learning opportunities, resources, and support.
D. Evaluate the effectiveness of training and development.
E. Support training and development advances and practice.

Stage 2: Key Roles
At the second level of analysis, Key Roles (coded A1, A2, A3, . . . ; B1, B2, B3, . . . ; etc.) are identified within each Area of Competence. For example:

D2. Evaluate individual and group achievements against objective.

Stage 3: Units of Competence
At the third level of analysis, the Key Roles are disaggregated into Units of Competence, coded A11, A12, A13 . . . ; A21, A22, A23 . . . ; A31, A32, A33 . . . ; . . . B21, B22, . . . ; . . . C11, C12 . . . ; etc. For example:

D23. Modify and adapt learning plans.

Stage 4: Elements of Competence
At the fourth level of analysis, Units of Competence are disaggregated into Elements of Competence,

coded A111, A112, A113 . . . ; A121, A122, A123
. . . ; A131, A132, A133 . . . ; B211, B212, B213
. . . ; C121, C122, C123 . . . ; etc. For example:

D231. Modify and adapt learning programs.

Performance Criteria
Standard D231, for which "Modify and adapt learning programs" is the Element of Competence, has
the following Performance Criteria:
a. Results of relevant evaluations are used to identify modifications and adaptations to learning programs.
b. Coherent and relevant proposals which have the
greatest potential for success are selected and
promoted.
c. Justifications for proposed modifications are presented clearly.
d. Learners and decision-makers are given opportunities to ask questions and seek clarification.
e. In cases where learners seek assistance in choosing between alternative modifications to the learning program, appropriate and realistic alternatives,
as well as clear choice criteria, are identified.
f. Agreements about modifications and adaptations
are conducted and concluded in a manner which
promotes goodwill.
g. Agreed modifications and adaptations are accurately summarized and made available to the appropriate personnel.

THE BREAKDOWN FOR AREA OF COMPETENCE "A," SHOWN SCHEMATICALLY, IS AS FOLLOWS:

Area	Key roles	Units of competence	Elements of competence
A	A1	A11	A111 A112 A113 . . .
		A12	A121 A122 A123 . . .
		A13	A131 A132 . . .
	A2	A21	A211 A212 . . .

Adapted from: Training and Development Lead Body (1992).

11

A Social Partnership:
The European Union
and Irish Vocational Education
and Training

By Jim Gleeson

This chapter discusses key aspects of Ireland's development of publicly funded vocational education and training (VET[1]), along with related policy issues. Like its economy, Ireland's public education system is undergoing significant change. Until recently, the postprimary education emphasized academic preparation for university study. However, Ireland's membership in the European Community resulted in the introduction of new thinking and values and the availability of very significant additional resources for VET.

Ireland's serious unemployment problems of the 1980s resulted in a major emphasis on social partnership to produce competitive enterprises and modernize public service. This led to the negotiation of partnership agreements that stress, among other things, the role of education and training in tackling social exclusion. The contribution of European Union (EU) membership and the partnership ap-

proach to VET policy and practice in Ireland, as well as the importance of vocational and technical education and training to developing human capital, round out the focus of this chapter.

THE GENERAL CONTEXT

The Republic of Ireland has a population of approximately 3.6 million, with a density of 50 per square kilometer. An important characteristic of the population is its youthfulness, which places enormous pressure on the education system (Clancy, Drudy, Lynch, & O'Dowd, 1995, p. 49). Expansion of the education system has been remarkable, with numbers at the second level growing from 98,800 in 1960 to almost 370,000 in 1997-98. Retention rates (up to the end of second-level schooling) rose from 20 percent in 1960 to approximately 80 percent in 1997 (higher for women), higher than the average in other Organization

[1]See the Appendix, page 160, for a list of acronyms used in this chapter, and their meanings.

for Economic Cooperation and Development (OECD) member states (OECD, 1997).

The number of students in higher education has grown from 18,500 in 1965 to almost 107,500 in 1996-97. It is projected to reach 121,000 by 2010 (OECD, 1997, p. 111). More than 40 percent of the school-leaving age cohort now progress to third-level education, and this proportion will approach 50 percent by the year 2000 as the size of the age cohort falls and more college places are provided (National Economic and Social Council [NESC], 1996, p. 8).

Ireland had the second lowest working population (in percentage terms) in the EU through the 1980s when unemployment rose steadily, reaching more than 17 percent in 1986. The working population dropped significantly over the next 12 years and stood at less than 8 percent in May 1998 (Central Statistics Office [CSO], 1987, 1998).

The Changing Face of Education

Until around 1965, Ireland had a dual, or bipartite, postprimary system of education. Its main element was the traditional, privately owned, usually parochial, secondary school that offered an academic, humanistic curriculum leading to higher education and, afterward, employment in the public service. Such schools were attended primarily by students from upper- and middle-class families. Secondary schools enjoyed higher status than the alternative system of vocational education, controlled by local authorities, which was of two years duration and led to technical education, apprenticeships, and entry to the workforce.

With the new emphasis on investment in education in the mid-1960s, the government permitted vocational schools to offer a full range of subjects and examinations previously available only in secondary schools. Around this time, also, a short-lived attempt was made to introduce comprehensive schools, but this endeavor found only limited success due to local political forces. Community schools were established during the 1970s, with provision for greater local and religious involvement in school management. As a consequence, Ireland has a complex system of postprimary schools, falling into three main types: (a) secondary (attended by approximately 60 percent of students); (b) vocational schools/community colleges (approximately 25 percent); and (c) community/comprehensive schools (approximately 15 percent).

Notwithstanding the differing traditions and subject specialties of each type of school, they do have similarities. All offer a comprehensive curriculum, though there is less vocational emphasis in secondary schools than in the other two types.

Vocational Education and Training

VET in Ireland is primarily the responsibility of two government departments: (a) Education and Science and (b) Enterprise, Trade and Employment (formerly Labour, later Enterprise and Employment). Relations between these departments have been characterized by tension and rivalry. The main quasi-independent governmental agencies responsible for training (outside of education) are

• FAS, the industrial training and employment agency, provides myriad programs ranging from apprenticeships to community training workshops for under-25s to community education programs for the long-term unemployed. It also offers placement and guidance to those who have left formal education.

• CERT, the training agency for the Hotel, Catering and Tourism Authority.

• TEAGASC, the advisory and training agency of the agricultural and food sectors.

The following aspects of the Irish situation have particular relevance for the VET issue:

1. Most students complete second-level schooling at 17 to 18 years of age, which is two years younger than in most EU-member states. Many complete university at age 20, having taken three-year degree courses.

2. Until recently, employers had the option of hiring workers home from the traditional migratory destination in neighboring Britain,

with the result that Ireland has not experienced specific skill shortages.

3. Educational opportunities are unevenly distributed across society (McCormack & Archer, 1998; Raftery & Hout, 1993). Hannan, Hovels, Van Den Berg, and White (1995) have drawn attention to the "sharp contrast between the returns [benefits] to taking or not taking qualifications in Ireland and the UK [United Kingdom]. These differences in returns are consistent with the rapid increase in qualification levels in Ireland and the slow advance of qualifications in the UK during the 1980s" (p. 336).

4. Education expenditure rose from 16 percent of total government expenditure in 1965 to 19 percent in 1998 and from 3.2 percent of gross national product (GNP) in 1965 to 5.8 percent in 1998. While these figures are around the OECD average, Irish expenditure per pupil is much lower than in other member countries (OECD, 1995, p. 73; 1998).

Impact of the European Social Fund

"It is clear that, without the support of the ESF [European Social Fund], Initial Vocational Education and Training in Ireland would be a pale shade of what it actually is," O'Connor (1998, p. 66) observed. The ESF was established in 1957 under Article 123 of the Treaty of Rome to improve job opportunities in the European Economic Community (EEC, as it was then known) by promoting employment and increasing worker mobility. During the 1960s and 70s, increasing rates of unemployment resulted in the restructuring of the ESF, with the result that over 90 percent of total funding was directed to vocational training measures aimed at specific categories of workers and at tackling structural unemployment (Hantrais, 1995). By 1977, the enlarged EEC found it necessary to broaden the scope of the ESF to include migrant workers; unemployed women over 25 years of age, or those wishing to return to work; and unemployed people under age 25, especially first-job seekers.

In response to the 1977 resolution, Ireland developed preemployment courses (PECs) at second-level schools. Certain courses in third-level regional technical colleges also received ESF support. PECs were initially confined to vocational, community, and comprehensive schools (which together would have catered to about 30 percent of all second-level students at the time) and were aimed at students who would otherwise have left school early in search of employment. Some 1,800 students, mostly males attending vocational schools, participated in the first year.

It soon became clear that youth unemployment was not a transitory phenomenon and that transition from school to work was a complex process rather than simply a matter of getting a job. The personal development of young people became a major concern. This was accompanied by a shift in emphasis from discrete job-specific skills toward a broader approach that included training in general skills, reflecting the need for young people to be adaptable at a time when traditional categories of jobs and skills were disappearing. Among the most significant influences on the postprimary curriculum were the European Commission's transition projects focusing on the transition from school to adult and working life in the nine member states. These initiatives were targeted at early school-leavers and those for whom the academic senior cycle was unsuitable (Gleeson, 1990).

With youth unemployment levels continuing to rise across Europe, the Social Guarantee was introduced in 1982 "to provide support for the implementation of a training guarantee for all young people and to promote a dynamic response to the problem of youth unemployment" (O'Connor, 1998, p. 58). At least 75 percent of the ESF was now earmarked for spending on schemes that would enhance the employability of young people under age 18 by combining vocational training and work experience, as well as that of unemployed persons in the 18- to 25-year age bracket.

This development was followed in 1983 by

an EEC resolution entitled "Vocational Training Policy in the Community in the 1980's." The resolution guaranteed access for unemployed school-leavers to full-time programs of basic training and work experience under the terms of the Social Guarantee.

In 1984, second-level schools introduced vocational preparation and training programs (VPTs), which replaced the earlier PECs and had similar curriculum lines. People in the 18- to 25-year age range who took middle-level technician courses in regional technical colleges were the beneficiaries.

This extension of aid from the ESF meant that secondary schools were permitted to introduce the new VPT program for the first time in September 1984. Of the 380 schools that offered VPT programs in the first year, 118 (out of 700 total) were secondary schools.

O'Connor (1998) explained that the adoption of the Single European Act in 1987 resulted in "a global integrated approach to working together towards the goal of economic and social cohesion and to the situation where the Funds began to shape policy because the Commission had discretion over approximately one third of the allocation to the Member States." ESF funding doubled between 1989 and 1993. Of the 20 billion European Currency Units (ECU) allocated over that period, Ireland received 1.5 billion ECU—almost 8 percent of the total amount available. The adoption of the principle of *additionality* meant that (a) the structural funds should not be used to replace national funds and (b) there should be an equivalent increase in overall national spending on relevant activities. In addition to the structural funds, 15 percent of the total budget was retained to fund community vocational education and training initiatives (known by their acronyms as EUROFORM, NOW, HORIZON, and PETRA), as well as innovative actions and studies relating to new approaches in vocational training and employment policies. Many of these initiatives facilitated transnational work experience for VET participants (Gleeson & McCarthy, 1996).

ESF eligibility rules were changed in 1988 and young people above the age of compulsory schooling who were being trained within the formal education system qualified for support. O'Connor (1998) commented that "this effectively finally abolished the 'ancient dichotomy' between education and training" (p. 3). Only four years earlier, the Ages of Learning policy proposal displayed a prominent distinction between postprimary education, on the one hand, and vocational education and training, on the other. The inclusion of that distinction was a matter of some heated debate (Department of Education, 1984).

Following the key principles of the European Commission's (1994) white paper, ESF aid to Ireland for the period 1993-1999 doubled again. Over the period 1994-99, the Department of Education received some 930 million ECU for programs in second- and third-level education. At present this supports curriculum reforms at the senior cycle (ages 15 to 18), which are discussed below (O'Connor, 1998, p. 65).

SOCIAL PARTNERSHIP AT THE NATIONAL LEVEL

Partnership has been an absolutely central plank of Irish policy during the past 12 years. During U. S. President Clinton's September 1998 visit to Ireland, the slogan "Celebrating the Success of Partnership in Ireland" was displayed prominently behind the speakers. The Tanaiste (Deputy Prime Minister), Mary Harney, Minister for Enterprise, Trade and Employment, speaking on September 24, 1998, at a Conference on EU Venture and Seed Capital Measure, referred to the Irish system of social partnership as "unique in Europe and unthinkable in America," adding that "it has now been virtually built into the fabric of our system of government."

The partnership approach to running Ireland was adopted in 1987 on the recommendation of the National Economic and Social Council. The then-Director of NESC commented that "in a context of deep despair in

Irish society, the social partners . . . hammered out an agreed strategy to escape from the vicious circle of real stagnation, rising taxes and exploding debt" (O'Donnell & Thomas, 1998, p. 122).

There were three main parties to the first partnership agreement, along with the elected government of the day: business and industry, trade unions, and the farming sector. These were joined by the community and voluntary sector, which constitutes the fourth pillar of the social partnership strategy.

The first agreement—the Programme for National Recovery—achieved trade union support for a radical correction of public finances in return for maintaining the value of social welfare payments and the promise of income tax reforms. This support was based on the understanding that there would be four such agreements. It was followed by the Programme for Economic and Social Progress from 1990 to 1993, the Programme for Competitiveness and Work from 1994 to 1996, and Partnership 2000 from 1997 to 2000 (Government of Ireland, 1987, 1991, 1993, 1996).

All four agreements followed a similar form: (a) setting out pay increases for the period in question; (b) making commitments to social equity and tax reform, as well as introducing policy initiatives such as "local pay bargaining;" (c) establishing partnership companies to tackle long-term unemployment; (d) developing a national center to promote partnership at enterprise level; and (e) developing the strategic management initiative for public service modernization. During the period 1986-1998, Irish gross domestic product (GDP) grew by an average of 6.5 percent a year compared with an OECD average of 2.7 percent, while employment grew 1.8 percent per year compared with an OECD average of 1.0 percent and an EU average of 0.4 percent. Ireland's debt-to-GDP ratio fell from 117 percent in 1986 to 73 percent in 1997, with growth accelerating especially during 1993-97 when GDP grew by 7.7 percent per year and employment rose by 4 percent each year (OECD, 1997, 1998).

Arising from the involvement of an increasing number of social partners and the recognized need for government and business to take social issues seriously, the National Economic and Social Forum (NESF) was established in 1993. It developed policy initiatives to combat unemployment and contributed to a national consensus on social and economic matters. The emphasis on greater social inclusion resulted in the development of a National Anti-Poverty Strategy which (a) intends to "poverty-proof" new policy, and (b) regards education and training as particularly important (National Economic and Social Forum [NESF], 1997).

The strategy of consensus through partnership was also used in the preparation of a 1994-1999 National Development Plan submitted to the European Community as a plan for employment (Government of Ireland, 1994, p. 9). The Plan's central objective is "to ensure the best long-term return for the economy by increasing output, economic potential, and long-term jobs. . . . It is further designed to reintegrate the long-term unemployed and those at risk of becoming so into the economic mainstream" (pp. 7, 31). Each of the four partnership programs includes a commitment to focus resources on the disadvantaged and to provide a range of education/training programs suited to their abilities and aptitudes. The focus rests on initial and prevocational preparation in school and nonformal education settings.

The Plan generally emphasizes human resource development and promises a "balanced and comprehensive range of programs covering initial education and training, continuing training for the unemployed and the employed, and training for the disadvantaged" (Government of Ireland, 1994, p. 36). The more recent social partnership agreements include the general population as well as the disadvantaged.

In Partnership 2000, the emphasis shifts perceptibly away from formal education toward nonformal education and training, with breaking of the intergenerational cycle of poverty and disadvantage as the primary objective (Government of Ireland, 1996). Partnership 2000's priorities include (a) tackling the issue of early school leaving, (b) improving access to second- and third-level education for disadvantaged groups, (c) increased participation rates of nonstandard applicants in third-level education, (d) expanding the number of places in Youthreach and Vocational Training Opportunity Scheme programs (discussed in more detail later), (e) strengthening the education service for travelers and the disabled, (f) deepening business-education links and cooperation, (g) enhancing the work of the Youth Service, and (h) increasing support for parental involvement in education.

O'Donnell and Thomas (1998) drew attention to the power of the partners and use of partnerships for legitimation purposes in Ireland. They supported this claim with a quote from a senior civil servant in the Department of the Tanaiste:

> The social partners are now a more powerful influence in the policy process, to the extent that some politicians feel that trade unionists, for example, have more power than back-benchers. It would be unthinkable to set up a task force or policy committee of any seriousness or weight without social partner representation. (p. 126).

As O'Donnell and Thomas (1998) further observed, "Informal, highly personalized interaction between the principal participants remains an integral feature of this emerging corporatist governance" (p. 126). There is a real danger, in the context of a small country, that the relationships that build up over the years between representatives of the partners can make it harder for them to address fundamental differences.

Beginning in 1984 with the Interim Curriculum and Examinations Board, the partnership approach has been increasingly adopted as a strategy for consensus seeking in education. The National Education Convention (NEC) represents Ireland's most celebrated example of the partnership approach in education. Some 42 bodies from diverse backgrounds participated in the 1994 convention. This included representatives of schools; managerial organizations at primary-, second-, and third-level education; teacher unions; national parent councils; and curriculum and assessment organizations; as well as social partners. The social partners were represented by farming and employer organizations, trade unions, and cultural groups. The Union of Students of Ireland, which normally represents the interests of third-level students, spoke on behalf of all school-goers (Coolahan, 1994).

The NEC agenda included provision for 15 discussion sessions, over a 10-day period, dealing with a wide range of topics not including VET. Analysis of the verbatim account of the NEC sessions shows that only 2 out of the 44 presentations referred specifically to VET: the National Council for Vocational Awards (NCVA) and the Irish Vocational Education Association (the umbrella body for the local vocational education committees). This neglect reflects the reality that VET was not a high-priority issue. Moreover, one presentation referred to post-leaving certificate courses (PLCs) as the "twilight zone of Irish education" (Coolahan, 1994, p. 4).

RECENT POLICY

The promotion of vocational education began to emerge as a major issue in Ireland in the 1980s, resulting from the belief that high levels of skill would bring more rapid economic growth. Policy statements of the time concentrated on the need to develop alternative curricula in postcompulsory education rather than on the reform of traditional curricula. They showed a greater concern for the education-work nexus and for students who performed poorly in the system and had poor employment prospects (Lewis & Kellaghan, 1987, p. 12).

In response, the Further Education Unit was established in the Department of Education. The NCVA (which is responsible for the development, professional support, assessment, and certification of vocational programs) was established in 1991. The National Economic and Social Council (1993), in considering the adequacy of vocational education and training policy, observed that

[o]ne of the most strikingly distinctive features of the Irish vocational education and training system from an international comparative perspective is the limited amount of structured training which occurs in the workplace and the peripheral role of employers in the education and training system. (p. 222)

Stokes and Watters (1997) identified the key principles of vocational training in Ireland as
• Access for diverse target groups.
• Provision for recognizing achievement through a comprehensive national framework of certification.
• Provision for progression through the system.
• The establishment of national standards of achievement quality, relevance, and partnership.
• The location of the learner at the center of the education and training process.
• An emphasis on lifelong learning (p. 11).
The 1990s saw a proliferation of policy statements related to education and training, beginning with the European Commission's (1994) white paper. The paper's policy statements were based on (a) the belief that education and training lead to increased competitiveness and employment and (b) the concept of the knowledge-based information society. Key principles of the paper included tackling long-term unemployment and social exclusion, promoting equal opportunities, and upgrading skills and basic training for new technologies

(p. 133). It made youth unemployment a special concern and proposed ESF support to implement guaranteed access to recognized education or training for all young people under age 18. The paper viewed prevention of unemployment and early school leaving as vital to the fight against social exclusion and urged further relaxation of regulations governing eligibility for ESF support to include those at risk of becoming long-term unemployed.

The white paper placed new emphasis on vocational guidance and placement supports and on enterprise education, as well as on training, guidance for workers facing change in industrial or production systems, and the promotion of vocational training as an alternative to university study. Problems were identified regarding the applications of science and technology; the interaction between science, technology, and society; and the low- and intermediate-level skills taught in these areas. The paper further recommended the development of (a) formulas of apprenticeship and inservice training in businesses and (b) initial vocational training in special training centers as alternatives to university study (European Commission, 1994).

The white paper also identified skills that are essential for integration into society and working life:
• Mastery of linguistic, scientific, and other knowledge, as well as skills of a technological and social nature.
• Ability to develop and act in a complex and highly technological environment, as characterized particularly by the importance of information technologies.
• Ability to communicate, make contacts, organize, and so forth—the fundamental ability to acquire new knowledge and new skills (European Commission, 1994, p. 136).

Another white paper, issued by the Department of Education (1995), recommended introducing and developing more work-oriented programs at the postcompulsory stage. The 1995 paper also emphasized the need to improve the working relationship between the

Ministry of Education and Science and the Ministry of Enterprise and Employment. It proposed establishing a new Further Education Authority "to provide a coherent national development framework, appropriate to the importance of vocational education and training (outside the third level sector) and adult and continuing education" (p. 71). At present, there is still no Further Education Authority.

A Further Education Section was established with responsibility for VET programs for early school leavers and travelers, along with various forms of adult and community education, as well as PLCs. The *Charting Our Education Future* white paper proposed the establishment of TEASTAS, the Irish National Certification Authority (Department of Education, 1995). By 1996, this body was established on an ad hoc basis. It has worked closely with various interests and existing certification bodies to establish a national qualifications framework and to advise on appropriate legislation. However, legislative progress remains slow for political reasons.

The Department of Enterprise and Employment (1996) published its white paper *Science, Technology and Innovation* against a background Tierney report entitled *Making Knowledge Work for Us* (Science, Technology and Innovation Council, 1995). The white paper noted Tierney's conclusion that "one of the main factors contributing to the general lack of public understanding of science and technology in Ireland has been the comparative lack of scientific and technological training in our schools in the past" (p. 120). Quinlan (1995) further drew attention to the scientific community's findings that "the failure to promote indigenous R & D [research and development] is one of the main reasons why industrialisation has failed to deliver on initial promises" (p. 103), with the result that Ireland has successfully attracted branch plants of large multinational companies (generally requiring low-skilled workers), while evaluations and reports questioned the benefits of such plants.

The third part of this Irish trilogy of white papers, *Human Resource Development*, was also prepared by the Department of Enterprise and Employment (1997). It expressed satisfaction with international comparisons that indicate that participation up to the end of second level is high in Ireland and that participation in full-time education for 18- and 19- year-olds is higher than the OECD average. However, the paper expressed concern about the comparatively low levels of overall educational attainment because of their impact on unemployment, especially considering Ireland's historically weak tradition of vocational education and relatively high proportion of school leavers. There has been a resulting enforced emphasis on remedial education and initial reintegration and training that "diverts a high proportion of national training resources from providing for the high-level skill requirements needed to help Irish firms to be more competitive. The result is a lower level of employment creation than would otherwise be the case" (p. 45).

CURRENT PROVISIONS

Early school leavers have access to initial VET programs in out-of-school Youthreach centers. The newly structured leaving certificate, particularly in the Leaving Certificate Applied Programme and the Leaving Certificate Vocational Programme, provides for VET. Formal VET comes through PLCs, based in second-level (mainly vocational) schools and in institutes of technology (formerly called "regional technical colleges") at third level.

The needs of those who leave school at or before the end of compulsory schooling are addressed by the Youthreach program. Some 4,500 young people participated in this program in 1996. They received a weekly allowance (IR£25 per week for 15- to 17-year-olds, IR£32 per week for 17-to 18-year-olds, and IR£52.50 per week for those over 18), along with meal and travel allowances. Participants had the option of taking NCVA Foundation Level and Level 1 courses and could move further up the NCVA ladder. Responsibility for

Youthreach is shared between FAS and the Department of Education. An additional 1,000 Youthreach places were provided during 1997-98.

The Vocational Training and Opportunity Scheme (VTOS), introduced in 1989, provides full-time education and training for unemployed adults and other socially disadvantaged people. There are currently 5,000 participants, of whom approximately 70 percent left school early.

The list below describes postcompulsory education options. Following the list is a description of specific leaving certificates beyond the enrichment level.

• Transition year (optional one-year enrichment program).

• Established Leaving Certificate (two-year program).

• Vocational Leaving Certificate (two-year program).

• Applied Leaving Certificate (two-year program).

• Post-leaving certificate course (one- or two-year program).

The Established Leaving Certificate student normally takes 7 from the menu of 31 subjects with an option of ordinary and higher levels of each subject. This two-year program (universally regarded as a very "academic") is evaluated through external written examinations. The more academically able students take most subjects at higher level and compete for places in university courses that lead to employment in more lucrative careers. However, many of the students who take this "established" leaving certificate cannot be described as academically gifted. More than half of the examinations are taken at ordinary or foundation level, with one-fifth of candidates taking all their subjects at ordinary or foundation level (National Council for Curriculum and Assessment [NCCA], 1995).

Vocational Leaving Certificate students are required to take (a) three work-related "link modules" (Preparation for Work, Work Experience, and Enterprise Education), (b) Irish language, (c) a Continental language (which may be taken at the Junior Certificate level), (d) two subjects from a list of vocational subject groupings (either Specialist or Services), and (e) at least one other subject from a prescribed list. Examples of a Specialist grouping of subjects are Accounting and Business Organization, and Engineering and Technical Drawing. An example from the Services grouping is Business Organization, combined with any Specialist subject such as Construction Studies.

The Applied Leaving Certificate program is a broad-based two-year prevocational education program, intended for those who do not wish to transfer directly to third-level education. It was designed as a real alternative to the Established Leaving Certificate in terms of breadth and balance, curriculum integration and organization, pedagogy, assessment and certification, student motivation, community involvement, and general focus (Gleeson & Granville, 1996). Now that participants in the nonformal VET sector (Youthreach, VTOS, and Traveler Education Centres) have begun to participate in this program, the suitability of the school-based approach for such audiences has come under examination (Department of Education, 1995, p. 53).

Post-leaving certificate courses (PLCs), which run for either one or two years, provide integrated education, training, and work experience in second-level schools and specialist colleges for those who have completed senior cycle education. "Their objective is to meet the needs of the economy, to equip young people with the vocational and technological skills necessary for employment and progression to further education and training, and to foster innovation and adaptability in participants" (Department of Education, 1995, p. 73) through technical knowledge, personal development, and work experience. These courses developed out of VPT courses funded through the ESF. There are currently 23,000 participants in this sector in over 1,000 courses in 210 centers, representing about one-third of the age cohort.

Apprenticeship is regarded as further education by policymakers. The number of statutorily designated apprenticeable trades is currently 24, with total annual intake set at 3,500. Registered apprentices numbered 11,695 at the end of 1994, about half the total in 1980. There has been a substantial upgrading in the educational requirements for apprenticeships—whereas some 40 percent of apprentices had a group certificate or less in 1980, the proportion with a leaving certificate had increased to 60 percent by 1998.

The National Economic and Social Council (1996) found that the Irish training system needed upgrading and suggested that employers have the main responsibility for investing in the ongoing training and development of the workforce. The low level of revenue to support training, based on a 1.2 percent payroll tax, was a major concern. But, in addition, the training effort within individual firms was found insufficient, the major constraint being firms' incapability and unwillingness to invest in upgrading the skills of their employees. "At production level, operatives and supervisors receive far less training in Ireland compared with Germany" (Government of Ireland, 1992, p. 54). Small employers, in particular, simply tend not to value training investments (O'Keefe, personal communication, October 7, 1997).

Despite the expansion of education and training, apparent skill shortages exist. More emphasis has gone toward expanding computer science programs at undergraduate and postgraduate levels and on multilingual teleservices/telemarketing skills. In October 1997, the Minister of Education announced the establishment of a new industry/college initiative to jointly recruit, educate, and train technicians and expressed concern that a qualitative skills gap separates many Irish firms from best practices in competitor countries (O'Keefe, personal communication, 7 October 1997).

KEY ISSUES

In this section of the chapter, I will examine four key issues: (a) the treatment of VET in education policy and the resultant opportunity cost, (b) the related issue of a perceived academic/technical imbalance, (c) the tension between quality and equality in the context of the strengthening relationship between education and economic development, and (d) the impact of social partnership.

Education Policy and the Opportunity Cost for VET

As vocational schools became part of mainstream education during the 1960s and 70s, a significant part of the vocational ethos was inevitably lost. Barber (1989) argued that

[h]ad the vocational schools been given the responsibility for the technical/vocational sector in the senior cycle, then the secondary schools would have been comprehensive in their intake. . . . If this had succeeded it would have been necessary for the vocational schools to have responsibility for many of the courses run by the national training bodies. . . . [Instead of that, however,] the higher technical colleges have clearly set their entry requirements in line with the academic courses of the traditional secondary schools. (pp. 95-96)

When they attempted curriculum reform in the 1960s, the ministers of the day saw comprehensive schooling, not as something ideological, but as a system of education whereby academic and technical subjects should be included in a broader curriculum. The comprehensive experiment proved unsuccessful, for largely political reasons, with the result that Ireland now has a "tripartite system" supporting a hierarchical order. At the top are privately owned and managed secondary schools, followed by publicly owned comprehensive/community schools. Vocational schools are at the bottom. Barber (1989) suggested that a major cause for this failure was

the decreasing commitment of the government to its own proposals in the face of the apathy of some and the hostility of others, and the shift of focus from curricular to political (the control and management of schools) and institutional (the relationship between the various sectors of post-primary education) considerations. (pp. 128-129)

The upshot was that in 1991

only 22 per cent of Irish upper secondary school students were involved in vocational education and apprenticeship programs, compared to a mean of almost 50 percent in OECD countries generally. Although the proportion in Ireland is similar to other English speaking countries and Japan, it is substantially below some European countries where 75 per cent of upper secondary school students are in such programs. (OECD, 1995, p. 84)

O'Connor (1998) locates Ireland's treatment of VET clearly in the context of an expanding system. As participation rates grew during the 1970s, the Department of Education's policy

focused, and quite rightly, on trying to provide free general education, using the resources that were available, and since those resources included the existing vocational schools, the result was that vocational training, as such, was effectively suppressed in those schools [in favor of more academic instruction]. . . . On balance, given the economic, demographic and

social pressures of the time, this was certainly the only way of reaching the goal of offering free secondary education to all, but it had the clear (though not obvious at the time) downside of devaluing the vocational tradition and vocational education in general. (pp. 66-67)

Ironically, the availability of EU support retarded the development of VET structures in Ireland in three further respects. The narrow interpretation taken of the EU regulations about the funding of mainstream education resulted in a significant opportunity cost for Irish VET in that ESF-funded skills training, part of upper secondary education, and training in Europe were all located in third-level colleges. O'Connor (1998) commented that "it may very well have been that a far-reaching decision was taken affecting the whole development of vocational education in Ireland on the basis of a suspect interpretation of a funding regulation" (p. 69). Second, the fact that the rival Department of Labour (now the Department of Enterprise and Employment) was Ireland's official interlocutor with the European Commission meant that "there is at least a suspicion that decisions about which programmes were developed and by whom were money decisions, rather than decisions with an education/training rationale" (p. 69). Third, the ESF support was project based up to the end of the 1980s, because unemployment problems were still viewed as transitory, needing ad hoc solutions using existing structures and delivery mechanisms. This meant that all funding was on a year-to-year basis, which made it possible to offer long-term or permanent contracts for project staff.

The Technical/Academic Imbalance?

During the 1980s and early 1990s, interest in reverting to a dual system of education and training arose. The argument was that a dual system that separated academic and vocational education streams could more efficiently meet the manpower needs for industrial enterprise development. Financial resources would be more clearly focused on domestic manpower requirements, and there would be less tendency for vocational programs to drift in the direction of academic-type education (Government of Ireland, 1991, pp. 53-54; 1992, p. 53).

The Industrial Policy Review Group recommended the introduction of the German dual system, concluding that

> there is not enough emphasis in Irish second-level education on technical and vocational training. Over the years the prestige of the academic Leaving Certificate programme has diverted students who would be much better adapted to a technical training programme. A high proportion of school-leavers describe their schooling in dismissive terms: they can see clearly its lack of relevance for them. (Government of Ireland, 1992, p. 53)

However, Ireland has traditionally favored a broad-based education for all—unlike many European countries where selection takes place at 15 or 16 years of age. While senior Department of Education officials and the National Council for Curriculum and Assessment are committed to the principle of a broad, unitary education system, the question of the appropriate balance between academic and vocational education continues to be contested.

In its policy statement *Social Policy in a Competitive Economy*, the Irish Business and Employers' Confederation (IBEC) (1996) emphasized "the need to develop a broadly based education system on which more specialist knowledge and skills can be built at a later stage and as the need arises" (p. 21).

However, it is easy to understate the extent of vocationally related education in Ireland.

Fuller (1990) drew attention to the "higher visibility, status and take up of applied subjects and . . . gradual erosion of the Humanities" (pp. 175-176). She traced the emergence of strong economic interests such as the Confederation of Irish Industry who were committed to shaping curricula, and observed that "the coalescence of State and economic interests provided the context for renewed efforts to redefine 'cultural capital' as legitimated in schools, in accordance with the perceived need to link education and economic planning even more closely" (pp. 175-176).

Lynch (1989) showed that postprimary schooling is characterized by competitive individualism, authoritarianism, and technicism, with an increasing proportion of young people following scientific, technical, or applied linguistic subjects within the so-called general stream of education. This is supported by OECD (1995) figures:

> The proportion of mathematics, science and engineering graduates in the 25 to 34 age group in Ireland is second only to Japan and is nearly 40 per cent above the mean in the OECD area despite a very high rate of emigration. In addition, the expansion of sub-degree higher education has been concentrated in the area of technical studies. (p. 84)

Yet, biology is the only science/technology subject in the 10 most popular leaving certificate subjects (NCCA, 1995, p. 30).

Parity of esteem for vocational education is an issue in Irish education as elsewhere. Young (1993) argued that "academic/vocational distinctions are a basic structural feature of all education systems of industrial societies [and are] inescapably embedded in other social divisions" such as workplace divisions between mental and manual labor. But there is the prospect that the combined pressures of new technology and global competition will force the abandonment of such forms of work organization in order to improve competitiveness, with the result that "overcoming academic/vocational divisions becomes an economic necessity" (pp. 212-213).

EFFICIENCY VERSUS EQUALITY

Ever since the *Investment in Education* report of 1966 (prepared for OECD), there has been tension between its twin goals—human capital production and equality of educational opportunity. O'Sullivan (1989) argued that "it is clear that equal opportunity, despite its frequent citation as an ideal, was never confronted as a concept demanding analysis and elaboration" (p. 243). Breen, Hannan, Rottoman, and Whelan (1990) described how the Irish state became interventionist in the late 1950s, thus developing a welfare system that resulted in high taxes and spending, but failed to "significantly reduce inequity and certainly failed to abate the importance of class in determining life chances" (p. 97). Hannan (1997), Research Professor at the Economic and Social Research Institute, observed that

> [o]ver ninety per cent of those who leave school without any qualifications come from lower working class or small farm backgrounds, over half have fathers who are not employed, and a very high proportion come from the most disadvantaged backgrounds. . . . [Ireland has] effectively built up a potential underclass, most of whose members are excluded from actively participating in the economy. (p. 8)

The tension between equity and efficiency is reflected in Ireland's National Development Plan and in the four social partnership agreements where both macroeconomic policy and tackling social exclusion were established as goals. However, as Hannan (1997) observed,

"[T]he national anti-poverty strategy does set brave objectives for itself—but given the competitive structure of Irish schooling it is difficult to see how these objectives can be achieved without more serious structural innovation than is proposed" (p. 9).

The current Irish Tanaiste, Mary Harney (1998), proposed a solution to the efficiency-versus-equality dilemma. Referring to the debate as to which economic model is ultimately the best—the enterprise model from America or the social model from Europe—she declared that

> Americans argue that their system is best able to deliver jobs. On the other hand, many Europeans argue . . . that social justice has been sacrificed in pursuit of economic growth. I would like to suggest that there is a middle way and that we in Ireland might have something to contribute to this debate.

She was referring to Ireland's experiment with social partnership.

While much of the credit for Ireland's current efficiency and success is attributable to the quality of the education system, some commentators remain unconvinced. Marie Geoghegan-Quinn (1998), a former senior government minister, asserted,

> [T]he reality is that for the vast majority of jobs, a narrow set of trainable skills is what is required, and if those skills can be delivered by a country where wages are one-eighth the European going rate and where industrial unrest is unheard of, so much the better. (p. 12)

TRANSLATING PARTNERSHIP INTO REALITY

As the newest and most innovative of the VET programs, the two-year Applied Leaving

Certificate raises interesting questions about partnership in practice. While the "ring-fenced" nature of the program allows considerable freedom for innovation on the one hand, it increases the fear of stigmatization on the other. Fears that participants in alternative, less-academic school programs are in danger of being "ghetto-ized," have been voiced, for example, at the National Education Convention: "Since the course will not lead to formal vocational qualifications and the course's certificands may only progress to limited courses of post-secondary education, there is a distinct danger that it will be seen as a 'soft-option' track and of limited value by students" (Coolahan, 1994, p. 76).

Recognition of the new award by employers and further education agencies puts the implementation of the partnership model to the test. While Applied Leaving Certificate students may progress to some forms of further education and training via a post-leaving certificate course, the primary concern of the typical participant is with the acceptability of the qualification to employers, including the State itself (Gleeson & Granville, 1996). NESC (1993) suggested that "the prospects for success of alternatives to the present general Leaving Certificate would be enhanced by linking such programmes, through structured and possibly exclusive routes, to further training and into the labour force" (p. 211). This proposal for preferential treatment asks a real question of the partnership approach as applied to VET. Notwithstanding the rhetoric of the partnership agreements in relation to the ending of social exclusion, the partners have not as yet shown any inclination to implement the NESC suggestion.

This leaving certificate throws up a second critical issue in relation to the partnership approach to national policymaking. The largest teacher union at postprimary level refused to implement the school-based assessment proposals that were an integral part of the program as designed. This refusal seriously curtails program effectiveness. While the Irish Congress of Trade Unions played a most responsible and strategically important role in the achievement of a partnership approach to government at the macro level, here we find one of its strongest constituent unions refusing to cooperate with a vital aspect of an initiative developed to address the needs of those most likely to experience the worst effects of inequality.

Social partnership is also coming under pressure: trade unions are becoming increasingly unhappy with the current situation. Roisin Callender (1998), National Equality Secretary of a major union, stated,

It's not enough to marvel at the fine words in chapters four and five of Partnership 2000, which deal respectively with Action for Greater Social Inclusion and Action Towards a New Focus on Equality. . . . The major point is that now, more than half way through the life of Partnership 2000, many of these commitments have not been honoured. (p. 4)

Callender (1998) goes on to warn that "our tiger-like economic performance cannot continue unless all members of our relatively close-knit society can share in its fruits" (p. 4).

A study at University College, Dublin, examined 450 workplaces across all private sector enterprises except construction. It showed clearly that the close working relationship between employers and unions at the national level is not being replicated in the workplace, and that most of the change is management driven. Yeates (1999) observed that "in spite of a decade of social dialogue and national wage agreements, the report states that 'deadlock, stalemate and ambivalence' characterise the activities of the social partners at workplace level much more than active collaboration to promote productivity coalitions" (p. 5).

CONCLUSION

The story of VET in Ireland essentially involves dealing with social exclusion on the one hand and promoting national economic well-being on the other. While social partnership has brought significant changes for the better on the economic front, resulting in new demands on VET provision, there are grounds for concern regarding the effort to eliminate social exclusion. As Sweeney (1998) concluded, "[T]he boom changed little for a substantial minority in Ireland. . . . [T]here is still a very serious problem of poverty as Ireland enters the twenty-first century" (p. 158). At the time of writing this chapter, there is much on-going speculation as to whether (a) partnerships will continue to benefit those who need help least or (b) the rhetoric of successive agreements in relation to tackling social exclusion will become reality. Also, Ireland faces another dilemma. Because of its well-publicized economic success, the good times that have accrued from Category 1 status within the European Social Fund are nearing an end. Proposals have been submitted to the ESF for continued inclusion of Ireland's western counties in Category 1. Will the educational reforms propelled by the Social Fund also end? Europe and partnership have served Irish VET well over the past 10 years, but a crossroad lies ahead.

References

Barber, N. (1989). *Comprehensive schooling in Ireland* (Paper No. 25). Dublin, Ireland: Economic and Social Research Institute.

Breen, R., Hannan, D., Rottman, D. B., & Whelan, C. T. (1990). *Understanding contemporary Ireland: State and class development in the Republic of Ireland*. Dublin, Ireland: Gill and Macmillan.

Callender, R. (1998, August 14). Economic progress hampered by social exclusion. *Irish Times* (Business This Week), p. 4.

Central Statistics Office. (1987). *Labor force survey: 1986*. Cork, Ireland: Author.

Central Statistics Office. (1998). *Quarterly national household survey: March–May*. Cork, Ireland: Author.

Clancy, P., Drudy, S., Lynch, K., & O'Dowd, L. (Eds.). (1995). *Irish society: Sociological perspectives*. Dublin, Ireland: Institute of Public Administration.

Coolahan, J. (Ed.). (1994). *Report on the national education convention*. Dublin, Ireland: National Education Convention Secretariat.

Department of Education. (1984). *The ages of learning*. Dublin, Ireland: Stationery Office.

Department of Education. (1995). *Charting our education future* (White paper on education). Dublin, Ireland: Stationery Office.

Department of Enterprise and Employment. (1996). *Science, technology and innovation* (White paper). Dublin, Ireland: Stationery Office.

Department of Enterprise and Employment. (1997). *Human resource development* (White paper). Dublin, Ireland: Stationery Office.

European Commission. (1994). *Growth, competitiveness, employment* (White paper). Brussels, Belgium: Author.

Fuller, L. (1990). *An ideological critique of the Irish post-primary school curriculum*. Unpublished M.Ed. thesis, Maynooth University, Maynooth, Ireland.

Geoghegan-Quinn, M. (1998, January 3). Success must be measured on more than share options. *Irish Times*, p. 12.

Gleeson, J. (1990). SPIRAL 2: The Shannon initiatives. In G. McNamara, K. Williams, & D. Herron (Eds.), *Achievement and aspiration: Curricular initiatives in Irish post-primary education in the 1980's* (pp. 63-86). Dublin, Ireland: Drumcondra Teachers' Centre.

Gleeson, J., & Granville, G. (1996). Curriculum reform, educational planning and national policy: The case of the leaving certificate applied. *Irish education studies* (Vol. 15, pp. 113-132). Dublin, Ireland: Educational Studies Association of Ireland.

Gleeson, J., & McCarthy, J. (1996). The recognition and certification of transnational training and work experience placements under PETRA—An Irish perspective. *International Journal of Vocational Education and Training, 4* (2), 60-80.

Government of Ireland. (1987). *Programme for national recovery*. Dublin, Ireland: Stationery Office.

Government of Ireland. (1991). *Programme for economic and social progress*. Dublin, Ireland: Stationery Office.

Government of Ireland. (1992). *A time for change: Industrial policy for the 1990's* (Report of the Industrial Policy Review Group). Dublin, Ireland: Stationery Office.

Government of Ireland. (1993). *Programme for competitiveness and work*. Dublin, Ireland: Stationery Office.

Government of Ireland. (1994). *Programme for national development* (1994-99). Dublin, Ireland: Stationery Office.

Government of Ireland. (1996). *Partnership 2000 for inclusion, employment and competitiveness*. Dublin, Ireland: Stationery Office.

Hannan, D. (1997). Social and educational exclusion: Why more serious in Ireland? *Ceide, 1* (2), 8-9.

Hannan, D., Hovels, B., Van Den Berg, S., & White, M. (1995). Early leavers from education and training in Ireland, the Netherlands and the United Kingdom. *European Journal of Education, 30*(3), 325-346.

Hantrais, L. (1995). *Social policy in the European Union*. Dublin, Ireland: Macmillan.

Harney, M. (1998, September 24). Unpublished address to Conference on EU Seed and Venture Capital Measure, Cork, Ireland.

Irish Business and Employers' Confederation. (1996). *Social policy in a competitive economy*. Dublin, Ireland: National Archives.

Lewis, M., & Kellaghan, T. (1987). Vocationalism in Irish second-level education. *The Irish Journal of Education, 21*(1), 5-35.

Lynch, K. (1989). *The hidden curriculum—Reproduction in education: An appraisal*. London: Falmer.

McCormack, T., & Archer, P. (1998). A response to Peter Lynch's revisiting of investment in education. In B. Farrell (Ed.), *Issues in education* (Vol. 3). Dublin, Ireland: Association of Secondary Teachers, Ireland.

National Council for Curriculum and Assessment. (1995). *The 1994 leaving certificate examination: A review of results*. Dublin, Ireland: Author.

National Economic and Social Council. (1993). *Education and training policies for economic and social development*. Dublin, Ireland: Author.

National Economic and Social Council. (1996). *Strategy into the 21st century: Conclusions and recommendations*. Dublin, Ireland: Author.

National Economic and Social Forum. (1997). *A framework for partnership—Encouraging strategic consensus through partnership*. Dublin, Ireland: Author.

O'Connor, T. (1998). The impact of the European Social Fund on the development of initial vocational education and training in Ireland. In A. Trant et al. (Eds.), *The future of the curriculum*. Dublin, Ireland: City of Dublin Vocational Education Committee.

O'Donnell, R., & Thomas, D. (1998). Partnership and policy-making. In S. Healy & B. Reynolds (Eds.), *Social policy in Ireland: Principles, practice and problems* (pp. 117-146). Dublin, Ireland: Oak Tree Press.

Organization for Economic Cooperation and Development. (1995). *Economic surveys—Ireland*. Paris: Author.

Organization for Economic Cooperation and Development. (1997). *Economic surveys—Ireland*. Paris: Author.

Organization for Economic Cooperation and Development. (1998). *Economic outlook*. Paris: Author.

O'Sullivan, D. (1989). The ideational base of Irish educational policy. In D. Mulcahy & D. O'Sullivan (Eds.), *Irish educational policy: Process and substance* (pp. 219-269). Dublin, Ireland: Institute of Public Administration.

Quinlan, K. (1995). *Research and development activity in Ireland: A spatial analysis*. Maynooth, Ireland: Centre for Local and Regional Development.

Raftery, A., & Hout, M. (1993, January). Maximally maintained inequality: Expansion, reform and opportunity in Irish education, 1921-1975. *Sociology of Education, 66*, 41-62.

Science, Technology and Innovation Council. (1995). *Making knowledge work for us: Report of the Science, Technology and Innovation Council* (Tierney report). Dublin, Ireland: Stationery Office.

Stokes, D., & Watters, E. (1997). *Ireland: Vocational education and training. A guide*. Dublin, Ireland: Leonardo Da Vinci, Leargas.

Sweeney, P. (1998). *The Celtic tiger: Ireland's economic miracle explained*. Dublin, Ireland: Oak Tree Press.

Yeates, P. (1999, February 19). Study challenges partnership notions. *Irish Times* (Business This Week), p. 5.

Young, M. (1993). Bridging the academic/vocational divide: Two Nordic case studies. *European Journal of Education, 28*(2), 209-214.

Appendix—List of Acronyms

ECU	European Currency Unit (now: Euro)
EEC	European Economic Community
ESF	European Social Fund
EU	European Union
GDP	Gross domestic product
GNP	Gross national product
IBEC	Irish Business and Employers' Confederation
NCCA	National Council for Curriculum and Assessment
NCVA	National Council for Vocational Awards
NEC	National Education Convention
NESC	National Economic and Social Council
NESF	National Economic and Social Forum
OECD	Organization for Economic Cooperation and Development
PEC	Pre-employment course
PLC	Post-leaving [certificate] course
VET	Vocational education and training
VPT	Vocational preparation and training [program]
VTOS	Vocational Training and Opportunity Scheme

12

National Vocational Training Agencies: The Latin American Model

By Dennis R. Herschbach

National vocational training agencies (VTAs) are attractive, because they provide an alternative to publicly funded vocational education and training institutions. Although specific forms vary from country to country, VTAs are generally administered through federations of enterprises empowered by legislative statutes to finance, organize, and conduct training. VTAs provide a variety of training services, but in Latin America most training is concentrated in established centers and focuses on preemployment training and upgrading. Although training agencies coexist with formal vocational and technical secondary schools, they were conceived as an alternative to regular school, and there is little formal articulation between the two. Qualifications attained in one institution do not transfer to the other. Training in VTAs is focused, specific, and designed for immediate use on the job. The populations served are mainly youth above age 14 and adults. The government has representation on VTA administrative boards, but employers provide the financing through various payroll tax and rebate schemes (Centro Interamericano de Investigación y Documentación sobre Formación Profesional/International Labour Office [CINTERFOR/ILO], 1991; Ducci, 1994).

National VTAs are a relatively well-established tradition in Latin America, having begun in the larger South American countries and spread throughout the region. An essential part of labor force development systems in more than 30 newly industrialized countries, VTAs now exist in all regions of the world. The concept, however, is less well established in North America and Europe (World Bank, 1986). Nevertheless, at a time when many countries face increased pressures on public budgets for all kinds of social services, finding better ways to finance workforce preparation is crucial. The demand for education and training services of all kinds has increased, but in most countries the government's financial constraints make it difficult to address additional demands. Public forms of vocational education and training no longer prove sufficient. Training agencies warrant examination because of their potential to overcome public financial and institutional constraints.

Vocational training agencies, however, are by no means free of conflict and problems. Considerable institutional inertia has plagued agencies in Latin America, in particular. High cost, excessive government control, and an inability to adapt training to employer requirements are other common problems (Atchoarena, 1998; Gasskov, 1994; Herschbach, Hays, & Evans, 1992). Nevertheless, considerable potential for experimentation and flexibility exists. Some of the most promising training forms are evolving out of relatively new agencies founded in countries challenged by the need to expand workforce preparation.

This chapter examines the organizational characteristics of VTAs. Attention is also given to the various institutional challenges VTAs struggle in their efforts to accommodate changing social and economic demands. Some newly evolving practices are also examined.

BACKGROUND

National vocational training agencies have a relatively long history. In 1942, the Brazilian government levied a special tax on enterprises to establish and maintain special training centers for compulsory technical training for youth under 18 years of age employed as apprentices, and to provide upgrading to young salaried workers and employed adults. Servicio Nacional de Aprendizagem Industrial (SENAI) was established as a training agency to serve industry, followed in 1946 by Servicio Nacional de Aprendizagem Commercial (SENAC) for training in commerce. Servicio Nacional de Aprendizagem Rural (SENAR) was established in 1991 for agriculture, and Servicio Nacional de Aprendizagem Transportes (SENAT) was set up in 1993 for the transportation industry (CINTERFOR/ILO, 1991).

Each training agency is administered by a federation of employers and governed through a board of directors that includes both private sector and government representatives. In SENAR, representatives from worker organizations also are included. The administrative structure is two-tiered: national and regional. The regional organizations have considerable autonomy and, in turn, administer training centers.

Financing is also decentralized so that regional organizations do not depend on the central administration for funding. Small employers contribute to a compulsory training fund through a special 1 percent wage tax; large employers pay 1.2 percent. In the case of SENAR, the tax rate is 2.5 percent to fund accompanying social programs for rural workers (Atchoarena, 1998; CINTERFOR/ILO, 1991, Vol. 2).

Following the example of Brazil, Argentina started the Committee for Training and Vocational Guidance in 1944. It was later absorbed into the formal educational sector. Its successor organization has taken a different direction: services are decentralized and vocational and technical education is mainly administered within the Ministry of Education and Culture as part of the secondary school cycle (CINTERFOR/ILO, 1991, Vol. 2).

In 1957, Servicio Nacional de Aprendizagem (SENA) was established by Colombia, followed by Instituto Nacional de Cooperación Educativa (INCE) by Venezuela in 1959, and Servicio Nacional de Adiestramiento en Trabajo Industrial (SENATI) by Peru in 1961, among other agencies throughout Latin America. Chile established Instituto Nacional de Capacitación Profesional (INACAP) in 1966, but it has since been reconstituted as a private agency responsive to market demands. Chile, like Argentina, provides considerable vocational and technical education through public schools and other public and private organizations (Espinoza, 1997).

The success of VTAs in the larger South American countries strongly influenced some of the smaller, neighboring countries. National training agencies were established in Central American and Caribbean countries throughout the 1960s and 1970s. However, smaller countries tend to have greater government domination of the agencies, and their programs have proven markedly less successful (Herschbach, Hayes, & Evans, 1992).

THE LATIN AMERICAN EXPERIENCE

Throughout Latin America, VTAs are the single largest source of vocational and technical education. Their development and spread resulted largely from lack of educational opportunity. Few public schools existed, but even as states expanded education, they emphasized secondary and higher education for the academically inclined, due to public pressure from the more affluent classes. Few children of the poorer classes attended school, and many youth lacked even the most rudimentary basic skills (Birdsall & Sabot, 1996; Ducci, 1994).

At the same time, large numbers of trained workers were needed to supply the early stages of industrialization. High levels of rural-to-urban migration throughout the 1940s, 1950s, and 1960s provided a supply of potential workers, but they lacked necessary skills. The situation exerted immense pressure to extend education and training opportunity, especially for urban populations. VTAs concentrated their activities on preemployment, apprenticeship training (plus a limited, but increasing amount of retraining for adults) in order to (a) accommodate the growing need for qualified, urban workers and (b) address work preparation for youth from the underprivileged and backward (marginal) populations, many of whom were school dropouts or had little access to formal education (CINTERFOR, 1991, Vol. 1).

VTAs were placed outside education ministries so they could respond more directly to the labor force and marginal populations. It was thought highly important to isolate work preparation from the formal schools' academic and intellectual tradition, to avoid emasculating the practical subjects. The education system also could not respond to the massive requirements of the large number of lower-class youth. However, placing VTAs outside formal education required an alternative source of financing. This financing came through a payroll tax on contributing firms. A significant level of resources was generated compared with that available for public education (CINTERFOR/ILO, 1991, Vol. 1). In recent years, the VTAs' monopoly on funds has been a matter of contention and a barrier to developing alternative training sources.

The Maturing of Vocational Training Agencies

During the 1970s, unemployment became a pressing issue throughout Latin America as large numbers of the population failed to find jobs in the modern industrial sector. Economic problems only intensified following renewed financial crisis. However, with the expansion of public education, greater numbers of young people could attend school, so the early emphasis on apprenticeship training for young nonschool attenders became less of a priority. Training agencies typically adjusted slowly to a new training profile, although the focus on services for employed workers increased. Short-term training revolved around upgrading, and activities were directed to job development in small enterprises and the informal economic sector, to generate greater employment opportunity. The marginal and disadvantaged urban and rural populations continued to be targeted. Human and social skills were emphasized along with occupational ones (CINTERFOR/ILO, 1991, Vol. 1). These developments were significant in that they marked a broadening of the VTAs' functions.

Today, however, the very concept of vocational training agencies is strongly contested. The economic restructuring that started in the Latin American region in the 1980s has placed new demands on workforce preparation systems. As in other regions of the world, international competition, rapid technological change, the opening of closed markets, and debt crises have combined to challenge existing policies and practices of human capital development. Furthermore, complex problems of chronic poverty, limited opportunity, and underperforming educational institutions continue to be widespread throughout the region, pointing to the limitations of current institutional forms. In many countries, public sector restructuring has accompanied economic reform, and has included ways to provide education and training. Current reforms call into question not only the funding monopoly of national training agencies but also the form and substance of their programming (Atchoarena, 1998; Birdsall & Sabot, 1996; Gallart, 1994).

Throughout the region, VTAs are trying to respond to the forces of economic, social, and political change. Some countries, such as Chile and Argentina, have moved radically away from the VTA model. Others, such as Brazil, have attempted to formulate change within the existing VTA structure. SENA in Colombia has adopted a middle course, earmarking a substantial percentage of its funding from employers to support social programs. To the extent that VTAs can refocus, they probably will survive, albeit in an altered institutional form. Following are major changes that are occurring in VTAs throughout the region.

Shift in Training Objectives

First, and importantly, there has been a measured shift from long-term initial training of young people for their first jobs to more short-term training. This includes preparation for initial qualifications and the upgrading of employed workers. Fewer young people, and more employed workers, are now served. This reflects the general extension of education and training opportunity through both more and better public schools, and the establishment of alternative training options, increasingly in the private sector (Atchoarena, 1998). The basic, initial training is at an increasingly higher level, reflecting changing employment requirements (Ducci, 1997). While in the early years VTAs focused primarily on workers at the lowest employment levels, currently there is a slow shift upward to include middle-level techni-

cians and supervisors. This change helps to accommodate the demand for more high-skilled, capital-intensive production, which is fueled by technological change and international competition.

More Technical Training

The provision for more technician training is an attempt by VTAs to fill the gap between semiskilled and skilled workers prepared through secondary-level vocational education programs and engineering and management personnel from professional schools. Although overall enrollment in technician-level training continues to be relatively modest, the growing trend is to designate specific centers as sites of specialized instruction. These centers then become known in their respective specialties as sources of highly trained workers. In many ways, the centers compare in level and function to technical and community colleges in the United States, but without the general education component.

Greater convergence also occurs now between VTAs and technical schools of the formal education system. VTAs in Argentina, Brazil, and Chile, for example, have formulated agreements with ministries of education to establish equivalent technician-level programming (Ducci, 1994).

Training in Firms

Yet another trend involves the increasing amount of training conducted within firms. In Sao Paulo, for example, where approximately 50 percent of Brazil's industrial employment is concentrated, more than 40 percent of employers receive at least a partial tax exemption for their in-firm training (Atchoarena, 1998). Ducci (1997) reported that most recent enrollment increases in SENAI result from increases in enterprise-based training, a pattern found throughout Latin America.

From the VTAs' early establishment, there was coordination with firms, but most initial training was, and still is, done through centers operated by VTAs. However, the introduction and use of technology requires increased in-firm training on a continuing basis. The training requirements of firms go beyond initial, first-job training, and their needs often shift rapidly. Established vocational training centers have limited ability to respond to employers reconstructing their workforce. Sensing this shift in the training market, VTAs in Argentina, Brazil, Chile, and Mexico have formulated joint financing agreements through which employers may exempt up to 80 percent of their statutory payroll contribution if they conduct training of equivalent value in their firms. In other countries, informal agreements have made possible the transfer of training to firms.

National vocational training agencies, however, hesitate to release their hold on resources. VTAs throughout the region retain control over the authorization, supervision, and implementation of in-firm training. Some employers invest considerable resources above the mandatory payroll level to support in-firm training and, while these resources complement the activities of VTAs, they also indicate their limitations. Then again, in-firm training exemptions cannot extend too far without endangering the primary institutional form of VTAs— that is, established vocational training centers.

The record of in-firm training has been mixed and the use of funds restrained. The monopoly of training resources by VTAs will continue to present a source of contention. The future viability of VTAs will probably depend on the extent to which they can respond to firm-specific training requirements.

Large firms tend to profit more from exemptions and conduct more in-firm training than small firms. Leite (1994) reported that, in Brazil, large international corporations and public companies are the major users of in-firm training exemptions. Large firms have complementary resources to put into training, can establish training departments, and can benefit from economies of scale. Small firms have less capacity to train in firm, and thus cannot make the best use of available funds (Herschbach, Hayes, & Evans, 1992).

Focus on Small- and Medium-Size Firms

Historically, the two most important client groups for VTAs have been large corporations and medium-size firms. This pattern is now changing to make medium- and small-size firms the focus of training. This shift acknowledges the fact that medium- and small-size enterprises constitute the largest employment market in Latin American countries. For these firms to continue to compete effectively in an increasingly global marketplace, they must have access to training. The large reservoir of poorly educated and trained individuals who find employment in small firms impedes development. While considerable educational gain has been made since the 1940s and 1950s, most countries in the region still lag in educational development, and their labor forces are characterized by large numbers of workers with marginal skills (Hanson, 1986; Martin, 1994; Plank, Sobrinho, & Xavier, 1996). Small employers, in particular, draw employees from the less-educated segments of the population while, at the same time, they have the least capacity to train.

Small firms also tend to be outside the mainstream of technological innovation and change and, consequently, do not have ready access to new knowledge and practice. However, since small firms have few resources to plow back into the business, they hesitate to invest their limited resources in training, given training's uncertain long-term benefits. In addition, employees who become very proficient are more likely to seek jobs in larger firms that offer better pay and benefits. Small firms' real cost of training is high because they cannot capitalize on economies of scale. Given the few employees they may need to train, it is not cost-effective to request outside assistance at the job site.

VTAs have attempted to address the training needs of small- and medium-size employers through specially designed courses offered through established training centers. This enables VTAs to assemble large enough groups to keep training costs reasonable. Also, by conducting courses in their facilities, rather than at the work site, financial resources are maintained within the training centers. One drawback, however, is the limited ability to tailor courses to the specific requirements of individual firms. VTAs have resorted to more generic forms of training, including management training. The incompatibility of grouping together personnel from different firms, all with very specific needs, presents complex issues that are yet to be resolved by training centers.

Diversification of Services

The most challenging trend among VTAs has involved the shift from exclusive training services to diversified services that support management development, product development, production improvement, and market expansion. Training is but one intervention in a comprehensive package of services linked together to make production more efficient and competitive. This development recognizes that training must often combine with other interventions to solve complex workplace problems. The need for training is seldom isolated from and independent of other, nontraining needs.

The broadening of the scope of activities has occurred gradually as both employers and VTAs realized that the same infrastructure and technical capacity could be used to deliver services such as the dissemination of new technology, product design, and management restructuring. Small- and medium-size employers, in particular, are not in a strong position to embark on development programs to accommodate technological change. The VTAs, moreover, can strengthen their own training markets by expanding the range of services they offer.

Ducci (1994, 1997) identified six kinds of service being provided by VTAs:

• Management consultancy services to enterprises, covering financing, budgeting, personnel, administration, and organizational restructuring.

• Technical assistance related to product design and development, production improvement, cost reduction, and machine and equipment layout.

• Production support in areas of equipment setup, materials testing and use, specialized tools and equipment, and quality control.

• Lease of specialized machinery and equipment; fabrication of specialty parts, tools, and fixtures.

• Applied research for product and production improvement.

• Dissemination of information on new technology, materials, production processes, and products, including assistance in upgrading the technical capacity of production units.

SENA in Colombia presents the best example of comprehensive training services offered to employers. The services include needs assessment, training design, training of instructional staff, and training evaluation. A short- and long-term action plan follows comprehensive, internal assessment of all operating levels. Following implementation, each component of the plan is evaluated.

Training takes place within the firm or at a training center, with the goal of developing in-firm self-sufficiency in training. Training commences with management and progresses down through the organization until lower levels of employees are also covered. Experience has demonstrated that supervisory and mid-level management training are crucial (Cuervo & Van Steenwyk, 1986). These services are designed to redirect resources to smaller firms. In the past, large- and medium-size companies have made the most use of training resources from VTAs.

ISSUES AFFECTING THE FUTURE

A number of institutional issues, however, continue to confront VTAs in Latin America. Some are systemic, rooted in the very policy and administrative structure of the institution itself. Others are more programmic, relating to conventional practices or institutional inertia. These issues have long dominated VTAs, and their resolution will largely determine whether this institutional form can accommodate the social and economic demands that confront countries in the region. Faced with similar constraints, national governments in other world regions have significantly modified the VTA model inspired by the Latin American experience. It is perhaps ironic that the newer training forms have proven considerably more effective in contributing to social and economic development.

Financing Vocational Training Agencies

The Latin American model of VTAs has attracted worldwide attention because it provides an alternative to public sector financing. To governments hard pressed to fund education and training programs, the payroll scheme pioneered by Brazil offers a way to mobilize substantial funds outside of regular public budgets. Government collects revenues and then channels funds to the vocational training agency.

In its most basic form, an earmarked tax for training is assessed as a percentage of the wage and salary bill of individual firms. This is a sheltered form of revenue, however, and the VTA tends to monopolize funds to support its established training centers. In the early stages of a country's economic development, when in-firm training capacity may be weak, established centers play an important workforce development. In Latin America, when VTAs were established, the quantitative expansion of education had not yet occurred to the point where it could supply a large pool of individuals with basic education skills, both general and vocational. VTAs supplied individuals with at least basic preemployment skills and, given the large size of the population served, could more easily justify monopolizing funds. As the economies of the regions developed, however, and as educational opportunity has grown more widespread, pressures have mounted to broaden the use of funds.

Technologically intensive production will

likely require more frequent training and retraining to a firm's specifications, thus requiring a financing pattern that supports more firm-based training. Moreover, as the proportion of the labor force that obtains higher levels of education increases, an associated need for more advanced forms of workforce preparation arises. VTAs in Latin America, however, have responded slowly. Although the funding and institutional framework tended to retard the emergence of alternative forms of training delivery, reforms are gradually occurring.

As previously observed, a number of Latin American countries have shifted more of their funding to support in-firm training, although VTAs still control a substantial amount of this training. Pressed by private industry, agencies throughout the region have slowly turned toward increased use of rebate schemes through which firms earn exemptions on part of the wage tax for conducting approved training. There is still reluctance, however, to grant rebates above a certain percentage of total revenues generated. Future support of VTAs will probably rest on extending the use of funds to more direct training by employers.

VTAs in Latin America face the precarious task of balancing revenue use with the requirements of the ever-present surplus of poorly educated, low-skilled, marginalized segments of the population who require basic training, and the increasing demands of firms introducing new technology and building export-oriented production. Both cannot be easily served through the same training form. So far, VTAs have opted to use most of their funding to support center-based training. However, in so doing, they risk being unable to respond adequately to the economic restructuring sweeping through the region—and thus they risk losing support from the very employer groups they depend on for funding.

Grant and rebate schemes largely developed and applied by VTAs outside Latin America provide the best examples of alternative uses of levy funds. Firms that establish or expand training programs receive grants or rebates, depending on the kind, level, and scope of training. These may be on a cost-incurred basis, as in Singapore and Tunisia, or in the form of a grant to establish an in-firm training system, such as that found in Nigeria and Zimbabwe. In both cases, VTAs' major role is to help firms develop training capacity, rather than to provide the training, as has been done in Latin America (Whalley & Ziderman, 1990).

Some of the most innovative and effective forms of training agencies appear in the industrializing Asian countries. A considerable amount of training tends to be financed through grants on a cost-sharing basis, with individual firms conducting the training and the training agency functioning more as a facilitator that assesses needs, channels funds to private firms, and monitors results. Training centers operated by the agency see little use. At the same time, a closer link is maintained with national development policy than we normally see in Latin American countries. This mainly has been achieved through the working relationship established between the training agency and national planning and economic development boards (Ashton & Green, 1996; Gasskov, 1994).

Singapore presents a good example. Its Productivity and Standards Board disperses funds for on-the-job and work-based training. To ensure a sufficient labor supply, training is coordinated with economic development objectives through the Economic Development Board. Those involved identify current and future labor needs, translate the needs into training specifications, and use training funds to bring labor supply and demand into approximate equilibrium. Moreover, to promote economic restructuring, the earmarked tax is levied mainly on low wages so as to encourage the use of high capital and advanced technology. The intended effect is to upgrade low-wage workers. Firms that train and raise wages receive an exemption from the tax. Assistance in the introduction of technology and advanced skills training now replace basic training

(Ashton & Green, 1996; Dougherty & Tan, 1997).

In Latin America, Chile has made the most substantial changes in the use of funds. Through the National Training and Employment Service (SENCE), the state subsidizes firm-based training with a tax rebate scheme. Firms that develop programs for new employees and organize training to upgrade worker skills can receive a tax rebate of up to 1 percent of their payroll. Certain training costs above the 1 percent are also tax deductible. In addition, the management of most work preparation programs was decentralized and privatized, with the government providing subsidies rather than direct funding to the various enterprise associations and private nonprofit corporations formed to conduct training.

SENCE has also developed a program of scholarships for youth, including unemployed youth. Financial support is given to individuals, rather than to the training provider. In this way, market forces come into play and individuals seek out the best providers of training services. So far, more than 400 training organizations have achieved eligibility for use of the funds. Serious administrative and political problems have accompanied the changes in Chile, but progress has been made toward breaking away from the more rigid funding and programming pattern characterizing VTAs throughout the region (Espinoza, 1997).

Crucial Question of Board Representation

National training agencies generally are statutory bodies but, not unexpectedly, the legal and institutional framework varies greatly among countries. In practically all cases, however, government has played an instrumental role in establishing and developing training agencies. In the Latin American model, in particular, agencies tend to be quasi-autonomous, operating under the umbrella of labor ministries and governed by a board of directors that has heavy government representation. The composition, representation, and defined authority of the board, as well as the government's role, are crucial to the effectiveness of training agencies.

The question of government representation is complex. In countries that have large public bureaucracies maintained as political constituencies, government representation in and control of VTA boards is often characterized by the same inefficiencies and lack of purpose found in other government agencies. The training fund becomes another source of revenue at the disposal of government. Some evidence suggests that when the government intervenes directly by requiring employers to provide training, or acts to control grant awards to training providers, the results are highly mixed (Salome & Charmes, 1988).

Government control, however, is not necessarily linked with less, or greater, effectiveness. The important consideration is how control is used. In Singapore, as suggested, training is an integral part of the government's employment and economic growth policy. Training is highly responsive to development policy since it is a tool used directly by government (Ashton & Green, 1996). Although government heavily influences Singapore's Vocational and Industrial Training Board, charged to carry out training, it functions effectively to accomplish national objectives. At the other extreme, national training agencies have proven ineffective when governments (a) used them to accomplish social and political, rather than educational and economic, objectives; (b) diverted funds to nontraining purposes; or (c) exploited, rather than assisted, employers. In such cases, government control has proven highly detrimental (Cuervo & Van Steenwyk, 1986; Herschbach, Hayes, & Evans, 1992).

Greater control by private sector representatives does not necessarily ensure increased effectiveness. There is no guarantee that the VTA board will be broadly representative. The tendency is for larger, more politically adroit employers to be represented on boards of directors, while the interests of smaller, less influential employers go largely ignored. To function successfully, a national training agency must (a) be free of self-serving domination by either government or private groups, (b) truly represent the constituencies that it serves, (c) control its budget, and (d) possess the autonomy to make policy and carry out decisions.

SENA in Colombia developed a formula for board representation that attempted to balance the interests of different constituency groups. Private sector members are appointed by the institutions they represent. National organizations for small and large employers, the Chamber of Commerce, and the agriculture association are represented. In addition, four members represent the public sector, including the Minister of Labor, who chairs the board, as well as delegates from the National Planning Department, and the Ministries of Education and Agriculture. One member represents the largest union in the country, and one member is appointed by the Episcopal (Catholic) Conference. Members are appointed for two-year terms with no limit on reappointments (Cuervo & Van Steenwyk, 1986).

The board of directors monitors and approves budgets and operational policy. A general secretary, reporting to the national director, has overall operational responsibilities and, along with four subdirectors, manages the various administrative offices. Training operations, however, are decentralized to SENA's 19 regional offices. More than 750 fixed training centers, 120 small community centers, and 60 mobile programs operate through the regional offices, which identify local training needs, establish training priorities, and conduct training (Cuervo & Van Steenwyk, 1986).

It is hard to make judgments about the effectiveness of different combinations of board membership, however, because it is hard to detach membership patterns from a host of interconnected variables that impact effectiveness in individual countries. In general, a situation in which employers and workers have equal or majority membership is probably positive, if for no other reason than that it indicates the existence of a constructive government policy toward issues of equity, representation, and efficiency, as well as social and economic development. On the other hand, to be most constructive, the policies of governing boards must fully integrate with a country's economic development policy. This can be achieved through measured government leadership. In most cases, however, government ultimately has considerable influence because it controls, directly or indirectly, the source of income.

Training boards that combine policy and coordinating functions with operational responsibilities within a single board or organizational level tend to be less effective than those that separate and delegate functions. Operations must be fully accountable to local employers. In an organization that combines functions, accountability is often solely to the board, and operational considerations may become subordinated to policy and coordination functions.

Constituency Links

For a training agency to provide effective services, it must have strong links to its constituency groups. These links, however, are often hard to forge. The agency can relatively easily work with publicly owned agencies and enterprises because they must comply with general training regulations defined by their departments. In the case of private sector enterprises, the scale of the establishment is an important factor. Large companies have greater visibility and more stable workforces. They also seem more receptive to training and have resources to support it.

In most countries, coordination with small- and medium-size employers is weak, and this is a shortcoming linked with vocational training agencies (Dougherty & Tan, 1997; Gasskov, 1994). Employer associations can play an effective role in coordination, and firms that belong to associations generally have greater access to training resources. Employer associations, however, generally do not have funds available to help build linkages with training agencies.

A strategy followed in some countries involves strengthening existing associations. In general, the most effective programs use the various professional, employer, and worker organizations to link with firms that can benefit from training agency services. In Hong Kong, for example, the Vocational Training Council uses professional and industry committees to link training provisions with employer needs. The various committees have responsibility for organizing and delivering training in their respective sectors, such as banking, electronics, and construction. Each committee comprises employer representatives and members of the Council, providing a way to link the administration of training with constituency needs (Ashton & Green, 1996).

In Indonesia, the National Training Council brings together the relevant ministerial departments, as well as involved public and private sector representatives, to discuss training issues and to make recommendations to the Ministry of Manpower. This constitutes a network, however, rather than an organizational structure. Nevertheless, a flexible, problem-oriented, decision-making process has been created.

Control Over Resources

In some countries, only a portion of the revenue generated through payroll tax goes to training, with the remainder allocated to the government's general funds. This can create serious problems. When resources earmarked for training are siphoned off to nontraining activities, employers end up paying for services they do not receive. Often, employers must then invest additional funds in their own training programs.

When payroll tax revenues lead to large unspent surpluses, there is a tendency to squander resources in top-heavy administrative structures, at both the agency and government levels. In addition, the government's temptation to dip into the large resource pool and use funds for other purposes often proves hard to combat. Consequently, the assessment must be continually monitored to adjust for surplus accumulation, while not endangering stable funding (Whalley & Ziderman, 1990).

An additional problem with resource use arises when funds are channeled to a disproportionate minority of firms. Large, formal sector firms tend to participate more in training, and thus end up being subsidized by smaller firms that receive little in return for their tax contributions (Dougherty & Tan, 1997).

When employers of all sizes have a major voice in policy and administrative issues, training funds will more likely go toward their designated purposes. Decentralized systems tend to suppress the central authority's use of funds. In addition, when there are co-financing agreements with industries, not only are additional training funds generated, but there tends to be greater overall responsibility in the use of all funds.

Responsiveness and Accountability

The more effective VTAs have developed functional links with their constituencies. Administrative regionalization has aided the development of closer working relationships with firms. Nevertheless, the lock on training resources tends to impede the development of broad-based collaborative arrangements. VTAs are not subject to market forces that would promote a higher level of responsiveness and accountability, and firms have little leverage over them.

Manufacturing Extension Partnerships (MEPs) in the United States are one example of the use of government funds to provide incentives to build collaborative arrangements with potential service providers. Administered and funded through the National Institute of Standards and Technology, the MEP program is a nationwide "system" of centers that supplies services and support to smaller manufacturers. The system aims to provide greater access to new technologies, resources, training, and expertise. At the heart of the system are 44 regionally based Manufacturing Exten-

sion Centers (MECs) located in 20 states, supported from multiple funding sources. Individual MECs vary greatly in the (a) particular services they provide, (b) sources of local financing, (c) organizational and management structure, (d) makeup of collaborating partners, and (e) locus of control.

The initiative for establishing an MEC typically comes from local economic development networks working in concert with state and local economic development officials. These networks are made up of influential community members spearheading economic revitalization efforts. They search for potential federal and state funds to support local training and economic development initiatives. MECs are formed to facilitate local and regional development efforts (Herschbach, 1997).

The Southeast Manufacturing Technology Center (SMTC), which serves small- and medium-sized manufacturers in North and South Carolina, exemplifies a regionally based MEC. SMTC provides three basic types of support, customized to the requirements of client firms: (a) classroom training and special seminars, given through technical and community colleges; (b) technical demonstrations, given through local universities and at SMTC locations throughout the region; and (c) consultant assistance to individual firms on specific technical problems. Use is made of the resources of SMTC's technical staff, its regional partners, and the National Institute of Standards and Technology. Advice and information are given on a broad range of topics, including business management, computer-aided technologies, process control, shop-floor layout, robotics, data collection, just-in-time inventory control, electronic data interchange with suppliers and customers, and quality control.

The Great Lakes Manufacturing Technology Center (GLMTC) provides an example of a locally managed MEC. The City of Cleveland's Advanced Manufacturing Program administers the program, which has ties to local economic development organizations. These organizations include numerous community development groups, the federal Small Business Administration, and surrounding technical and community colleges as well as universities. A manufacturing resource facility houses equipment for hands-on training as well as demonstrations. This equipment includes upgraded machine tools, laser-based inspection systems, and a fully automated robotic computer-integrated manufacturing cell. There is also a teaching facility. A staff of manufacturing engineers and technical specialists provide related financial assistance and help in risk analysis and cost justification. Specific programs include modernization and continuous improvement projects; factory, environmental, and human resources assessment; workplace training; business planning assistance; and pollution prevention.

Individual MECs attempt to respond to the particular requirements of small enterprises. This calls for offering courses in the evenings, at work sites, in various time blocks, and in other unconventional ways. In addition, MECs must aggressively reach out and offer services to employers who may have little knowledge of what assistance they need or can get. For this purpose, MECs employ marketing specialists.

Federal funds are used to initiate programs and are matched by (a) state and local funding, (b) fees for services and training contracts from firms, and (c) industry contributions. The regional sponsor must contribute at least 50 percent of the center's capital, operating, and maintenance costs. As a center's program becomes more established, federal funding decreases, and the program relies increasingly on user fees.

MEPs are several steps away from the financing and administrative structure of VTAs, but they indicate the direction that the Latin American model probably must move to gain relevance and accountability. There are similar developments in other countries, such as the County Labour Market Boards in Sweden, and the Industrial Funds and National Apprenticeship Bodies in the Netherlands (Gasskov, 1994).

Similar to the MEPs, these bodies are designed to respond to the needs of the clients they serve. Stakeholders influence funding; local participation is supported; there are multiple and flexible ways to deliver training; and the concept of social partnership dominates.

THE EXPERIENCE IN SMALL COUNTRIES

Vocational training agencies appear to be a useful institutional form in small countries where individual firms have difficulty providing training. Small, local employers may incorrectly or inadequately assess training needs or lack resources to train. Often, they do not know where to find assistance. They also cannot realize economies of scale. In theory, at least, vocational training agencies can overcome these limitations, lowering individual firms' training costs by assembling groups. VTAs can also deliver a range of services. Nevertheless, for a variety of reasons, VTAs have been less successful in small countries with weak economies. The use of the payroll tax as the financing mechanism has been one of the major limitations, especially in the low-income countries of the Caribbean and Central America, where tax evasion presents a major problem.

The tax collection rate among modern sector companies is high, particularly for those employing 25 or more workers. But, evasion is a general practice for small firms, nonunion establishments, and informal as well as agricultural employers, who make up a major part of the economy. For this reason, generating sufficient revenues may prove difficult.

As previously suggested, the payroll tax is often an over-sheltered source of income outside of regular government channels. There may be few checks on how it is used. On the one hand, a vocational training agency may overindulge itself and, on the other, the government may siphon off considerable funds for nontraining purposes. In Panama in the 1980s, for example, only 15 percent of the income generated through a payroll tax went to financing the national vocational training authority.

As a consequence, the organization was seriously underfunded and training quality was low. Employers felt dissatisfied because they paid taxes for training services but got little in return, and their training needs went unmet. While this is an extreme case, the diversion of funds is common practice (Herschbach, Hayes, & Evans, 1992).

Administrative control of both the training agency and funds is crucial. In some Caribbean and Central American countries, governments tend to exert greater control over the vocational training agency than in the larger South American countries with well-established training traditions. This fact alone may account for the relatively poor performance of vocational training agencies in these countries. The training agency is often characterized by the same inefficiencies found in other government agencies, and it may be maintained by a large public bureaucracy that mainly serves as a political constituency.

In general, then, in the case of small, low-income countries such as those found in the Caribbean and Central America, vocational training agencies have not succeeded as an institutional form for delivering training services. Restricted economies, limited financial resources, weak management and staff capabilities, and an inability to capitalize on economies of scale all work against the successful establishment of viable training organizations. A national vocational training agency also may be too complex an institutional form, given the low supporting capacity found in some countries.

LINKING WITH DEVELOPMENT

As economies evolve, so must their educational and training institutions. Throughout Latin America there has been a strong tradition of preemployment institution-based work preparation. VTAs promote this kind of training and at one time it was appropriate. However, as the countries of the region have moved toward more skill-intensive economic growth, their need to diversify delivery of training ser-

vices and types of services provided has grown. Closer links with employers also must be developed. As economic structures become more diverse, and as more high technology processes are incorporated into work, there is a corresponding need for a higher level of technical training and for more focused, specialized, in-service training programs delivered in various forms on a continuing basis (Salome & Charmes, 1988). More training must be given in-house by firms, and less through established institutions. In a limited way, VTAs are responding to the changing social and economic context.

However, in many Latin American countries, the educational system's performance is so limiting that large segments of the population lack even the basic rudimentary skills needed for job preparation above the most elementary level. These groups of youth will more likely find themselves in VTAs if they pursue job training. VTAs continue to provide the main source of formal job preparation for marginal and disadvantaged populations, but the training is restricted both in scope and level. At the same time, there are constraints on the VTAs' ability to reconstruct their own training, given the low educational level of the primary population that they continue to serve. Thus, VTAs see limits in their ability to respond to economic restructuring and to the forces of technological change and international competition.

A comparison with VTAs in the Asian region proves instructive. A main factor accounting for the higher level of skill training achieved through VTAs in the newly industrializing Asian countries is the educational level of the entering population. In contrast to Latin America, East Asian countries have invested more in basic education. Primary and secondary education is widely accessible, and enrollment, achievement, and completion rates are all higher. Youth who enter VTAs are equipped to perform at a more advanced level than comparable youth in Latin America. Also, the relatively large, unequal distribution of income and widespread poverty in Latin America further constrain the ability to shape a high-skilled workforce. The educational, economic, and political environment throughout the region has not been conducive to either strong educational expansion or social development (Ashton & Green, 1996; Birdsall & Sabot, 1996). The lack of fundamental educational and social reform will continue to work as a detriment to the VTAs' ability to forge a new training role.

VTAs also are hindered in part by their own institutional history and inertia. In general, Latin American vocational training agencies are not flexible enough and are too inward looking. Once institutions are established, it is hard to change their mode of operation. Resources have been monopolized, and center-based training has dominated as the major mode of service delivery. Significant changes are occurring, however. The perception and practice has been that services are provided primarily through training center staff, even though there are alternative ways that position VTAs as facilitators, rather than as direct suppliers of training and related services. As long as revenue continues to go primarily to VTAs, the agencies will tend to monopolize resources and concentrate services in the hands of their own personnel. Whether some of the more established training agencies can adapt quickly and fully enough to maintain the support of the business and industrial community is open to question (Ducci, 1997). To achieve fundamental change, the funding mechanism itself must be restructured to shift the locus of control over funds and programming to the firm itself.

Finally, compared with the VTAs established in newly industrializing countries, there is a relatively weak link between the agency and the economic development priorities of individual Latin American countries. Mechanisms for coordinating the two are simply not in place. One reason is that programming does not center solely around the needs of economic restructuring, but rather arises from a compromise between the social objective of addressing the marginalized segments of the population and the evolving requirement of economic growth.

In a real sense, VTAs serve to absorb the social tensions arising from conditions found throughout the region: deep poverty, restricted opportunity, the highly unequal distribution of income, and the monopolization of political representation and power (Birdsall & Sabot, 1996; Hanson, 1986). This social objective conflicts with the objective of efficient training targeted to economic restructuring. There is an obvious need for a strong implementing apparatus to link the use of training resources and program development and delivery with economic transformation policies and strategies. The VTAs work independently, responding to the most vocal and powerful of their constituencies, but they do not necessarily address the most important or critical needs. In addition, through the monopoly of training resources, firms have been bound to the particular form of centrally developed and administered training programs, while the development of alternative forms of training has waned.

The Latin American model of the national training agency has existed for more than 50 years. Its spread through all world regions attests to its influence. In the early stages of industrialization, countries found it an appropriate model to adopt, but as economies mature, VTAs need alteration. It is the newer forms of VTAs found outside the Latin American region that embody the most functional development. Many of them (a) are structured on a stronger public elementary and secondary education system, (b) have a less rigid funding mechanism, and (c) provide incentives to employers to train. Employers are the major decision-makers, and more training is based directly in the firm and focused on high-skilled, capital-intensive production fueled by technological change and international competition. In Latin America, however, VTAs have been markedly slower to adapt and have not yet been able to break out of their own institutional constraints.

References

Ashton, D., & Green, F. (1996). *Education, training and the global economy.* Cheltenham, England: Edward Elgar.

Atchoarena, D. (1998). The alternatives for the financing of vocational training: The example of emerging countries in Latin America. *Vocational Training European Journal, 13,* 56-65.

Birdsall, N., & Sabot, R. H. (Eds.). (1996). *Opportunity foregone: Education in Brazil.* Washington, DC: Inter-American Development Bank.

Centro Interamericano de Investigación y Documentación sobre Formación Profesional/International Labour Office. (1991). *Vocational training on the threshold of the 1990s* (Vols. 1 & 2). Washington, DC: The World Bank.

Cuervo, A. G., & Van Steenwyk, N. (1986). *Columbia's Servicio Nacional de Apprendizaje (SENA). A qualitative analysis of a technical training system.* Colombia: United States Agency for International Development.

Dougherty, C., & Tan, J.-P. (1997). Financing training: Issues and options. *International Journal of Manpower, 18*(1/2), 29-62.

Ducci, M. A. (1994). Latin America: National training agencies. In T. Husen & T. N. Postlethwaite (Eds.), *The international encyclopedia of education* (2nd ed., pp. 3262-3267). Oxford, England: Pergamon.

Ducci, M. A. (1997). New challenges to vocational training authorities: Lessons from the Latin American experience. *International Journal of Manpower, 18*(1/2), 160-184.

Espinoza, E. M. (1997). *Chile: Experiences in a market-oriented training system.* Geneva, Switzerland: Training Policies and Systems Branch, Employment and Training Department, International Labour Office.

Gallart, M. A. (1994). Latin America: Articulation of education, training, and work. In T. Husen & T. N. Postlethwaite (Eds.), *The international encyclopedia of education* (2nd ed., pp. 3256-3262). Oxford, England: Pergamon.

Gasskov, V. (Ed.). (1994). *Alternative schemes of financing training.* Geneva, Switzerland: International Labour Office.

Hanson, E. M. (1986). *Educational reform and administrative development: The case of Colombia and Venezuela.* Stanford, CA: Hoover Institution Press.

Herschbach, D. R. (1997). *Training partnerships in the United States: Linking enterprise and government.* Geneva, Switzerland: Training Policies and Systems Branch, Employment and Training Department, International Labour Office.

Herschbach, D. R., Hayes, F. B., & Evans, D. P. (1992). *Vocational education and training: Review of experience.* Washington, DC: Bureau for Latin America and the Caribbean, United States Agency for International Development.

Leite, E. M. (1994). Levy-based co-financing agreements in Brazil. In V. Gasskov (Ed.)., *Alternative schemes of financing training* (pp. 63-68). Geneva, Switzerland: International Labour Office.

Martin, C. J. (1994). *Schooling in Mexico.* Brookfield, VT: Ashgate.

Plank, D. N., Sobrinho, J. A., & Xavier, A. C. (1996). Why Brazil lags behind in educational development. In N. Birdsall & R. H. Sabot (Eds.), *Opportunity foregone: Education in Brazil* (pp. 117-145). Washington, DC: Inter-American Development Bank.

Salome, B., & Charmes, J. (1988). *In-service training: Five Asian experiences.* Paris: Development Center of the Organization for Economic Cooperation and Development.

Whalley, J., & Ziderman, A. (1990). Financing training in developing countries: The role of payroll taxes. *Economics of Education Review, 9*(4), 377-387.

World Bank. (1986). *Regional review of alternative modes of vocational training and technical education.* Washington, DC: Author.

13

Combining School and Work: New Pathways for Learning in Australia

By James A. Athanasou

In addition to their links to universities, in recent years Australian schools have developed an emphasis toward vocational education and training. Many schools now train existing staff to deliver courses that previously were not considered the province of secondary education. These include courses in accounting, agriculture, avionics, commercial cookery, computing studies, electronics, engineering science, furniture manufacturing, metal manufacturing, retailing, sheep husbandry and wool technology, and travel.

One reason for the wide acceptance of workplace learning is that many students seek courses that have immediate relevance and that lead to a career. This reflects significant changes in the nature of education and training, as well as adolescent employment, that parallel the experiences of other nations.

In the past, adolescents in Australia found low-skill jobs readily available, and only a minority completed secondary schooling. By the early 1990s, however, more than 75 percent completed school, even though school-based vocational education had been available for only a short time (Lepani & Currie, 1993). Most vocational education programs occurred in government-sponsored technical and further education colleges with courses for apprentices as well as other postschool technician and commercial courses.

THE CHANGING FACE OF EDUCATION IN SENIOR SCHOOLS

A decade ago, it would have been unthinkable for Australian schools to rush to develop vocational education and training programs. Yet, a nationwide consultation (Sweet, 1995) revealed that by 1995 some 600 programs operated throughout Australia. In part, this reflects a concerned reaction to changes in senior school demography and the realization that for some students more schooling does not necessarily equate with more education. It also reflects fundamental changes in the way Australians think about the purpose of education and training and the efforts of individual teachers and various boards of studies throughout Australia to provide a balanced curriculum for each student in the senior school.

For some people, this transition has not been easy, and vocational education in schools is only slowly coming to be seen as a natural extension of the curriculum. Parallel overseas developments, however, have offered useful examples. Cooperative education in the United States provides a practical model (Stern, Finkelstein, Stone, Latting, & Dornsife, 1994), which, along with youth apprenticeships, career academies, and other "traditional" forms of vocational education, has served as a source of program ideas.

School-industry programs, a feature of Swedish education, are another attractive concept. Industry supports schools' efforts to provide a wide range of courses in the workplace. Legislation in Sweden mandated that three-year vocational courses be at least 15 percent workplace-based. Similar programming approaches are highlighted by organizations such as the Organization for Economic Cooperation and Development and the World Bank.

The federal government recognized the social importance of these developments and, among other initiatives, supported the development and expansion of vocational education and training. In particular, it endorsed the development of high-quality partnership-based workplace learning and, in so doing, said that

• Industry has the capacity and facilities to educate and train.

• Students want to learn in realistic circumstances.

• Vocational education ought to be accredited by industry.

• Local community-based programs offer a flexible form of delivery.

This chapter outlines Australia's efforts to implement such school-industry programs.

AUSTRALIAN STUDENT TRAINEESHIP FOUNDATION

A model of school-based vocational educa-

tion, or student traineeships, has now been supported formally. In its policy paper *Working Nation*, the federal government (Commonwealth of Australia, 1994) announced the formation of an Australian Student Traineeship Foundation (ASTF). For the first time, the federal government is helping students throughout Australia obtain vocational education and training in the workplace and seeking to develop local school-industry workplace learning programs with recognized pathways to further education and training through an autonomous independent authority. This vocational education program operates in parallel with existing postschool apprenticeships and traineeships.

The ASTF received AU$39 million in funds over four years to assist a wide variety of programs that fall within its charter. The key principle underlying the ASTF is development of quality workplace learning programs. The foundation established a number of essential criteria for the support of school-industry programs. To meet the essential criteria, programs must

• Form part of the curriculum of years 11 and 12.

• Require substantial learning and assessment in the workplace.

• Combine on- and off-the-job training.

• Reflect industry and local community requirements.

• Receive school accreditation and industry recognition.

Other desirable features of workplace learning programs include (a) shared management between industry and education, (b) encouragement of joint resourcing by education and industry, and (c) an agreed quality-assurance process.

The ASTF criteria are based largely on insights from overseas programs such as cooperative education, but also on the development of pilot national workplace learning programs, such as TRAC. TRAC originally stood for Training in Retailing And Commerce, but it has expanded well beyond these areas. Given the central importance of the concept of TRAC to school-industry programs, it may be helpful to describe this program in some detail as an Australian model of community-based vocational education.

TRAC

TRAC was established in 1989 by the Dusseldorp Skills Forum, a nonprofit foundation formed to improve training and education opportunities for young people. The TRAC program was recognized as a model and example relevant to the Australian context for workplace learning at the senior school level. TRAC now runs in 45 regions across Australia, with programs coordinated through the Centre for Workplace Learning in partnership with employers and government as well as nongovernment schools. The aim is for student-trainees in TRAC programs to complete part of an industry qualification before leaving school. TRAC was designed initially as a nontertiary entrance subject for students who do not plan to attend university. Eleventh-grade students receive more than 300 hours of on-the-job training; 12th graders undergo at least 200 hours. A local industry and school steering committee manages TRAC in conjunction with a full-time coordinator who is responsible to the steering committee. The coordinator manages work placements and provides individual support for students.

A panel of teachers and local employers selects TRAC students. Employers also nominate an employee as a dedicated "mentor" for each TRAC student. Each term, students are placed in a different business (one day per week for seven weeks); they also receive specialized training (one day per week for three weeks) at a TRAC center. Employers train students and pay a fee for each student placement, but, unlike co-op programs in the United States, Australian students do not receive pay for their work placement.

Industry designs the TRAC curriculum and has an opportunity for local customization. Available strands include (a) customer service

(retail careers), (b) business service (office careers), (c) hospitality/tourism, and (d) automotive service. On completion of the program, students receive their higher school certificate, credit toward technical and further education studies, a nationally recognized industry certificate, a record of their skill attainment, and a local Chamber of Commerce certificate. TRAC is dually accredited by (a) the state Vocational Education and Training Accreditation Board and (b) an accrediting organization for each strand. The hospitality strand receives accreditation through the Australian Hospitality Review Panel; the Retail Traders Association recognizes the customer service strand; and the Automotive Training Board recognizes the automotive service strand. Linkages to federal Career Start Traineeships are provided for the customer service and hospitality strands.

Evidence indicates that 92 percent of 1993 TRAC graduates either found employment or went on to full-time study. Other specific outcomes included

• 92 percent of students in year 11 continued on to year 12.

• 59 percent continued with TRAC in year 12.

• 83 percent of year 12 TRAC students were not aiming for tertiary entrance.

A more important outcome of the TRAC program is the enhanced self-esteem and motivation of participating students. In postprogram monitoring, students emphasized the value of their work experiences, with comments such as

• Provided new knowledge and skills (53 percent).

• Increased confidence and self-esteem (46 percent).

SCHOOL-INDUSTRY PROGRAMS

This chapter does not purport to advocate TRAC, but the discussion does offer an example of what is happening in Australia. Also, TRAC is important because of its similarities with, as well as variations from, school-based vocational education in the United States and other countries. Moreover, TRAC programs have served as the national template for thinking about cooperative vocational education in the Australian context and a number of variants have been developed, including programs that offer credit toward university entry. They all contain elements of successful overseas programs and, like vocational education programs in most developed nations, have reformed secondary schooling by

- Introducing local involvement in curricula and industry participation in education.
- Lessening rigid subject domination of upper secondary schooling.
- Introducing experiential education on a large scale.
- Imposing new demands on teachers as coordinators of learning.
- Reducing centralized control and forcing schools to adapt their administrative framework.
- Breaking down barriers, offering more students a legitimate basis for learning.
- Establishing criterion-based assessment.
- Recognizing the development of individual talents outside school.
- Creating new pathways from schools into tertiary education.

Now that vocational education has come to demand a greater role, it has the potential to change the face of secondary schooling in Australia. It will impact commercial and industrial training and harness the talents of those students who do not find the curriculum satisfying. Vocational education has always been an integral component of professional university courses (e. g., law, medicine, dentistry, veterinary science, accounting, engineering) and has been a familiar aspect of high school programs in courses such as woodworking, metalworking, and so forth. The positive results, from programs such as TRAC, provide evidence that vocational education and school-industry programs deserve further attention.

Secondary schooling is clearly changing. It is unlikely that the introduction of vocational education into the formal and less formal aspects of upper secondary school in Australia will be reversed. Despite the barriers and stigma that some individuals face in taking these courses, students throughout Australia seem to appreciate the opportunity to learn in the workplace. It has been estimated that some 35 percent of senior school students now participate in vocational education. There is a realization that learning in real workplaces, integrated with classroom learning, is needed to develop long-lasting work skills.

References

Commonwealth of Australia. (1994). *Working nation: Policies and programs*. Canberra, Australia: Australian Government Publishing Service.

Lepani, B., & Currie, J. (1993). *Workplace learning in NSW senior secondary courses*. Sydney, Australia: Dusseldorp Skills Forum.

Stern, D., Finkelstein, N., Stone, J. R., III, Latting, J., & Dornsife, C. (1994). *Research on school-to-work transition programs in the United States*. Berkeley, CA: National Center for Research in Vocational Education.

Sweet, R. (1995). *An ear to the ground: A report on a national consultation with regional Australia*. Sydney, Australia: Australian Student Traineeship Foundation.

14

How the Japanese Prepare for Work

By Dennis R. Herschbach and Takao Kamibeppu

In spite of a recent severe and protracted economic crisis, Japan's industrial achievement has been remarkable. Known in the world marketplace of the post-war 1940s as a producer of inexpensive, unsophisticated toys and gadgets, Japan today occupies a place in the world economy as a formidable export machine. Between 1950 and the economic oil shock of 1973, Japan's economy grew at an extraordinary average of 10 percent per year. Following a short-lived recession after 1973, economic growth continued until 1991 at the still impressive average rate of 4 percent per year.

Product diversification, exemplary engineering, superior organization and production methods, high productivity, and low cost led to the penetration and domination of new markets. Japan made deep competitive inroads in shipbuilding and steel, photographic and optical equipment, semiconductors, automotives, machine tools, processed foods, and computers, as it captured large chunks of the international export market (Berggren, 1995). Although challenged by an economic crisis, as

well as by new Asian competitors, Japan maintains its place as the world's second-largest economy. Its economy is massive, diverse, pervasive, and powerful. What accounts for this remarkable achievement?

Intense international study has focused on the Japanese industrial system to determine the basis of its achievement. Inquiry has focused on management systems and shop floor practices: quality control circles; just-in-time-delivery; lean, flexible, and zero-defect production; and other ways of combining human resources with materials and machines to achieve superior products and high productivity. The work culture itself has been extensively examined, as have the business and political cultures.

While education is acknowledged as a crucial factor underpinning the quality of the Japanese workforce, it has been examined primarily through the lens of the academic/vocational duality that permeates much of Western educational thought. Japan's high academic achievement usually catches the eye of Western observers. Relatively little attention has gone to education and training for work or to the role of general academic learning in forming the foundation for subsequent specialized skill development in the workplace. In a real sense, in Japan, all education involves preparation for work. From preschool to higher education, the single overriding purpose of education is to develop the capacity of youth to successfully enter Japan's work culture.

To be sure, at various points in the education system groups are sorted out to concentrate on vocational studies, with all of the attending differences in status, opportunity, and monetary gain. Nevertheless, in contrast to Western systems, Japanese divisions do not so much follow academic/vocational lines as fall between different levels of occupational preparation. Underlying all of Japanese education is the conviction that vocational preparation must be based on a solid foundation of excellence in educational basics. Good general educational preparation grounded in moral responsibility is considered good vocational education.

It follows then that, if one wants to examine how the Japanese prepare for work, it is not enough to focus on individual institutions designed specifically for vocational and technical education and training. The scope of inquiry must encompass all of the education system. It is the whole education system, in its various public and private institutional forms, that has achieved the high-skill formation underpinning Japan's economic success. However, an examination of the link between school and work also must take into account the social and work context. Work preparation is shaped in part by deeply held social perceptions concerning the role of the individual and society. Moreover, the work culture has exerted a profound influence on education and work preparation (Ashton & Green, 1996; Koike, 1981; McLean, 1995). With this introduction, the remainder of the chapter examines how the education system in a comprehensive sense prepares citizens for work, as well as how social and work contexts condition this preparation.

CHARACTERISTICS OF JAPANESE EDUCATION

Japan's education system, when compared with that of other countries, has very high enrollment, achievement, and completion rates at all levels. The preschool kindergarten, supported through tuition, enrolls about a third of all 4-year-olds and most 5-year-olds. Ninety-nine percent of all children enroll in the nine-grade compulsory public school (6- to 15-year age group), and 97 percent continue on to upper secondary school (ages 15 to 18). From the high-school level, more than 66 percent matriculate into university or some other form of higher education, including vocational schools. Dropout rates are low at all levels (Ministry of Education, Science, Sports and Culture [MESSC], 1997).

The Learning Culture

One reason for the high level of participation is that entrance to education beyond the compulsory level comes through examinations, and individual schools do not accept students unless those students have a reasonable possibility of succeeding. Moreover, at each school level there is a concentrated effort to work with students who lag behind, even if this means that the student must attend one of the many after-hours cram schools (*Juku*). Parents make a substantial contribution in paying for cram schools or individual tutors and, in fact, parents of high-achieving students may also send their children to cram schools to better prepare them for entrance examinations to the best schools.

All educational levels emphasize general, rather than specialized, education. While changes have started to occur, general preparation is valued because it indicates an individual's ability to master difficult intellectual content and, therefore, the capability to undergo additional advanced education and training. Vocational preparation rests on a strong foundation of math and science, and average Japanese pupils who go on to join the workforce have a higher level of general educational attainment than their counterparts in other industrialized countries. Moreover, the overall level of educational attainment in the workforce is higher than that found elsewhere (Prais, 1987).

Moral education is a central concern of schools. Showing respect for society, knowing one's place within the group, and demonstrating diligence and hard work are outcomes reinforced though instruction. They are considered at least as important as intellectual outcomes. Japanese society values conformity and consensus over individuality. It is strongly believed that success in life and work rests on the formation of the crucial and fundamental values that society considers important. In Japan, there is a high degree of consensus concerning core social values, appropriate standards of behavior, and the importance and value of education. Japan views its education system as an instrument for achieving cultural identity and national unity (McLean, 1995).

Parents and students alike are expected to take education and learning seriously, and to devote family resources and energy to promoting achievement in school. The young are expected to improve themselves so that they can become fully contributing members of society. As an individual and a member of society, it is each person's obligation to work hard, achieve in school, value group above individual goals, contribute to society, and respect the established order. While there is great respect for learning in general as a means to personal improvement, there also is a strong consensus that success in school is crucial to later economic and social status (McLean, 1995).

The Public/Private Link

Twenty-four percent of high schools are private, as are 84 percent of junior colleges and 74 percent of universities. However, in all cases, the government contributes funding, so the definition of "private" embraces the concept of government support and regulation. Nevertheless, government's main investment comes at the comprehensive-school level. Government

policy concentrates public funds at the elementary and junior school levels so that the largest possible number of pupils can attain the maximum general educational achievement. Solid intellectual and moral development in the lower grades is considered the foundation for all subsequent specific skill development (Dore & Sako, 1998; Dorfman, 1987; Koike, 1996).

Educational financing comes from national, prefectural, and municipal governments. The national government makes a relatively modest contribution compared with that of other industrialized countries: 4.78 percent of gross national product (GNP) in 1994 (MESSC, 1997). At the post-compulsory-school level, tuition and fees augment public funding. Nonprofit, private institutions play a major educational role, and they rely on tuition, fees, and government subsidies. At the postsecondary level, private companies may also contribute to specific institutions.

The national government exerts considerable influence over public and private education. The Ministry of Education, Science, Sports and Culture (*Monbusho*) prescribes curricula, standards, and administrative requirements; approves textbooks; sets budgets; and provides financial assistance to prefectures and municipalities. In addition, it (a) establishes and operates national educational institutions, primarily universities, junior colleges, and technical colleges; (b) regulates the establishment of private schools and provides general supervision of private institutions of higher education; and (c) issues directives to, monitors, and investigates local boards of education. In critical manpower and training areas, *Monbusho* expands opportunities through incentives and extended programming. The state also influences access to employment through active assistance in work placement (Dore & Sako, 1998; Imada, 1993).

The governing structure for education, including vocational education, is three-tiered: national, prefectural, and municipal, with the national government playing the strongest role. Both the prefectural and municipal levels are under the general supervision and authority of *Monbusho*. At the national level, consensus in the formation of educational policy is achieved by drawing on the advice and recommendation of standing advisory councils composed of individuals from outside the Ministry. Through the Central Council for Education, the most powerful policy group for education, the Ministry works with the national cabinet and parliament (*Diet*) to formulate budgets and education legislation. In terms of governance of the education system, the Ministry exerts considerable authority (Dorfman, 1987).

The Japanese education and employment systems are closely interrelated. Formal education qualifications are the most important prerequisite for employment in a leading firm or a prestigious government bureaucracy. These qualifications indicate one's ability to undergo successful firm-based training. The government also shapes policy to align human resource development and use with national economic and social development priorities, builds policy support, and mobilizes resources to support national goals (Ashton & Green, 1996; Cummings, 1995).

Employers tend to select students with good general education backgrounds because they prefer to provide specific skill training on the job. They also consider it essential that the prospective worker demonstrate the values and behaviors needed to function in the work culture of a specific firm. Unlike the systems of work preparation in most industrialized countries, in Japan the majority of specific skill training takes place inside the firm once the individual becomes an employee (Ishikawa, 1991; Koike, 1996; Yahata, 1994).

The various components of the education and training system form a loose hierarchy, with one level flowing into another. Students either progress upward through the various levels, or they exit at strategic points into the labor market. However, not all institutions at a given educational level have equal status.

THE EDUCATION AND TRAINING SYSTEM

While public and private schools exist at all educational levels, this is particularly the case in the postsecondary vocational and technical education tracks, and includes colleges of technology, special training schools, and miscellaneous schools. There are two categories of public schools: national schools (established and funded by the national government) and local public schools (established and supported either by the prefectural or municipal government, but funded by all three government levels).

Compulsory Education

Compulsory education is free in Japan and open to all children from the ages of 6 to 15. Most children attend tuition-supported private preschool kindergartens or day-care centers that ease the transition from home to school by helping children learn to respond to group responsibilities. The "head-start" achieved through preschool underscores the importance parents place on the compulsory school years. The first nine years of school life largely dictate the social and economic options that children will have later, when, as young adults, they enter the labor force.

Certain individual high schools, including vocational ones, enjoy higher status with the public. Attendance in these schools determines not only which university students can eventually enroll in but also which particular firms will offer employment once they have completed their formal education. Entrance into high school is very competitive, and only the highest-performing students gain admittance to the best schools. The economic and career stakes related to doing well in compulsory school are very high for Japanese youth.

Emphasis on achievement and values. In a real sense, formal preparation for work starts with entrance to compulsory school and rests on a foundation of academic studies and social conditioning. Unlike Western systems of vocational preparation, little emphasis goes to specific skill training. Employers will provide specific skill training later. The Japanese value demonstrated ability to follow a rigorous course of study, pass difficult examinations, and gain entrance to the best schools. Considerable weight also goes to moral education and cultural conditioning. Schools receive strong support to develop moral attitudes, personal habits, and group cohesiveness.

Classes are organized into small groups that serve as the basic units of instruction. In these groups, students develop loyalty and learn to (a) subordinate their own interests to common goals and (b) achieve as a coordinated unit. The traits of respect for society and the established order, diligence and responsibility, well-organized and disciplined study, and self-criticism and conformity in behavior are believed not only to promote academic achievement but to form the foundation for successful work careers. Subsequent entrance to the best high schools, postsecondary institutions, and companies rests on high test scores and evidence of the development of proper values, attitudes, and habits. From their very first educational experiences, children travel down an educational road that parents hope will lead to a secure, high-status job (Dorfman, 1987).

Compulsory schooling is uniform. Virtually all students follow a standardized national curriculum and use government-approved textbooks. Except in some exclusive private schools, students at the same grade level throughout the country study the same material at the same time. There is no internal tracking, such as that found in schools in the U.S., and no remedial classes, ability groups, or electives. However, some teachers, on their own initiative, give students extra help after school. While some changes are occurring, they have met resistance. All students must master subject matter to approximately the same level so that very little difference in the range of achievement exists. Japanese society believes that student differences in achievement result primarily from a lack of effort, and not from innate differences in ability. Japan emphasizes

individual responsibility for learning (McLean, 1995).

However, in practice, some students lag behind others. These slower students receive help in four ways: (a) additional graded textbook exercises; (b) "remedial" tutoring after school at the initiative of some teachers; (c) attendance at private, supplemental classes (*Juku*) during evenings and weekends; or (d) tutors hired by parents (Dorfman, 1987). To be sure, differences exist among Japanese students, but no other country matches Japan's level of uniform achievement.

In the elementary grades (1-6) of the compulsory school, all students study a broad-based curriculum: Japanese language, social studies, arithmetic, science, music, art and handicraft, homemaking (for girls and boys), physical education, and moral education. Lessons follow sequenced textbook material, and all mandated material must be covered for each grade level. Schools stress development of habits such as diligence, perseverance, and attention to detail. Throughout all grades, heavy emphasis goes to math and science (Dorfman, 1987).

Lower secondary school. In the three upper grades of the compulsory school (7-9), emphasis on academic preparation intensifies in preparation for high school entrance examinations. More stress goes toward the acquisition of factual knowledge and the development of basic skills. Mathematics for all students includes basic algebra and geometry. Ninety percent of all Japanese students take some calculus before leaving the compulsory school; science includes laboratory instruction and field work. Additional subjects are social studies, music, art, health, foreign language (usually English), physical education, and moral education. Although specific vocational education does not begin until after compulsory schooling, all students take industrial arts or homemaking in the 7th, 8th, and 9th grades. Considered prevocational, these courses are designed to help students acquire practical skills and to develop appropriate attitudes about work and home life (Dorfman, 1987).

The emphasis on regulating individual habits and values intensifies. Students must wear uniforms in many schools; personal appearance and accessories are regulated; discipline is stressed; and conformity and achievement are expected. In moral education, core themes continue to be emphasized and infused throughout the curriculum:

• Importance of order, regularity, cooperation, thoughtfulness, participation, manners, and respect for public property.

• Endurance, hard work, and high aspirations.

• Freedom, justice, fairness, rights, duties, trust, and conviction.

• The individual's place in groups such as the family, school, nation, and world.

• Harmony with nature and its appreciation.

• Need for rational and scientific attitudes toward human life (Dorfman, 1987).

PREPARING FOR THE WORK WORLD

The academic track in upper secondary schools prepares students for university entrance examinations. University attendance is viewed as the most desirable form of work preparation since it leads to the best jobs in large corporations. Traditionally, to be a "salary man" has been the goal of most Japanese youth. Advancement opportunities and lifetime employment have been virtually assured for loyal, hard-working employees in prestigious companies.

Six public and private institutional forms are used to prepare non-university-bound youth for entry into the labor market. Five are administered under the jurisdiction of *Monbusho*:

• Vocational tracks in comprehensive secondary schools and specialized vocational secondary schools.

• Colleges of technology.

• Junior colleges.

• Special training schools.

• Miscellaneous schools.

The sixth form, vocational training centers, falls under the jurisdiction of the Ministry of Labor. A considerable amount of vocational training takes place within firms, and this is no insignificant fact. As previously discussed, in Japan, firms, rather than schools, are the major source of specific skill training.

Upper Secondary Education

High school attendance in Japan is desirable but not free. Parents pay substantial fees. As students end the compulsory education cycle at the age of 15, they must formally apply for admission to high school, which requires good scores on an entrance examination. The application includes written recommendations and "placement guidance" from teachers and, when combined with examination results, determines whether the student may enroll in a high-status school. Individuals who do not perform well academically in comprehensive schooling usually pay a heavy price for the rest of their lives, working in low-prestige, low-paying jobs. The particular educational institution a person attends, and not necessarily the individual's talent, greatly impacts initial employment and subsequent job advancement (Dore & Sako, 1998; Dorfman, 1987; Koike, 1996).

The great majority of upper secondary schools are public institutions. Of the more than 1,300 private schools, some are among the best high schools in Japan, while others cater to middle- and low-achieving students whose parents can and will pay to improve their sons' or daughters' performance.

The student participation and completion rates in secondary education are the highest of those in any country in the world. Of the 97 percent of students who enroll in some form of upper secondary education, only 2 percent do not complete it. Strong parental and student demand has driven the expansion of the three-year upper secondary school, where about 94 percent of the enrollment is concentrated (MESSC, 1997).

Striving for status. Approximately 70 percent of all students who attend high school enroll in the academic, college preparatory track although, as suggested, high schools differ greatly in their individual status and, hence, their value for college entrance purposes. At the point of attending high school, education stratification becomes most obvious. Relatively few students gain admission to elite schools and, as Rohlen (1983) suggested, "the educational tracks into which students are shunted at this stage are both more diverse and more fundamental than at the college stage to the overall structure of society" (p. 122). In the minds of parents and students, there is a clear, definite, and absolute ranking among schools, including schools that offer vocational education.

Except for vocational education, students follow a uniform, unspecialized, and encyclopedic curriculum, with few electives. They study a great deal of factual information that they expect to need on university entrance examinations. During the 10th grade, everyone takes virtually the same core subjects: Japanese language, mathematics, science, English, and social studies. They may also take physical education, health, and art. In the 11th and 12th grades, students choose to concentrate in either literature or science, and some separation by ability levels occurs.

Despite the enormous pressure on students to excel, some have difficulty with the content and pace of instruction. As a result, they may elect to attend a private academic preparatory school or forego college attendance by enrolling in postsecondary vocational education. Large numbers of students also attend *Yobiko*, specialized cram schools that offer intense preparatory training for university entrance examinations. *Yobiko* instruction often is tailored to the requirements of specific institutions.

Feeding the labor market. Of the approximately 70 percent of students who pursue the academic track in upper secondary school, 29 percent enter university, 8 percent opt for jun-

ior colleges, and 21 percent enroll in postsecondary vocational education (MESSC, 1997). The remainder seek employment. In a real sense, then, the "academic" upper secondary track makes a major contribution to the high quality of the Japanese labor force. Students who cannot qualify for university entrance, but who nevertheless have a relatively high level of academic achievement, take jobs or enter some form of vocational preparation. Most students who attend postsecondary programs complete them, which indicates their competitive and selective nature, the level of previous preparation, and the value attached to achievement. In general, entrance to postsecondary education in all forms is highly competitive. Students do not gain admittance unless they show considerable promise of successful completion.

Secondary-Level Vocational Preparation

At the upper secondary school level, both comprehensive and specialized schools offer vocational preparation. Of the more than 5,000 upper secondary schools in Japan, 16 percent offer exclusively vocational programming, while 31 percent offer both vocational and general subjects. At any one time, approximately 23 percent of all secondary school students are enrolled in vocational preparation programs in either comprehensive or separate vocational schools (MESSC, 1997).

In both cases, students study general as well as vocational subjects. Vocational students take nearly the same broad-based curriculum as academic students for the first two years of the upper secondary school, including courses in Japanese language, history, geography, mathematics, science, art, and physical education. Of the 80 credits needed to graduate, at least 30 are in vocational preparation. However, vocational studies also are broad based, rather than job specific. The more general vocational preparation is valued as a way to develop foundation skills considered essential for a successful working life. Typically, much attention goes to the more general and theoretical aspects of vocational studies as the basis of practical application. This provides the foundation for further vocational development, either through additional schooling or in individual firms (Prais, 1987).

In general, six instructional concentrations are offered: agriculture, commercial, economics, fisheries, health, and technical/industrial. Each concentration includes specialized courses. In the technical/industrial concentration, for example, students select from among electricity, machinery, electronics, information technology, architecture, and civil engineering. Male enrollments tend to center in technical concentrations, and female enrollments in commercial ones (Dore & Sako, 1998; Dorfman, 1987).

The dividing line between vocational and academic students seems less sharp in Japan than elsewhere. Prais (1987) observed, for example, that 39 percent of students who took the vocational school entrance examination scored higher than the median score for all school-leavers. It is incorrect to assume that vocational enrollments come primarily from the lower half of the ability range—vocational students actually represent a broad range of ability levels. Similarly, the institutions and programs that they attend vary. Some schools screen specifically for high-ability students. These schools tend to specialize in what are considered the most important fields, such as electronics, civil engineering, industrial chemistry, and machinery. On the other hand, some technical schools cater specifically to lower-ability students. Moreover, differences appear in the enrollment profile for individual programs since students are screened according to their examination scores. Higher-scoring students are admitted to higher-status vocational programs.

A striking characteristic of Japanese vocational education is its high level of student achievement, particularly in math and science. Vocational students as a group, for example, pursue a more rigorous curriculum and achieve at a higher level than comparable student groups in either the United States or England (Prais, 1987). Unlike the United States, Japan has no large group of underachievers who lack even the most basic academic skills. This results in a workforce that as a whole has a high overall level of technical competence. This is particularly true in the case of intermediate-level workers. Employers can make better use of average- and below-average-ability individuals since they possess the foundation skills necessary for high-skill, high-wage work (Koike, 1996). Indeed, the strength of the Japanese production system, Prais (1987) observed, rests in its large, competent, and disciplined technician class, which can outperform comparable workers in other industrial countries.

How does Japan achieve such uniformly high performance levels? First, and primarily, the solid foundation in basic skills that individuals achieve at the compulsory school level is fundamental to all subsequent education and training, including job preparation within a firm. The standardized national curriculum is coupled with classroom instruction focused on getting all group members to perform at nearly uniform levels. Educators and parents alike believe that virtually all students have the potential to achieve if they work hard and long enough (McLean, 1995). With education so important to economic and social advancement, Japanese students have strong incentives to perform, and they receive strong parental support. More than 65 percent of lower secondary school pupils attend private evening classes—and the number jumps to 75 percent in the year before students take high school entrance examinations. In large cities, attendance may be consistently 75 percent or more (Dorfman, 1987). Prais (1987) suggested that the "strong parental motivation that supports these supplemental classes goes a long way towards explaining how such a large proportion of pupils are able to attain such very high standards by age 15" (p. 45).

Students cannot graduate from a vocational program until their performance is judged satisfactory based on assessments within the individual school. Even lower-performing and -ability students understand that they must attain acceptable performance levels if they expect to graduate. Since students pay fees, they feel pressure to perform. On the other hand, teachers and employers know that variability exists among schools and programs. In schools that cater to weaker students, the curriculum may cover the same content, but not at the same depth (Prais, 1987).

Some students from vocational secondary schools matriculate into university, but they often find it hard to keep pace with students from the nonvocational track. Most vocational school completers occupy places in industry somewhere between operators and engineers or managers. Large firms rely heavily on university graduates, however. It is the small firms that tend to recruit vocational school graduates. They cannot afford extensive in-house training, and they look to secondary vocational programs to provide students with technical skills.

Colleges of Technology

Colleges of technology (*Koto Senmon Gakko*) are designed to prepare skilled technicians for industry and commerce. Students enroll in these colleges at the beginning of 10th grade, after completing compulsory lower secondary education. They follow a rigorous, five-year course of general education and technical studies. Enrollment is almost exclusively male and concentrated in engineering-related fields. The colleges are well equipped and staffed, and they provide quality programs.

This type of institution was established in the 1960s in response to the need for an intermediate level of training that lies between the technician and the university graduate levels. Of the 62 colleges of technology, only 3 are private and 4 municipal, while the remaining 55 are national. Their combined enrollment is approximately 56,000 students. Most graduates enter the labor force directly, but roughly 24 percent continue on to university, typically

entering at the third year of study (MESSC, 1997; Sako, 1994).

Junior Colleges

Women make up around 90 percent of the enrollment in the 588 junior colleges. Admission to the two-year programs is open to upper high school graduates. Roughly one-third of the more than 417,000 students concentrate in general educational studies (humanities, social sciences, and general culture), while the remainder enroll in vocational programs. Almost one-fourth of the vocational-program students enroll in home economics (homemaking), with the remainder studying such fields as engineering, agriculture, health, and teaching. Teachers prepared in junior colleges tend to find jobs at the preschool level. More than 80 percent of the junior colleges are private (Dorfman, 1987; MESSC, 1997).

Special Training Schools

The system of special training schools (*Senshu Gakko*) offers continuing education courses to everyone. Many of those who enroll are looking for a second chance after they failed to gain admission to college or get a job in a prestigious firm. They hope that additional schooling will open the door of opportunity (Dore & Sako, 1998). Two kinds of special training schools exist: upper secondary (*Koto Senshu Gakko*), which provide a three-year course to lower secondary school graduates; and two-year training colleges (*Senmon Gakko*), which offer courses for upper high school graduates. Students take general education courses along with vocational ones so that they will acquire both vocational skills and "education for daily living." These schools prepare individuals for jobs in midlevel occupations in such fields as engineering, agriculture, health, and commerce. Instruction is linked closely to occupational qualification and certification requirements.

About 90 percent of special schools are private, which gives them considerably more institutional and instructional flexibility than publicly supported institutions in terms of responding to market demand. For this reason, special schools fill an important niche in the workforce preparation system, since they can quickly adapt to changing technology and labor market requirements. Special schools have been quick to set up new courses in response to local demand. They fill the gap left by the slower-to-respond public schools. In particular, special schools play an important role in preparing workers in cutting-edge, high-technology, and computer fields. Special schools are a major source of technically trained individuals.

In 1995, there were more than 83,800 students enrolled in upper secondary-level special schools and 650,000 students attending postsecondary special colleges for upper high school graduates. Reforms over the past decade have contributed to the attractiveness of these schools.

Since 1985, individuals who have completed an upper secondary level course of at least three years' duration that satisfies established standards may be granted qualifications for university entrance. Beginning in 1991, individual special-college courses that meet established standards have been recognized for university credit. Since 1995, the title of "Specialist" can be awarded to individuals who complete a course at a special training college that satisfies established standards. The enhanced status resulting from reforms, combined with the market value of the instruction provided, has contributed to making special schools an attractive and increasingly important form of workforce preparation (Dore & Sako, 1998; MESSC, 1997).

Miscellaneous Schools

Miscellaneous schools (*Kakushu Gakko*) give both adults and young people additional educational opportunity outside of the formal education system. They offer courses at both upper secondary and postsecondary levels. Their programs vary in length and substance, ranging from highly specific occupational

preparation in dressmaking, cosmetology, and nursing, for example, to more general occupational subjects such as home economics, business studies, and computer science. General subjects, such as foreign language studies, also are offered. As of 1997, there were about 2,600 miscellaneous schools with a total enrollment of 281,000 students, of which approximately half were female. Almost all miscellaneous schools (98 percent) are private, supported through student fees (Dorfman, 1987; MESSC, 1997; Sako, 1994).

THE MINISTRY OF LABOR

A national system of 370 vocational training centers (VTCs) (*Shokugyo Kunrenko*) is administered through the Ministry of Labor. These centers were originally established to combat skill and labor shortages by training 15-year-olds who were leaving school and going directly into the labor market. Their purpose, however, has expanded to include retraining displaced workers, retraining and upgrading employed workers, and providing career development activities that address the needs of both youth and mature workers. Courses in the VTCs tend to focus on craft- and trade-based occupations, such as auto mechanics, construction, welding, painting, plumbing, and woodworking. Initial two-year training courses enroll more than 30,000 youth annually. About 225,000 employed adults take either full-, part-time, or correspondence upgrading courses, and around 46,000 displaced workers undergo retraining each year in VTCs.

Other ministries conduct limited training activities in such fields as marine occupations, health, and transportation. Apart from this, subcontracting of training to the private sector has been encouraged since the 1980s. In addition, a 1985 amendment to the Human Resources Development Promotion Law supported career development activities provided through employers.

Many individuals prepared through the VTCs and other programs administered by government ministries make up the large category of employees termed *peripheral workers*. They generally work in the thousands of small- and medium-size establishments that offer lower pay and less-secure jobs than the large, prestigious national corporations. These individuals may experience periods of unemployment, or part-time or temporary work. While the work that they do is important, their jobs demand less rigorous education, have lower status, and require long hours. Such training programs, while they cannot fully address questions of status, security, and opportunity, at least provide an outlet for individuals trying to better themselves (Chalmers, 1989; Dore & Sako, 1998; Ishikawa, 1991).

JOB STANDARDS
AND QUALIFICATIONS

Most employees in technical fields take rigorous periodic tests to establish and maintain their qualifications. However, those who hold a university degree (or graduation certificate) may be either fully or partially exempt from professional examinations. The purpose of the testing is to raise the efficiency of those already employed, a process called *leveling up.*

Qualification requirements in different fields strongly influence the curriculum of training institutions. A considerable amount of the training done in special training schools, miscellaneous schools, and VTCs is preparation for a qualification exam. Employees in some fields must take such examinations as frequently as every three years to maintain their certificates or licenses. Most are seasoned employees, which reflects the emphasis on continuing career development. More employees in large firms take qualification examinations than do those in small firms (Dore & Sako, 1998).

The state is the primary participant in maintaining the standards and qualification system, with associations of employing organizations and training associations playing only minor roles. Rather than intervene directly in job preparation, the government can indirectly shape skill development, at a relatively modest cost, through the qualification system. To do this, the state directs its efforts to individual firms, the site of specific skill development. Firms participate because it is in their best interest: Participation encourages loyalty and enhances a firm's status. Qualification exams are perceived primarily as being linked to job performance and employment in a specific firm. They are not viewed as a way to acquire a better job in a different firm. The exams grow out of work and ratify the skills acquired, rather than reflect attendance in routine training courses (Dore & Sako, 1998; Koike, 1996; Yahata, 1994).

Many large firms have their own qualification examinations. Although individuals who demonstrate sufficient proficiency can take government-administered qualification exams, these exams may not have high currency within a firm because the important thing is an employee's ability to address the skill requirements defined by the job. Individual companies carry out the functions of training, quality control, and advancement to maximize their employees' potential. Employees accept the system because they perceive the cultural climate of the company as promoting their own welfare (Alexander, 1993; Dore & Sako, 1998; Koike, 1996).

THE TRANSITION
FROM SCHOOL TO WORK

Their first employer may be the only employer many Japanese youth will ever have. Although the ethic of loyalty to the firm is weakening, individuals who secure a job after graduation in a large, prestigious firm tend to stay with that employer. More job mobility exists, however, among workers in smaller firms, and extensive job changing is common among peripheral workers who have temporary and part-time jobs. Nevertheless, in general, Japan has considerably less occupational mobility than that found in many Western industrialized countries. Furthermore, in Japan, the first job that school leavers get often determines their subsequent work career: Firm status and occupational level are established. Because the first job is so important, the search process is not left to chance.

The Transition of Non-University-Bound Youth

Only about 3 percent of students begin work directly after they finish the compulsory grades. These individuals generally find employment in low-prestige, low-skill, low-paying jobs that have limited career prospects. Among upper high school graduates, approximately 30 percent enter directly into the labor force, while the remainder go on to postsecondary training. The latter have much better job prospects.

The Ministry of Labor operates a job referral system through its Public Employment Security Office (PESO). By law and in order to prevent exploitation, only PESO and other nonprofit organizations, including schools, can supply job placement assistance. The referral system aims to minimize the unemployment period of school completers and to ease their transition to work. The system makes extensive use of teachers, placement counselors, and advisors. Schools spend a considerable amount of time placing students in the best possible jobs to enhance their reputation, while avoiding inappropriate placements. Employers know the status ranking of individual schools, and they tend to hire from the best ones possible. In this way, a stable relationship develops between schools and employers. Furthermore, linking school completion directly with job placement encourages students to enroll and complete a program, which partially explains Japan's high secondary school attendance rates. As Imada (1993) recounted, "The system of schools acting as job-placement channels enables them to get these students involved in school work. Knowing that academic performance counts when finding employment . . . students steer themselves toward school" (p. 7).

Direct contact between high school students and company personnel is prohibited. Company representatives sent to the schools can meet with placement counselors, but not with individual students. Placement counselors also consult with students about their employment interests, advise them on job selection, and prepare them for company examinations and interviews. Every effort is made to match students with appropriate jobs (Dorfman, 1987; Imada, 1993).

Students' job applications are submitted to employers by their schools. Job interviews take place at the firm, and potential employers look not only for evidence of solid academic achievement, but also for a record of positive values, habits, and attitudes. In addition to an interview, the student may take a written examination, an intelligence/aptitude test, and a physical examination (Dorfman, 1987).

From Postsecondary Education to Work

College and university graduates may contact firms directly or seek employment through a school placement office or personal acquaintances. PESO does not play a significant role in the placement of university graduates. However, the Ministry of Labor, as a public service, operates placement offices throughout the country. Nevertheless, the pattern of employer contact with university faculty or departments tends to dominate. Firms and specific faculty members in special fields often develop direct working relationships. It is through these personal contacts that important hiring decisions are made. For example, a firm that wants to hire an electrical engineer relies on its connections with faculty members in programs of known quality to recommend well-qualified students. Since the students have a continuing obligation to the professor, they accept the offered positions (Dorfman, 1987; Stern, 1995).

Employers tend to place more faith in the quality of a program than in a detailed assessment of a particular student's knowledge. Applicants almost always take a written exam, but the exam is generally used to confirm a hiring decision rather than to screen candidates. However, the personal interview is extremely important. Employers use the interview to assess applicants' personality, leadership potential, attitude toward professional development, and compatibility with the firm's culture (Dorfman, 1987; Stern, 1995).

TRAINING IN INDUSTRY

When discussing Japanese firms, what first comes to mind are the large, internationally known corporations that dominate industries: Toyota, Nissan, and Honda in automobiles; Sony, Fujitsu, and Toshiba in electronics; Minolta and Canon in cameras; Hitachi and Panasonic in televisions; and Mitsubishi in heavy equipment. Small- and medium-size enterprises, however, prevail in Japanese business and industry. More than 80 percent of all employees work in privately owned, small- and medium-sized firms. More than 50 percent of nonagricultural workers are employed in firms that have fewer than 30 employees, and 42 percent work in firms smaller than 10 employees (Chalmers, 1989; Koike, 1996). What is striking about the Japanese industrial structure is that the division between firms is not sharp. Smaller firms work under the umbrella of larger ones, with the transfer of new technology and skills from the large to the small (Dore & Sako, 1998). Nevertheless, substantial differences exist in employee selection, training, and skill level.

In general, individuals who have the lowest level of educational attainment work in the smaller firms. As firm size increases, so does employees' educational achievement, with the best students from the best universities finding work in large, premier firms. Smaller firms also tend to employ more older workers and more women. In addition, smaller firms tend to have lower pay and job security, as well as greater job mobility. Small firms that do mainly subcontracting work are most vulnerable to economic cycles, so they tend to maintain an expendable workforce of nonregular workers. This both protects the firms' own permanent, core workers from layoffs and forms a buffer

for large firms (Chalmers, 1989; Koike, 1996).

Smaller firms tend to recruit more workers from the labor market itself rather than directly from schools, and they rely more on external training sources to prepare their workforce. There is less in-firm training among small firms (Dore & Sako, 1998). However, a full 80 percent of all Japanese firms provide some type of training, either through external sources or in-house. In smaller firms, training is designed mainly to facilitate the introduction of new equipment and processes, "level-up" new operations, and improve the quality of services. Long-term career development is emphasized less in small firms, as compared with the practice in large firms. Small firms that cannot afford training may rely on technology transfers from large customer companies for whom they do subcontracting. They also may request skill or upgrading courses through the Ministry of Labor's VTCs. During periods of low economic activity, training increases as firms take advantage of worker availability to prepare for an economic upturn (Sako, 1994).

Japanese industries can situate their specific skill training and career development in-firm for two fundamental reasons. First, the high level of general education within the workforce as a whole enables employees at all levels to undergo productive training and career development. Japanese firms rely on schools to provide intellectually able and motivated graduates who have demonstrated their potential by following a rigorous course of instruction. Comprehensive and wide-ranging preparation works better than specialization because it provides the foundation for future learning within the firm in a variety of capacities. A school's status and reputation hold more importance than particular subjects studied because they demonstrate the individual's capacity to learn in a demanding environment. Also, formation of good behavior and attitudes is valued as much as intellectual background because it indicates leadership potential and the ability to work within a firm's culture

(Koike, 1996; Stern, 1995). Prais (1987) concluded that the high level of general competence in the workforce as a whole is the overriding strength and achievement of Japan's work preparation system.

Second, because there is virtually lifetime employment within larger firms, these firms can make considerable investments in training employees without the danger that trained individuals will leave to take other jobs. Firms can develop specific, long-term career development plans with the expectation that initial training will be followed by periodic retraining, job rotation, and individual career advancement (Dore & Sako, 1998; Koike, 1996). Stern (1995) reported that when graduates search for employment, they look for firms that offer the best training opportunities, which they view as a good indicator of future advancement and promotion possibilities.

Larger firms, those with more than 1,000 employees, almost always link training to promotion. Moreover, unlike in the United States, where the considerable sums that firms spend each year on training go mainly to the management level, Japan takes a broad-based approach to employee development to improve the performance of all employees. The goal is to cultivate over time a productive, all-embracing work culture that can respond to a changing economic environment. The work culture itself is considered a key to success. As Koike (1981) suggested, the concept of human capital development as a long-term investment policy is instrumental to understanding Japan's high economic achievement.

Large firms typically recruit graduates as regular employees at full salary, even though they will undergo a one-year combination of on- and off-the-job training. Older employees who have passed a special examination to qualify as instructors act as trainers and supervisors and pass on their specific knowledge and skills. Training courses within and outside the firm supplement this basic training, although in large firms in-house training predominates. The firm continually monitors beginning employees to identify their special skills or skill deficiencies. Each firm tailors training to its specific requirements. Most training, moreover, is application related in narrowly defined, single activities. Retraining, provided when necessary, is the major method for transferring new skills to workers. Adaptation to technical and production changes tends to occur rapidly (Alexander, 1993; Ishikawa, 1991; Koike, 1996).

After basic training, as a result of their experience and demonstrated performance, employees are assigned to new, usually higher-skill and higher-paying jobs. This generally occurs every three to five years. Frequent retraining is seen as a necessary and expected part of a career. Employees deliberately rotate through key departments to maximize the breadth of their experience. In each new job, preparation again starts with on-the-job training, coupled with organized retraining and, where needed, training outside the firm (Alexander, 1993; Koike, 1996; Yahata, 1994).

Systems of workforce preparation that provide high concentrations of specific school-based skill training have the initial advantage of providing new employees with skills that they can immediately use. However, such systems are more likely to reproduce skills already in use than to develop the capability to enter new phases of productive activities that in-firm training offers. Training in Japanese firms is linked directly to new product development and changed production mix.

DISCUSSION

There are many explanations for the remarkable post-World War II achievements of Japanese business and industry (Berggren, 1995). However, the education system and its role in work preparation are major factors. From the very first grades of compulsory education, Japanese children start down the road of workforce preparation. High academic achievement during the compulsory school years, coupled with training in core values and behaviors, provides the foundation for all subsequent education and training in schools and on the job. Japanese youth attend and complete school and achieve at a higher level than youth in any other country. A broad cross section of the workforce receives a distinctly higher level of education than is found elsewhere. At intermediate vocational levels, in particular, students reach a high level of educational attainment. Even the lower levels do not have large numbers of dysfunctional individuals who lack even the basic rudiments of learning, as seen in some Western countries (Dore & Sako, 1998; Dorfman, 1987; Prais, 1987).

General, rather than highly specific, preparation is preferred. A solid record of academic achievement is considered the best vocational preparation. Firms hire graduates based on the reputation of their schools, and not necessarily because of specific courses followed. Students select employers for the potential for training and advancement. In fact, firms play a central role in the Japanese system of work preparation. Firms—not schools—serve as the major source of specific skill training. Through training, companies can develop a sense of loyalty among employees, while cultivating a highly skilled, broad-based, and adaptable workforce well versed in multiple aspects of work.

However, the relationship between firms and schools plays a crucial role. Schools provide the basic foundation skills needed by all workers at every level. Work preparation in the different occupational strata is delivered through different institutions and, below the university level, schools play a major role in the transition to work. Japanese youth use school completion as a passport to work. Companies influence both the substance and quality of instruction by their hiring and in-firm qualification practices.

The education and training system is not ideal in all aspects, however. Women face significant problems. Increasingly, youth are rebelling against the rigidity and social sorting. There are high human costs not only for those

driven to excel, but also for those who do not perform to expectation. Critics also suggest that, while the quantitative accomplishments of Japan's education system are unquestioned, large gaps exist in the full range of cognitive and social skills, with soft spots in basic research and creativity most evident (Berggren, 1995; Cummings, 1995; McLean, 1995). Perhaps most challenging, the work culture itself is changing. Company loyalty and the system of elite selection are breaking down under the pressures of economic recession and international competition. Job opportunities are fewer; companies are more cautious in hiring; and the time-honored system of in-house training is being severely tested (Berggren, 1995).

To what extent, however, can work preparation in Japan provide lessons for other countries? The high participation and achievement rates in Japan's intensely competitive education system, where individuals are expected to achieve, result from deeply ingrained societal values. Practices within industry are rooted in these same values. Whether other societies with different historic traditions can emulate Japanese educational performance is highly questionable. McLean (1995) observed, for example, that "elements of Confucianism have underwritten a drive for educational achievement among large numbers of people in ways that have eluded Western societies. They help to explain why, also, educational achievement becomes a mass characteristic yet is based on individual responsibility" (p. 43).

Nevertheless, the twin forces of globalization and rapid technological change are driving the quest worldwide for more effective education and training. Even if other countries cannot fully emulate the Japanese approach to preparing for work, at least there are important policy lessons that require studied consideration.

References

Alexander, P.-J. (1993). *The German dual training system in Japan*. Tokyo: German Chamber of Industry and Commerce in Japan.

Ashton, D., & Green, F. (1996). *Education, training*

and the global economy. Cheltenham, UK: Edward Elgar.

Berggren, C. (1995). Japan as number two: Competitive problems and the future of alliance capitalism after the burst of the bubble boom. *Work, Employment & Society, 9* (1), 53-95.

Chalmers, N. J. (1989). *Industrial relations in Japan: The peripheral workforce*. London: Routledge.

Cummings, W. K. (1995). The Asian human resource approach in global perspectives. *Oxford Review of Education, 21*(1), 67-81.

Dore, R., & Sako, M. (1998). *How the Japanese learn to work*. London: Routledge.

Dorfman, C. H. (1987). *Japanese education today*. Washington, DC: U.S. Department of Education.

Imada, S. (1993, October 1). Transition from school to work. *Japanese Labor Bulletin*, pp. 5-8.

Ishikawa, T. (1991). *Vocational training* (Japanese Industrial Relations Series). Tokyo: The Japan Institute of Labour.

Koike, K. (1981). The inner workings of Japanese diligence. *Japan Eco, 8*(2), 30-43.

Koike, K. (1996). *The economics of work in Japan*.

Tokyo: LTCB International Library Foundation.

McLean, M. (1995). *Educational traditions compared: Content, teaching and learning in industrialized countries*. London: David Fulton.

Ministry of Education, Science, Sports and Culture. (1997). *Japanese government policies in education, science, sports and culture*. Tokyo: Author.

Prais, S. J. (1987, February). Educating for productivity: Comparisons of Japanese and English schooling and vocational preparation. *National Institute Economic Review, 119*, 40-56.

Rohlen, T. P. (1983). *Japan's high schools*. Berkeley, CA: University of California Press.

Sako, M. (1994). Japan: Vocational education and training. In T. Husen & T. N. Postlethwaite (Eds.), *The international encyclopedia of education* (2nd ed., pp. 3086-3092). Oxford, England: Pergamon.

Stern, S. (1995). Education and work in Japan: Implications for policy. *Educational Policy, 9*(2), 201-217.

Yahata, S. (1994, May 1). In-house training and OJT. *Japan Labor Bulletin*, pp. 5-8.

15

Maximizing Human Potential and the Process of Economic Growth in Singapore

By David Ashton and Johnny Sung

Notwithstanding the crash of 1997-98, the four Asian "Tiger" economies (Hong Kong, Republic of [South] Korea, Singapore, and Taiwan) have experienced a higher growth rate than any other industrial societies. Central to this burst of economic growth was the intentional development of human resource potential to ensure that continued growth would not be impeded by shortages of skilled labor at all levels of the economy.

The first part of this chapter presents the patterns of economic growth among the high-performing Asian economies (HPAEs[1]) and explores ways in which their experiences differ from those of other societies. The second part examines Singapore's experience in more detail to identify the part in the growth process played by human resource development (HRD). The final part of the chapter explores implications of this case study for understanding HRD's role in economic growth.

The argument put forward here is that the governments of the four Asian Tigers, in general, and Singapore, in particular, have played a major role in enhancing the speed of their economic growth. This was done by coordinating the actions of both capital and labor. Government influenced capital by developing a coherent industrial strategy that focused on moving the economy away from low-value-added forms of production to higher-value-added ones. This ensured having appropriate forms of capital in place to produce high-value-added goods and services. Regarding labor, this change required the development of a workforce that had the skills that new industries needed. Singapore and the other Tigers proved particularly innovative in establishing mechanisms that enabled the government to coordinate changes in the spheres of employment, education, and training. This ensured that employers always had employees with appropriate and necessary skills available, which kept investment from being held back by shortages of skilled labor and facilitated attracting appropriate forms of capital. Consequently, economic growth took place more rapidly than if the government had left the coordination of capital and labor entirely to market forces.

[1]*See the Appendix, page 212, for a list of acronyms used in this chapter, and their meanings.*

TABLE 1—EMPLOYMENT, LABOR, AND GDP GROWTH

Countries	Employment growth	Labor growth	GDP growth
	[Average annual growth percent]		
Developed Economies (1974-1995)			
Australia	3.0	1.9	3.0
Canada	1.8	2.0	2.9
France	0.2	0.7	2.2
Germany	1.2	1.6	2.6
Italy	0.2	0.5	2.4
Japan	0.9	1.0	3.2
New Zealand	1.5	1.3	1.5
Portugal	1.1	1.3	2.6
Spain	−0.2	0.8	2.4
United Kingdom	0.1	0.4	1.8
United States	1.8	0.5	2.5
High-Performing Asian Economies (1975-1993)			
Hong Kong	3.2	2.8	7.0
Republic of [South] Korea	3.0	2.4	8.6
Singapore	3.7	2.5	7.5
Taiwan	NA	NA	NA

Note: NA = Information not available. Data sources: International Labour Office (1996) and Pacific Economic Cooperation Council (1993).

SHIFTING FROM LOW-VALUE-ADDED TO HIGH-VALUE-ADDED PRODUCTION

Between the 1960s and the financial crisis of 1997, the HPAEs of the four Tigers grew consistently at a rate two to three times that of the rest of the world. The HPAEs also significantly outperformed developed economies in North America and Europe. With this spectacular growth came major labor market changes. Changes included the maintenance of a high level of employment growth, the transfer of labor from low-value-added sectors to high-value-added sectors, and the continuous upgrading of the labor force through national education and training (ET) systems.

Table 1 shows that the rate of employment growth in all but one of the developed economies was very slow compared with that in the HPAEs. In the period 1974-1995, most countries in the European Union (EU) achieved a rate of employment growth of less than 1 percent, while the United States' average rate for the same period was 1.8 percent. The HPAE equivalent was more than 3 percent. These figures are not necessarily surprising as the HPAE countries started from a lower base. However, considering the figures in relation to the rate of labor growth, it is clear that the HPAEs could create jobs faster than the growth in labor supply. This stands in marked contrast to the developed economies, where the reverse was true, which resulted in relatively high levels of unemployment.

Table 1 also shows that in the HPAEs, employment growth always ran ahead of labor supply. This led to low unemployment rates

TABLE 2—UNEMPLOYMENT RATES IN HIGH-PERFORMING ASIAN ECONOMIES, 1986 AND 1990

Countries	1986	1990
	[Annual percent]	
Hong Kong	2.8	1.3
Republic of [South] Korea	3.8	2.2
Singapore	6.5	1.3
Taiwan	2.7	1.7

Note: Data source: *The Other Hong Kong Report* (1991).

Maximizing Human Potential and the Process of Economic Growth in Singapore

TABLE 3—STRUCTURE OF PRODUCTION: DISTRIBUTION OF GDP BY MAJOR SECTORS

Countries	Agriculture		Manufacturing		Service	
	1970	1993	1970	1993	1970	1993
	[Annual percent]					
Developed Economies						
Australia	6	3	24	15	55	67
Canada	4	NA	23	NA	59	NA
France	NA	3	NA	22	NA	69
Germany	3	1	38	27	47	61
Italy	8	3	27	25	51	65
Japan	6	2	36	24	47	57
New Zealand	12	NA	24	NA	55	NA
United Kingdom	3	2	33	25	52	65
United States	3	NA	25	NA	63	NA
High-Performing Asian Economies						
Hong Kong	2	0	29	13	62	79
Republic of [South] Korea	25	7	21	29	46	50
Singapore	2	0	20	28	68	63
Taiwan	24	4	22	34	46	53
Latin America						
Brazil	12	11	29	20	49	52
Chile	7	NA	25	NA	53	NA
Mexico	12	8	22	20	59	63

Note: NA = Information not available. Taiwan figures for 1965 and 1990. Data sources: World Bank (1993) and Pacific Economic Cooperation Council (1993).

(see Table 2), which caused these economies to struggle with tight labor markets. These developments created pressures for wage increases. To ensure that the wage increases were "real" (in terms of productivity), there were pressures on both employers and governments to upgrade the skill and productivity content of new and existing jobs. In addition to these internal pressures, external events, including intensified competition from new low-labor economies such as Indonesia and China, led to a gradual change in the structure of production.

As a result of these pressures, the economies of the developing countries now share many of the same characteristics as the developed countries; for example, they are now dominated by manufacturing and service industries (Table 3). However, Table 3 reveals two clear trends that have implications for ET systems in the HPAEs. First, in at least two of the four HPAEs (Republic of Korea and Taiwan), the rate of change from agricultural production (and hence, employment) to other sectors has been drastic. Primary production has fallen almost to the level found in the developed economies. Comparing these with the Latin American economies, which were at positions more similar to the HPAEs' in the 1960s, the rate of change in the HPAEs is even more pronounced. Both Korea and Taiwan started with a higher proportion of agricultural workers and, within the same 24-year period, the HPAEs reached a lower level than the Latin American economies. Given the fact that labor supply in the HPAEs has lagged behind

TABLE 4—STRUCTURE OF MANUFACTURING: DISTRIBUTION OF MANUFACTURING VALUE ADDED

Countries	Food, beverage & tobacco		Textiles & clothing		Machinery & transport	
	1970	1993	1970	1993	1970	1993
	[Percent]					
Developed Economies						
Australia	16	18	9	24	24	20
Canada	16	17	8	23	23	26
France	12	14	10	26	26	30
Germany	13	NA	8	31	31	NA
Italy	10	10	13	24	24	33
Japan	8	10	8	34	34	38
New Zealand	24	27	13	15	15	14
United Kingdom	13	15	9	31	31	30
United States	12	13	8	31	31	31
High-Performing Asian Economies						
Hong Kong	4	11	41	35	16	21
Republic of [South] Korea	26	20	17	12	11	30
Singapore	12	4	5	3	28	54
Taiwan	NA	NA	NA	NA	NA	NA
Latin America						
Brazil	16	15	13	11	22	22
Chile	17	29	12	7	11	5
Mexico	NA	24	NA	5	NA	25

Note: NA = Information not available. Data source: World Bank (1995).

employment growth, such a structural change cannot be accommodated solely by enhancing the skills of new entrants to the labor market. It can happen only if the labor market has enough flexibility to enhance the skill base of all workers. This means not only the training of new workers but also the large scale reskilling of existing workers.

Efforts to raise productivity have accompanied the changing structure of production in the HPAEs. Table 4 uses manufacturing industries to illustrate the shift and shows two important trends. First, value-added output deriving from the traditional labor-intensive industries, such as food processing and textiles, has been in decline (except in Hong Kong). Second, value-added output deriving from skill-intensive industries, such as machinery

and transport equipment, increased dramatically during the 24-year period. These trends illustrate the economies' success in making the transition from low-value-added to higher-value-added forms of manufacturing production. A similar trend occurred in the service sector, where the economies of Hong Kong and Singapore became leading providers of finance and business services within the region. Thus, there was a shift in the output from these countries, away from the production of labor-intensive goods and services toward higher-value-added goods and services that were previously a preserve of older industrial countries. However, nothing was inevitable about this shift because, as Table 3 also illustrates, it has not happened in the Latin American economies. They have sustained their economies by staying with low-value-added production.

Changes of this magnitude have important implications for the demand for skills. Employers no longer require a disciplined labor force that is sufficiently literate to learn quickly on the job to perform the tasks required for textile and clothing production. They increasingly need skills of a higher and more complex nature required for the production of sophisticated machinery and financial and business services. This is precisely what happened in the HPAEs. Moreover, some of these skills are knowledge intensive and therefore unlikely to be "picked up" through on-the-job training. Rather, they require the kind of professional and scientific knowledge best acquired through formal education and training.

SINGAPORE CASE STUDY

Why the four Asian Tiger economies could make the transition to high-value-added forms of production is still a matter of some debate. However, various schools of thought agree about the involvement of many interrelated factors, including the (a) characteristics of the states, (b) government policies, and (c) investments in education and training. On one side, a World Bank (1993) analysis focused on the importance of an efficient administrative system and the "market-friendly" strategies of the governments and their functional interventions. On another side, developmentalists stressed the role of strong state and government intervention in the economy, while evolutionary economists emphasized the selective interventions by government in building up the HPAEs' technological capabilities (Lall, 1996).

The following analysis draws on insights from all three schools of thought, including examining the (a) characteristics of the state and political systems of Singapore and (b) ways in which the government was instrumental in helping develop high-value-added forms of production. The government's interventionist strategies are briefly examined, along with the political conditions that were necessary for their success. This is followed by a more detailed examination of how the economic transformation came about and the role played by education and training in the growth process.

Political Structures

It is universally agreed that Singapore, like Hong Kong and Taiwan, had efficient administrative systems that were an essential prerequisite for economic development. This ensured a stable legal framework and attracted talented and technically competent officials who could effectively implement political and administrative directives. Also of crucial importance in light of the financial crash in some Asian economies in 1997, Singapore's stable legal framework maintained the autonomy of the state vis-à-vis the interests of both capital and labor (Ashton & Sung, 1997).

At the political level, Singapore also had distinctive features. It has long been ruled by political elites who hold power for decades. The resulting political stability enabled the elites to focus on long-term goals needed to initiate the process of industrialization. They could not foresee their long tenure at the outset, but they believed that bringing about economic development would legitimize their party's long-term presence in power. This is a main theme in analyses of the "developmental state" theories. It contrasts with the situation in the West, where most economies experience frequent political change and coalitions tend to focus politicians' attention on short-term measures, and where government actions are legitimated through their adherence to the rule of law (Weber, 1947).

The political elite's focus on long-term goals also resulted from the geopolitical context within which Singapore developed. As with the other three Tigers, Singapore's political situation threatened its very existence. Expelled from the Malaysian Federation, it faced regional political turbulence. With a population of approximately 3 million, Singapore was a vulnerable island state. The political uncertainty surrounding its future viability put pressure on political leaders to actively promote industrial development, not as an end itself, but as a way to establish independence and national survival. Thus, in the case of Singapore, the state had to play an active part in developing industry if it was to achieve industrial take-off and thereby create the wealth necessary for political security.

Economic Growth

Singapore's economic growth has had three main phases. In the first phase, during the 1960s and 1970s, the economy moved from a very narrow base, centered around the trans-shipping trade, with its high levels of unemployment, to a broader manufacturing base in the 1970s with essentially full employment. At first, the government sought to stimulate the economy through import substitution policies, but it soon abandoned these policies in favor of export orientation policy (Ashton, Green, James, & Sung, 1999). Between 1965 and 1979, manufacturing output as a proportion of gross domestic product grew from 19.8 percent to 28.8 percent in response to increased demand for petroleum and related products in the wake of the Vietnam War and the investment by multinational companies (MNCs) in the electronics and electrical manufacturing industries (Goh, 1995). By the early 1970s, unemployment had virtually disappeared due largely to the demand by MNCs for semiskilled and unskilled labor. Such was the extent of the demand that immigrants from Malaysia were attracted into the economy to sustain its growth.

During the mid to late 1970s, the economy started to move in the direction of more higher-value-added forms of production (the second phase of economic growth). Other economies in the region provided political stability and extensive pools of low-cost, literate labor that attracted foreign investment. Wages in Singapore were rising and more capital-intensive forms of manufacturing were being encouraged. In addition, Singapore was rapidly becoming a center of finance for the region and a source of expertise in business services. The expansion of trade within the region during the 1980s and 1990s fueled economic growth in these areas. Growth of more sophisticated forms of production in the electronics, computing, and engineering industries resulted. However, during the 1980s, financial and business services became the main growth engine, replacing manufacturing. By 1993, Singapore was the world's fourth-largest foreign exchange market (Huff, 1995). This was reflected in a dramatic shift in the composition of the labor force, with production workers falling from 42.9 percent of the labor force in 1984 to 31.0 percent in 1996. At the other end of the labor market, technicians and associate professionals increased from 9.6 percent in 1984 to 17.6 percent in 1996, and professionals rose from 12.2 percent to 19.7 percent, during the same period (Ashton et al., 1999).

During the third phase of economic growth, the economy became increasingly integrated through the development of the regional Growth Triangle, which consisted of Singapore, Johor in Malaysia, and the Riau Islands in Indonesia. Consequently, companies in Singapore could move productive capacity for low-value-added goods to areas of low-cost labor while retaining their headquarters in Singapore (Low, Toh, Soon, Tan, & Hughes, 1993). This, in turn, enabled Singapore to retain its role as a leading center for finance and business services as it began servicing growth and developments in other parts of the region.

Government Intervention

The rapid economic transformation away from low-value-added goods and services to high-value-added forms of production resulted partly from government policies. It has been widely acknowledged, especially since the late 1980s, that Singapore was characterized by government use of interventionist trade and industry policies. For political leaders to develop their industrial base, they had to break into world markets already dominated by older industrial countries and increasingly by Japan. Singapore had no natural advantages, so political leaders had to identify where their possible competitive advantage lay in world markets. The solution initially came in the form of an export-oriented industrialization strategy that was targeted toward low-value-added product markets where Singapore's surplus labor and low wage costs had a competitive advantage.

The initial thrust to develop low-value-added forms of production involved taking advantage of their factor endowments and thereby competing in markets where Western countries, and increasingly Japan, were losing competitive advantage due to increased labor costs. Singapore had little capital and a labor force with only basic skills. As a consequence, the government sought to attract MNCs to provide the capital, technology, and management skills required to modernize production. To help in this task it used the Economic Development Board (EDB). This government organization, dedicated to ensuring implementation of industrial strategy, succeeded remarkably in its initial task of attracting MNCs to use Singapore's low-cost labor. By the mid-1980s, MNCs accounted for 70 percent of gross manufacturing output and 50 percent of employment (Bello & Rosenfeld, 1990).

The government took an active role in ensuring labor force discipline. Industrial relations were reformed, communism was marginalized, and the National Trades Union Congress was incorporated into the decision-making process at government level. This ensured the trade union movement's active cooperation in economic development.

The subsequent shift in economic activity in the direction of higher-value-added goods and services also resulted, in part, from government policies. As MNCs started to move their production of low-value-added goods into neighboring countries in the 1970s, the government saw that the expanding global production system had no predefined frontiers. The comparative advantage that Singapore had enjoyed by way of low-cost labor would prove unsustainable at some future stage of economic development. Countries such as Malaysia, the Philippines, Indonesia, and nations in Latin America had an obvious advantage in labor costs and also sought to attract capital. In addition, the 1973-74 worldwide recession led to trade protectionism in most developed countries. Given the situation, Singapore urgently needed to upgrade the value content of industrial output.

This meant that the government of Singapore could either (a) seek to maintain a competitive position in low-value-added product markets by restricting wages or (b) endeavor to sustain high rates of growth and a continued increase in the standard of living by moving toward higher-value-added forms of production. Singapore's government adopted the latter course of action, in part because the very legitimacy of the political regime had come to depend on the government's ability to deliver continual improvements in the standard of living for the majority of the population (Castells, 1992).

Left to the market as the only mechanism for adjustment and coordination, Singapore's move into higher-value-added product markets might never have happened or could have taken generations. Instead, Singapore avoided market failures within firms by helping them develop technological capabilities. Similarly, it prevented market failures in inter-firm relations by coordinating investments, clustering firms, and promoting linkages between them. Finally, Singapore avoided market failures in factor markets by direct intervention, for example, in education and training (Lall, 1996). These interventions reduced the normal commercial risks involved in such decisions, while making available a wider range of resources for the development process.

Singapore's strategy carried considerable risks. Initially, the government encouraged existing MNCs to move toward higher-value-added forms of production through the use of market forces by increasing their labor costs. To do this, the government introduced a "wage-correction" policy, which allowed unions to obtain large wage increases (Peebles & Wilson, 1996). It also introduced a tax that discouraged employers from using low-paid labor. The tax proceeds went largely to worker retraining. However, employers resisted the government's strategy, inward investment lessened significantly, and growth faltered.

In 1986, for the first time, Singapore experienced negative growth. Learning from this failure, the government switched its efforts to concentrate more on developing the growing financial services industries and sought to attract new capital for the higher-value-added industries. To this end, it invested heavily in telecommunications equipment and systems. However, it continued to build on its existing industrial strengths. Singapore's government chose to move into high technology manufacturing in electronics where it already had a strong industrial base on which to build. The government made mistakes and growth ceased, but lessons were learned. It was not a question of picking winners and sitting back. The government had to learn from mistakes and adapt its strategy accordingly. During the third phase of growth, the government continued to take the lead, this time through its policy of developing the Growth Triangle and encouraging Singaporean companies to invest abroad.

For interventions to succeed, certain political preconditions were essential. In particular, the state (politicians and civil servants) had to establish a degree of independence from the immediate interests of capital and labor in order to be in a position to influence them (Ashton & Sung, 1994). In the first phase of industrial growth, this state independence enabled the political leadership to provide the industrial discipline and control over labor costs essential for the successful establishment of labor-intensive industries (Ashton & Green, 1996). This resulted in both a disciplined labor force and control over labor costs in the first phase of industrial growth.

Of equal importance, the political elite also had to exert some degree of control over the business community to assure success in the later industrialization stage of moving from low-value-added to high-value-added forms of production. Companies engaged in labor-intensive forms of production had to be persuaded to change their strategy or relocate. Here, the interests of the national community, as defined by the political leadership, had to take precedence over the business community's immediate interests in maintaining existing companies. This was necessary to move the economy as a whole in the direction of higher-value-added forms of production.

The economy's success in maintaining steady high rates of growth and structural change in the productive system, both domestically and in relation to the international economy, produced substantial increases in the standard of living and a relatively egalitarian distribution of income (World Bank, 1993). As a result, the state and the political elite could actively compete in world markets. For them, the international economy became the arena of market competition, with the national economy viewed as a unit of competition in the larger arena. Involvement in the international economy would correct any distortions introduced by government interventions.

THE ROLE OF EDUCATION AND TRAINING IN SINGAPORE'S ECONOMIC GROWTH

This part of this chapter investigates the vital role that education and training has played in ensuring that Singapore maintains high economic growth rates. We might argue that one reason for government intervention was to remedy market failures in the delivery of skills. This involved anticipating changes in skill demands and ensuring that the ET system would respond rapidly by providing the needed skills.

The government's role in providing education and training was one aspect of its more general interventions to accelerate the economic growth process. As with the establishment of technological capability, if the market had been left to its own devices to deliver education and training, imperfections would have delayed the growth process (Lall, 1996). For example, employers would have bid up wages in areas of skill shortages; recognizing this, parents would have pressured schools to provide appropriate skills; and schools would eventually have adjusted their curriculum. The process could have taken decades as it did in Western countries. Instead, Singapore's government ensured that, over a short span of time, the ET system delivered the appropriate skills for the rapidly developing economy. Thereby, it prevented skill shortages that would have restricted growth.

To do this, the government invested in, and managed, the ET process at two levels. First, regarding interventions involved in providing general education and training, it had to ensure the appropriate updating and improvement of skills being taught at the same time the new higher-value-added industries were being established. Second, as new targeted industries were established, the government had to ensure that secondary and tertiary schools and training institutes taught the appropriate specialized skills, or that alternative sources would provide them. Their success in this allowed them to achieve skill levels in three decades that older industrial countries had taken generations to acquire.

With regard to the first phase of growth of the Tiger economies, there is general agreement about how the process operated, especially with regard to the functional interventions identified by the World Bank (1993) team. Briefly, the government expanded primary and secondary education and refrained from overinvesting in tertiary education. This approach generated a steady supply of semiskilled labor for the new manufacturing and service organizations. However, this explanation does not work as well when it comes to understanding the part played by education and training in the second phase of industrial growth, as the economy moved into higher-value-added forms of production that required more selective ET interventions.

In its analysis of the HPAEs, including Singapore, the World Bank (1993) group accepted high levels of investment in education as an important explanation for rapid economic growth. These high levels of investment were possible because the HPAEs' growth was characterized by a relatively equal distribution of income that translated into generally higher incomes. In Asia, the income growth made more resources available for education. Furthermore, a rapid decline in the growth rate of the school-age population during the same period enabled more resources to be devoted to each pupil, which enhanced the quality of teaching.

The World Bank (1993) group also pointed out that education-related policy decisions followed the maxims of conventional economic analysis. Thus, the difference between private and social returns is higher for primary- and secondary-level education than for university- or tertiary-level education. In addition, vocational education tends to produce high social returns. In effect, the four Tiger governments followed this pattern in their investment decisions. They made primary and secondary education the main focus of their initial investments during their first growth phase, when employers demanded a literate, disciplined labor force. Unlike some other developing societies, they refrained from overinvesting in tertiary education, at least in the early stages. Thus, although they did not invest more public resources in education than other developing countries, they did allocate more to primary and secondary education.

Subsequent work by Campos and Root (1996) reinforced the World Bank's interpretation of the effects of investment in primary and secondary education vis-à-vis economic growth. Others found that the higher the enrollment rates in primary and secondary education, the higher the growth in the country's per capita gross domestic product (GDP) — ". . . a 10% increase in primary school enrollments in 1970 (among a sample of 98 developing countries) would have increased average annual growth in real per capita GDP between

1980 and 1985 by 0.21%; a 10% increase in secondary enrollments would have increased the growth rate by 0.33%" (Birdsall & Sabot, 1993). Birdsall and Sabot (1993) claim that, as in the case of Korea, basic education increases the supply of skilled workers, which is vital in avoiding labor market bottlenecks when demand for exports expands. A steady supply of skilled workers also reduces the likelihood of upward wage pressure and lowers the scarcity premium, thereby decreasing income inequality.

These conclusions explain the impact of government policies vis-à-vis education investments in the first phase of growth. What they do not explain is the constant reassessment and reform of public provision in education and the expansion of public investment in vocational education and training, especially training that characterized the economy as it moved in the direction of high-value-added forms of production. It is not known how selectivity in the delivery of specialized skills was brought about, and in what way the process was managed to ensure that other considerations, such as the desire of many parents for an academic education for their children, did not create imperfections in the market for skills.

The constant reassessment and reform of ET provision resulted from the government recognizing the need to have an appropriate skill base in place in order to ensure the effectiveness of the policies that directed the move to higher-value-added forms of production. The government knew that human capital investments can contribute to economic growth. Consequently, throughout the past three decades, the government has actively upgraded its ET system.

The educational system inherited from the colonial past was reformed to ensure that the new society would transmit a cohesive set of values to the next generation. Emphasis went to delivering the "basics" at the primary level, engendering a sense of loyalty to the nation, and recognizing the importance of individual discipline. At the early stages, industry demanded unskilled and semiskilled labor. Thus, it was important that schools deliver a supply of disciplined, literate labor. When the economy edged toward higher-value-added forms of production, the demands on the ET system changed dramatically.

Vocational Education and Training Reforms

As a result of the Goh (1979) report, changes were made in the ET system to support economic diversification and general upskilling. The report recommended introducing streaming into primary and secondary education and placed greater emphasis on language teaching. Strong central control of the curriculum was maintained and a vocational route was introduced for those less gifted academically. The Singapore Institute of Technical Education (ITE) was also established (Yip & Sim, 1994). Furthermore, the activities of the old Adult Education Board and the Industry Training Board merged in a new body called the Vocational and Industrial Training Board (VITB). This board provided a unified national training authority for providing vocational and industrial training, at subprofessional level, for young people who did not follow the academic route.

These reforms were supported by measures aimed at upgrading the skills of older workers who had left school with only a primary education and who therefore could not compete for highly skilled jobs. Because of Singapore's labor shortage, the government could not wait for the ET system to upgrade the stock of skills by increasing the skill level of those entering the labor market. This would take too long. The government had to find ways to upgrade the skills of people already in the workforce. It accomplished this through a series of programs financed by the Skills Development Fund.

In 1983, the Basic Skills for Training Programme was introduced for those groups (largely immigrants) who had not completed primary education. In 1986, the Modular Skills

Training Programme followed, to upgrade semiskilled workers in manufacturing. Worker Improvement through Secondary Education was introduced in 1987, to enable those with only a primary education to move to secondary level. The same year also saw the introduction of Core Skills for Effectiveness and Change, aimed at enhancing the skills of workers in the service sector. Taken together, these programs provided means by which the government significantly increased the stock of skills in the labor force by training lower-skilled workers.

During the 1980s, the establishment of industries such as business and financial services and telecommunications, intended to create higher-value-added forms of production, brought demands for new skills. Intermediate- and higher-level technical skills were required, as were more professional and managerial skills. This led to further reform in the ET system. The 1991 reform focused on three main areas: identification of skills required for effective participation in advanced industrial society, production of intermediate technical skills, and expansion of higher education.

Singapore studied the education systems of more advanced industrial societies, especially Germany and Japan, and, as a consequence, enhanced language and mathematics instruction. In addition, the minimum number of years of education was extended to 10. Upgrading by the VITB produced intermediate technical skills. Vocational training started only after young people had mastered the basics of their general education. The vocational route now leads to polytechnics and universities. Building on higher participation rates (with more than 90 percent of 15- to 19-year-olds in education), tertiary education expanded with a Year 2000 target of 25 percent of the age group in universities, 40 percent in polytechnics, and 25 percent in the Institute of Technical Education. By the late 1990s, levels of educational achievement compared to those of the United States and Britain (Felstead, Ashton, Green, & Sung, 1994; Department for Education

and Employment & Cabinet Office, 1996).

During this phase, the government also continued to help those currently in the labor market to further enhance their skills. The new growth industries of the 1990s require not only technical competence but also problem-solving skills and the ability to increase task performance flexibility. Singapore again studied the workplace learning approaches of Germany and Japan for methods it could apply. From the Germans, Singapore learned the importance of combining on- and off-the-job training. This was introduced through a New Apprenticeship Scheme instituted by the ITE in 1991. From the Japanese, Singapore learned how to structure on-the-job learning. This lead to the launch of a series of structured on-the-job training (OJT) programs, tailored to the needs of each of the targeted industries that the government identified as being at the leading edge of world markets. The Productivity and Standards Board worked with major companies to refine the structured OJT programs before they were made available, as industry-based blueprints, to other companies within the industry. The government launched the program in 1993, and by 1997 it had surpassed the initial target of 100,000 OJT program graduates (Ashton et al., 1999). These programs aim to train employed workers, not merely in the technical job skills but also in the intellectual skills needed to cope with rapid change—a process know as "skills deepening."

The government has actively worked to transfer the latest knowledge and techniques directly to the labor force. It did this through joint industrial training centers in the first phase of growth and, later, by securing the cooperation of foreign governments and several MNCs. The latest institutes provide the necessary "hardware, software, and teachware" needed to establish and develop the knowledge- and technology-intensive industries that the government seeks to promote (Soon, 1993). All this helped ensure transformation of the occupational structure noted earlier and resulted in technology-intensive exports. The most sophisticated of the product categories increased its share of total exports from 6.2 percent to 43.2 percent between 1970 and 1993 (Cheah, 1997).

Government actions were not only general functional forms of provision but also highly targeted interventions. In the face of scarce resources, Singapore had to exercise care concerning the type of education and training in which to invest. In view of the skill demands made by new forms of higher-value-added production, it could no longer invest only in primary and secondary education. Singapore was developing its own distinctive industry clusters that made different demands on the skills of the labor force and on methods for delivering those skills. Therefore, it must be stressed that these reforms were more than a mere general upgrading of skills. Singapore made very selective reforms to its ET system regarding the skills being developed.

All the Tiger economies were selective in the types of industry and technology they sought to develop. Singapore established very different industries in the form of MNCs with skill requirements that differed from those of the large conglomerates in South Korea and the small- and medium-sized enterprises of Taiwan. Singapore's industries required a different knowledge and skill base and different institutional forms of delivery. In Lall's (1996) words,

> If the pattern of investment in skills is closely geared to industrial promotion by protection or credit direction, then the former becomes just as selective [intervening] as the latter. The Asian evidence suggests that many education and technology import policies were in fact extremely selective, with close government direction of the content of enrolments and curricula to ensure conformance with the thrust of industrial policy. (p. 7)

As in the case of other government interventions, those in education and training were highly selective in places and designed to support the buildup of capabilities in designated industries.

Government Coordination and Control

Given the highly selective forms of intervention, how could the government ensure that output from these programs would conform to market demands for skilled workers? Part of the answer lies in the fact that, unlike governments in the West or Japan, the Singaporean government could influence the demand for future skills. Singapore did this through its trade and industry policy, which specified the types of industries it sought to move into. From this, it was only one more step to identify the human resources required for such industries. Precisely because government agencies such as the Economic Development Fund (EDF) had active involvement in helping establish the industries, they could provide feedback regarding requisite information about skilled worker demand to appropriate decision-making authorities.

This led to a very different approach to defining national skill requirements than that conventionally followed in Western countries. Singapore determines skill needs in part to address the requirements of the industrial strategy and in part to address the requirements of existing employers. Existing employers' needs alone are not the basis for identifying the skill needs, as they are in the West (Ashton et al., 1999).

In Singapore, the knowledge required to identify skill needs comes from a variety of sources. Some arises from the government's "vision" of Singapore's future. For example, the current developmental focus, as specified in the "Next Lap" document, aims to achieve by 2030 the standard of living enjoyed in the United States today (Ministry of Trade and Industry, 1991). The document specifies the various aspects of development (e. g., the types of industries, housing, health care, transportation systems, and so forth) that Singapore needs to take it closer to its vision.

A more immediate source is the EDB, which must ensure that the inward investment is forthcoming to provide the necessary capital and know-how for the new industries. In performing this function, the EDB also takes charge of the human resource requirements for those industries. Schein (1996) studied the extent to which the EDB would go into minute detail to persuade foreign investors to come to Singapore. In effect, the work of the EDB forms a "one-stop" investment package organization. But, as part of this one-stop function, the EDB has to ensure that the ET system can produce the skills required for the new industries. As a result, both the Ministry of Trade and Industry and the EDB feed this information into the Council for Professional and Technical Education (CPTE), the main decision-making body for determining the output of the ET system.

The CPTE provides the means of focusing all the information that comes into the government about the economy's human resource demands. It enables the government to use this knowledge to adjust the output of the ET system. The CPTE is a national body chaired by the Minister of Trade and Industry. On the supply side, education and training institutions produce data on their existing and projected outputs. Academics provide an analysis of national data which, together with input from employers, is used to identify national skill requirements. Based on this analysis, judgments are made about the future level of output from education and training institutions and whether any gaps require filling through recruitment of appropriately skilled labor from outside the country. The CPTE then uses this information to establish specific targets for the various components of the ET system—the universities, polytechnics, schools, and the ITE. In this way, the CPTE institutionalizes the links between trade and industry policy and the ET system. It thereby ensures that the human capital demands of new industries inform the targets (Selvaratnam, 1989).

Interaction between the EDB and the political leadership also gives indications for forward planning. For example, the government recognizes the need to incorporate research and development capability for the next stage of economic development. This requires an increase in the output of scientists and engineers. The CPTE is charged with meeting those targets.

In the West, governments purchase this type of information from consulting firms that specialize in market intelligence. The ET system could not access this information to inform its decision-making process directly and without cost. In Singapore, this information is collated by the government and shared among relevant industrial sectors and the CPTE. In this sense, market intelligence, including information on world market trends, takes on the character of a public good.

Regarding workplace training, Singapore's Productivity and Standards Board sets targets for on-the-job and work-based training and for the level of investment in training by employers. The Board adjusts targets to meet the demands of existing and new industries. The CPTE and Productivity and Standards Board together control the output quality and quantity.

This process differs greatly from the Western idea of manpower forecasting, which relies on sophisticated extrapolation of historical data. In Singapore, civil servants or academicians who are not involved in implementing policy related to economic growth conduct the exercise.

A further characteristic of this approach involves the way that the decision-making process is weighted so that the economy's future takes precedence over all other interests and pressures in decisions regarding the output of the ET system. Singapore achieves this by ensuring that the agenda of the Ministry of Trade and Industry dominates the decision-making process.

Once output decisions are made, the government has responsibility for ensuring implementation. It does this through a highly centralized system of control over the ET system (Ashton et al., 1999). Control was first established to secure the social and political objectives of nation-building. On receiving independence from Britain, Singapore urgently needed to create a unitary nation to tackle the issue of economic survival. However, economic considerations soon dominated decisions on the structure of the ET system. The government has since strictly controlled the curriculum. At the tertiary level, the distinction between polytechnics, with their emphasis on technical and technological skills, and universities, which cover the more academic subjects, has been retained. Universities and polytechnics have also been subject to strong central direction, with quotas established for different disciplines. In the field of training, the government can control finances for training through the use of the Skill Development Fund administered by the Productivity and Standards Board.

The centralized system of control allowed the government to manage the demand for education in the interest of the economy as a whole and thereby prevent market distortions. Given the emphasis in Confucian societies on academic education, the government had to restrict access to meet the needs of the economy. In the early phase, the limited availability of places restricted entrance to university, which avoided both wasting resources and producing too many graduates. Only when it appeared that the economy would require a high proportion of university-educated personnel for the new higher-value-added industries was university education expanded. There was a fear that, left to market forces, Singapore would be burdened by an oversupply of university graduates long before its economy could support them.

Thus, to adjust the supply of labor to meet employer demands, the government uses its central levers over the ET system to continually fine-tune the output to meet changing needs. This was easier to achieve in the field of academic/vocational education and initial training than in workplace training, where the government had to influence foreign employers. Such strategies have, as one would expect, changed over time as the nature of the "training problem" changed.

To summarize, a series of mechanisms ensure that the government can continuously fine-tune the output of the ET system to meet the economy's emerging demand for new skills (Ashton et al., 1999). Key to this is the dominance of the Ministry of Trade and Industry's agenda to ensure that the economy's future demands will inform the decision-making process. Second, mechanisms such as the CPTE ensure that the ET system as a whole responds in a coherent manner to these demands. Finally, the government maintains control over the ET system so that decisions, once they are made by bodies such as the CPTE, will be implemented.

While all this seems relatively straightforward, in practice it involves a complex process of passing information back and forth between civil servants and politicians who struggle to ensure that the right decisions have been made and that they are implemented. For example, the CPTE's attempt to increase the proportion of science and engineering graduates to fuel growth in research and development could not be achieved just by increasing university quotas. The CPTE also had to find ways to ensure that more children opted to study science and that the products of the process would meet employer needs. To achieve its aims, the CPTE had to act on a number of fronts and the outcomes are by no means certain. They require constant monitoring and corrective action.

CONCLUSIONS

To achieve rapid economic growth, the Singapore government had to work with business to change the relationship between its factor endowments. Since the country did not have a wealth of natural resources, it focused on changing the relationship between land, labor, and capital.

In the West, movement from labor-intensive, low-skill-based industries to capital-intensive, high-skill-based industries, using the market as the main mechanism of adjustment, took generations. Following the example of the Japanese manufacturing industry, Singapore sought to achieve the shift in only a few decades. It accomplished this goal by targeting specific industries that political leaders believed could achieve an economic competitive advantage in world markets. The government's role was to ensure that the companies involved built their capabilities as rapidly as possible. This is where ET policies came into their own. With the various mechanisms detailed in this chapter, the government could ensure that appropriate, highly specific skills were available when needed.

This was not a matter of government providing the population with a good general education and leaving industry to develop the specific skills. It involved the government in identifying the skill types and levels required by the economy at each stage of its growth and, in light of that, reengineering the ET system to ensure delivery of targeted skills. It necessitated continuous educational reforms as the economy moved toward higher-value-added forms of production. It also involved finding ways to upgrade the skills of those already in the labor force without imposing unnecessary financial or administrative burdens on employers. Singapore did this by adapting techniques from other countries to address its situation.

To achieve these objectives required a different approach from government officials than that used by civil servants in the West. As Schein's (1996) analysis of Singapore's EDB demonstrated, Singapore's civil servants created in the EDB a "learning organization" in the best tradition of modern management theory. The organization is geared to achieving business targets (in this case, the specific types of inward investment required to establish high-value-added industries) by focusing on improving productivity and maintaining sustained learning and rapid decision-making in a complex business environment. When backed by resources at the national level, control of land, fiscal incentives, preferential credit, and skilled labor, such an organization represents a formidable business resource. It provides the government with (a) excellent intelligence on trends in world markets and (b) access to leading MNCs.

Civil servants and politicians had an advantage in that they could learn from older Western countries and Japan. They could, therefore, identify the high-value-added industries—for example, high-tech electronics, information technology, and financial services—in which they sought to compete and learn. Then they simply had to ensure that they could secure part of the market for their producers. Also, because of their export-oriented strategies, they depended on world markets and were, therefore, sensitive to changes in the level of competition and pattern of demand. Thus, the EDB set up offices in some of the major economies to facilitate the acquisition of inward investment, as well as information for the government on patterns of demand.

In this context, the government ET policies were but one element, albeit an important one, in a complex strategy aimed at ensuring that Singaporean companies remained competitive in world markets. The strategy was also to ensure that the economy would continue to attract and support companies that could compete at the cutting edge of those niches in world markets where Singapore had a competitive advantage.

The government adopted a number of support mechanisms to help overcome market failures and to develop the economy's technological capabilities, which promoted what Lall (1996) refers to as "a healthy and dynamic learning process." This involved coordinated and integrated interventions in both product and factor markets. Such interventions were cumulative, used to build on existing skills and knowledge. Singapore adopted a strategy of targeting MNCs aggressively, using a one-stop service approach provided by the EDB to attract capital for targeted industries. The government delivered technological capability by ensuring (a) the establishment of industry clusters, for example, high-tech engineering companies to supply the machinery and components for electronics manufacturers; (b) advanced training sponsored by leading MNCs in conjunction with the government, to deliver appropriate technical skills; and (c) preferential financial services.

Singapore's strategy presents a number of risks. If the government makes a bad investment decision, it suffers the same consequence that a company would, except on a much larger scale. The government made a mistake in trying to push MNCs into higher-value-added production through its wage correction policy. Singapore paid a price for this in the form of negative growth for one year (1986) and the drying up of foreign investment. If the negative growth had persisted, the government's failure to sustain the population's increased standard of living could well have resulted in loss of its legitimacy. However, the government was sensitive to its mistake and rectified it quickly.

Southeast Asia's financial crisis revealed another major threat to the overall strategy. In countries at the center of the crisis, such as Indonesia, Thailand, and to a lesser extent Malaysia, governments failed to effectively insulate their activities from those of banking and financial institutions. The lack of transparency in financial dealings enables the private interests of political officials to influence the outcome of investment decisions. This was not the case in Singapore where, in spite of close collaboration between state officials and business, the autonomy of government officials was never compromised. Singapore's government suffered as a result of its regionalization policy, which encouraged Singaporean firms to put substantial capital at risk by investing in Indonesia. In this and other ways, because of its role as a provider of business services to the region, Singapore's economy was influenced by the overall crisis in the region, but only as a knock-on effect, not as a causal factor. This is reflected in the fact that, in spite of the crisis, leading business figures and analysts still place Singapore at the top of the league for foreign investment.

References

Ashton, D., Green, F., James, D., & Sung, J. (1999). *Education and training for development in East Asia*. London: Routledge.

Ashton, D., & Green, F. (1996). *Education, training and the global economy*. Cheltenham, England: Edward Elgar.

Ashton, D., & Sung, J. (1994). *The state, economic development and skill formation: A new East Asian model?* (Working Paper Series, No. 3). Leicester, England: The Center for Labour Market Studies, Leicester University.

Ashton, D., & Sung, J. (1997). Education, skill formation and economic development: The Singaporean approach. In A. H. Halsey, H. Lauder, P. Brown, & A. S. Wells (Eds.), *Education: Culture, economy and society*. Oxford, England: Oxford University Press.

Bello, W., & Rosenfeld, S. (1990). *Dragons in distress: Asia's miracle economies in crisis*. London: Penguin Books.

Birdsall, N., & Sabot, I. (1993). *Virtuous cycles: Human capital growth and equity in East Asia* (Background paper for The East Asian Miracle, Policy Research Department). Washington, DC: The World Bank.

Campos, J. E., & Root, H. J. (1996). *The key to the Asian miracle: Making shared growth credible*. Washington, DC: The Brookings Institution.

Castells, M. (1992). Four tigers with a dragon head: A comparative analysis of the state, economy and society in the Asian Pacific Rim. In R. Appelbaum & J. Henderson (Eds.), *States and development in the Asian Pacific Rim* (pp. 33-70). Newbury Park, CA: Sage.

Cheah, H. B. (1997). Can governments engineer the transition from cheap labour to skill-based competitiveness? The case of Singapore. In M. Godfrey (Ed.), *Skill development for international competitiveness* (pp. 92-138). Cheltenham, England: Edward Elgar.

Department for Education and Employment & Cabinet Office. (1996). *The skills audit: A report from an interdepartmental group*. London: Author.

Felstead, A., Ashton, D., Green, F., & Sung, J. (1994). *Vocational education and training in the Federal Republic of Germany, France, Japan, Singapore and the United States*. Leicester, England: The Center for Labour Market Studies, Leicester University.

Goh, K. S. (1995). *Wealth of East Asian nations*. Singapore: Federal Publications.

Goh, K. S., et al. (1979). *Report on the Ministry of Education 1978*. Singapore: Ministry of Education.

Huff, W. G. (1995). The developmental state, government, and Singapore's economic development since 1960. *World Development, 23*(8), 1421-1438.

International Labour Office. (1996). *World employment report 1996/97: National policies in global context.* Geneva, Switzerland: Author.

Lall, S. (1996). *Learning from the Asian tigers: Studies in technology and industrial policy.* New York: St. Martin's Press.

Low, L., Toh, M. H., Soon, T. W., Tan, K. Y., & Hughes, H. (Eds.). (1993). *Challenge and response: Thirty years of the Economic Development Board.* Singapore: Times Academic Press.

Ministry of Trade and Industry. (1991). *The strategic economic plan: Toward a developed nation.* Singapore: Singapore National Printers.

The other Hong Kong report (Yearly report). (1991). Hong Kong: The Chinese University Press.

Pacific Economic Cooperation Council. (1993). *Human resource development outlook, 1993-1994.* Singapore: Times Academic Press.

Peebles, G., & Wilson, P. (1996). *The Singapore economy.* Cheltenham, England: Edward Elgar.

Schein, E. (1996). *Strategic pragmatism: The culture of Singapore's Economic Development Board.* Singapore: Toppan.

Selvaratnam, V. (1989). Vocational education and training: Singapore and other third world initiatives. *Singapore Journal of Education, 10*(2), 11-23.

Soon, T. W. (1993). Education and human resource development. In L. Low, M. H. Toh, T. W. Soon, K. Y. Tan, & H. Hughes (Eds.), *Challenge and response: Thirty years of the Economic Development Board* (pp. 235-270). Singapore: Times Academic Press.

Weber, M. (1947). *The theory of social and economic organisation.* London: Collier Macmillan.

World Bank. (1993). *The East Asian miracle: Economic growth and public policy* (A World Bank policy research report). New York: Oxford University Press.

World Bank. (1995). *World development report, 1995.* New York: Oxford University Press.

Yip, J. S. K., & Sim, W. K. (1994). *Evolution of educational excellence: 25 years of education in the Republic of Singapore* (2nd ed.). Singapore: Longmans.

Appendix—List of Acronyms

CPTE	Council for Professional and Technical Education
EDB	Economic Development Board
EDF	Economic Development Fund
ET	Education and training
EU	European Union
GDP	Gross domestic product
HPAEs	High-performing Asian economies (Singapore, Hong Kong, Taiwan, and Republic of [South] Korea)
HRD	Human resource development
ITE	Institute of Technical Education
MNC	Multinational company
OJT	On-the-job training
VITB	Vocational and Industrial Training Board

16

Vocational and Technical Education in a Transitional Economy: A Case Study of Laos

By Marvin E. Lamoureux

Classified as a "least developed country" by the United Nations, the People's Democratic Republic of Laos faces classic development challenges: poor telecommunication and transportation systems, meager national revenues, a high dependency on foreign assistance, serious urban-rural disparities, as well as poor quality education and health services with limited access. Expenditures on education and health rank among the lowest in Asia. Recent surveys showed that 65 percent of the population live in conditions of poverty, with two-thirds of these in "severe poverty." Laos is striving to build its human resource base so that it can effectively compete with its regional neighbors. Increased rural productivity and enabling nonfarm economic activity are crucial to the country's long-term economic growth strategies. As pressure to enhance productivity increases throughout the economy, especially in rural areas, a guaranteed supply of well-trained workers becomes vital to forging the country's competitive economic structure (Asian Development Bank [ADB], 1995).

The country's labor force lacks the skills required for economic development. This is due, in part, to the absence of vocational/technical education (VTE) policies and plans and to a resulting inability to define a clear and supportable approach to workforce training implementation schemes. These constraints are found in most, if not all, developing nations. And, as in the case of transitional economies, which are moving away from centralized planning to a market-based structure, Laos serves as a valid case study of a country that needs to formulate cost-effective VTE policies and operational plans.

This chapter examines Laos's education and training capabilities and identifies existing constraints and deficiencies. Policies and practices to strengthen the human resources capacity of the country are also considered.

THE EDUCATION AND TRAINING SYSTEM

Since 1975, the main thrust of the government's social policy has been to provide accessible educational opportunities on a mass scale throughout the country. The objective is to enhance social and economic welfare wherever possible. Basic education (grades 1 to 11), higher education (National University of Laos), and nonformal adult education and literacy programs have received the most support. The vocational and technical education sector (secondary vocational schools and technical colleges) has received less fiscal attention from the government. Although Laos has implemented a significant expansion in the education sector overall, enrollment, repetition, and dropout rates continue to indicate that the population's capacity to absorb these benefits remains limited. The system itself lacks essential infrastructure to respond to the needs of an effective and efficient educational development and delivery mechanism.

Special measures are being implemented to meet the future human resource requirements for planned economic and social progress. Initiatives include (a) founding of the National University of Laos (NUOL); (b) extending and improving the general education system; (c) intensifying nonformal education programs, especially in rural and remote areas; and (d) emphasizing the education of girls and minorities. Vocational and technical education plus nonformal skills training are moving in the same positive direction. There has been, and will continue to be, a significant involvement of outside donor agencies in nonformal skills training and employment promotion. In addition, since the early 1990s, the German Agency for Technical Cooperation (GTZ) has concentrated on upgrading Laos's vocational secondary education, technical college-level programming, and nonformal skills training, as well as on developing a country-wide, government-endorsed VTE strategy (Groeber, 1994).

Educational Structure

The educational structure in Laos has five levels: preschool (preschool and kindergarten), primary (five years), lower secondary (three years), upper secondary (three years for a general education diploma or two for a vocational diploma), and postsecondary (two to six years). In 1994-95, there were 685 preschools and kindergartens, 7,591 primary schools, 105 lower secondary schools, and 129 upper secondary schools. Before 1996, there were 36 postsecondary institutions, including technical colleges, higher technical colleges, and other degree-granting institutions. These were, for the most part, responsible to specific government ministries.

During 1996, and as a result of a technical assistance project sponsored through the Asian Development Bank (ADB) and a resulting loan, the National University of Laos was created under the jurisdiction of the Ministry of Education (MOE). A number of postsecondary institutions were removed from other ministries and amalgamated under the NUOL. In cooperation with these ministries, the MOE, through its Higher and Technical Vocational Education Department (HTVED), is restructuring the remaining postsecondary institutions into a "regional comprehensive college" system.

Expenditures allocated to different educational levels have remained fairly constant, with more than 40 percent allocated to primary education, about 25 percent to secondary education, about 13 percent to higher education and teacher training, and 7 percent to administration. Vocational/technical education and training has seen a significant rise over the years.

Vocational/Technical Education

The country's VTE subsector is composed of government-operated formal training institutions and a small number of private sector institutions. By government decree, the MOE's Higher and Technical Vocational Education Department has responsibility for VTE. There are three subsector levels: secondary vocational schools; postsecondary technical colleges; and, at NUOL, the faculties of (a) engineering and architecture, (b) forestry and agriculture, (c) medical sciences, (d) law, (e) economics and management, and (f) education.

Although the VTE subsector is dominated by government-funded institutions, the majority of workers in the rural subsistence sector, including skilled weavers and craftsmen, work in the informal economy and have little or no formal vocational training. Most acquire their skills through a traditional extended-family "master craftsman to apprentice" method.

Secondary Vocational Schools

Presently there are 25 secondary vocational schools (SVSs) in Laos that offer two-year trade-related programs. Seven different ministries plus provincial governments are involved in establishing and operating these schools. They are the Ministries of (a) Education, (b) Post and Telecommunication, (c) Labor and Social Welfare, (d) Agriculture and Forestry, (e) Industry and Commerce, (f) Health, and (g) Culture. The MOE directly supervises eight of the schools (plus three teacher-training institutions), of which seven are actually operated by provinces. Seventeen SVSs were established and are administered by other ministries.

In most instances, a director, one or two deputies, plus a number of department heads operate the SVSs. Political advisors also have involvement at the management level. The director usually has responsibility for administration and the department heads for overseeing instruction in the various occupational fields.

Entry into an SVS normally follows completion of the lower secondary level (grade eight) for the training of skilled workers. Selection is based on aptitude, interest, and academic ability. SVS enrollment, or intake, is further governed by a quota system, which is based on the principle that continuous upgrading and the systematic distribution of training opportunities to the provinces will match their development plans with human resource requirements.

The intake process for SVSs consists of the following steps:

1. The appropriate industries estimate intake requirements for the year.
2. The MOE consolidates information regarding intake requirements for each program.

3. A quota distribution plan for provinces and ministries is prepared.
4. Ministries and provinces receive advice on quota distributions for all programs.

The responsibility for selecting qualified students and cadre representatives from provinces and districts lies with a selection committee that operates within each Provincial Education and Sports Service. The committees nominate candidates to the MOE's Central Selection Committee, which finalizes the list of candidates. The final candidate list is then returned to the provincial selection committees, which have the final authority on student selection for schools in their respective province. As can be seen, the intake process is highly structured and subject to political influence.

As a matter of policy, vocational school graduates are expected to return to the province and district that nominated them. Under the quota system, their employment should be assured by the provincial authorities or ministries. However, there are situations under which they cannot find employment due to market conditions, and some graduates simply do not return to their former province/district.

The purpose and program objectives of SVSs vary considerably and depend on the perceived needs of the ministry concerned, plus the identified priorities of the province or region in which the schools are located. Therefore, the same programs do not offer admissions every year.

Teachers prepare the curriculum for most vocational education programs at the school level. In some cases, foreign experts, provided through bilateral grants, aid the teachers. A typical curriculum of a two-year SVS program consists of about 2,600 contact hours. Approximately 24 percent of the time goes to the study of general education subjects, 20 percent to technical theory, and the remaining 56 percent to trade-related practical skills instruction. On-the-job training, usually after the second year, may be available depending on the requirements of government ministries, provincial authorities, and private businesses. Employers commonly complain that SVS graduates lack practical skills, job-related theoretical knowledge, appropriate work attitudes, and essential problem-solving capabilities.

Postsecondary Technical Colleges and the National University of Laos

With the advent of the ADB's Postsecondary Education Rationalization Loan Project in 1996, the country's postsecondary education and training structure was recast, establishing three major development phases. Phase one (the creation of NUOL) and phase two (the amalgamation of the higher technical colleges and degree-granting institutions into NUOL faculties) have both been actualized. Thirty-six postsecondary institutions had previously existed under the jurisdiction of various ministries. They included 28 technical colleges, 5 higher technical colleges, and 3 degree-granting institutions. Eleven are now part of the NUOL faculty structure and therefore come under the jurisdiction of the MOE.

Phase three, the development of a regional comprehensive college system, will see the amalgamation of the remaining technical colleges into a demand-driven education and training system, also under the MOE's jurisdiction. The colleges will provide (a) national and regional technical programs, (b) university transfer into third year at the NUOL, (c) transferability from the regional and national technical program completion into NUOL engineering programs, and (d) expansion of adult/continuing education opportunities for the local population. Phase three is being formulated for external funding by the HTVED. It will involve the transfer of the remaining technical colleges from other ministries to MOE jurisdiction and, after a thorough evaluation, the restructuring of the remaining locations.

Nonformal Vocational/Technical Education

The Department of Labor (DOL) functions under the Ministry of Labor and Social Welfare (MOLSW) and oversees workforce preparation for the unemployed. In addition, DOL collects labor statistics, addresses labor management and labor relations issues, and promotes employment. Thus, inasmuch as the MOE, through the Higher and Technical Vocational Education Department, has responsibility for the country's formal vocational/technical education, the Department of Labor generally has responsibility for nonformal, short-term (less than one year) vocational and skills training. There is, as might be expected, some overlap between the DOL and HTVED.

This demarcation of authority and responsibility has been recently portrayed in a series of strategy meetings among a number of organizations involved in the country's education and training subsectors. Cooperation between the DOL and HTVED is ongoing in the areas of curriculum development; relationships between formal and nonformal vocational programming; and use of facilities, equipment, and instructors.

Nonformal training under the DOL is presently confined to the operation of only two small-scale vocational schools, the Vientiane Skills Training Center and the Center for Skills Development. The Vientiane Skills Training Center runs in cooperation with the Labor and Social Welfare Division of the Municipality of Vientiane. The Municipality established the center with the assistance of the United Nations High Commission for Refugees (UNHCR), to assist refugees who returned to Laos in 1985. It offers three- to six-month courses in sewing, radio/TV repair, electrical work, and administration/secretarial work. The center's capacity is about 170 trainees at any given time, and it trains 250 to 350 individuals each year.

The Center for Skills Development, also located in Vientiane, actually belongs to the MOE, but it has been leased by the MOLSW until its Employment Promotion Centers are built under a proposed ADB loan. The former U. S. S. R. supplied the Center with training equipment, about 20 years ago, that is unsuited to current industrial requirements. Near Vientiane, there is also a Farmers' Skills Training Center that will be operated by the Vientiane Municipality, under the supervision of the MOLSW, after its renovation and refurbishment.

Private Sector Training Initiatives

Because the private sector is so vital to social and economic development, it is useful to briefly examine recent initiatives. The government decided in 1990 to allow the establishment of private schools. Even though an ADB (1998) survey revealed that their number was still small, the MOE opened a department that has a mandate to develop and manage private education, including skills training. Presently, approximately 30 proprietary vocational training centers exist, including some that offer (a) English-language preparation; (b) computer training; and (c) business administration, clerical, and secretarial skills. With few exceptions, skills training programs are not well equipped. Generally, they form part of a business concern (e. g., a computer training center operated as an adjunct to a computer products, software, and repair firm) or are operated by individuals (e. g., English language and secretarial centers).

It appears that, for the country's major cities, a small but growing proprietary training subsector is emerging. Unfortunately, the rather unregulated process of the past did not allow for a good fit into the countrywide human resources plan. For the most part, private training schools follow the traditional path of similar schools in both developing and developed countries. The classes, courses, and programs that have been developed and presented to the public are so-called "soft" courses where (a) curriculum is readily available, (b) facility and equipment needs are minimal and not capital intensive, and (c) traditional classroom methods suffice. Nevertheless, the public perceives the training as valuable and leading to employment. Due to a lack of commitment to capital-intensive training courses and programs, a number of industries that could benefit from expanded private training can employ only graduates with business, computer, secretarial, or English-language competencies.

Training provided by employers is relatively limited, but essential. A training needs assessment survey conducted by the ADB/Netherlands Economic Institute (1994) covered 120 firms in seven growth sectors: manufacturing, construction, services, trade, transportation, utilities, and finance. The Institute surveyed approximately 10,000 employees, of whom 56 percent were male. A need for four types of training was identified: (a) on-the-job training; (b) formal training; (c) training by suppliers; and (d) miscellaneous nonformal training such as seminars, tours, and workshops. Another study noted that a number of enterprises would access training centers if they existed in their region. Both managers and workers expressed interest in training.

The most common type of training provided by employers was on-the-job training, for about 12 percent of the workforce. The other three types of training were each provided to 2 to 3 percent of the workforce. On-the-job and supplier-provided training were considered least costly. Training fields included management, finance, service, and sales, as well as clerical and computer skills. Employees paid for approximately 29 percent of their training, mainly in the areas of management and office skill training. The most striking outcome was that employers apparently see no real need to train their production workers. Several reasons were cited for not providing training: (a) lack of time (especially in smaller firms), (b) possibility that a worker would leave the firm after being trained (a main concern of larger firms), and (c) lack of training centers.

WORKFORCE PREPARATION CONSTRAINTS

Three studies commissioned by the GTZ found that the economy's skilled and semi-skilled workforce requirements are not being met. As noted earlier, employers have repeatedly complained that VTE graduates lack practical skills and their training often has little relevance to the functions they must perform. Most private enterprise managers and their public sector counterparts complain that the current quality of vocational training is not only poor but also is not responsive to the changing needs of the market-driven and growing economy (Pedersen, 1996; Weidmann, 1996).

The problems appear to stem from a shortage of instructional materials and equipment, lack of qualified teachers, outdated curricula, low student quality due to the quota system, inadequate financing, and poor educational administration. Shortages of facilities and up-to-date equipment means that students do not receive training and practice in meaningful practical skills. The lack of qualified teachers compounds this deficiency, which is due mostly to low wages and little or no in-service training.

A number of studies, commissioned by international donor agencies, revealed a clear pattern of the issues surrounding Laos's VTE system. Furthermore, there is broad consensus as to the seven issues listed below, which the remainder of this chapter addresses.

- Training capacity.
- Administrative structure.
- Internal and external efficiency.
- Staff development.
- Programs.
- Facilities, equipment, and instructional materials.
- Private sector participation (Ministry of Education/German Agency for Technical Cooperation [MOE/GTZ], 1997; Weidmann, 1996).

Training Capacity

Capacity involves the quantity, quality, and management of human and capital resources in education and training institutions to meet social and economic expectations. Concern has been expressed about the VTE institutions' ability to develop and conduct relevant programs that meet both employers' and government policy expectations.

As early as 1992, it was obvious that the small number of public vocational schools and their limited enrollment could not meet planned government economic targets. The yearly vocational school output averaged only about 1,500 and was limited to preparation in carpentry, masonry, general mechanics, food and cooking, and sewing. Furthermore, the schools' limited capacity prohibited any significant increase in student enrollment. Consequently, output will fall far short of projections for the year 2002, which indicate a demand for more than 95,000 skilled workers and 14,000 semiskilled workers. Private sector schools cannot make up the shortfall, since their output is only about 3,000 semiskilled and skilled graduates per year, who will largely receive training in trade and commerce and the English language.

Regarding postsecondary technical colleges, there has been a presumption that the number of skilled-worker and technician graduates could meet both current and future market demand. However, the following issues impede the colleges' progress:

- A training focus and capacities geared to specific ministry requirements.
- Unpopularity among young people and therefore low intakes.
- Lack of employer satisfaction with overall graduate skill levels.
- Their impending transfer to MOE jurisdiction.

Thus, it appears that the present postsecondary training capacity may be less than adequate. In addition, the ADB's Employment Promotion and Training Project (1996) and the subsequent fact-finding mission found that the MOLSW and its DOL division did not provide sufficient training opportunities in their skills and employment promotion centers to meet employer demands for skilled and semiskilled workers.

To fill the gap created by the absence of qualified Laotian workers, employers hire foreigners. According to the Department of Labor, the number of applicants approved by the government has increased significantly over the past few years. However, the government conceded that the number of illegal workers is also quite high. This indicates the existence of a demand for skilled and semiskilled workers that goes unmet at present. Without significant improvements in the local labor force, economic growth will likely stagnate, given the increasing costs of employing foreign workers. Under this assumption, Laotians cannot benefit from the increased earnings they would receive if they could perform the required skilled and semiskilled tasks.

Simultaneously, the unemployment rate among nonagricultural households increased from less than 4 percent a decade ago to almost 7 percent in 1994. Unemployment is highest among secondary school leavers and institute graduates, but relatively low among technical college and university graduates. This unemployment rate is increasing as experienced workers lose their jobs due to privatization and/or downsizing of state-owned enterprises and government departments.

Laos's mismatch of demand and supply results from the wide gap between industry's current and future skills demand and the capacity of both public sector schools (secondary vocational schools, postsecondary technical colleges, and skills centers) and proprietary vocational training centers to provide an adequate supply of skilled workers. Increased capacity in short-term nonformal training, longer-term formal education and training aimed at human resource development, and upgrading of currently needed skills must be provided for the situation to improve.

Administrative Structure

From the outset of education sector reviews through the most innovative proposal for the reformulation of vocational education and training in 1997, the administration, management, and planning of the country's education sector, and especially its VTE subsector, have received significant criticism. The main problems relate to legislation planning and budgeting, along with role perceptions of staff and their development, supervision, and monitoring.

Although a systematic planning process, which commences with the schools and moves upward through the hierarchy, is theoretically being adopted, the linkage between provinces and the MOE remains relatively weak. This weakness exists because the submission and approval process for provincial education plans to the government goes through the Ministry of Economy, Planning and Finance, rather than through the Ministry of Education, which results in poor communication. Also, no coherent policy or administrative framework exists for integrating all providers of education and training services, regardless of their government affiliation, level within the system, output agenda, or geographic location.

Government policy on quality improvement and socioeconomic linkages for each geographic area is not explicitly translated into concrete actions at the school or program level. Nor does policy receive adequate consideration in the planning of school improvements. The absence of norms and standards for vocational schools, postsecondary institutions, and training centers has led to wide variations among buildings and other physical facilities, funding, expenditure patterns, and performance.

The MOLSW, in particular, lacks the experience and management capability needed to mount an effective VTE operation. At the school, institute, and training center levels, a number of administrative and management problems have also been identified. A lack of oversight exists regarding (a) provision of adequate buildings, (b) funding, (c) appointment of personnel, (d) procurement of equipment and materials, (e) student intake, and (f) staff salaries. In addition, the decision-making responsibilities of school directors are not well defined, staff has little or no opportunity for in-service training, and the institutions have weak formal administrative structure.

Internal and External Efficiency

Efficiency generally describes the relationship between inputs and outcomes of the VTE subsector. SVS graduation rates average 64 percent. This is low for two-year programs in relation to their high operating costs. Poor performance most likely arises from unsatisfactory student amenities in the schools, a defective system of student selection, and loss of student interest due to poor quality learning environments. Technical colleges have better student completion rates, with a range of 75 to 83 percent.

The low internal efficiency rate results partly from irrelevant curriculum, poor quality instructors, inadequate instructional processes, and the student selection process. Another factor that has reduced the efficiency of these institutions is low student-to-instructor ratios. The ratios vary from 0.6 to 28.0 (only one school had the highest level) in SVSs, with an average of 6.9. In the technical colleges and former higher technical colleges, the ratio ranged from 3.3 to 12.4, with an average rate of 3.7 students for each instructor.

The level of graduate employment and the attitude of employers toward VTE graduates and their institutions also serves as an indicator of the sector's external efficiency. It is generally conceded that graduates of SVSs have difficulty achieving their employment objectives. Groeber (1994) reported that, on average, 40 to 50 percent enter employment and 10 to 15 percent become self-employed, while 35 to 50 percent remain unemployed. This is due to employers' contention that both SVS and technical college graduates lack practical skills and demonstrate poor work attitudes.

Until recently, the SVSs and technical colleges operated by ministries other than the MOE were goal-directed toward meeting their own ministry-based human resource requirements. Thus, graduates were virtually assured of employment. This was also the case for the quota students in MOE schools, whose employment was assured by provincial authorities. With the change in economic policies,

graduate employment is no longer assured. This applies to non-MOE school graduates as well as quota students.

Staff Development

From the outset, staff development has been a key VTE issue. A significant number of instructors working in SVSs, technical colleges, and training centers are underqualified and lack industrial experience. They need updating and upgrading in instructional knowledge and skills, as well as related industrial on-the-job experience. Approximately 70 percent of the SVS instructors are graduates of technical colleges or former higher technical colleges, with the remainder coming from the secondary vocational school system. Very few have industrial experience and, given the salary variance between public service and the private sector, this situation will not likely change in the foreseeable future. There also appears to be a deficiency in initial training as well as further upgrading of VTE instructors in shop management, equipment maintenance, and the development of instructional materials.

In many respects, a similar problem exists at the technical colleges and former higher technical colleges (now NUOL faculties). The staff of these institutions are also generally underqualified, with few possessing a qualification higher than that for the level at which they teach. The majority have neither industrial experience nor instructional training in curriculum/program development, teaching methods, and student evaluation techniques.

With the exception of the SVSs and technical colleges serviced by the GTZ, teachers still have limited opportunities to upgrade their skills. Provincial education services and the Faculty of Education at NUOL have organized short seminars and workshops; however, no sustained system to upgrade VTE instructors in their content area, vocational skills, or instructional techniques appears to exist. As noted previously, at all VTE levels (secondary schools, technical colleges, and training centers), the knowledge and skills of the educational managers (directors and deputy directors) also need significant upgrading. A vocational education system strategy paper clearly defined the enormity of the staff development issue (MOF/GTZ, 1997).

Programs

There is considerable evidence of growth in several sectors of the economy, particularly in construction and civil projects. This includes residential, commercial, and industrial buildings; roads and bridges; and large-scale hydroelectric projects. Commercial and trade activities have grown rapidly, with continued growth expected in the transition to a full market economy. Services, particularly in finance and banking, social services, and tourism and hospitality, have also grown rapidly and are forecast to continue performing well under the current development plan. However, all of these economic improvements depend on the availability of a well-educated and skilled workforce. This directly impacts the existing training system, which cannot provide the type and level of skills in demand, a problem that will increase due to on-going or planning-stage industrial developments.

Pedersen (1996) concluded, based on his labor market research, that there is a nationwide demand for skilled workers in (a) construction trades, including carpentry, masonry, electrical installation, plumbing, and welding; (b) commerce and trade, including accounting, finance, office management, bookkeeping, computer operations, and clerical and secretarial work; and (c) repair and maintenance services, including motor vehicles, tractors, motorcycles, small engines and pumps, rice mills, mechanical equipment, commercial electronics (radios, televisions, recorders, etc.), household and commercial appliances, and equipment. Unfortunately, however, Pedersen noted that there is presently insufficient capacity to meet these demands. There is a need, therefore, for significantly increased training in these specializations. Local area surveys should confirm the type and amount of training in each specialization.

Laos cannot determine which of the current VTE programs to eliminate, expand, or upgrade, as well as what programs to add, because it has no labor market information to inform program decision-making. Nor is there reliable data or information that could help respond to the inherent issues surrounding overall program quality. Also lacking is determination of the individual course components that would make programs viable, useful, and, therefore, effective and efficient.

More specifically, information is lacking on
• Training standards—standard norms for determining the efficiency with which the process of training is conducted, including quality of curriculum, instructional design, instructor qualifications, delivery methods, and so forth.
• Skill standards—standard norms for determining the effectiveness of training and thus defining the skills required and benchmarks against which performance (competency) can be measured.

Without these two fundamental components, a skill standards, testing, and certification system (SSTC)—which could be used to certify that an individual has a specific level of competency, and which employers would accept as a valid and reliable measurement—cannot exist. In addition, without standard norms and a database, neither a program nor an institutional accreditation system is possible.

Facilities, Equipment, and Instructional Materials

An in-depth review of VTE institutions confirmed that they generally lack adequate physical facilities as well as funds to provide textbooks, teaching materials, and consumables of all kinds. A VTE study by the GTZ noted that

> there is a lack of equipment and educational materials. All schools complain about the shortage of instructional material in print or

non-print. Teachers' guides,
student manuals, instructional
sheets, illustrated charts, handouts, transparencies, and, moreover, exercise material are in
many cases non-existent. Financial assistance from the state for
these objects is generally not
available in the necessary extent.
(Weidmann, 1996)

The situation is somewhat better in schools
supported by a donor country development
project (e. g., the Lao-German Technical School
in Vientiane supported by the GTZ). The materials in these schools were either prepared
by individual teachers (and then copied by the
students) or adopted from other countries.
However, efforts from interested civil servants
to translate suitable (written) material are not
always encouraged or successful.

In 1996, there was another review of
nonformal facilities, equipment, and instructional resources on behalf of the MOLSW and
its Department of Labor skills center initiatives. This study further confirmed that the
problems experienced by formal VTE were also
apparent in nonformal VTE. The study reported that a

major constraint of the DOL is
the availability of buildings,
equipment and training materials.
. . . [T]hose [facilities] of the
existing center of Vientiane need
to be upgraded to meet the
requirements. . . . [T]he possibility of renting or utilizing existing
facilities of vocational schools in
these provinces is remote as
such schools do not possess the
kind of facilities, equipment and
materials demanded. (Weidmann,
1996)

With the exception of those SVSs, technical
colleges, or NUOL faculties that participate in
either bilateral grant programs with other
countries, or the ongoing Postsecondary Education Rationalization Loan Project, the state
of the country's VTE facilities, equipment, and
instructional resources is in difficult straits. The
entire subsector needs a significant infusion
of capital and other resources for educational
facilities and equipment, student facilities,
learning resources centers, water and sanita-
tion, as well as corresponding technical assistance and expertise to upgrade the instructors, maintenance staff, and school administrators in their use of these resources.

PRIVATE SECTOR PARTICIPATION

Private sector involvement is important to
VTE systems in developed and developing
countries. Without a visible and workable relationship with local employers, it is virtually
impossible to develop a strong, market-driven
vocational school, institute, or center. This
proposition is true at the secondary,
postsecondary, and higher education levels, as
well as for training centers involved in short-
term, nonformal programs.

Even though Laos's vocational and technical education subsector is criticized for having poor private sector linkages and poor quality graduates, it does not fully avail itself to
employers and generally ignores program-link-
ing activities. Furthermore, although directors
and instructors at VTE institutions have awareness of the need for program advisory committees (PACs), so that local employers can
offer advice about program quality and activities, very few of these PACs exist. This state of
affairs—combined with the lack of (a) access
to labor market information, (b) a program
and/or institutional accreditation mechanism,
and (c) a skill standards and testing certification system—has placed the country's VTE
system in its difficult position.

POLICY AND STRATEGIES

Laos is attempting to make the difficult and
complex transition from a centralized, com-

mand economy to an open, market-driven one. However, the country is captive to its political, administrative, and bureaucratic heritage. Its institutions are slow to respond to the challenges of economic and social transformation. Realizing that the situation is becoming critical, the government embarked on a national education reform effort, including strategic planning for vocational education and training. The government commissioned a task force in 1997 as a first attempt to emphasize the importance of VTE to the country's social and economic development. Through this initiative, an integrated VTE subsector strategy involving formal vocational and technical education, as well as nonformal basic vocational education and skills training, was formulated.

Overall, the purposes of the strategy are to (a) provide a political framework for the further planning and development of a vocational education system that responds to economic and individual needs, (b) improve cooperation between and among all vocational education and skills training providers, (c) encourage the private sector to contribute to the development of the vocational education and training system, and (d) clarify areas where further assistance from donors should be sought.

Criticisms

Vocational and technical education has been under considerable strain since its first external review in 1989. Criticisms leveled then have been reinforced throughout the 1990s. Issues that have befallen the country's VTE subsector include

• A lack of training capacity, including quantity, quality, and relevance for both urban and rural employers, as well as rural and agricultural communities, combined with little or no labor market information.

• An administrative structure that has too many decision-making participants who have unclear authority and responsibility, combined with unclear policies and plans, and an untested strategic vision.

• Inadequate databases, including the absence of an education information system that is linked to a labor market information system.

• Low internal and external efficiency outputs, which cause discontent within stakeholder groups, uneasiness in international financial institutions and other countries that might invest in the subsector, and rejection by parents and students who fail to see VTE as worthwhile.

• Large numbers of inappropriately trained instructors and administrators who lack relevant expertise (including program/course planning, instructional techniques, and evaluation methods) as well as on-the-job experience, combined with a lack of readily accessible upgrading opportunities.

• A range of programs and related curriculum that have little or no realistic value to employers and, most disturbingly, that are not part of a program accreditation mechanism or a skills standards, testing, and certification program.

• An inventory of facilities and equipment that is inadequate for training, unsafe, and in need of maintenance, repair, and/or replacement.

• A less than satisfactory relationship with the private sector, wherein few if any VTE institutions (a) have program advisory committees or other forms of employer involvement, (b) extensively employ work-based activities that link students to on-the-job experiences as part of their learning activities, or (c) arrange on-the-job industry-based practicums for their instructors (MOE/GTZ, 1997; Pedersen, 1996).

Each of these eight issues presents a major impediment to the successful conduct of activities within the VTE subsector, yet it must be quickly positioned to significantly contribute to Laos's human resource needs. The VTE subsector must also respond to the expectations of both private and public sector employers and, most significantly, provide a wide range of target groups with a specific set of income-generating opportunities.

Policy Elements

Key policy elements in a comprehensive human resource development strategy include the following:

• Linking the supply of trained personnel (quality and quantity) to labor market employment needs, where monitoring of present and future skill requirements is achieved through a labor market information system that has (a) an appropriate method to analyze the input and distribute the results for VTE institutions to use in making programming decisions and (b) a follow-up procedure to see what the VTE institutions accomplished.

• Linking the supply of trained personnel with local development needs, since about 80 percent of the population live in rural areas and skill requirements differ from one region to another. (For example, employment opportunities may arise from the need to enhance development of agricultural-based services such as processing, storage, distribution, and marketing activities.)

• Developing and delivering a broad range of formal and nonformal training and education specialties based on the demands of different economic sectors, such as training that focuses not only on clearly defined employment opportunities but also on self-help work at the community or family level.

• Building the quality and quantity of human and capital resources for all VTE institutions, which requires significant effort to increase the internal and external efficiency of the institutions through installation of an education information system, a program accreditation mechanism, and a skills standards, testing, and certification process.

• Planning and delivering courses and programs in cooperation with local employers and other stakeholders through program advisory committees to create on-going links with business and industry, as well as with public sector employers.

• Implementing courses and programs that have a work-based learning component. This involves building into each formal and nonformal program external activities (work experience, practicums, internships, cooperative education, production processing, etc.) that enable students/trainees to apply their knowledge and skills in on-the-job activities with local employers.

• Implementing a programming system that has clearly visible upward mobility opportunities for all VTE graduates. (For example, using a combination of course/program credit transfer, SSTC, program accreditation, and prior learning experience mechanisms to offer graduates from all VTE programs [including in-house, employer-based training courses and short-term training at skills centers] an opportunity to move upward in the system from unskilled, to semiskilled, to skilled, to technician, to technologist, and to professional/engineer. This would include recognizing knowledge and skill acquisition across occupational categories.)

Moreover, any VTE implementation strategy needs to include some clearly defined form of decentralized decision-making (and therefore, accountability) to the local levels, even to the school-/college-/center-based management level.

Policies help to define a country's human resource vision by stating what should be accomplished under given circumstances and within specified time periods. Plans focus on how and who will accomplish the activities, while specific organizations conduct the tasks. It appears, however, as is the case with most successful VTE structures in other countries, that the authority and responsibility for accomplishing VTE's key outputs should lie with those who must perform the training and implement the tasks in the most effective and efficient manner—namely, the institutions, agencies, businesses, skills centers, and so forth.

References

Asian Development Bank. (1995). *Lao People's Democratic Republic: Country profile*. Manila, Philippines: Author.

Asian Development Bank. (1998). *Final report: Employment promotion and training project*. Manila,

Philippines: Education, Health and Population Division (West), Asian Development Bank.

Asian Development Bank & Netherlands Economic Institute. (1994). *Training needs assessment survey*. Manila, Philippines: Education, Health and Population Division (West), Asian Development Bank.

Groeber, K. (1994). *Management of vocational education and training in Lao PDR*. Vientiane, Lao PDR: German Agency for Technical Cooperation.

Ministry of Education & German Agency for Technical Cooperation. (1997). *Development of the vocational education system (VES): Strategy paper*. Vientiane, Lao PDR: Author.

Pedersen, D. (1996). *Labour market training needs for technical and vocational education and training in Lao PDR* (Vols. I - II). Vientiane, Lao PDR: German Agency for Technical Cooperation.

Weidmann, W. (1996). *Strategy paper: Technical and vocational education and training*. Vientiane, Lao PDR: German Agency for Technical Cooperation.

Vocational and Technical Education in a Transitional Economy: A Case Study of Laos

Appendix—Terminology and Definitions

By Clifton P. Campbell

The following terms and definitions were adopted for use. While this glossary serves as a ready reference for the meaning of words, terms, and abbreviations, it is not definitive or universal. Nevertheless, it should facilitate more exacting study and communication.

ability: The power to do something; the result of learning and practice. A characteristic that indicates an individual's skill, expertness, or competence.

adult vocational and technical education: A formal or nonformal education/training endeavor developed and provided for adults who need or want upgrade or continuing training. Emphasis is on preparing for occupational roles.

affective learning: Learning that involves feelings and personal judgments (opinions, attitudes, and values) about knowledge needed and behaviors demonstrated during the performance of job tasks.

alternative learning: Periods of training in a school, center, academy, or institute, alternating with periods of work experience.

apprentice: A qualified person of legal work-ing age who has entered into an apprenticeship agreement with an employer. Under such an agreement, the employer pays wages and provides training and work experience in a skilled occupation.

apprenticeable occupation: An occupation customarily learned by practical, on-the-job training and work experience. Occupation is clearly identified and commonly recognized and accepted throughout the industry. Also, it involves the development of a skill broad enough to apply in similar occupations.

apprenticeship agreement: A written agreement, also known as an indenture, that imposes obligations on both the apprentice and employer and provides for a stated number of hours of reasonable continuous employment that offers an approved schedule of training and work experience, supplemented by related instruction. The agreement is registered with an apprenticeship and training council, chamber, government agency, and so forth.

apprenticeship standards: Document that incorporates procedures for training apprentices, terms and conditions of employment, training on the job, and related instruction. The duties and responsibilities, including administrative procedures, of the Joint Apprenticeship Committee (where applicable) are also set forth.

articulation: A planned process that enables students/trainees who choose more than one level of instruction to move from level to level or from one institution to another without unnecessary duplication or gaps in their instructional program.

assessment: The act of determining the amount or value of learning.

barriers to transfer: Actual or perceived factors that act as impediments (inhibitors) to the transfer of training from school-based learning experiences to a job.

basic training: Training given off the job in an institution or other undertaking that aims to impart the fundamentals of an occupation or group of occupations. May qualify trainee for employment or provide a basis for specialization. May be recognized as a phase of initial training or constitute a part of retraining.

behavior: An individual's (visible, audible) action, performance, operation, or product which can be measured by an observer according to specific and discreet criteria.

behavioral objective: See *learning objective*.

certification: A process whereby an individual's competence in defined occupational/job skills is assessed and recognized by an organization, agency, association, or other group.

coaching: An activity in which an instructor and/or supervisor provides individual oversight during the practice of a skill or procedure.

collective bargaining: The process by which representatives of employers and those of employees negotiate the various aspects of their relationship with a view toward arriving at a mutually acceptable labor agreement (contract).

competency: Proficient performance based on knowledge, skills, and attitudes that are collectively measured when an individual is evaluated as to ability to perform a job-related task(s) under specified conditions to a specified level of proficiency. Required to enter and perform effectively in a job.

conditions: Circumstances that exist during performance of a behavioral action. Specify what the trainee is given—inputs including the environment (setting); tools, equipment, and so forth.; safety considerations; job performance aids; and special physical demands. Used in terminal and enabling objectives.

context: The multiple interrelated conditions (environment) in which instruction, performance, and practice are embedded.

cooperation: Working together to accomplish mutual goals.

cost-benefit analysis: An assessment of the specific costs and benefits (expressed in economic terms) involved in a course or program.

cost-effectiveness: A comparative evaluation derived from an analysis of two or more alternatives (actions, methods, approaches, equipment, support systems, etc.) in terms of the interrelated influences of cost and effectiveness in accomplishing a learning objective.

counseling: Purposeful assistance aimed at (a) understanding an individual's apparent impediment to learning (e. g., lack of knowledge, personal problem, or difficulty relating to others) or job-related performance and (b) developing a strategy to eliminate or reduce the impact of that impediment. Counseling is best done before a problem becomes a deterrent to success in a learning situation.

course documentation: Information describing the content of a course (instructional materials, tests, instructor's manual, evaluation plan, trainee's manual) and its developmental history (job analysis, criteria for selecting tasks for training, previous revisions, etc.).

course objective: A description of the ultimate purpose of a course, including a statement of who is to be trained, what they will be trained to do, the degree of qualification brought about by the training, and where and under what general conditions the graduate will perform on the job.

criterion (criteria): A standard or test against which something, including learning, can be measured and/or judged.

criterion-referenced performance test (CRPT): A sample work situation in which trainees perform a task that requires them to demonstrate their acquisition of necessary knowledge and skills. Trainee performance, under predetermined conditions, is compared with attainment standards (criteria) derived from an analysis of what a particular task requires. The term *job performance measure* (JPM) is also used.

curriculum: Activities that are planned, carried out, and evaluated by the instructor of an occupation to prepare students/trainees for work on the job.

day release: Authorized absence of a trainee from work, with or without pay, to attend courses of related instruction for a number of hours or days each week.

duty: A major subdivision (a large segment) of the work performed by an individual. A job is made up of two or more duties. Duties are groups of closely related tasks.

efficiency: Resource control, accomplishing more or the same results with fewer resources (money, time, etc.); reducing or containing costs. How well someone or something performs compared with expectations. Also, reducing barriers and inefficiencies of learning. Evaluation at the efficiency level is process oriented and formative in nature.

enterprise: A business, company, commercial or industrial establishment, firm, organization, or plant that employs workers.

entry behavior: The skills, knowledge, and attitudes required before a trainee begins instruction. Also may refer to the intended trainee's capability prior to new learning.

entry-level job: One that employers offer to individuals who (a) lack on-the-job experience or (b) have received some training outside of the hiring enterprise.

entry skills: Specific, measurable behaviors determined, through the process of analysis of learning requirements, to be basic to subsequent knowledge or skill in the course or program.

entry test: Contains items based on the learning objectives that the intended trainee must have attained to begin a course or program.

evaluation: The process of collecting information/data using tests, CRPTs, and so forth, and interpreting it for the purpose of making a judgment or decision on the worth or value of instruction or on an individual's success.

evaluation instruments: Tests, rating forms, checklists, reaction forms/opinionnaires, questionnaires, interview guides/schedules, and other devices used to (a) gather information and data; (b) determine achievement; or (c) determine the relative standing of an individual, group, or objective (attitude, performance, etc.).

evaluation plan: A method or outline of the set of procedures that will be used to gather information and data to assess a course or program.

experiential learning: A technique in which students/trainees undergo a particular experience, through role playing or group or individual work, so that they can evaluate the experience and learn from it.

external evaluation: The collection and analysis of feedback data from outside the instructional setting to (a) evaluate the graduates' success in applying at the workplace the knowledge, skills, and attitudes being trained and (b) determine whether the job requirements have changed.

feedback: Information on trainee performance is "fed" back to the (a) trainee, to reinforce or improve proficiency; (b) instructional designer, so that materials and procedures can be improved on the basis of trainee needs; and (c) management system, so it can monitor the internal and external integrity of the instruction and make appropriate revisions.

formal education: A system with a hierarchic structure and chronological succession of grades, from kindergarten through the university, that, in addition to academic studies, comprises a variety of specialized programs and full-time training institutions. Classes are conducted within specially built institutions. Strictly controlled credentials form the basis of legitimacy.

formative evaluation: The process of collecting information and data on instructional materials, media, procedures, instruction, and tests, while they are being developed and tried out, to improve their relevance, effectiveness, and efficiency. The term *developmental testing* is also used.

front-end analysis: Refers to needs assessment, job analysis, selection of tasks for training, and the development of CRPTs.

further education: Full- or part-time general or vocational education for persons who have left school. Includes higher education and adult education.

further training: Global term that encompasses any type of training subsequent and complementary to initial training.

general education: Education that, in its choice of subject matter, does not envisage any kind of specialization with a view to preparing individuals for work.

grading: The process of assigning a mark or rating to trainee deliverables and examinations.

higher education: Term used in connection with education at the postsecondary, college, or university level.

individualized instruction: A management scheme that permits making individual characteristics a factor in determining the kind and amount of instruction given. It nearly always implies some form of pacing controlled by the individual (as opposed to the instructor and/or group) and guided by instructional materials.

informal learning: Requires a conscious effort throughout life to take advantage of available opportunities to learn through the environment, for example, the library, open learning centers, and communication media (magazines, television, computers, etc.).

initial training: First complete course of training for an occupation. Often divided into two parts: basic training followed by specialization.

in-plant training: Any training (including apprenticeship) provided on the premises of an enterprise in which the trainee is in an employment situation. May be given on the job or off the job or through a combination of the two.

institution: A school, center, academy, institute, or college that provides instruction.

instructional materials: Tangible trainee-oriented resources, with instructional content. These resources support the learning process and are an essential component of effective and efficient training courses and programs. Instructional materials can be categorized as (a) printed materials, (b) audiovisual media, and (c) manipulative aids. The term *training materials* is also used.

instructional methods: Methods (techniques, strategies) of presentation, practice, and evaluation that specify the ways in which the desired learning outcomes should be achieved in the instructional setting (e. g., tutorial, lecture/discussion, demonstration, role playing, case studies, programmed instruction, and so forth).

instructional setting: The environment, place, or facilities in which instruction is provided. For example, (a) the schoolhouse—classroom, shop, laboratory, library, and so forth and (b) the workplace—factory, garage, construction site, supermarket, hotel, hospital, and so forth.

instructional system: An integrated combination of resources (trainees, instructors, materials, equipment, and facilities), techniques, and procedures performing effectively and efficiently the functions required to achieve specified learning objectives.

instructor: A person who instructs; teacher, tutor, or trainer. One who directs the development of individuals by helping them accomplish learning objectives.

instruments: Questionnaires, interview guides/schedules, and opinionnaires or reaction forms used to gather information and data from respondents.

internal evaluation: The collection and analysis of feedback and management data from within the instructional setting to assess the effectiveness of instruction in terms of trainee attainment of learning objectives.

interpersonal skills: Human relations skills that enable individuals to recognize, judge, and balance appropriate behavior; cope with undesirable behavior in others; absorb stress and deal with ambiguity; listen to others; inspire trust and confidence in others; structure social interaction; share responsibility; and easily interact with others in a positive manner.

job: All the duties and tasks performed by a single job incumbent constitute that individual's job. If several individuals perform identical tasks, they all hold the same job. The job is the basic unit used in carrying out the personnel actions of recruitment, selection, training, classification, and assignment.

job analysis: The process used to prepare a detailed listing of the tasks and elements necessary to perform a clearly defined, specific job. Often involves observations of workers and interviews with those who know the job well, to describe accurately and completely the work performed and the requirements for successful performance.

job content: The functions, requirements, and tasks of a particular job. May differ for the same job title due to variations in type of machinery, production method, and so forth.

job description: A detailed description of a job including: qualifications, duties, work environment, tools, equipment, references, and most important, a list of the tasks to be performed.

job incumbent: An individual who performs a job.

journeyman: A worker who has satisfactorily completed an apprenticeship and is classified as a skilled worker in a trade or craft (occupation).

knowledge: Specified information, principles, rules, or facts that are not directly observable. Involves the use of mental processes. Used in developing the skills and desired attitudes to effectively accomplish prescribed tasks and jobs.

labor mobility: Refers to the ability of individual workers to move in and among labor markets.

labor supply: Denotes not only the size of the workforce, but also its skills and geographic location and its willingness and ability to be productive.

learner characteristics: Traits or qualities possessed by students/trainees that could affect their ability to attain course/program learning objectives (e. g., academic background, age and maturity, intelligence, motivation, aptitude, temperament, reading grade level, physical ability, and so forth). Same as *trainee characteristics*.

learning: Measurable change(s) in a trainee's behavior as a result of experience. The behavior can be intellectual (knowledge), physical and overt (skills), or attitudinal.

learning activities: Specific activities the individual engages in to facilitate attainment of a learning objective (e. g., taking a field trip, mowing a lawn, painting a house).

learning alternatives: Instructional experiences that are made available to individuals with the intent that they would help attain a learning objective or set of objectives.

learning categories: Learning can be classified into one of three categories (called *do-*

mains in cognitive psychology): mental skill/knowledge (cognitive learning), physical skill (psychomotor learning), or attitude (affective learning).

learning hierarchy: Graphic portrayal of the relationships among learning tasks in which some tasks must be attained before others can be learned.

learning objective: A statement that specifies measurable behavior (performance) that must be exhibited after instruction.

management plan: Program for the assignment, monitoring, and assessment of the personnel, materials, and resources dedicated to an instructional setting (schoolhouse or workplace).

mandatory training: Participation in a training course or program as a condition of employment or continued employment.

mastery: In terms of learning, refers to meeting or exceeding all the specified requirements for a learning objective.

mentor: A highly skilled worker who guides the learning process of another worker who lacks workplace knowledge, skills, attitudes, and/or experience.

methods: See *instructional methods*.

modular training: System in which the training content is divided into independent units or modules of learning. The modules can be combined to form a program suited to the needs of the individual, to technical developments, to occupational structure, and so forth. It permits continuous program adaptation.

module: A combination of the directions, instructional content, activities, and postinstruction questions that facilitate the attainment of learning objectives. Often called self-learning packages, modules are designed for individual use. May include both printed materials and audiovisual media. The terms *training*, *learning*, and *instructional package/packet/guide* are also used.

needs assessment: A method of determining training needs by reviewing job tasks, iden-tifying performance factors and objectives, and defining learning objectives and recommendations. Often includes a study that collects and analyzes data as well as opinions to identify problems.

nonformal training: Training organized and conducted outside the formal education system for employees to attain particular learning objectives. Examples include on-the-job, vestibule, and apprenticeship training.

occupation: A skilled worker's trade, craft, vocation, profession, or job.

on-the-job training (OJT): Workplace-based training and practice under close supervision, designed specifically to train an individual, without the necessity for a long-term interruption to work assignments. Uses actual processes and products of commercial value for instruction and practice purposes. OJT ranges in complexity from a program for an entry-level trainee to become qualified in simple tasks, to a program designed to take an individual who possesses the fundamental principles required to understand the tasks from the entry level to that of an individual who is fully qualified to perform all the tasks of a job.

outputs: Influences training has on the trainee; products of the training process.

peer tutoring: Instruction in which trainees at a more advanced level of knowledge and/ or skill provide instruction to other trainees.

performance-based training (PBT): Training based on the products of job and task analysis (learning objectives, etc.) so that the training relates directly to job performance requirements.

performance deficiency: Inability to perform job tasks to established standards.

planning: The application of foresight, approaching the future with the aid of systematic analysis, so as to minimize uncertainty and mistakes.

policy: A course or method of action established to guide an organization toward attainment of its goals/strategic objectives.

practice: The physical rehearsal of a task (skill) undertaken with the intention of achieving proficiency in performing that task (skill).

prerequisite: Knowledge, skills, or behavior that individuals must have attained before beginning instruction.

probationary period: A period of time served by apprentices during which the apprenticeship agreement can be canceled at the request of either party. After completion of the probationary period, the agreement may be canceled only by the sponsor after adequate cause has been shown and all parties to the agreement have had an opportunity to be heard.

productivity: The amount of goods/products and services produced by a skilled worker.

proficiency: Ability to perform a specific behavior (task or learning objective) to the established standard to demonstrate mastery of that behavior.

progress tests: Examinations administered (daily, weekly, etc.) throughout the training course or program to measure trainee progress.

public finance: The finances of the state, including fiscal policy, taxation, and so forth.

qualification: Describes all the knowledge, skills, and attitudes acquired during an individual's educational, training, and socialization processes. These qualifications serve individuals not only in their working life, but also in their role as citizens and family members. Thus, in addition to their vocational dimensions, qualifications encompass social and societal aspects as well.

quality control: Process of measuring and evaluating to maintain course or program standards through adjustments in instructional materials, methods, or setting.

reliability: The consistency with which (a) a test measures the amount of achievement and (b) an instrument's results are predictable, dependable, and stable.

retraining: Training for the acquisition of skills and knowledge for practicing an occupation other than the one for which the individual originally trained. May require basic training plus specialization.

return on investment (ROI): The rate at which training returns the investment (costs). It is a calculative approach to comparing results (monetary benefits) to investment (monetary costs). Usually expressed as a percentage.

self-pacing: A mode of instruction whereby trainees progress through instructional materials at their own rate of speed. This enables slower learners to take the time they need while faster learners finish more quickly.

sequencing: Ordering instruction. Proper sequencing enables trainees to make the transition from one skill or body of knowledge to another, and it assures the acquisition of supporting skills and knowledge before dependent performances are introduced.

simulation: A technique whereby job-world phenomena are mimicked, often in a low-fidelity situation, in which costs are reduced, dangers eliminated, and time compressed. The simulation may focus on a subset of the features of the actual job environment.

situational constraints: Environmental conditions and circumstances that interfere with an individual's performance. Include availability and adequacy of place of employment; funds; tools, equipment, furniture, materials, and so forth.; safety clothing; reference documents; and time.

skills: Involve physical or manipulative activities. They generally require knowledge for their execution. All skills are actions that have special requirements for proficient performance.

specialist training: Advanced level training to deepen knowledge of a particular task, function, or aspect of an occupation.

standards: Describes the measurable criteria or standards of performance (level of proficiency) that trainees must attain.

structural unemployment: Unemployment caused by changes in the structure of the economy resulting from such factors as technological change or relocation of industry, or by changes in the composition of the workforce.

subject matter experts: Qualified individuals who are recognized for their skill and experience in the performance of a specific job and who are consulted by a job analyst or an instructional developer in the process of job and task analysis, instructional material and test preparation, and so forth.

systems approach: Refers to the orderly process of analysis, design, development, evaluation, revision, and operation of a collection of interrelated elements. In a systems approach, one element builds on another.

target population: The pool of potential trainees for whom instructional materials are prepared and tested.

task: A distinct measurable work activity that constitutes specific and necessary action by a job incumbent for a meaningful purpose. The work unit that deals with the methods, procedures, and techniques by which parts of a job are carried out. Tasks vary in complexity but are made up of at least two elements. Related tasks grouped together make up a duty.

technical school: Vocational school. The functions and objectives of the technical and vocational school tend to overlap. The terms are often used synonymously from one educational system to another.

trade-off: A compromise between what is desirable and what is possible—a necessity in any systematic approach to instruction. Ordinarily, trade-offs involve increases or decreases in time, money, facilities, equipment, or personnel. The use of simulators is an example.

trainee: Person undergoing training or education for an occupation.

trainee characteristics: See *learner characteristics*.

training: Providing individuals with practical know-how and theoretical insights, through applied learning experiences in a schoolhouse or at a workplace, necessary for gainful employment as skilled workers, technicians, or entry-level professionals. Training imparts the knowledge, skills, attitudes, understandings, work habits, and appreciations needed to enter and progress in a career.

training allowance: Stipend or other payment made by an employer or from public funds to an employee undergoing training for a certain period. Training usually takes place outside the workplace.

training by stages: Training given in stages of increasingly higher specialization. The first stage consists of broad basic training for skills and knowledge common to a range of economic activities. Each subsequent stage both prepares for the next and permits employment at a recognized level of skill.

training levy: Tax imposed on employers with a view to financing training activities.

transfer of training: Ability or lack of ability of a course/program graduate to apply (use) knowledge and skills acquired in a school-based learning experience on the job.

tutoring: A one-to-one relationship between a trainer (tutor) and an individual for the purpose of learning how to perform a job task. Effective tutoring requires good communication skills (e. g., eye contact, positive tone of voice, encouragement, praising), as well as a positive learning and work environment with the goal of increasing occupational competencies.

union: The duly recognized contractual bargaining agency for a specific enterprise, trade area, or industrial group or groups.

validation: The process of developmental testing and revision of instruction until the instruction effectively realizes its intent.

validation process: Testing instructional materials on a sample of the target population to insure the effectiveness of the materials.

validity: The extent to which (a) a test measures what it claims or is intended to measure and (b) an instrument gathers the information and data it is designed to gather.

vestibule training: Training in which on-the-job conditions are duplicated in a more favorable environment that allows trainees to learn job tasks without the adverse effects of production requirements.

vocation: A trade, craft, occupation, or profession; a calling.

vocational counseling: A part of vocational guidance that consists of helping individuals develop a career or vocational plan to be periodically reviewed and revised on the basis of new information, goals, and progress.

vocational education and training (VET): Initial and continuing VET is provided in public and private (proprietary) schools, postsecondary colleges, and other institutions, as well as in the workplace and military. It uses practical work experiences and theoretical insights to prepare trainees (students/apprentices) for (a) gainful employment as skilled workers, technicians, or entry-level professionals in recognized occupations or (b) enrollment in advanced technical education programs. VET uses a full range of training delivery methods—formal (school-based) and nonformal (workplace-based). VET is concerned with the development of skills, abilities, understandings, attitudes, work habits, and appreciations needed by trainees to enter and progress in employment on a useful and productive basis. It provides a range of skill levels, from basic entry-level skills to technical skills that require a high degree of specialization and competence. VET generally excludes preparation for a baccalaureate or higher degree.

work experience: Schemes in which students can participate, to a limited extent, in work in trades, industry, commerce, or other fields.

work study: Detailed examination of the manner in which a particular job is performed, with a view to rationalizing performance and thus increasing productivity.

workplace: The enterprise in which graduates, apprentices, and trainees are employed to perform the skills trained.

About the Authors

The following biographical summaries provide information on the authors' background and expertise in the various chapter topics. Author entries appear in alphabetical order by last name.

David Ashton

David Ashton is Director of the Centre for Labour Market Studies, which he founded in the 1980s, at the University of Leicester, United Kingdom (U. K.). The Centre specializes in postgraduate teaching and research into labor market and training issues, including an ongoing research program into national human resource development systems. It currently has one of the largest master's degree programs in training utilizing a distance education delivery format.

Dr. Ashton graduated from Leicester University and taught sociology there as well as at the University of Reading. He has also been a Visiting Professor at the State University of New York (U. S. A.) and the University of Alberta (Canada). In addition to his education experiences, he has served as a consultant to a number of national and international organizations, including the International Labour Organization as well as the U. K.'s Department of Employment and Institute of Personnel and Development.

Dr. Ashton has published widely in the field of employment and training. His current research interests are in national systems of skill formation. He also took part in a research project comparing the education and training systems of Singapore, Hong Kong, Taiwan, and Republic of [South] Korea. His latest books include *Education, Training and the Global Economy*, with Francis Green (published by Edward Elgar, Cheltenham, 1996) and *Education and Training for Development in East Asia: The Political Economy of Skill Formation in Newly Industrialised Economies*, with Johnny Sung and others (published by Routledge, London, 1999).

James A. Athanasou

James Athanasou is Associate Professor and convenor of the Vocational Education Training and Employment Group in the Faculty of Education at the University of Technology, Sydney, Australia. He is a psychologist and teacher by training who lectures mainly in the areas of measurement and evaluation. His research focuses on the role and development of educational and vocational interest.

Dr. Athanasou has been a visiting fellow at the Dusseldorp Skills Forum, Universitat der Bundeswehr Muenchen (Germany), and the University of Illinois, Urbana-Champaign (U. S. A.). He formerly served as Secretary of the Commerce and Industry Training Council [of] the State Training Authority, and Deputy Director of Vocational Services with responsibility for the Government Recruitment Agency.

Dr. Athanasou is the author of *Introduction to Educational Testing* (Social Science Press), *Career Interest Test* (Hobsons Press), *Selective Schools Tests* (Pascal Press), and *Adult Educational Psychology* (Social Science Press).

Megan Birch

Megan Birch is a high school English teacher in Prince George's County, Maryland. She holds a B. S. degree in Secondary Education for English, with a minor in Women's Studies, from Pennsylvania State University, and is pursuing a Master of Education degree from the University of Maryland. She expects to complete her master's in the summer of 2000.

Clifton P. Campbell

Clifton P. Campbell is a professor in the Department of Human Resource Development at The University of Tennessee and an international consultant. His varied background includes leadership roles in training and technical assistance projects with the Royal Saudi Naval Forces, U. S. Department of Labor, International Labor Organization, International Center for Advanced Technical and Vocational Training, U. S. Navy, Kuwait Public Authority for Applied Education and Training, World Bank, Taiwan (R. O. C.) Ministry of Education, and multinational corporations. His research focuses are the development, implementation, and evaluation of performance-based education and training, as well as workforce development policy and practices.

Professor Campbell has authored and co-authored numerous publications, including books, monographs, and journal articles in the United States and overseas, dealing with human resource development issues. His latest book was a two-volume edited set entitled *Education and Training for Work* (published by Technomic). He is active in professional, fraternal, and civic associations and has held offices at the local, state, national, and international levels. Dr. Campbell has received awards for his research, writing, and professional service in vocational and technical education and training and for his accomplishments in developing countries.

Sharon Coursey

Sharon Coursey is a doctoral student in Education Policy, Planning and Administration at the University of Maryland, College Park. Previously, she worked at the U. S. Department of Agriculture, Animal and Plant Health Inspection Service, as an Education Specialist, then as Deputy Director for International Training, and, most recently, as the agency's Director for Organizational and Professional Development. As part of her Ph.D. program, Ms. Coursey recently served an internship with the Office of Education Research and Improvement, U. S. Department of Education, where she studied the impact of school-to-work legislation as well as the types of programmatic activities and efforts it has engendered at the state and local levels.

Ms. Coursey holds a Master of Arts degree in International Education from The American University in Washington, D. C. She has worked in the field of adult education and training for more than 15 years, including both domestic and international experience as an education consultant, instructional designer, teacher trainer, and program manager. Her international experiences include work in West Africa, the Philippines, Mexico and Central America, and the South Pacific.

Jeanette R. Daines

Dr. Jeanette Daines works for the Minnesota State Colleges and Universities (MnSCU) as the System Director for International Education. Prior higher education responsibilities in Minnesota have included Academic Program Director for MnSCU; Senior Fellow and Leadership Academy Coordinator (University of Minnesota); and State Board of Vocational and Technical Education positions involving special projects development, international education, tech prep, community-based organization projects, human resource development, licensure and equity, planning, research, and policy development.

Dr. Daines's background includes 10 years experience at the University of Wisconsin, Stout, where she taught in the areas of Education, Early Childhood Education, and Home Economics Education, and served as the program administrator for the Office of Educational Strategies Development. Originally from South Dakota, she holds B.S. and M.S. degrees from the University of Wisconsin and the Doctor of Philosophy degree from the University of Minnesota. She has been a Fellow in the Educational Policy Fellowship Program and the Kellogg Leadership Program, and currently serves as President-Elect of the International Vocational Education and Training Association.

Cynthia Davis

Cynthia Davis is Associate Dean in the Division of Information Technology at Barry University in Miami, Florida, where she is responsible for planning and delivering the distance education program. Before coming to Barry, she was Assistant Director of the Instructional Television System in the College of Engineering, University of Maryland, College Park. She began her career teaching high school English and later taught at The American University and University of Maryland, Overseas Division.

Dr. Davis received her Ph.D. in Education Policy, Planning and Administration from the University of Maryland. Her dissertation was titled "Planning Education in Developing Countries: A Critical Theory Approach." In addition to educational planning and critical theory, Dr. Davis's research interests include North-South transfer of technology and distance learning.

She has published articles on educational planning in a number of journals, including *The Journal of Industrial Teacher Education*, for which she won the journal's Best Conceptual Manuscript award.

Hermann Diedrich

Hermann Diedrich is the Training Manager of DEULA (German Training Institute for Agricultural Engineering), which provides initial vocational training, adult rehabilitation, and job-related continuing education. Herr Diedrich has held various positions in government agencies, secondary and postsecondary schools, as well as in the private sector. His teaching experience spans more than 22 years and includes secondary education, postsecondary technical education, and instructor training. His background includes positions in in-service education for vocational instructors, technical educators, and industrial trainers. Prior to entering the field of vocational education, he completed an apprenticeship, then worked as a journeyman, master craftsman, and engineer in the tractor and heavy equipment sector. He also has extensive work experience in vocational/technical training in developing countries.

Herr Diedrich's educational background is bipartite: he is authorized to act in business as a worksite mentor (*Meister*) and in academic vocational training as a teacher; hence, he is all-embracing the German apprenticeship (dual) system. He received his master craftsman's certificate from the Chamber of Crafts and his university degree from the teacher college of the Gesamthochschule Wuppertal. He has authored and coauthored a number of research articles and curriculum publications, all focusing on best practices in workforce training through the dual system as practiced in Germany.

Vladimir Gasskov

Vladimir Gasskov received a diploma of engineering from the Moscow Steel and Alloys Institute and an advanced degree in industrial sociology from the Institute of Sociological Studies, U. S. S. R. Academy of Sciences. He also received, in 1989, a Ph.D. degree in management sociology from the International Research Institute for Management Sciences, Moscow University.

Since 1989, Dr. Gasskov has been employed by the International Labour Organization as a specialist in the Training Policies and Systems Branch. His research and professional activities focus on the financing and management of vocational and technical education systems.

His recent major publications include *Managing Vocational Training Systems: Handbook for Senior Administrators, Skills Promotion Funds,* and *Alternative Schemes of Financing Training.* He is a frequent consultant to governments and has participated in numerous workshops and training programs on management and financing.

Jim Gleeson

Jim Gleeson holds postgraduate degrees in theology, philosophy, and education. He is a lecturer in the Department of Education and Professional Studies at the University of Limerick, Ireland, where he teaches curriculum studies and works in the areas of initial and continuing teacher education. He was formerly Head of that department and is currently Course Leader of the Masters in Educational Management program.

Mr. Gleeson's experience over 25 years includes teaching and administrative positions in second- and third-level education. He has been actively involved with vocational education and training (VET) related programs funded by the European Union (EU) and has conducted a number of external evaluations for the national ministry and the EU in areas as diverse as European studies, gender equality, and transition from school to adult and working life. Centrally involved in curriculum

development at the local and national levels over much of his career, he has a particular interest in education policy matters. The author of many papers and reports, he has also edited curriculum materials for various VET programs.

Annette A. Hartenstein

Annette Hartenstein is a Special Projects Officer of the International Federation of Training and Development Organisations, Ltd. (IFTDO), a global nongovernmental organization affiliated with the United Nations and devoted to furthering human capacity development worldwide. She recently served as project manager for an IFTDO/United Nations "Work and Family" study in Argentina, Egypt, India, and the Netherlands.

Dr. Hartenstein has also worked as a U. S. Government official as well as a management consultant to improve human resource management and development systems internationally and to identify and transfer "best human resource practices" globally. She has managed and served in international development projects, including a U. S. Aid for International Development project to improve the Egyptian Capital Market.

Dr. Hartenstein holds a doctorate degree in public administration from the University of Southern California. Her dissertation was titled "Organization Effectiveness in a Federal Government Agency." She has authored several articles on human resource development.

Dennis R. Herschbach

Dennis Herschbach is the coordinator of the Comparative and International Studies program in the Department of Education Policy, Planning and Administration, College of Education, University of Maryland, College Park. He has worked in the field of human resource development for a number of international development agencies and organizations. He was formerly the Deputy Director of the International Labor Organization's training center in Turin, Italy. His experience includes development work in Africa, the Middle East, Eastern Europe, Central America, and the Caribbean. He was a Fulbright Senior Research Scholar at the University of Twente, Enschede, the Netherlands. Most recently, he has been involved with establishing a technical high school in Albania.

Dr. Herschbach's publications include work on instructional design, curriculum development, and classroom instruction. He has also published a number of works on policy and planning issues related to workforce programs in developing countries. His current research involves issues of program quality and sustainability. He is a former editor of the *Journal of Industrial Teacher Education* and the *International Journal of Vocational Education and Training*.

Takao Kamibeppu

Takao Kamibeppu is a Ph.D. candidate in the Department of Education Policy, Planning and Administration, College of Education, University of Maryland, College Park. After getting a B.A. in Law from Kumamoto University, Japan, he served the Japanese Ministry of Education, Science, Sports and Culture in Tokyo for eight years including a three-year stint with UNESCO in Bangkok as an Associate Expert in basic education. At the Ministry and UNESCO, he managed various educational development projects in developing countries in Asia and the Pacific.

Mr. Kamibeppu arrived in the United States in 1993 on a Fulbright scholarship to study at the School for International Training, Vermont, where he received his M.A. in International and Intercultural Management. At the University of Maryland, he is currently working on his dissertation on the role of subgovernmental processes in Japanese policymaking in education aid. His research interests include education aid policy and practice, internationalization of Japanese education, and minority and cross-cultural issues in education. He is also a cross-cultural consultant to the International Center for the Study of Education Policy and Human Values in the College of Education, as well as a research fellow at International Christian University in Tokyo.

Marvin Lamoureux

Marvin Lamoureux was a business administration university/college instructor for eight years in the United States and Canada. For 13 years, he was also Dean of Instruction at one of Canada's largest postsecondary institutions. Throughout his instructional and administrative career, Dr. Lamoureux was involved in education and training at both the national and international levels. Since 1981, his formal training, experience, and expertise have been applied especially to education and training policy, planning, and administrative topics.

In addition to his work in education, Dr. Lamoureux has been a project manager, team leader, and specialist consultant on projects funded by the World Bank, Asian Development Bank, Canadian International Development Agency, as well as a host of private and public organizations including Deloitte and Touche Management Consultants (Kenya); TADS Education, Ltd. (U. K.), Organization for Educational Resources and Technology Training (U. S. A.); and KPMG/ARA Consulting Group (Toronto), Sandwall Engineering (Vancouver), Eduplus Management Group (Montreal), and the Canadian Real Estate Association. Dr. Lamoureux has had in-country project experience in 23 countries representing the Caribbean and Central America, Middle East, North America, East and Southern Africa, Central Europe, and Asia. He has authored or coauthored a multitude of technical reports and has delivered numerous guest lectureships and workshops throughout the world.

Johanna Lasonen

Johanna Lasonen, Senior Researcher at the Institute for Educational Research of the University of Jyväskylä, Finland, gained a Teacher's Diploma in 1974, a Master of Arts in Pedagogics in 1977 from the University of Jyväskylä, and a doctoral degree in Vocational and Technical Education from the Virginia Polytechnic Institute and State University (U. S. A.). Her dissertation concerned vocational teachers' gender-role attitudes and received an Omicron Tau Theta award in the U. S. A. She is President of the International Vocational Education and Training Association for 1999-2000.

Dr. Lasonen taught 10 years as a Senior Lecturer at the Vocational Teacher Training College of Jyväskylä. After a three-year fellowship with the Academy of Finland, she received the tenure of a senior researcher at the Institute for Educational Research. Her research has focused on analyzing the effects of learning environments on musical skills among school-age children, surveying the link between attitudes and the promotion of equality among teachers in vocational education institutions, and the learning of young adults using both quantitative and qualitative methods. Dr. Lasonen has participated as an expert in national and international educational evaluation projects and served as a trustee for professional organizations. She is the author of numerous journal articles and monograph chapters in Finnish and English. Her recent research focuses on European upper secondary education reforms and work-related learning.

Stuart M. Niven

Stuart Niven is President Emeritus of the International Vocational Education and Training Association. He is a recipient of the Joel Magissos Award for exceptional service to the Association and the Silvius/Wolansky Foundation Award for Outstanding International Leadership in Vocational Education and Training. He is Chairman of the Board of Management of Clydebank College (Scotland) and is an active researcher and consultant.

Mr. Niven is a graduate of Glasgow University, and pursued postgraduate studies in education at Glasgow and Strathclyde Universities. His current interests are in the governance of vocational/technical education institutions. He is a Fellow in the Institute of Management and a member of the Executive of the Scottish Association for Educational Management and Administration. He is also a member of the Royal Philosophical Society of Glasgow.

Mr. Niven has served on various United Kingdom and Scottish committees and boards, including the Further Education Board of the National Council for Academic Awards; the United Kingdom Central Council for Nursing, Midwifery and Health Visiting; the Further Education Committee of the General Teaching Council; and the Editorial Board of the *Journal of Lifelong Learning Initiatives*. He was formerly Director of the Scottish School of Further Education, and served as the first Chairman of the Editorial Board of the *Journal of Further and Higher Education in Scotland*.

Mr. Niven has been a visiting scholar, visiting professor, and consultant at colleges and universities in Asia, Australia, Europe, and North America. He has written widely in the professional press and in journals and has given keynote addresses on vocational education and training issues at international conferences in the United States, U. K., Europe, the Middle and Far East, and Australia.

Pentti Rauhala

Pentti Rauhala is the President of Espoo-Vantaa Polytechnic (Institute of Higher Education) in the Helsinki Region of Finland. He formerly worked in the field of vocational education for about 25 years, including positions as Director of Planning for the National Board of Vocational Education, which was participating in the reform of secondary stage vocational education in Finland; Executive Director of the Union of Vocational Schools in Finland; Principal of Järvenpää Vocational School; Executive Director of the Intermunicipal Federation for Vocational Education; and researcher at the University of Tampere (Finland).

Dr. Rauhala has also served as President of the Union of Vocational Principals Association in Finland, engaged in many national and international developing projects, and served as an advisor in Phare projects concerning vocational school management in Estonia and the Czech Republic. He is a member of the subcommittee of Leonardo, addressing initial vocational education in the European Union. He received his Ph.D. degree from the University of Tampere, where his dissertation focused on flexible vocational education. He has published in the areas of vocational school reform and the development of vocations in working life.

Jan N. Streumer

Jan Streumer is an Associate Professor in the Department of Educational Science and Technology at the University of Twente, the Netherlands. His specialty is in vocational education and training as well as training for business and industry, and he has developed and facilitated numerous performance and learning interventions in companies.

Dr. Streumer was a visiting professor in the Human Resource Development Research Center at the University of Minnesota, and serves on the board of directors of the Academy of Human Resource Development.

Dr. Streumer has written numerous articles and books on a range of topics dealing with training and vocational education, including *Key Qualifications in Work and Education* (Kluwer Academic Publishers) and *Flexibility in Training and Vocational Education* (Lemma Publishers).

Johnny Sung

Johnny Sung is Deputy-Director and Senior Research Fellow of the Centre for Labour Market Studies at the University of Leicester, United Kingdom. His research interests include learning styles and the learning environment, open and distance learning, and national education and training systems in Asia. Together with Professor David Ashton, he is involved in the delivery of master's and diploma programs (in training, development, and human resource management) by distance learning worldwide.

Professor Sung has researched the role of the Singapore government in delivering rapid

economic growth and was part of a research project comparing the education and training systems of Singapore, Hong Kong, Taiwan, and Republic of [South] Korea. His recent publications include a book coauthored with David Ashton and others, entitled *Education and Training for Development in East Asia: The Political Economy of Skill Formation in Newly Industrialised Economies*, as well as a book chapter, "National Consensus, Changing Vocational Policy in Rapid Economic Growth: The Case of Singapore" in *Recent Vocational Training Policy: A Comparative Studies*.

Stephanie P. Young

Stephanie Young was appointed Director, Lifelong Learning, with Glasgow Development Agency (Scotland) in April 1998 with the ambitious task of developing Glasgow as a Learning City. Prior to joining the Agency, she was Director of the Advisory Scottish Council for Education and Training Targets. Previous to that, she held a variety of senior positions in Scottish economic development in both the Scottish Enterprise and Enterprise Trust Network. Her experience spans all aspects of strategic planning, organization development, and human resource management.

Ms. Young's key interests are lifelong learning and the development of national education and training systems. She has written for national newspapers, professional journals, and contributed to a number of books on education and training. She chairs the Glasgow Learning Alliance, and the Government's National Development Project on Literacies. She is also Editor of the *Journal of Lifelong Learning Initiatives*, and a Board Member of Anniesland College (Scotland).

Since graduating with an M.A. (with Honors) in Economic History from Edinburgh University, Ms. Young has studied Economic Planning at the University of Budapest (Hungary), and completed a Diploma in Training Management at Strathclyde University, as well as an M.S. in Training and Human Resource Management at Leicester University.

Topic Index

Index of Countries and Regions

Index of Boards, Councils, Ministries, and Other Bodies